Keynes's Theoretical Development

Keynes was probably the most important and without doubt the most influential economic thinker to emerge in the era spanning the decline and disintegration of the Pax Britannica and ending with the Second World War. After his death, his influence in the spheres of macroeconomics and economic policy-making became, over the course of the third quarter of the twentieth century, so overwhelmingly dominant that the period from the 1950s to the 1970s may with some justification be designated the 'Age of Keynes'.

The principal objective of this book is to elucidate Keynes's development as an economic theoretician through examining his books, his articles, various manuscripts, lecture notes (very often taken by his students) and controversial correspondence. Hirai is not so much interested in relating a narrative, but instead in analysing the processes of theory-building and re-building which constitute Keynes's intellectual journey from the *Tract* to the *General Theory*. In short, the book aims to put forward Keynes's theoretical development as a theoretical hypothesis (and, collaterally, to show how this study differs from other studies).

This book will be of great interest to students and researchers interested in Keynes and more widely the history of economic thought and macroeconomics.

Toshiaki Hirai is a professor in the Faculty of Economics at Sophia University, Tokyo.

Routledge Studies in the History of Economics

1   **Economics as Literature**
    Willie Henderson

2   **Socialism and Marginalism in Economics 1870–1930**
    Edited by Ian Steedman

3   **Hayek's Political Economy**
    The socio-economics of order
    Steve Fleetwood

4   **On the Origins of Classical Economics**
    Distribution and value
    from William Petty to
    Adam Smith
    Tony Aspromourgos

5   **The Economics of Joan Robinson**
    Edited by Maria Cristina Marcuzzo, Luigi Pasinetti and Alesandro Roncaglia

6   **The Evolutionist Economics of Léon Walras**
    Albert Jolink

7   **Keynes and the 'Classics'**
    A study in language, epistemology and mistaken identities
    Michel Verdon

8   **The History of Game Theory, Vol. 1**
    From the beginnings to 1945
    Robert W. Dimand and Mary Ann Dimand

9   **The Economics of W. S. Jevons**
    Sandra Peart

10 **Gandhi's Economic Thought**
    Ajit K. Dasgupta

11 **Equilibrium and Economic Theory**
    Edited by Giovanni Caravale

12 **Austrian Economics in Debate**
    Edited by Willem Keizer, Bert Tieben and Rudy van Zijp

13 **Ancient Economic Thought**
    Edited by B. B. Price

14 **The Political Economy of Social Credit and Guild Socialism**
    Frances Hutchinson and Brian Burkitt

15 **Economic Careers**
    Economics and economists
    in Britain 1930–1970
    Keith Tribe

16 **Understanding 'Classical' Economics**
Studies in the long-period theory
Heinz Kurz and Neri Salvadori

17 **History of Environmental Economic Thought**
E. Kula

18 **Economic Thought in Communist and Post-Communist Europe**
Edited by Hans-Jürgen Wagener

19 **Studies in the History of French Political Economy**
From Bodin to Walras
Edited by Gilbert Faccarello

20 **The Economics of John Rae**
Edited by O. F. Hamouda, C. Lee and D. Mair

21 **Keynes and the Neoclassical Synthesis**
Einsteinian versus Newtonian macroeconomics
Teodoro Dario Togati

22 **Historical Perspectives on Macroeconomics**
Sixty years after the 'General Theory'
Edited by Philippe Fontaine and Albert Jolink

23 **The Founding of Institutional Economics**
The leisure class and sovereignty
Edited by Warren J. Samuels

24 **Evolution of Austrian Economics**
From Menger to Lachmann
Sandye Gloria

25 **Marx's Concept of Money**
The God of commodities
Anitra Nelson

26 **The Economics of James Steuart**
Edited by Ramón Tortajada

27 **The Development of Economics in Europe since 1945**
Edited by A.W. Bob Coats

28 **The Canon in the History of Economics**
Critical essays
Edited by Michalis Psalidopoulos

29 **Money and Growth**
Selected papers of Allyn Abbott Young
Edited by Perry G. Mehrling and Roger J. Sandilands

30 **The Social Economics of Jean-Baptiste Say**
Markets and virtue
Evelyn L. Forget

31 **The Foundations of Laissez-Faire**
The economics of Pierre de Boisguilbert
Gilbert Faccarello

32 **John Ruskin's Political Economy**
Willie Henderson

33 **Contributions to the History of Economic Thought**
Essays in honour of R. D. C. Black
Edited by Antoin E. Murphy and Renee Prendergast

34 **Towards an Unknown Marx**
A commentary on the
manuscripts of 1861–63
Enrique Dussel

35 **Economics and
Interdisciplinary Exchange**
Edited by Guido Erreygers

36 **Economics as the Art of
Thought**
Essays in memory of
G. L. S. Shackle
*Edited by Stephen F. Frowen and
Peter Earl*

37 **The Decline of Ricardian
Economics**
Politics and economics in
post-Ricardian theory
Susan Pashkoff

38 **Piero Sraffa**
His life, thought and
cultural heritage
Alessandro Roncaglia

39 **Equilibrium and
Disequilibrium in Economic
Theory**
The Marshall–Walras divide
Michel de Vroey

40 **The German Historical
School**
The historical and ethical
approach to economics
Edited by Yuichi Shionoya

41 **Reflections on the Classical
Canon in Economics**
Essays in honour of Samuel
Hollander
*Edited by Sandra Peart and
Evelyn Forget*

42 **Piero Sraffa's Political
Economy**
A centenary estimate
*Edited by Terenzio Cozzi and
Roberto Marchionatti*

43 **The Contribution of Joseph
Schumpeter to Economics**
Economic development and
institutional change
Richard Arena and Cecile Dangel

44 **On the Development of
Long-run Neo-Classical Theory**
Tom Kompas

45 **F. A. Hayek as a Political
Economist**
Economic analysis and values
*Edited by Jack Birner, Pierre
Garrouste and Thierry Aimar*

46 **Pareto, Economics and
Society**
The mechanical analogy
Michael McLure

47 **The Cambridge Controversies
in Capital Theory**
A study in the logic of theory
development
Jack Birner

48 **Economics Broadly
Considered**
Essays in honour of
Warren J. Samuels
*Edited by Steven G. Medema,
Jeff Biddle and John B. Davis*

49 **Physicians and Political
Economy**
Six studies of the work of
doctor-economists
Edited by Peter Groenewegen

50 **The Spread of Political Economy and the Professionalisation of Economists**
Economic societies in Europe, America and Japan in the nineteenth century
Massimo Augello and Marco Guidi

51 **Historians of Economics and Economic Thought**
The construction of disciplinary memory
Steven G. Medema and Warren J. Samuels

52 **Competing Economic Theories**
Essays in memory of Giovanni Caravale
Sergio Nisticò and Domenico Tosato

53 **Economic Thought and Policy in Less Developed Europe**
The nineteenth century
Edited by Michalis Psalidopoulos and Maria-Eugenia Almedia Mata

54 **Family Fictions and Family Facts**
Harriet Martineau, Adolphe Quetelet and the population question in England 1798–1859
Brian Cooper

55 **Eighteeth-Century Economics**
Peter Groenewegen

56 **The Rise of Political Economy in the Scottish Enlightenment**
Edited by Tatsuya Sakamoto and Hideo Tanaka

57 **Classics and Moderns in Economics, Volume I**
Essays on nineteenth and twentieth century economic thought
Peter Groenewegen

58 **Classics and Moderns in Economics, Volume II**
Essays on nineteenth and twentieth century economic thought
Peter Groenewegen

59 **Marshall's Evolutionary Economics**
Tiziano Raffaelli

60 **Money, Time and Rationality in Max Weber**
Austrian connections
Stephen D. Parsons

61 **Classical Macroeconomics**
Some modern variations and distortions
James C. W. Ahiakpor

62 **The Historical School of Economics in England and Japan**
Tamotsu Nishizawa

63 **Classical Economics and Modern Theory**
Studies in long-period analysis
Heinz D. Kurz and Neri Salvadori

64 **A Bibliography of Female Economic Thought to 1940**
Kirsten K. Madden, Janet A. Sietz and Michele Pujol

65 **Economics, Economists and Expectations**
From microfoundations to macroeconomics
Warren Young, Robert Leeson and William Darity Jr.

66 **The Political Economy of Public Finance in Britain, 1767–1873**
Takuo Dome

67 **Essays in the History of Economics**
Warren J. Samuels, Willie Henderson, Kirk D. Johnson and Marianne Johnson

68 **History and Political Economy**
Essays in honour of
P. D. Groenewegen
Edited by Tony Aspromourgos and John Lodewijks

69 **The Tradition of Free Trade**
Lars Magnusson

70 **Evolution of the Market Process**
Austrian and Swedish economics
Edited by Michel Bellet, Sandye Gloria-Palermo and Abdallah Zouache

71 **Consumption as an Investment**
The fear of goods from Hesiod to Adam Smith
Cosimo Perrotta

72 **Jean-Baptiste Say and the Classical Canon in Economics**
The British connection in French classicism
Samuel Hollander

73 **Knut Wicksell on Poverty**
No place is too exalted
Knut Wicksell

74 **Economists in Cambridge**
A study through their correspondence 1907–1946
Edited by M. C. Marcuzzo and A. Rosselli

75 **The Experiment in the History of Economics**
Edited by Philippe Fontaine and Robert Leonard

76 **At the Origins of Mathematical Economics**
The economics of A. N. Isnard (1748–1803)
Richard van den Berg

77 **Money and Exchange**
Folktales and reality
Sasan Fayazmanesh

78 **Economic Development and Social Change**
Historical roots and modern perspectives
George Stathakis and Gianni Vaggi

79 **Ethical Codes and Income Distribution**
A study of John Bates Clark and Thorstein Veblen
Guglielmo Forges Davanzati

80 **Evaluating Adam Smith**
Creating the wealth of nations
Willie Henderson

81 **Civil Happiness**
Economics and human flourishing in historical perspective
Luigino Bruni

82 **New Voices on Adam Smith**
Edited by Leonidas Montes and Eric Schliesser

83 **Making Chicago Price Theory**
Milton Friedman–George Stigler
correspondence, 1945–1957
*Edited by J. Daniel Hammond
and Claire H. Hammond*

84 **William Stanley Jevons and
the Cutting Edge of Economics**
Bert Mosselmans

85 **A History of Econometrics
in France**
From nature to models
Philippe Le Gall

86 **Money and Markets**
A doctrinal approach
*Edited by Alberto Giacomin and
Maria Cristina Marcuzzo*

87 **Considerations on the
Fundamental Principles of
Pure Political Economy**
*Vilfredo Pareto (Edited by
Roberto Marchionatti and
Fiorenzo Mornati)*

88 **The Years of High Econometrics**
A short history of the generation
that reinvented economics
Francisco Louçã

89 **David Hume's Political
Economy**
*Edited by Carl Wennerlind and
Margaret Schabas*

90 **Keynes's Vision**
Why the Great Depression
did not return
John Philip Jones

91 **Monetary Theory in
Retrospect**
The selected essays of
Filippo Cesarano
Filippo Cesarano

92 **Keynes's Theoretical
Development**
From the *Tract* to the *General
Theory*
Toshiaki Hirai

Keynes's Theoretical Development
From the *Tract* to the *General Theory*

Toshiaki Hirai

Routledge
Taylor & Francis Group

LONDON AND NEW YORK

First published 2008
by Routledge
2 Park Square, Milton Park, Abingdon, OX14 4RN

Simultaneously published in the USA and Canada
by Routledge
270 Madison Ave, New York, NY 10016

*Routledge is an imprint of the Taylor & Francis Group,
an informa business*

© 2008 Toshiaki Hirai

Typeset in Times New Roman by
Newgen Imaging Systems (P) Ltd, Chennai, India
Printed and bound in Great Britain by
Biddles Ltd, King's Lynn

British Library Cataloguing in Publication Data
A catalogue record for this book is available
from the British Library

Library of Congress Cataloging in Publication Data
A catalog record for this book has been requested

ISBN10: 0–415–36279–2 (hbk)
ISBN10: 0–203–01295–X (ebk)

ISBN13: 978–0–415–36279–5 (hbk)
ISBN13: 978–0–415–01295–6 (ebk)

Contents

List of tables		xiv
Acknowledgements		xv

Introduction   1

    I   *Keynes 1*
    II   *The outline of the book 2*
    III *Main conclusions 4*
    IV *Note on methodology 5*

1   The relative decline of the British economy   7

    I   *The workshop of the world 7*
    II   *Relative decline 8*
    III *The interwar years 11*

2   Wicksell's influences on Keynes and his contemporaries   17

    I   *Wicksell 17*
    II   *Keynes and his contemporaries 19*
    III *Interpretations of Wicksell's influences 29*
    IV *Conclusion 30*

3   The life of Keynes   31

    I   *The making of an economist 31*
    II   *The First World War 34*
    III *The 1920s 36*
    IV *The 1930s 37*
    V   *The Second World War 39*

4   From the *Tract* to the *Treatise*   41

    I   A Tract on Monetary Reform *41*

II   A Treatise on Money *43*
III *Comparison 44*
IV   *The* Treatise *vision 44*
V   *Examination through primary material 45*
VI   *Conjectural conclusion 54*

5 The *Treatise*   56

I   *The theoretical structure 56*
II   *Two problems 63*
III *The key concepts 69*

6 After the *Treatise*   71

I   *Hawtrey's criticism 71*
II   *June 1931 to early 1932 73*
III *'The Monetary Theory of Production' manuscript 77*
IV   *The 'Cambridge Circus' criticism: May 1932 82*
V   *Two tables of contents (1932) 85*
VI   *Conclusion 86*

7 The turning point   88

I   *'The Parameters of a Monetary Economy' manuscript 88*
II   *The 1932 Michaelmas lectures 95*
III *Kahn's contribution 98*
IV   *Malthus and Keynes 100*
V   *Conclusion 102*

8 Searching for a new theory of employment   103

I   *Three manuscripts 103*
II   *Comparison of the 1933 three tables of contents 115*

9 Establishment of the investment and consumption theories   118

I   *The 1933 Michaelmas lectures 118*
II   *The two undated manuscripts 120*
III *Conclusion 127*

10 The eve of the *General Theory*   130

I   *'The General Theory' 131*
II   *'The Summer Manuscript' 140*
III *The 1934 Michaelmas lectures 143*
IV   *Conclusion 145*

11 The proofing process (I): from 'The Pre-First Proof
Typescript' (Summer 1934) to 'Galley 1(III)'
(June–July 1935)   146

    I   *Introduction 146*
    II   *'The Pre-First Proof Typescript' 147*
    III   *Galleys 1, 2 and 3 149*
    IV   *Galley 1(I) (chapters 1–19) 150*
    V   *Galley 2 154*
    VI   *Galley 1(II) (chapters 20–25) 154*
    VII   *Galley 3 155*
    VIII *Galley 1(III) (chapters 26–28) 156*

12 The proofing process (II): 'The Great Revision'
and the 1935 Michaelmas lectures   159

    I   *'The Great Revision' 159*
    II   *The 1935 Michaelmas lectures 171*
    III   *Conclusion 176*

13 The *General Theory*: the monetary economics of
underemployment equilibrium   177

    I   *Views on earlier economists 177*
    II   *The monetary economics of underemployment
        equilibrium 180*
    III   *The essence of the Keynesian Revolution 191*

14 Interpretations of Keynes and the development of
postwar macroeconomics   194

    I   *Interpretations of the* General Theory *195*
    II   *Interpretations of the development of Keynes's
        economics 200*
    III   *Keynes and postwar macroeconomics up to
        the 1970s 203*
    IV   *The situation of macroeconomics during the last
        thirty years 210*

Notes   214
Bibliography   240
Index   265

Tables

7.1	From the *Treatise* to 'The Parameters of a Monetary Economy' manuscript	93
9.1	The situation in 1933–1934	128
11.1	The proofing process	150
12.1	The process of development of the chapters of the *General Theory*	173
12.2	Michaelmas lectures: 1932–1935	175

Acknowledgements

The principal precursor of this volume is my Japanese book, *A Study of Keynes* (University of Tokyo Press, 1987, pp. ix+206), which owed a great deal to many scholars, and above all to Professor Emeritus Takashi Negishi (University of Tokyo). During my stay as a Visiting Scholar at the University of Cambridge, I translated it into English (1988; it is listed in Skidelsky (1992. p. 651)).

However, I avoided making it public, for at that time I was eager to articulate the main theme there more fully, and in a wider perspective. As it turned out, the task required unexpectedly longer and harder work. The final result was 'A Study of Keynes's Economics (I)–(IV)' (*Sophia Economic Review*, December 1997–March 1999). Thereafter I translated it into Japanese, and it was published as *Looking at Keynes's Economics from Multiple Points of View* (University of Tokyo Press, 2003, pp. xv+842).

The present book is a condensed and updated version of this Japanese book. Thus it had behind it many scholars for whose suggestions, encouragement and comments I should express my great gratitude. It would not have been published but for the strong recommendation and encouragement given by Professor Maria Cristina Marcuzzo (University of Rome 'La Sapienza') while I was studying there as a Visiting Professor (October 2003–April 2004). I would also like to express my great gratitude, among others, to Professor Emeritus D. P. O'Brien (Durham University), and Professor Roger Backhouse (University of Birmingham) as well as those who have attended both the International Conferences on the Cambridge School at Hitotsubashi University since 2002 and the International Conferences on Keynes at Sophia University since 2005 (see www2u.biglobe.ne. jp/~olympa/cambridge/kokusai/kokusai.htm), and those who attended the ESHET and the HES annual meetings, for their invaluable suggestions, comments on and criticisms of my papers which are based on the old versions of several chapters of this book.

I would like to express my gratitude to the University of Tokyo Press, the *History of Economic Ideas*, the *European Journal of the History of Economic Thought* and the *Journal of the History of Economic Thought* for copyright licence, and to Mr Graham Sells for his excellent proofreading.

Last but not least, my wife, Fusako, who has shown a complete understanding of the scholar's life and unflaggingly helped me with my work, should also be considered a great contributor to this work.

The Author, Faculty of Economics,
Sophia University, Tokyo
7 June 2007

Introduction

I Keynes

There is widespread agreement that the greatest contribution of John Maynard Keynes (1883–1946) to modern economics was the construction, for the first time, of a model explaining how the level of employment is determined. At the same time, although the term 'Keynesian Economics' is frequently used with considerable nonchalance by Keynesian and anti-Keynesian economists alike as if there could be no doubt about the exact meaning of the expression, certain facets of the evolution of Keynes's ideas have been somewhat overlooked. Although documentation of the great changes and evolutionary developments in Keynes's thought has been readily available in the *Collected Writings of John Maynard Keynes* (*JMK*) and in Keynes's Economic Papers (on microfilm), with the notable exception of the pioneering work of Patinkin there have been remarkably few studies attempting to trace the complicated route from *A Tract on Monetary Reform* (December 1923. Hereafter the *Tract*) to *The General Theory of Employment, Interest and Money* (February 1936. Hereafter the *General Theory*). This book is the result of my research to address this neglected, yet crucial, aspect of the genesis of Keynes's Economics.

Keynes was probably the most important – unquestionably the most influential – economic thinker to emerge in the era spanning the decline and disintegration of the Pax Britannica and ending with the Second World War. After his death, his influence in the spheres of macroeconomics and economic policy-making became, over the course of the third quarter of the twentieth century, so overwhelmingly dominant that the period from the 1950s to the 1970s may with some justification be designated the 'Age of Keynes'.

The evolution of Keynes's thought was informed as much by the events of the real world, in which he was himself deeply engaged, as by the world of theoretical economics. He developed a monetary approach to economics, centring on the theory of effective demand, and, on that foundation, advocated a fiscal policy to address the crushing problem of mass unemployment which marked the interwar years. The stance Keynes took in theoretical economics and in practical affairs was closely linked to his social philosophy – the 'New Liberalism'– which insisted on the necessity for judicious intervention on the part of government to facilitate the orderly functioning of the economy – an outlook set squarely against nineteenth-century laissez-faire. The other influence on Keynes's thinking, his active involvement in policy-making, continued into his final years, when as the top UK representative in negotiations with the United States he contributed important proposals for the design of the postwar world order.

II   The outline of the book

The principal objective of this study is to elucidate Keynes's development as an economic theoretician by combing through his books, his articles, various manuscripts, lecture notes (very often taken by his students), controversial correspondence etc. Our main work is not to recount a narrative but to analyse the processes of theory-building and re-building which constitute Keynes's intellectual journey from the *Tract* to the *General Theory*. In short, the book aims at putting forward Keynes's theoretical development as a theoretical hypothesis (and, collaterally, at showing how our study differs from other studies).

The structure of our investigation is as follows. Chapter 1, 'The relative decline of the British economy', charts the changing position of the British economy in relation to the international economy from the late nineteenth century through the interwar period. Chapter 2, 'Wicksell's influences on Keynes and his contemporaries', deals with the tradition of monetary economic stemming from Knut Wicksell, and developed by a number of economists of diverse theoretical persuasions among whom the Keynes of the *Treatise*, Myrdal and Hayek are mainly examined, though touching on Lindahl and Mises.

Chapter 3, 'The life of Keynes' focuses on the academic and policy-making aspects of Keynes's life.

Chapters 4–13 form the core of the present book.

Chapter 4, 'From the *Tract* to the *Treatise*' deals with the development of Keynes's theory from the *Tract* (1923) to the *Treatise* (1930). In Chapter 5, 'The Treatise on Money', we clarify the theoretical structure of the *Treatise*. We argue that one of the most significant features of the theoretical framework of the *Treatise* is the uneasy co-existence of a Wicksellian theory and a theory peculiar to Keynes ('Keynes's own theory'). We further argue that it is the latter which is more relevant to an understanding of Keynes's theoretical development, as the following chapters will make clear.

Chapter 6, 'After the *Treatise*', discusses the period following the completion of the *Treatise* up to the middle of 1932. We find that the basic outlook of the *Treatise* – that is, 'Keynes's own theory' – was maintained in Keynes's thinking throughout this period.

In Chapter 7, 'The turning point', we deal with the qualitative shift in Keynes's thinking from the *Treatise* world to that of the *General Theory*, which occurred around the end of 1932. The manuscript entitled 'The parameters of a monetary economy' dates from this time. Keynes here abandoned the idea of constructing a dynamic model using excess profit and the 'TM supply function' (see p. 59).

Probably Keynes's most important contribution to modern economics lies in his establishment of the theory of underemployment equilibrium. One of the keys to comprehending how Keynes changed his theory in this sphere is to observe how he treated the TM supply function. To put this another way, abandoning the TM supply function entailed a severe upheaval in the foundations of the theoretical framework held by Keynes up to mid-1932. The main elements which comprise the *General Theory* were worked out in accordance with this fundamental transformation.

It should be noted, however, that Keynes did not completely abandon the TM supply function at least in his own opinion.

In Chapter 8, 'Searching for a new theory of employment', we see Keynes use the concepts we shall refer to as the 'pseudo-TM supply function' (see p.105) and the 'pseudo-TM supply function mk2' (see p.108) which, though essentially different from the TM supply function, were regarded as its successors. We have adopted these terms in order to mark out a path through this somewhat confused feature of Keynes's thinking.

In this chapter we examine the three manuscripts of 1933. Keynes first formulated his theory of the determination of the level of employment in the 'First Manuscript' of 1933. This formulation was the prototype of the 'principle of effective demand' put forward in Chapter 3 of the *General Theory*. In the 'Second' and 'Third' manuscripts of 1933, effective demand is defined in terms of the 'expected sale proceeds over variable cost'. We call this function the 'pseudo-TM supply function mk2', which can be interpreted as a stability condition for the equilibrium level of employment.

In Chapter 9, 'Establishment of the investment and consumption theories', we concentrate on the two undated manuscripts (reckoned to have been written either towards the end of 1933 or in the first half of 1934). As far as the existing man-uscripts are concerned, it is in 'The First Undated Manuscript' that Keynes appears to have first established the fundamental psychological law and the multiplier theory, and in 'The Second Undated Manuscript' that he first put forward an investment theory close to that of the *General Theory*.

At this stage Keynes already had in place the theory of the determination of the employment level with almost all the elements comprising the theoretical structure of the *General Theory*, as we shall see. We can therefore say that he had essentially arrived at the position of the *General Theory* by the end of 1933.

In Chapter 10, 'The eve of the *General Theory*', we examine the manuscript entitled (for short) 'The General Theory' written in the spring of 1934, and also the manuscript containing the revised versions of Chapters 8 and 9 written in the summer of 1934 which we will call the 'The Summer Manuscript'. This chapter focuses on the state of development of Keynes's employment theory, pointing out the ambiguity in the concept of effective demand, as well as some theoretical inconsistencies, while still recognising that in 'The General Theory' Keynes put forward almost the same theoretical framework as that of the *General Theory* in the areas of both the consumption and the investment theories.

In Chapters 11 and 12, 'The proofing process' (I) and (II), we deal with the gestation of the *General Theory* from the summer of 1934 up to publication. Here we examine the production of the *General Theory* in terms not only of substance but also of form. With regard to the substance we examine the evolution of the employment function and of such fundamental concepts as effective demand, investment and prime cost.

It should be noted that in tracing Keynes's theoretical development, we also examined Keynes's 1932–1935 lectures and incorporated the results in the above analysis.

In Chapter 13, 'The *General Theory*', our aim is to clarify the theoretical structure of Keynes's magnum opus. The *General Theory* has two striking features. First, it sees the market economy as possessing two contrasting aspects: stability, certainty and simplicity on the one hand; instability, uncertainty and complexity on the other. Second, it can be characterised as a monetary economics which deals with underemployment equilibrium. We examine the theoretical structure, and the essence of the Keynesian revolution.

The topics discussed in Chapter 14, 'Interpretations of Keynes and the development of postwar macroeconomics', include: the two recognised areas of interpretation relating to the *General Theory* (interpretations of the *General Theory*, and of the development of Keynes's economics), an outline of postwar macroeconomics in relation to Keynes until the 1970s, and an outline of the situation of economics during the last thirty years.

In 'Acknowledgements' I touched on the relation between my 2003 Japanese book and the present one. In writing the present book, I was forced to delete or shorten several topics such as the rise of neoclassical economics, Keynes's social philosophy and Keynes's lectures. My 2003 Japanese book had 'Looking at Keynes's economics from multiple points of view' as the English title. But, for the above reason, I chose 'Keynes's Theoretical Development' as the title. (However, when it has seemed to me opportune, I have tried to direct the readers' attention to the place in my 2003 Japanese book and its corresponding working paper written in English.)

III   Main conclusions

Finally, for the sake of convenience, let us summarise here our main conclusions.

1   It is crucially important to pay attention to the question of how Keynes dealt with the relation between profits and the volume of output. In the *Treatise* the importance of this relation (the TM supply function) is stressed as expressing the dynamic mechanism. Keynes adhered to this function after the *Treatise*, in spite of many criticisms. Towards the end of 1932, however, he abandoned it, though showing some hesitation, and put forward a new formula of a system of commodity markets which led up to the *General Theory*.

2   The *Treatise* belongs to the 'Wicksell's influences', which includes Myrdal, Lindahl, Mises, Hayek and others. We regard 'Wicksell's influences' as propounding monetary economics critical of neoclassical orthodoxy. The *Treatise*, however, included two theories – a 'Wicksellian theory' and 'Keynes's own theory'. Immediately after the *Treatise*, Keynes abandoned

the former theory, and strove to maintain or improve upon the latter. We regard the Keynes after the *Treatise* as departing from the Wicksell's influences, with the result that the *General Theory* is completely independent of them.

3 The *Treatise* and the *General Theory* have in common the following points: (i) both belong to monetary economics and were pitched against neoclassical orthodoxy; (ii) prices and output are treated as endogenous variables; (iii) the importance of both monetary and fiscal policies are stressed. (Throughout his life Keynes believed in the efficacy of interest rate policy in controlling the economy.)

4 The *General Theory*'s revolutionary feature lies in its showing, through presentation of a clear-cut model, that the market economy, if left to itself, falls into an underemployment equilibrium. The model shows how the volume of employment is determined, on the basis of an equilibrium analysis, contrary to the arguments of Post-Keynesians, 'Disequilibrium Approach' Keynesians and others. It was not until 1933 that Keynes came to put forward a model of how the volume of employment is determined. Thereafter he took pains to elaborate his model, continuing to revise the concept of effective demand, the concept of marginal efficiency of capital, the theory of liquidity preference and other things. We have indeed traced his efforts to such a meticulous degree. At the same time, however, we argue that in the *General Theory* Keynes sees the market economy as possessing two contrasting potentialities: stability, certainty and simplicity on the one hand; instability, uncertainty and complexity on the other.

5 We put forward the essential theoretical framework of the *Treatise* in terms of Mechanisms 1 and 2 (the determination of the price levels of consumption and investment goods, respectively), and 3 (the TM supply function). We also reconstruct the theoretical framework of the *General Theory* in terms of the 'heterogeneity-expectations approach', pointing out some flaws in the original.

IV   Note on methodology

Needless to say, the study of the history of economic doctrines ought to be as objective as possible. However, to suggest that this particular subject can be approached straightfowardly in this way is rather misleading. As soon as we depart from the simplest facts, such as who wrote what, when and where, we cannot but perceive reality through the filters of our own value judgements and presuppositions, whether consciously or unconsciously. Hence, however objective we strive to be, we can never completely eliminate an essential subjectivity from our work, as this is inherent in the nature of our subject itself. All we can do is to strive to be as impartial as we can; an extremely delicate and difficult task. This is also why the spectrum of interpretation of the work of any great economist is often so wide. Predictably, the greater the impact of the economist is, the wider the spectrum of opinion tends to be. Moreover, the range of the interpretations is bound to be subject to considerable fluctuation in accordance with changes in social, political and economic conditions. One particular understanding may be in the ascendant for a long time only to be superseded by a completely different one as the prevailing conditions change. Furthermore, influential economists often tailor a powerful traditional theory to accommodate their own tastes and predilections, or to support their own ideas. Such is the stuff of which the history of economic doctrines is made. Under these intellectual conditions, the researcher must persevere in his/her work while being exposed to yet two further pressures, namely the influences of both present and past interpretations. To progress in the study of the history of economic doctrines, his/her starting point must be to establish his/her own understanding of individual texts. In the case of Keynes these strictures are perhaps especially pressing.

Scholars inevitably draw their views of the market society, as with other economic issues, from the alternatives offered by current economic thought. While undoubtedly useful, the effect is often to distort our grasp of the history of economics unconsciously by forcing us to view earlier doctrines from ideologically biased perspectives.

From what viewpoint research should be oriented – in particular whether to take an ahistorical or a historical approach (i.e. whether to endeavour to interpret historical doctrines in their original settings or not) – is necessarily a delicate problem. The approach adopted in this book is the latter; that is, we have sought to interpret Keynes's theories in the spirit of their original meanings. But this does not mean that theorisation has had no place in our reasoning. It has rather been vital in enabling us to articulate (hopefully) cogent interpretations of Keynes's correspondence, manuscripts, books and related materials. It is worth noting, too, that this approach may help us either to reaffirm the correctness of, or to locate crucial flaws in, current orthodox thinking. In any case, one cannot avoid a certain amount of intellectual tension in confronting the dilemmas posed by the various approaches one might take.

1 The relative decline of the British economy

The purpose of this chapter is to outline how the British economy proceeded in relation to the world economy from the early 1800s to the Second World War. This will go a long way towards helping us grasp Keynes's activities as a theoretical economist and an economic policy adviser and critic in the broad historical context.

The course of the world economy here can be divided into three periods: the early 1800s to the third quarter of the nineteenth century, when Britain was the workshop of the world and dominated the international economy; the last quarter of the nineteenth century to the First World War, which witnessed the relative decline of the British economy due to the rapid economic growth of the United States and Germany; and the interwar years, which saw the demise of the old international economic order, and during which Keynes was actively involved in the economic problems of the United Kingdom as well as the worldwide issues.

I The workshop of the world

The United Kingdom was the first country to experience an 'Industrial Revolution'.[1] Starting in the 1760s, the process was completed by the 1830s. Propelled by technological innovations such as Watt's steam and rotative engines, Crompton's 'mule', and so forth,[2] Britain saw unprecedented advances in cotton, iron and steel, and civil engineering. These advances were transforming the British economy, and with the final stage of the Industrial Revolution the transformation was complete. It was then that the United Kingdom came to dominate the international economy as 'the workshop of the world', meeting with no serious challenge until the 1880s.

We now see, thanks to Harley (1982) and Crafts (1983), that two industrial revolutions are distinguishable: 'the wave of gadgets which occurred in the last third of the eighteenth century, and the economy-wide changes accompanied by rapid growth of the industrial sector which became dominant after 1815' (Mokyr, 1985, p. 4). Actually, just a few industries (above all, the cotton industry) grew at a truly amazing rate, but industry as a whole did not: 'the macroeconomic effects of the Industrial Revolution are not overwhelming before 1820' (p. 5).

After 1820 the British economy developed spectacularly. Up to 1870, British industrial production grew by 37.7 per cent with each passing decade.[3] The dimensions of this expansion can be grasped by calculating indices for raw cotton consumption and pig iron production: the former had risen to 1,322 by the year 1870 (the base year: 1815);[4] the latter to 1,836 by the year 1870 (the base year: 1818).[5]

This progress was considerably sustained by exports. In the cotton manufactures, the ratio of exports to total production had reached 63.8 per cent by the 1880s from 56.4 in the 1830s.[6] In the steel industry, the ratio doubled from 16.5 per cent in the 1830s to 32.8 in the 1880s.[7] This excessive dependence on foreign markets was to leave the British economy vulnerable to competition from other exporting nations as the international competitiveness of the British industries weakened.

The Industrial Revolution was also to bring far-reaching reforms in economic structures and policies, two of which in particular deserve mention.[8]

The first was the tariff and financial reforms introduced by the Peel (1840s) and Gladstone (1850s) governments, through which the United Kingdom established a free trade system. The second was a reform of the banking system. In 1825 and 1837 the British economy suffered severe depressions, in response to which two schools arose: the Currency School (Overstone and Torrens) ascribed the cause of the depressions to over-issue of notes by local banks, while the Banking School (Tooke and Fullarton) maintained that the issue of notes was automatically regulated by the needs of trade. The Currency School carried the day, as a result of which, through the Bank Charter Act of 1844, a monetary system was established under which the Bank of England became the nation's de facto central bank, with sole authorisation to issue notes based on gold reserves. The Bank was also entrusted with the task of stabilising foreign exchange rates by means of the bank rate.

Thus the United Kingdom was to dominate the world economy over the ensuing decades.

II   Relative decline

The period covering the last quarter of the nineteenth century[9] to the First World War[10] saw the beginnings of Britain's relative decline as an industrial power.[11] Three factors were largely responsible for this state of affairs: the industrialisation of the United States and Germany; Britain's failure to exploit technological innovation; and the weakening of the entrepreneurial spirit.

1   *Industrialisation of the United States and Germany*

The US economy took off in the period 1843–1860[12] with the spearheading growth of the cotton industry,[13] the major thrust arriving in the 1865–1914 period.

The rise of Germany as an economic power took place in the period 1851–1873.[14] Industrialisation gained impetus with formation of the Zollverein (the Customs Union) in 1834, and the rapid development of the railways backed by the coal and steel industries, and Germany's industrial revolution was accomplished in the period 1873–1914.

Germany was also in the ascendant politically. Having won the Austro-Prussian War of 1866, Prussia embarked on war with France which was crowned with victory, culminating in proclamation of the German Empire in 1871. Germany was also rewarded with 5,000 million francs in reparations and the iron-rich region of Alsace-Lorraine.

Both similarities and dissimilarities are discernible in the economic advances of the United States and Germany. The two countries were alike in seeking to promote their domestic industries through protectionist policies to counteract the British industrial superiority, but differed in that the US economy developed through private enterprise, while the German economy developed thanks to the initiatives of the bureaucracy's top echelon.

Some statistics will suffice to give an idea of the extent to which the economic fortunes of both the United States and Germany surpassed those of the United Kingdom over the period 1870–1913. Industrial production in the United States increased at the rate of 4.7 per cent per annum, and in Germany at the rate of 4.1. The corresponding rate for the United Kingdom was 2.1 per cent.[15] The United States' share of world pig iron production increased from 15.6 per cent in the period 1875–1879 to 40.2 in the period 1910–1913; Germany's share rose from 12.7 to 21 per cent. By contrast, Britain's share decreased from 46 per cent to 13.9.[16] As for the share of manufactured goods in world trade, the figure for the United States increased from 2.8 per cent to 12.6 between 1880 and 1913; Germany's figure from 19.3 per cent to 26.5. Meanwhile, the United Kingdom's share declined from 41.4 per cent to 29.9 over the same period.[17] By 1914 the national income of the United States had reached three times that of Britain, while Germany's came to almost 96 per cent of Britain's.[18]

The new industrial prowess of Germany and the United States enabled their firms to enter the United Kingdom, bringing further dismay and anxiety for the British in their wake. The 'Fair Trade' movement of the early 1880s and the 'Tariff Reform' campaign in the early 1900s symptomised the apprehensions engendered with British industry's relative decline.

2   *The failure to exploit technological innovation*

The second factor was Britain's failure to exploit technological innovation. The American and German entrepreneurs' active pursuit of technological innovation resulted in new industries, while the traditional industries also benefited from the adoption of new methods. In the steel industry, for example, not only were large-scale mills constructed, but new processes, such as the Bessemer and Thomas methods, were introduced.

In Germany, industry was committed to intra-firm research and development, based on which the 'New Industries' – such as the chemical and electrical industries – made such outstanding headway[19] that they soon held dominant positions in these fields.

Economic development in the United States[20] was equally remarkable. Mineral resources were exploited on a large scale: the coal mining industry, for instance, doubled production every decade during the period 1850–1910, while capital stock increased 14-fold between 1860 and 1920. Furthermore, the population trebled between 1860 and 1910, thanks mainly to the massive inflow of European immigrants, which was accompanied by an acceleration of westward migration. Stimulated by the establishment of new cities and the geographical spread of the population, American entrepreneurs developed new methods of marketing, including department stores, chain stores and mail order houses, and improved production methods applying the 'scientific management' techniques devised by F.W. Taylor.

In the United Kingdom, on the other hand, entrepreneurs were slow to adopt new technologies and new managerial methods.[21] There was no attempt to introduce innovations into the traditional industries, nor were new ones being created. In the steel industry British industrialists continued to content themselves with the old small-scale mills. In the cotton industry innovation was similarly spurned. To put it another way, British industry became 'overcommitted' to the established industries and tried-and-tested technologies.[22] Britain also failed to create a chemical industry, although the basic research which provided the foundations for this industry abroad was being done there.

3   *The decline of entrepreneurial spirit*

The third factor is the decline in that entrepreneurial spirit which had been the powerhouse of the Industrial Revolution. This was due to several influences, two of which were particularly significant.

First, 'gentlemanship' was established as the guiding ethos of the British society in the mid-nineteenth century.[23] In the light of this ethos, originating in the aristocracy, business was looked down upon as crude money making, while the aristocratic lifestyle and gentlemanly pursuits represented the true values. Not only the business class but also the middle class came to embrace this ideal. The top of the business class was continually being creamed off into the gentry and land-owning classes, acquiring estates, titles and the associated mode of life. Thus active involvement in business had a tendency to be abandoned the instant a man had garnered sufficient wealth to emulate the ways of his social superiors. The successful business class and the upper-middle class would marry their well-dowried daughters into the old elite, and send their sons to the newly reformed public schools to be inculcated with upper class values, and to be prepared for futures as members of the higher professions, or in the Civil and Colonial Services, whose intake was broadened through the introduction of competitive recruitment examinations.

Shaped by the educational tenets of Thomas Arnold,[24] education in public schools[25] emphasised the Classics and Evangelical Christianity, sidelining the sciences. This tendency was not confined to the public schools, which produced the ruling class: so entrenched was the prevailing ethos that even the working class, most of whom received little or no education, was infected with gentlemanly aspirations. The educational system created a nation that neither could nor would adapt to technological innovation. Successive educational commissions, as well as the press, criticised the shortcomings of British education, especially in science and technology, but in vain.[26]

Second, the emergence of the United Kingdom as a nation of rentiers contributed to the decline of the entrepreneurial spirit. Above all, two economic developments seem to have accelerated the decline:

1   After a long time lag, the free trade policy eventually led to a rapid increase in agricultural imports. Prices fell sharply, in consequence of which landlords and tenant farmers who had invested in the land ceased to do so. British agriculture was forced to shift from wheat to stock raising and horticulture. Directing their resources towards financial investment, the landowners became a rentier class.
2   After 1905 the British were increasingly inclined to invest abroad – a trend that peaked immediately before the First World War. The average annual revenue from interest and dividends, standing at 50 million pounds in the period 1871–1875, reached 188 million pounds in 1911–1913.[27] The interest revenue from foreign investments grew to such an extent that it exceeded the outflow of new foreign investment; although Britain's continued success required more resources to be invested at home, the tendency to invest abroad continued to escalate – a phenomenon we may characterise as capital flight.

III   The interwar years

From 1900 onwards German expansionism repeatedly came into collision with the national interests of the United Kingdom. Two particular sources of tension were the development of the Mark Clearing Zone in northern, southern and eastern Europe from 1907,[28] which signalled the retreat of the Sterling Clearing Zone there, and the advance of Germany into the Middle East (e.g. the construction of the Baghdad Railway Line).

The resulting conflicts, together with the eruption of ethnic tensions in the Balkans, led to the First World War. As we know, the war ended with the defeat of Germany, but the United Kingdom was unable to recover the position she had enjoyed before. The First World War completely destroyed the conditions which had sustained the old international order – the Pax Britannica. Furthermore, the war established not only the military and political pre-eminence of the United States, but also her industrial and financial dominance.

The Versailles Peace Conference was a grand assembly of nations, but the significant issues were in fact decided by the United States, Britain and France. Despite the treaty, the new international order was doomed from the start, because (i) the US Congress vetoed ratification, and (ii) the United States held back from joining the League of Nations, which thus lacked the necessary clout to mediate or intervene in international disputes. Moreover, Versailles left many important issues, particularly reparations and war debts, unsettled.

1   *The American economy*

Around 1910 two overriding factors began to make themselves felt in the American economy. The first was the introduction of mass production in the automobile industry. Initiated by Henry Ford, its impact was phenomenal: the number of cars owned by Americans jumped from 2.33 million in 1915 to 23.06 in 1929.[29] Although the United Kingdom gained the place of second largest car producer, she was left far behind the United States. Given the importance of the motor vehicle industry in the modern economy, this is a good index of the widening gap between the two.

The second factor was the meteoric development of the US chemical industry during the war. Not only did the Americans acquire the technology to produce synthetic dyes, hitherto monopolised by the Germans, but they also succeeded in developing synthetic fibres such as nylon.

The war turned America into a creditor country, Allied war munitions requirements being for the most part financed by American loans – from J.P. Morgan & Co. to begin with, and later on from the US government.[30] American lending continued through the 1920s when the United States increased exports by extending credit. Direct investment abroad was also rising, making America's position as a creditor country even stronger. In the period 1914–1919 net capital exports reached 14.1 billion dollars, and in the period 1920–1933 they were still showing 7 billion.[31] Consequently the net return from foreign investment amounted to 8.5 billion in the period 1920–1933. Thus New York pushed its way to the centre-stage of international finance.

Despite the decisive enhancement of America's industrial and financial status, the United States persisted in maintaining a policy of strict protectionism: for example, the Fordney-McCumber Act (1922) and the Smoot-Hawley Tariff Act (1930)[32] were enacted to prevent any fall in the price of agricultural goods. Industrialists took advantage of the protectionist mood to get tariffs on manufactured goods raised as well. The United States failed to observe the resolutions against high tariffs by the Brussels International Economic Conference (1920), the Genoa International Economic Conference (1922), and the Geneva World Economic Conference (1927).

Up until the mid-1920s, the United States behaved as a good internationalist in the realm of international finance. Thereafter, however, a monetary policy aimed solely at stabilising the domestic economy was adopted, totally disregarding the adverse international repercussions. The curtain finally came down on the old international economy when President Roosevelt unilaterally launched his attack on the London World Economic Conference (1933). At this point the United States shook off her responsibilities as the international economy's leading nation, with the result that the interwar period failed to generate a climate in which a new internationalism might have flourished. This isolationist attitude on the part of the United States contrasts sharply with Britain's stance during the Pax Britannica: it was one of the principal factors that brought the interwar international economy plunging into instability. In Kindleberger's formulation, while Britain had the will to stabilise the world economy but lacked the power, America had the power but lacked the will.[33]

2 The British economy

Britain's economic performance in the interwar years requires assessment from both the domestic and the international perspectives.

From the domestic perspective, the first point to note is that British industry actually made rather impressive progress during this period. The new motorcar and electrical industries were particularly successful, with output growing at a rate of 6 per cent per annum in the period 1924–1937, thereby outstripping 3.3 per cent growth rate shown by manufacturing industry as a whole.[34] Labour productivity even increased in the traditional industries thanks to technological innovation.

In the period 1920–1929 British industrial production grew at a rate of 2.8 per cent per annum, and industrial productivity at a rate of 3.8.[35] The latter figure was actually the highest for the entire period from the 1860s to the 1930s. At the end of the 1920s, therefore, the British economy, aided by the introduction of advanced American technology during the war, had, at least to a degree, succeeded in catching up with the United States. Even in the Great Depression of the 1930s, the United Kingdom experienced no severe decline in economic activity. Indeed, it could be said that these years witnessed some notable economic successes. For instance, GNP grew annually at the rate of 3.9 per cent in the period 1933–1939,[36] in sharp contrast to the economic performance of the United States, where the national income, which had been rising at an annual rate of 3.3 per cent over 1923–1929,[37] plummeted sharply in 1933 to less than 50 per cent of what it had been in 1929. The Roosevelt administration came up with the New Deal in response to the crisis, but the exodus from the Depression did not occur until the outbreak of the Second World War.

The second point is that in spite of good economic performance in terms of production and national income, Britain experienced unemployment on a scale previously unknown. The chief culprit was the stagnation of investment in both domestic and exporting industries; the return to the Gold Standard at pre-war parity in 1925 exacerbated the situation. The average annual rate of unemployment in the period 1921–1929 was 7.7 per cent, far higher than in any previous decade since the 1860s. Unemployment worsened in the 1930s, when it reached 11.1 per cent.[38]

The third point is that the United Kingdom continued to invest abroad on a vast scale throughout the interwar period: some 209 million pounds per annum in the form of interest, profits and dividend in the private sector during the period 1920–1938.[39]

The fourth and final point is that exports stagnated in the interwar period. The average annual balance of visible trade, which had fallen to minus 153 million pounds in the period 1907–1913, plunged to a precipitous minus 361 million pounds in the period 1925–1938.[40] Two main factors account for this. One was the 1925 return to the Gold Standard at pre-war parity, which meant a 10 per cent upward revaluation of sterling against the dollar (while other European countries were keeping their exchange rates low), creating a situation unfavourable to exporting industries. The other problem was that Britain's exports still came mainly from traditional industries, such as spinning. These, however, were heavily dependent on the Asian market, where they were now facing strong competition from Japan. Thus exports of the British spinning industry – 55.8 per cent of total exports in 1870 – fell to just 18.8 per cent in 1938. Even so, the industry retained its position as the top exporter, followed by machinery, which accounted for 12.9 per cent.[41]

From the international perspective, the continuing relative decline of Britain's position in the world economy in the interwar years is all too evident. The share of British industries in total world exports of manufactured goods, for example, fell from 37.1 per cent in 1885 to 19.1 per cent in 1938; the share of British industries in terms of the world production of manufactured goods tumbled from 31.8 per cent in 1885 to 9.2 per cent in 1938.[42]

The evolution of the British economy in the interwar period can be summarised as follows:[43]

1   *The domestic side.* The economy was in a state of imbalance: on the one hand, it suffered from a high rate of unemployment, stagnating exports, and an outflow of capital; on the other, satisfactory economic growth was achieved due to the development of new industries based on the introduction of technological innovations.
2   *The international side.* Britain suffered continuous decline relative to other major economies in terms of both share of world exports and industrial production. Even in the field of international finance, New York caught up with London as a consequence of the First World War.

During this period the British government pursued a deflationary policy. The immediate return to the Gold Standard at pre-war parity, for instance, was seen as being of the utmost urgency for the stability of both the price level and the exchange rate (and therefore, it was thought, for the stability of the world economy). However, in order to facilitate this, sterling had in fact to be re-valued upward against the dollar. To achieve this, the government actually had to lower the price level, clinging to a policy of retrenchment (i.e. of maintaining a balanced or surplus budget).[44] The government also rejected a public spending policy, accepting the so-called 'Treasury View'[45] that this would have no lasting beneficial effect on the economy.

The government had furthermore to deal with the huge amount of interest owed on government bonds[46] that had accumulated as a result of the war effort. It tried to decrease the debt and lengthen the term structure of the bonds, and was successful in the latter objective in the period 1925–1929.

The United Kingdom had persisted in maintaining a policy of free trade over a long period, though the principle of laissez-faire was increasingly being superseded by that of collectivism as from around 1880. After the First World War, however, a great political debate arose over protectionism. The Bonar Law (1922) and Baldwin (1923) governments insisted that a protectionist policy would help to ease unemployment.[47] The general election of December 1923, together with that of 1906, was exceptional in British history, protectionism being a central issue, and the result was a resounding defeat for the Conservative Party which favoured it.

However, in February 1932 the MacDonald government forcibly enacted the Import Duties Bill despite its having been voted down in the House of Commons by 454 votes to 78. Even the United Kingdom was forced to give up the attempt to restore the old international economic order, which then became divided into a number of more or less separate economic blocs.

3   *The international monetary crisis*

In the interwar period, the world economy was subject to chronic monetary crisis. The main reason for this was that, as a consequence of the First World War, the foundations underpinning the Gold Standard had collapsed.

Before the war the smooth operation of the Gold Standard rested on four pillars.

> Britain's basically favourable balance on its current account, the premier financial position of London in relation to other centres, the common money market instruments of the time, and the willingness of other centres to let gold go in the short run, secure in the knowledge that it would return once the crisis was over.
>
> (Moggridge, 1972, p. 13)

The First World War destroyed these pillars. The United Kingdom was now suffering from stagnant exporting industries. While the United States became a creditor country, Britain joined the ranks of the debtors. Meanwhile, the war left Germany obliged to pay huge sums in reparations, though her industrial base was in ruins. Furthermore, the Allies were left owing substantial amounts in war debts to the United States, whose industrial superiority was now overwhelming. It was under these changed circumstances that Britain, followed shortly after by many other countries, returned to the Gold Standard in 1925. Sterling's consequent upward revaluation against the dollar left Britain's ability to export badly damaged.

Then, from the middle of 1928, Wall Street began to experience a speculative boom.[48] Enormous sums of money started to flow into New York, leaving the London money market in a tough predicament. Germany was forced to pay reparations with money borrowed from the United States, but because of the stock boom American loans to Germany were sharply reduced from the latter half of 1928 onwards. The Germans then directed their attention towards London, with the result that the outflow of gold from London further increased. While the

Federal Reserve raised its official discount rate to try to check the stock boom, this only served to accelerate the inflow of gold into New York.

Following the 29 October crash on Wall Street, the German economy, which had boasted the second highest growth rate of industrial production in the world during the period 1924–1929,[49] plunged into depression in 1930. To make matters worse, the Müller and Brüning Cabinets, under the dictates of the Young Plan, implemented a deflationary policy. The number of unemployed increased by 4.2 million between 1928 and 1932 to reach a figure of 5.6 million. Furthermore, the structure of foreign loans to Germany was very fragile because the country was heavily dependent on short-term debts.

The monetary crisis started with a run on the Kredit Anstalt Bank in Austria in May 1931. It immediately spread to Germany, and although President Hoover issued a moratorium, this was to no avail. In July 1931 the crisis spread to Britain. Despite desperate efforts, the United Kingdom lost a huge quantity of gold and was eventually forced to abandon the Gold Standard. Twenty-five other countries immediately followed suit. In April 1933 the United States also abandoned the Gold Standard, prohibiting the export of gold and devaluing the dollar. It was not until after the Second World War that a new international monetary system was to be established.

2 Wicksell's influences on Keynes and his contemporaries

A century after Thornton (1802), monetary economics came to the fore with Wicksell (1898), and the influence on economic theory was powerful, above all in the 1920s–1930s.

In this chapter we set out to examine that strand of thought, taking in Keynes, Myrdal and Hayek as well as Wicksell. How did Wicksell's theory influence them? How did they evaluate it as monetary economics, and in doing so come to take a critical stance on the neoclassical orthodoxy?

This chapter runs as follows. Section I deals with Wicksell, Section II with Keynes, Myrdal and Hayek, concentrating on their views on the state of economics and their own theories. We then look into similarities and differences among them. In Section III we show how Wicksell's influences are now interpreted, and in Section IV we draw our conclusions.

I Wicksell

1 *The state of economics*

Wicksell was a neoclassical economist who argued that a successful economic theory should comprise a theory of relative prices and one of absolute prices, the two being separable. On the former, Wicksell (1893) regards Walras' general equilibrium theory as accurately describing the system of production, distribution and exchange, except for capital theory.[1] On the latter, seeing serious flaws[2] in the quantity theory of money as the theory of absolute prices, Wicksell (1898) puts forward his theory of cumulative process.[3]

Wicksell criticises the quantity theory on three points:

1 It assumes constancy in the velocity of money;
2 It assumes that the medium of exchange consists of notes and coins only, so that the quantity of money is inelastic if the quantity of currency remains constant;
3 It holds that an increase in the quantity of money induces an increase in money prices and a fall in the money rate of interest.[4]

2   *Wicksell's theory of cumulative process*

Wicksell's theory[5] (hereafter the TCP) explains changes in money prices in terms of the relation between the natural rate and the money rate of interest.[6] The quantity of money is assumed to adjust to changes in money prices and trade.[7]

The natural rate of interest is defined as 'the rate of interest which would be determined by supply and demand if... all lending were effected in the form of real capital goods' (Wicksell, 1898, p. 102). It fluctuates incessantly due to technical progress, which belongs to the theory of relative prices. Any change in the natural rate triggers a change in the price level.

The banking system is assumed to have no rapid access to the information on changes in the natural rate which industry is taken to have. It is also assumed that money be lent at a certain rate of interest whatever the demand for it might be.

Thus the divergence between the two rates of interest can persist over an appreciable period. They become equal only as a result of the movement of prices.

Suppose that in an organised credit economy the market rate of interest is kept lower than the natural rate for a certain period of time. The entrepreneurs borrow money from the banking system, using it as a 'wage-rent' fund, and advance it to labourers, landlords and so forth, who, in turn, purchase consumption goods from the capitalists by spending their income. The capitalists earn interest by depositing the sale proceeds which they made at the beginning of the period. The entrepreneurs engaged in production in the current period sell their output (consumption goods) to the capitalists and repay borrowed money to the banking system. As a result, the entrepreneurs obtain excess profits equal to [the natural rate – the market rate] × advanced capital.

If the entrepreneurs continue to reap excess profits, their desire to expand production grows (no actual expansion occurs, the structure of roundabout production being assumed to remain constant). The demand for labour, raw materials, durable investment goods and so forth increases, which induces rises in money wages and rent (full employment is assumed).[8] The entrepreneurs need to borrow more money from the banking system. This is advanced to labourers and landlords, and the same process as described above proceeds.

Once the entrepreneurs take rising prices into account in the conduct of their business, the rise in prices accelerates due to the 'law of continuity and inertia'. Eventually this process comes to an end as the market rate of interest catches up with the natural rate and prices find stability at a new equilibrium.

At the root of the TCP lies the determination of the price level of consumption goods by aggregate supply and aggregate demand. Aggregate supply is assumed to remain constant while aggregate demand depends on the entrepreneurs' willingness to expand production.[9]

In order to see how this works, let us formulate the TCP as originally stated:

$$D_t = D_t(\pi_t - 1) \tag{1}$$

$$M_t = D_t \tag{2}$$

$$\pi_{t-1} = D_{t-1} \cdot (n - r) \tag{3}$$

$$C_{t-1} = D_{t-1} \cdot r \tag{4}$$

$$S_t = Y_{t-1} - \frac{\pi_{t-1} + C_{t-1}}{P_{t-1}} \tag{5}$$

$$D_t = P_t \cdot S_t \tag{6}$$

$$Y = Y_{t-1} = f_{t-1}(T) = \text{constant} \tag{7}$$

where D is the money demand by entrepreneurs; M the money supply by the banks; C the amount of money obtained by capitalists; π excess profit; Y, S, P respectively. the volume of output, the supply, and the price level, of consumption goods; $f(\cdot)$ the production function; n the natural rate of interest; r the money rate, and t time.

Here n and r are exogenous variables, D_{t-1} and P_{t-1} predetermined variables. The system contains six endogenous variables $(D_t, \pi_{t-1}, M_t, S_t, C_{t-1}, P_t)$ and six equations.

Entrepreneurs determine the money requirement based on π_{t-1} (1). This is financed by the banks (2). π_{t-1} equals [the money requirement in the previous period $\times$ the difference between the two rates of interest] (3). The amount of interest in the preceding period is equal to [the money requirement in the previous period $\times$ the money rate] (4). The amount of consumption goods supplied in this period equals $[Y_{t-1} - $ (the volume consumed by entrepreneurs + the volume consumed by capitalists)] (5). Entrepreneurs are assumed to possess the excess profit in the form of consumption goods, and to consume it. Capitalists are assumed to possess an equivalent to the amount of interest in the form of consumption goods, and to consume it.

The price level of consumption goods is determined in such a way that the supply from capitalists (aggregate supply) equals the demand from the factors of production (aggregate demand) (6).[10] This should be the 'fundamental equation'. The volume of output remains constant (7).

II Keynes and his contemporaries

How did Keynes and his contemporaries evaluate Wicksell's theory and set about constructing their own monetary economics? This is the theme of the present section.

1 *Keynes*

A *The* Treatise

Let us start with Keynes as the author of the *Treatise*.[11]

a THE STATE OF ECONOMICS

The views that Keynes expressed in the *Treatise* had to do, above all, with bank rate theories, investment/saving and the quantity theory of money.

Bank rate theories – Keynes identifies four theories, so far developed, regarding the bank rate as:

1   the means of regulating the quantity of bank money (Marshall, Pigou and Hawtrey);
2   the means of protecting a country's gold reserves (Goschen and Bagehot): Keynes evaluates and uses it in his open system;
3   a psychological influence on price levels (Pigou);
4   influencing investment and savings: Keynes regards this as expressing the essence of the bank rate, seeing Wicksell (1898) as representing this view and coming close to his 'fundamental equation'.[12]

Some explanation is required. First, although the bank rate plays a pivotal role in Keynes's theory, money supply also has its part to play. This may have something to do with Wicksell's construction in an 'organised credit economy',[13] and Keynes's criticism that Wicksell does not succeed in 'linking up his theory of bank rate to the quantity equation' (*TM*.1, p.167).

Second, the 'fundamental equation' should be

$$\Pi = E/O + (I-S)/O$$

where Π denotes the price level of output as a whole, E money earnings, O the total output, I the value of investment and S the volume of savings.

On the other hand, Keynes criticises Marshall's monetary theory as found in his testimony before the Gold and Silver Commission (1887) and the Indian Currency Committee (1898) (*TM*.1, pp. 172–173).

Keynes calls his theory – an extension of perspective (iv) – the 'General Theory of Bank Rate', which is explained as follows:

(i)   Suppose that the market rate of interest, say, rises above the natural rate, which causes the demand price of investment goods (and so of investment goods) to fall, resulting in a decrease in the volume of investment while it causes savings to increase, though not by an equal amount. Thus the decrease in investment is greater than the increase in savings.
(ii)   A fall in the price level of investment goods causes production to decrease. And as an increase in savings means a decrease in consumption, the price level of consumption goods decreases. Thus, the price level as a whole falls.
(iii) When producers incur losses, they cut the level of employment at the existing rate of earnings. If this continues, unemployment increases until the rate of earnings is reduced.

(*TM*.1, p. 171)

Keynes argues (i) with the 'second fundamental equation' in mind. The first point in (ii) is based on the 'TM supply function' (to be explained below) in the investment goods sector, the second on the 'first fundamental equation'.

Investment/savings – According to Keynes, the distinction between investment and savings was clarified by Mises (1912),[14] and introduced into the Anglo-Saxon world by Robertson (1926).[15]

Keynes's understanding of savings and investment runs as follows. The income of society is partly spent on consumption, the rest being saved. Saving is a passive act of individuals while investment is a positive act of entrepreneurs. Keynes takes investment from the supply side, which reflects the lack in investment theory in the *Treatise*.

Keynes stresses that investment is not usually equal to savings, offering two reasons: (i) those determining the division of the total output are not the same as those determining that of the total income; (ii) earnings and savings do not include entrepreneurs' profits, while the value of investment does.

Quantity theory – Keynes criticises it[16] with two convictions in mind:

1   Without considering the influence of the bank rate upon investment and saving and the distinction between earnings and profits, the dynamic process of price formation cannot be captured;
2   Any analysis failing in distinguishing between various kinds of transactions will cause confusion.

With the former point Keynes asserted the advantage of the 'fundamental equations' over the quantity theories (see *TM*.1, pp. 198–199), offering two reasons.

1   A change in the bank rate influences factors such as the volume of output and the rate of profits, which means that the quantity of money related to any one of them cannot be estimated.
2   The causation runs as follows: changes in the bank rate cause the market rate of interest to shift relative to the natural rate, which in turn causes the quantity of money, and consequently the price level, to move.

He classifies the demand for money in terms of people's motives and explains the determination of the price level of investment goods in terms of the relation between savings deposits and equities.[17]

In Chapter 14 he examines three versions of the quantity theory: the *Tract* version, the Marshall–Pigou version and the Fisher version, pointing out the following:

1   They deal with various kinds of ambiguous price levels;
2   They fail to distinguish between income, business and savings deposits, so that disturbances arising from changes in the relative proportions of different deposits cannot be explained;
3   They cannot analyse a dynamic process in which the disturbance of the price level arises from a divergence between saving and investment.

Unlike the other Wicksellians, Keynes goes into analysis of the relationship between bank rate and quantity of money. He also offers two reasons for giving priority to the bank rate over the quantity of money.[18]

b   THE *TREATISE* THEORY

The *Treatise* has two theories – a Wicksellian theory and 'Keynes's own theory'. As they are explained in Chapter 5, we shall here touch on the bare bones only.

The *Treatise* belongs to the Wicksellian strand of thought in explaining the fluctuations of the economy in terms of the natural and money rates of interest, and in accepting Wicksell's three conditions for monetary equilibrium.

At the same time, however, the *Treatise* has its own theory, consisting of two parts, one of which addresses the determination of the price level of consumption goods (to be called 'Mechanism 1') and that of the price level of investment goods[19] (to be called 'Mechanism 2') in 'each period'. The other part deals with the determination of variables between one period and the next (to be called the TM supply function or 'Mechanism 3'. Now, this theory can be expressed as the dynamic process consisting of Mechanisms 1, 2 and 3 (see Section I(1(B)) of Chapter 5 of the present book).

B   *After the* Treatise, *and the* General Theory

After the *Treatise* Keynes went on applying 'Keynes's own theory' until mid-1932, disregarding Wicksellian theory. Subsequently, he proposed a simultaneous equation system at the end of 1932.

We should note, moreover, that the *General Theory* rejects the TCP. Rather, he stresses the need to allow for interaction in the working of the economy, and to admit equality of saving and investment (see Section I(1) of Chapter 13 of the present book).

2   *Myrdal*

A   *The state of economics*

Myrdal's criticism of neoclassical orthodoxy went further than Wicksell's. He noted the then growing dissatisfaction over the lack of internal integration between price theory and monetary theory in Walrasian theory,[20] where the problem of production and exchange is dealt with as a theory of relative prices, while the quantity theory is used as a theory of absolute prices.

How did orthodox economics come to incorporate a division between the two theories? Myrdal argues that the marginal utility theory overthrew the classical cost theory with the result that money came to be regarded as nothing more than the power to purchase goods and services.

He deems closer integration of the quantity theory with general price theory logically impossible, for they are based on different principles.[21]

Actually, the quantity theory has serious defects:[22]

1   During a dynamic process the money velocity varies, ruling out any simple relation between the money supply and the price level.
2   The relation between the money supply and the price level cannot be one-way, for both simultaneously depend on factors outside the payment mechanism.
3   The price level in the context of the theory cannot be defined in terms of the multiplicative factor required by the theory of relative prices.
4   Although the quantity theory stresses movements of the price level, no homogeneous price level exists: it ignores change within the price level.
5   The price level as treated in the theory is a curious concept including the prices of pecuniary rights.
6   The quantity theory challenges practical possibility by adopting total sales as weighting principle of a price index.

Points (1) and (2) are made by Wicksell, but not points (3) and (4), for he accepts the autonomy of relative prices.

Myrdal, for his part, proceeds to criticise the central price theory:[23]

1   Failing to provide the 'multiplicative factors', the price theory remains abstract and unreal.
2   The theory has prices concerning a single point in time, and is inapplicable to time contracts. Thus the credit problem is relegated to the quantity theory, which proves unfit for the task, dealing only with the price level. Credit is crucial not only to the price level but also to price relations.
3   Because the price theory embodies Say's Law, it is inapplicable to business cycles.

B   Myrdal's theory

Myrdal endeavoured to construct his own monetary theory through careful study of Wicksell's 'monetary equilibrium', that is (i) equality between the two rates of interest; (ii) equality between investment and saving; and (iii) price level stability.[24]

Myrdal's conclusion is as follows:

1   What matters to monetary equilibrium is condition (ii).
2   Condition (i) does not hold good. But the argument based on condition (i) contains an investment function important in the theory of cumulative process.
3   Condition (iii) does not hold good.

Myrdal formulates monetary equilibrium as

$$R_2 = W = S + D \tag{1}$$

where R_2 is the production cost of gross investment, W free capital disposal, S savings proper, and D total anticipated value-change of the real capital.

All are expressed in ex-ante terms. The money rate of interest which satisfies (1) is 'normal'.[25]

R_2 is the discounted value anticipated at the initial point of time, which the entrepreneurs calculate by discounting various kinds of cost needed for a certain amount of investment. It is a money demand for new investment.

The amount of money which the public freely dispose of is expressed in ex-ante terms. Savings proper (hereafter savings) are defined as the part of income not used for consumption.[26]

$$Y - C = S \tag{2}$$

where Y is income, C consumption and S saving.

Income synonymous with 'net return' is an ex-ante concept defined as

$$Y = B - (M + D) \tag{3}$$

where B is the discounted sum of all anticipations of gross returns in the next period, M the discounted sum of all anticipations of gross cost in the form of operating cost of the co-operating means of production in the same period.

Gross investment and free capital disposal are ex-ante concepts determined by different economic agents, and thus not equal. They are, however, ex-post equal, for the banks make up for the difference.

Monetary equilibrium has two characteristics: (i) a position departure from which produces a cumulative movement; (ii) it fixes certain specific price relations. Myrdal considers that in monetary equilibrium relative prices, the price level, and production might change.

Now suppose that the economy starts off by monetary equilibrium.

The investment function expressed as (4) works as the driving force.

$$R_2 = F(Q) \tag{4}$$

where $F(\cdot)$ is the investment function, and Q the profit margin.

This shows that the entrepreneurs as a whole determine the amount of investment based on the profit margin.

Q is given by

$$Q = \Sigma_w (c_1' - r_1') \tag{5}[27]$$

where c_1' and r_1' are, respectively, the value and the reproduction cost of the existing real capital, and w the investment–reaction coefficient of each firm's investment function.

Equation (5) says that the profit margin as a whole is the sum of the profit margin of individual firms, which is the difference between the value and the reproduction cost of the existing real capital possessed by each firm, weighted by w. Myrdal assumes that the value of capital fluctuates violently while the reproduction cost is inflexible because it includes various kinds of inflexible prices.

Turning to consumption goods, we find two kinds of argument.

The first concerns determination of the price level of consumption goods. The part of income not saved is always equal to the volume of consumption goods sold, O, multiplied by its price level, P_1:

$$Y - S = P_1 \cdot O \tag{6}$$

The left-hand side is the demand for consumption goods, C. The volume of output is determined ex-post by the roundabout production structure. Thus P_1 is determined.

Equations (2)–(6) complete the system. This holds good in each period. Income and the profit margin are subjectively expected concepts. The entrepreneurs determine, based on the profit margin, the amount of investment, which is realised due to 'freie Valuta' and is injected into the production stage of intermediate goods. The demand for consumption goods ascertained through equation (2) determines the price level together with the volume of production ascertained through the roundabout production mechanism.

The second argument concerns the idea that a rise (fall) in the price level of consumption goods induces, through its effect on expectations, a rise (fall) in the value of capital, C_1, in the next period:

$$\Delta C_1 = \Phi \left(\Delta P_1 \right) \tag{7}$$

This influences the profit margin through equation (5). Myrdal's model is thus completed as a dynamic system.

What we need to take into account is the way in which Myrdal deals with the natural and money rates of interest. He argues that in a money and credit system the natural rate of interest should be redefined as a rate of return of planned investment, and that the difference between the two should be understood as the difference between the existing capital and its reproduction cost. Believing that even in monetary equilibrium there exists a profit margin which stimulates investment, he rejected Wicksell's first condition.[28]

Thus Myrdal explains the cumulative process in three cases in which a primary change take place in: (i) anticipations; (ii) the money rate of interest; (iii) savings. What is explained is the situation in which divergence between investment and free capital disposal cumulatively expands, due to the change.

The basic account comprises two stages. In the first stage change comes about along three routes, in the second along two.

The first stage: Route 1 – Suppose that some primary change takes place in a monetary-equilibrium economy. The initial impulse induces a change in the value of real capital but no change in the cost of production, so that the profit margin changes. This leads to a change in the demand for investment.

Route 2 – The initial impulse induces a change in income through a change in 'total anticipated value-change of the real capital', which brings on a change in saving or consumption. Consequently, free capital disposal changes.

Route 3 – Due to Routes 1 and 2, the economy begins to move upwardly or downwardly. Free capital disposal is money capital on the part of the public. The difference between the demand for investment and saving is provided by the banks.

The second stage: Route 4 – A change in the demand for investment goods and in that for consumption goods induces a change in the roundabout production structure, which leads to a change in the volume of production of both goods.

Route 5 – A change in the price level of consumption goods and a change in anticipations are brought about.

3   Hayek

A   The state of economics

Hayek divides the development of monetary theory into four stages:

1   The quantity theory of money;
2   The theory of the chain of cause and effect between the amount of money and prices;
3   The theory of the influence of the amount of money on the rate of interest, and the theory of its influence, through the rate of interest, on the relative demands for consumption and capital goods;
4   The theory of relative prices and roundabout production.

Rejecting the first stage as inadequate from the point of view of methodological individualism (see 1931, pp. 4–7), Hayek argued that the fourth stage, which lies ahead of the second and third stages, is what monetary theory should now be aiming at. He opposed the neoclassical system, arguing that monetary theory is by virtue of the quantity theory detached from general economic theory.[29]

Hayek considered that the fourth stage could be constructed partly on the foundations laid by Wicksell, and partly along the corrected lines developed by Mises (1912).[30]

B   Hayek's theory

Hayek advocates a monetary theory that analyses the process by which a change in the quantity of money influences the structure of roundabout production through a change in relative prices.[31]

Hayek's theory of roundabout production runs as follows:

People spend their money income on consumer goods or producer goods. The relative prices change depending on whether the relative demand for each good increases or decreases. Changes in relative prices apply to consumer goods and various producer goods. Thus there occurs a change in the price margin between successive stages of production. Producer goods consisting of non-specific and specific goods shift so as to be used in higher (lower) stages of production. The production structure becomes longer (shorter), and the volume of output of consumer goods increases (decreases).

Hayek applies this to two states of the economy: the cases of 'voluntary saving'[32] and 'forced saving'. The demarcation is whether the quantity and velocity of money remain constant and fail to influence the real economy.

The former characterises the normal state of the economy which the monetary authority should aim at, while the latter represents its disruption, prolonging disequilibrium.

Let us see what happens in the case of forced saving.

When additional money is injected into an equilibrium-state economy, how are normal prices disturbed and how is the production structure affected? Two cases can be distinguished: the new money is provided to (i) producers, who desire to obtain producer goods; or to (ii) consumers, who wish to buy consumer goods.

In case (i), investment is equal to the sum of voluntary saving and new credit. In case (ii), investment is equal to voluntary saving. In either case, the amount of money increases due to the provision of credit, causing the money rate of interest to fall below the natural rate. Crucially, case (ii) follows as a result of case (i). Let us begin with case (i).

Would-be entrepreneurs provided with credit can now purchase producer goods, but only if they offer to pay prices higher than do the existing entrepreneurs. Due to the fall in the money rate of interest, together with a rise in the price of the original means of production, and a rise in the prices of non-specific producer goods, the existing entrepreneurs will find it rational to reduce expenditure on the original means of production and increase expenditure on new intermediate products.

Thus the new entrepreneurs can generate a more roundabout stage of production. In this way the production process comes to be drawn out.

The volume of output in the stage of production from which the original means of production and non-specific producer goods were withdrawn and directed towards a higher stage of production decreases, and, consequently, the volume of output of consumer goods will decrease. Due to the decrease in the production of consumer goods and the invariable consumption expenditure, the prices of consumer goods rise. Consumers would restore their real consumption to its former level, if possible, by spending more money. The money income of labourers in the producer goods sector increases, and they can now spend their extra income on consumption. Thus they increase their expenditure on consumption, but supply is not rising at the same rate: consequently, the prices of consumer goods mount ever higher.

This argument is crucial to Hayek's theory. The lengthening of the roundabout production structure must eventually increase the output of consumer goods, but, in the case of forced saving, no actual increase occurs. The increased expenditure on consumption due to the increased income of the labourers also plays an important role in Hayek's theory. The output of consumer goods will temporarily decrease due to the lengthening of the roundabout production structure, while expenditure on consumption will continue to increase. Consequently, the prices of consumer goods go on rising cumulatively.

As the public's expenditure on consumption rises on the strength of increased income, there eventually occurs a reverse in the movement of the ratio of demand for consumer goods to demand for producer goods, so that the prices of consumer goods rise relative to those of producer goods.[33]

In this step we see the origins of case (ii). The reverse movement of the ratio of demand for consumer goods to demand for producer goods is the same as in case (ii), where the economy moves in the opposite direction from that in case (i).

4   *Similarities and differences*

At this point it may prove useful to summarise the theories of Wicksell, Keynes, Hayek and Myrdal (adding Lindahl and Mises) in terms of similarities and differences:[34]

1 Wicksell, Keynes, Hayek, Myrdal and Mises adopt period analysis, while Lindahl analyses disequilibrium given that equilibrium is attained at each period;

2 Wicksell, Myrdal, Lindahl and Mises assume an organised credit economy, while Keynes does not, and what matters to Hayek is whether the quantity of money is kept constant;

3 Wicksell, Keynes, Hayek and Mises adopt 'divergence between the two rates of interest' as an analytical tool, drawing critical response from Myrdal and Lindahl;

4 Myrdal and Keynes adopt divergence between investment and saving as an analytical tool; what matters to Hayek is the distinction between voluntary saving and forced saving, while Lindahl assumes that for each period investment equals saving;

5 Myrdal, Lindahl, Mises and Hayek adopt a roundabout production theory. Mises and Hayek regard it as crucial in monetary economics, while Wicksell, Myrdal and Lindal do not; only Keynes does not adopt it;

6 Wicksell, Myrdal, Keynes and Mises accept the concept of the price level; Hayek does not;

7 Wicksell looks to the fluctuations in money prices while the others keep their eyes on the fluctuations in relative prices;

8 Wicksell assumes full employment while the others consider fluctuations in employment;

9 Wicksell, Lindahl, Myrdal and Keynes regard expenditure from income as crucial in determining the price level of consumers' goods;

10 Wicksell adopts the wage fund doctrine while the others do not;
11 Wicksell, Keynes and Lindahl stress the price level stability achieved through bank rate operations. Myrdal and Hayek are critical of it;
12 Hayek develops a doctrine of forced saving while Keynes is critical of it.

III Interpretations of Wicksell's influences

A broad survery of the evaluations accorded to Wicksell's theory should help to clarify our viewpoint.

1 *Positive evaluation*

Leijonhufvud (1981) points to a maladjustment of the rates of interest as the core of Wicksell's influence, regarding the Keynesian Revolution as 'the *Treatise* plus the quantity adjustment' or 'the *General theory* minus the liquidity preference theory'.[35] He supports the loanable funds theory as a theory of interest, and the 'dual decision hypothesis' as a theory of effective demand.

Shackle (1967, chapter 9) takes Wicksell's influence as working against the general equilibrium theory. He regards the *Treatise* and the *General Theory* as manifestations of Wicksell's influence, the *General Theory* and Myrdal (1939) as 'one and the same theory' (1967, p. 126), and the *Treatise* and Hayek (1931a) as two sides of the same coin.

Akashi (1988, pp. 28–29) defines the 'Wicksellian Paradigm' as consisting of the real system and the TCP, seeing it as casting doubt on the quantity theory and yet retaining the remnants of the classical dichotomy. In the line of the Paradigm he made a distinction between Hayek, on the one hand, and the Stockholm School (Lindahl and Myrdal) and the Cambridge School (Robertson and Keynes) on the other, the former focusing on the real fluctuations, the latter looking to the monetary fluctuations. Akashi (1988, pp. 202–204) explains the 'Keynesian Paradigm' in terms of the IS-LM formula.

Hishiyama (1990; 1993) sees the TCP as a challenge to the classical dichotomy and the quantity theory, and as a denial of the ability of the rate of interest to adjust the economy automatically. The *Treatise*, in contrast with the *General Theory*, is regarded as exemplifying the 'Wicksellian mode of adjustment'.

Chiodi (1991, p. 39) upholds the TCP against Ricardo's classical/neoclassical monetary theory. Examining Lindahl and Ohlin, Chiodi (1991, chapter 8) takes a critical position on the concept of Wicksell's influence. He also argues, criticising Patinkin and Leijonhufvud, that Wicksell's monetary theory has been misinterpreted.

Laidler (1991, p. 119) agrees with Ohlin (1937) in regarding the TCP as 'an amplification' of the quantity theory, recognising that Wicksell's followers rejected the quantity theory. Focusing on Wicksell's softening attitude towards the quantity theory between Wicksell (1898) and Wicksell (1915), Laidler ultimately defines Wicksell as a persistent exponent of the theory.

The Horizontalists and Circuitists (Graziani, 2003; Rochon, 1999) rate Wicksell's influence highly in terms of money endogeneity or the circuit point of view.[36] They reject the TCP and the loanable fund theory in Wicksell's theory, accepting the *Treatise* while tempted to reject the *General Theory* (especially the liquidity preference theory).[37]

Woodford (2003) is highly appreciative of the TCP. He stresses Wicksell's 'pure credit economy' in which the quantity theory does not hold.[38]

2 *Negative evaluation*

Milgate (1982, p. 76) and Garegnani (Eatwell and Milgate, 1983, chapter 7) criticise Wicksell's influences, arguing that Wicksell's theory (inclusive of Hawtrey, 1913, 1923; Robertson, 1926; Lavington, 1922) constitutes 'embellishment' rather than overthrow of neoclassical economics.

Amadeo (1989; pp. 130, 158) sees the *Treatise* in line with the 'post-Wicksellian tradition', the *General Theory* departing from it. Amadeo (1994b) regards the Wicksellian analysis in Lindahl and Hayek as the 'static finite period' method, as opposed to Keynes's 'dynamic equilibrium method'.

Rogers (1989) criticises Wicksell's monetary theory as an extended version of the quantity theory pertaining to 'real analysis' in contrast with long-term 'monetary equilibrium' in the *GT*'s chapter 17.

IV Conclusion

Wicksell put forward the TCP as an alternative to the quantity theory. It is a theory of how price fluctuations are caused by the divergence between the two rates of interest in the organised credit economy. Wicksell assumed the classical dichotomy.

The TCP greatly influenced the younger economists, all of them rating Wicksell's theory highly in the evolution of monetary economics, and seeing their own theories as following in Wicksell's line. They did not, however, accept the dichotomy, arguing that monetary theory should not be confined to the determination of absolute prices, although they differed as to how and on what points they should accept the TCP.

3   The life of Keynes

The present chapter briefly surveys Keynes's life,[1] which spans the period from late nineteenth century to the Second World War, and falls into five stages (dealt with here in as many sections). We will take it in relation to the external events forming the background against which it unfolded.

I   The making of an economist

John Maynard Keynes was born in 1883, the eldest son of John Neville Keynes,[2] a Cambridge economist remembered for one text in particular (Keynes, 1890), and Florence Ada Keynes,[3] who studied at Newnham Hall, Cambridge. From John Neville's diaries we gather that Keynes's early years were passed in an enlightened, affectionate home atmosphere. As a child, he displayed many of his characteristic adult traits, such as the ability to grasp the essence of things instantly, and a vigorous, eclectic, intellectual curiosity.

In 1897 Keynes entered Eton College, followed by King's College, Cambridge in 1902, and in 1903 he was elected a member of the 'Society' or the 'Apostles'.[4] Under the guiding spirit of G.E. Moore – whose ethical precepts and moral philosophy drove Russell to turn his back on Hegelianism – the Society's meetings attracted the best students of Cambridge. In this milieu of intense intellectual engagement in philosophy, ethics, aesthetics and literature, Keynes forged the views, value, and friendships which defined his social and intellectual life. A particularly potent influence was Moore's 'religion', with its insistence on a consciousness of the fundamental importance of human relationships and a sense of beauty as the supreme values in life.[5] Influenced by this ethic, Keynes, together with Lytton Strachey among others, advocated atheism, and set himself up against the still-powerful Victorian, middle-class 'double standard'.

In 1905 Thoby Stephen, an apostle and the son of Leslie Stephen, determined to turn his home in Bloomsbury into a meeting-ground for his Cambridge friends, who were joined by the artistic circle of his sisters, the future Vanessa Bell and Virginia Woolf. Out of this grew the 'Bloomsbury Group',[6] which for several decades stood at the cutting-edge of English literary, artistic and intellectual life. It combined a rational and philosophical spirit close to that of the Apostles with the free, intuitive spirit of artists of Post-Impressionism. This fusing of principles found expression in the pursuit of an ethic transcending Victorian morality in their personal affairs and in their attitude to the prevailing order. At the same time, the Group maintained a firm foothold within the political, social and economic establishment, with Keynes as a central member.

Keynes's personality was dominated by two conflicting facets: (i) loyalty to convention; (ii) revulsion against the tradition.[7] The former facet manifested itself in his affection towards his parents and friends, and in his scrupulous commitment to his non-academic affairs including administrative and business obligations.[8]

The other facet accounted for his unflagging readiness to absorb new ideas and indeed to seek out the new in many areas. One field of speculation that he was drawn to by his intellectual curiosity, sparked off by Moore in this case, was probability theory: into it he channelled a great deal of his intellectual energies in his twenties. Revulsion is also seen in his response to the still-dominant Benthamite ethic of the supremacy of economic value; this went hand in hand with his rejection of Victorian pseudo-morality.[9]

Keynes's mind was fortunately able to accommodate this duality; bowing to convention and kicking against tradition somehow managed to co-exist without causing him too much inner unease, although he was not entirely immune to the dilemma.

One of his significant works dealt with probability, starting on his critique of Moore's justification of the accepted rules of conduct and consequentialism[10] with the paper, 'Ethics in Relation to Conduct', which was read to the Apostles in 1904. He thereafter pursued the logical relationship between propositions based on Russell-Whitehead's analytical philosophy and Locke-Hume's empiricism.

Keynes's active career started when he entered the India Office[11] in October 1906. 'Neville's Diaries' describe Keynes's activities in detail.

When Keynes took the Civil Service Examination in 1906, Florence accompanied him to London where they rented a flat. Florence reported on Keynes's frame of mind in detail to her husband. His entry for 5 August, for example, reads: 'Maynard had Political Science on Friday. F[lorence] writes, "He liked the morning papers best, but in neither were quite so many facts required as he would have liked." ' His entry for 26, 'He has gone through his various subjects with me, making an estimate of the marks he will get in each'. The result was second place, and Maynard decided to go to the India Office. On 1 October Neville wrote: 'He is going to the India Office, the top man having chosen the Treasury we are a little disappointed'. On 11 October, the diary notes: 'I have been going very carefully into the prospects at the India Office, & I find the results rather depressing'. Four days later Neville records: 'Florence half wishes that the boy had stayed on at Cambridge, working for a Fellowship, and taking a chance of some career opening out for him'.

The job at the India Office left him feeling intellectually unfulfilled, and he continued to devote much of his spare time to his probability theory. In December 1907 he submitted a thesis to King's College, only to be disappointed. But in 1908 he was able to secure a lectureship. This was contingent on a special arrangement whereby Pigou, Marshall's successor,[12] on Marshall's personal suggestion, paid Keynes £100 per year out of his own pocket.

On 20 March 1908 Neville quoted the letter from his son:

> I have had letters from Macaulay...as well as from Pigou. ...It is evident
> that the dissertation was severely criticised in detail – at which I don't
> wonder, for I exposed an enormous amount of surface & said the greatest
> possible number of controversial things. Hence everybody disagreed
> with something, but with this proviso their remarks are complimentary which
> cheers me....

The next year Keynes was made a fellow on the strength of a revised version
of his thesis.[13]

Keynes started as an economist, lecturing mainly on finance and financial
institutions from 1908 until 1913.[14] In June 1913 he published his first book,
Indian Currency and Finance (ICF). The book was the outcome of a snap
decision in November 1912, which was motivated by

1   a wave of political and public concern over the state of the Indian currency
    in the aftermath of the 'Indian Silver Scandal'.[15]
2   the lack of any considered analysis to explain the actual condition of the
    Indian currency.

In this book Keynes embarked, theoretically and empirically, on his critical
examination of the Gold Standard, which had originated in 1717 when Newton set
the mint price for gold at 77s. 10.5d. per ounce. So quickly was it institutionalised
that 'by the 1830s, the gold standard had become an unquestioned article of faith
to most economists and bankers, remaining so until 1914' (Moggridge, 1972, p. 3).

According to Keynes, the Gold Standard did not represent a unified international
monetary system. Rather, the world had three different monetary systems. At one
end of the spectrum was the United Kingdom, where cheques were used as the
principal medium of exchange, and the bank rate was used as a means of
equilibrating the balance of payments. Mid-spectrum were many European
countries, which maintained gold currency systems and a bank rate, but where a
gold currency never became the main medium of exchange, and the bank rate
never became an effective means of equilibrating the balance of payments.
How well a country succeeded in adjusting the balance of payments through the
bank rate depended on its position in the international short-loan market. There,
in fact, notes were the principal medium of exchange, and the balance of payments
was equilibrated by the amount of gold reserves, suspensions of free payment in
gold, and holdings of foreign credits and bills. At the other end of the spectrum
stood India and Japan, with monetary systems that worked as a gold-exchange
standard:

> The gold-exchange standard is simply a more regularised form of the same
> system as theirs [Russia and Austria-Hungary].
>
> *(ICF*, p. 20)

On the face of it the book was an exposition of the Indian currency and monetary systems, together with proposals for improvement. Keynes identified three characteristics in India's monetary system. First, the actual medium of exchange was the local currency. Second, when the need arose, the government acquired international currencies in exchange for local currency on the London markets. Third, the government maintained both local and international currency reserves as emergency funds.

The significance of the book went beyond its ostensible purpose. Rather, Keynes used the Indian case as a vehicle to advance the 'Gold-Exchange Standard' as the world monetary system for the future:[16]

> ... in the last ten years the gold-exchange standard has become the prevailing monetary system of Asia. ... [I]t is also closely related to the prevailing tendencies in Europe. ... [I]t contains one essential element – the use of a cheap local currency artificially maintained at par with the international currency ... – in the ideal currency of the future.
>
> (*ICF*, p. 25)

In 1911 a career boost came to Keynes in the form of his appointment to the editorship of *The Economic Journal*. He was in an unrivalled position to keep his finger on the pulse of new developments in economics.

II   The First World War

In August 1914 the United Kingdom declared war on Germany. In January 1915, probably on the recommendation of Edwin Montagu, Keynes became assistant to George Paish (Advisor to the Chancellor). He quickly made his mark and in May was promoted to 'No. 1' Division responsible for the financial management of the war, and subsequently, in 1917, to head of 'A' Division responsible for reporting directly on international financial affairs to Robert Chalmers (Joint Permanent Secretary) and the Chancellor.

At this juncture, the United Kingdom was facing a financial crisis. In order to continue the war effort, dollar loans from America were needed desperately. Throughout 1916, though, political relations between the two nations were at a low ebb.

Symptomatic of this was a memorandum issued by the FRB in November 1916 advising member banks to cut down their credit to foreign borrowers: for Britain, this meant huge gold losses. But for an all-out German U-boat offensive, the American government would not have relaxed its uncompromising stand on British borrowing[17] – nor would it have joined in the war. Keynes played a central role in the difficult financial negotiations.

Keynes was devoted to his friends, as the following episode – just one of many – illustrates. When Lytton Strachey, Duncan Grant and others had to appear before tribunals as conscientious objectors, Keynes went to great lengths to defend them. In this connection, on 11 September 1916 he wrote to Duncan Grant, who had been assigned to do agricultural labour: 'I went to the Pelham this morning, feeling almost as nervous as though it was a Tribunal over again. ... The commissioner was very polite, the chairman slightly hostile..., the three others friendly.... They supposed that...you were really spending your time painting away as heretofore...'. Keynes also managed his friends' money. To Duncan Grant he writes on 5 November 1917: 'I invested for you £528. This now yields an annual income of £42 and has increased in capital value to £573. ... I can't promise to do so well as this again!'. In a similar vein he writes to Vanessa Bell on 5 January 1919: 'I have sold out your £300 Sharp Trust at a small profit (including dividend received, the profit is 10.5 per cent for 9 months)... I bought ten steel shares very luckily, as your holding went up £40 in value two days after I bought them'.

The war ended in November 1918 with the victory of the Allies, followed by the Peace Conference in January 1919. Keynes described the situation in the memoir, 'Dr Melchior: A Defeated Enemy'[18] (*JMK*.10, pp. 389–432). Even the highest officials in Britain, says Keynes, were kept in the dark as to when the Conference would be held because of Lloyd George's secrecy. The memoir dealt mainly with the negotiations over the provision of food in exchange for either German ships or gold, interweaving Lloyd George's eloquence and the guile of the French.

Keynes, who participated in the Conference as chief Treasury representative of the United Kingdom, was mainly concerned with two issues. One was the problem arising from the destruction of the three pillars of the pre-war German economy, namely: (i) overseas commerce connections; (ii) the exploitation of German coal and iron; (iii) the German transport and tariff system (see *ECP*, p. 41). The other was the problem of German reparations.

The Versailles Treaty was signed on 28 June. By this time, however, Keynes had handed in his resignation,[19] protesting the Allied terms, and especially the amount of reparations. As soon as he was back in England Keynes embarked on a book revealing the inner mechanisms of the Conference, and criticising the level of reparations stipulated by the Treaty. He wrote to Duncan Grant on 17 July 1919: 'Most of the day I think about my book,.... So that I get on fairly well and am now really half way through the third chapter out of eight'.

The result was *The Economic Consequences of the Peace* (1919. *ECP*), which caused a sensation around the world.[20] Three years later he published a sequel, *A Revision of the Treaty* (1922. *RT*), which has the following summary of *ECP*:

(1)...the claims against Germany...[of] the Allies...were impossible; (2) [because of] the economic solidarity...the attempt to enforce these claims might ruin [Europe]; (3)...the...damage done by the enemy in France and Belgium had been exaggerated; (4)...the inclusion of pensions and allowances in our claims was a breach of faith, and (5)...our legitimate claim against Germany was within her capacity to pay.

(*RT*, p. 69)

Keynes's vivid portraiture of the 'Big Four' caused a sensation. In terms of economics, though, the most valuable part is chapter 5, 'Reparation', in which Keynes attempts to calculate the most appropriate level of reparations.[21]

Moreover, in chapter 6, 'Europe after the Treaty', he discussed three points: (i) the arbitrary wealth redistribution which occurs when inflation causes the collapse of a capitalist economy (*ECP*, pp. 148–150); (ii) the danger of adopting a price control policy to cure inflation (pp. 151–152); (iii) the unfavourable influence on foreign trade of adopting price control and anti-profiteering policies to cure inflation (p. 152).

III   The 1920s

The question of reparations and war debts[22] remained the most serious problem confronting the postwar world. In April 1921 the Reparations Committee managed to decide what the indemnity should amount. Faced, however, with Germany's incapacity to pay, terms and payment schedules were revised (e.g. the Dawes Plan (1924) and the Young Plan (1929)). Then, in 1931, the Hoover Moratorium brought in a suspension of payment because of the European financial crisis. Finally, at the Lausanne Conference of 1932, the reparations plan was scrapped.

Britain's enormous war debts – accruing from the huge loans from the United States for the war effort – were another issue. The United States had declined reparations, and was exclusively concerned with debt repayments. Not only was the Allied proposal to link reparations and war debt turned down, but also the British proposal to cancel the inter-Allied war debts. The United States settled for one-by-one debt agreement.

The terms of British war debt repayments were set with the Anglo-American Agreement (June 1923), but in 1933, with recurrent financial crises raging throughout the world, it was virtually abandoned.

What the issue of war debts and reparations reveals is that pre-eminence had irrevocably passed from the United Kingdom to the United States in military and financial terms. The return to the Gold Standard at pre-war parity in April 1925[23] can be interpreted in terms of Britain's struggle to retain hegemony.

The Cunliffe Committee, in its final report of 1919, recommended a return to the Gold Standard at pre-war parity, stressing a deflationary policy to attain it. The Genoa International Economic Conference[24] (1922) adopted the same resolutions, affirming: (i) a return to the Gold Standard; and (ii) a policy of retrenchment.

The problem was further discussed in the Chamberlain-Bradbury Committee. Testimony to the committee saw opinion divided along three different lines: (i) support for an immediate return to the Gold Standard at pre-war parity (Paish, Cannan); (ii) support for the return in principle, but with uncertainty about the timing (Goschen, Schuster); and (iii) opposition to the return (Keynes, McKenna).

The BOE Governor, Norman, who conferred with the New York FRB Governor, Strong, supported the first option. In April 1925, the Chancellor, Churchill, finally declared return to the Gold Standard at pre-war parity, and persuaded the Netherlands, New Zealand, and various others to follow suit.[25]

Keynes continued to observe and comment on these developments. The question of reparations and war debts continued to preoccupy him, as is shown by *A Revision of the Treaty*, the purpose of which was to 'provide facts and materials for an intelligent review of the reparation problem, as it now is' (*RT*, p. xv). He also remained critical of the return to the Gold Standard at pre-war parity, as is shown in *A Tract on Monetary Reform* (1923) and *The Economic Consequences of Mr Churchill* (1925; *JMK.9*, pp. 207–230. *ECC*).

In the latter text Keynes argued thus. As a return to the Gold Standard at pre-war parity means a rise of no less than 10 per cent in sterling, this would force money wages to be cut. This could be effected either (i) with a policy of credit restriction or (ii) with an all-round cut in money wages by agreement. If money wages were cut, the cost of living would fall after a process of adjustment, and real wages would return to the former level.

The Baldwin government favoured option (i), which Keynes opposed because of 'its unequal effects on the stronger and on the weaker groups, and . . . [an increase in unemployment] while it is in progress' (*ECC*, p. 228). For his own part, Keynes favoured option (ii).

Keynes was also engaged in the Liberal Party's policy-making providing, among other things, a major contribution to *Britain's Industrial Future*,[26] published by the party in 1928.

Other involvements included work on various government committees. Keynes was an assiduous member of the Macmillan Committee,[27] set up with the aim of examining important economic issues mainly through hearings from top leaders in various fields. He had a major hand in the Committee's final report (*Macmillan Report*), which included two particularly significant points:

1   The level of employment could be increased with public investment (or a subsidy to domestic investment), and import controls (or export bounties).
2   Increasing the level of employment with a cut in money wages would be difficult.[28]

IV   The 1930s

In January 1930 Keynes was appointed member of the Economic Advisory Council,[29] and subsequently chairman of its sub-committee – the Committee of Economists.[30] His policy stance emerges clearly from the following points: (i) he opposed Pigou, who advocated cutting money wages cut to fight unemployment;[31] (ii) based on the multiplier theory,[32] he maintained that an increase in the amount of investment effectively influences the level of employment; (iii) he stressed the importance of recovery of business confidence to promote investment, followed by a low interest rate policy, and a public investment policy.

Meanwhile, Keynes had been working on the *Treatise*, which appeared in October 1930. It had taken him six years to write, and met with critical response from several economists, spurring him on to follow up with another book. So it was that in February 1936 the *General Theory* saw the light of day.

It is widely believed that the *General Theory* was deeply influenced by the Great Depression. The influence was, however, much less than has often been argued. We should say, rather, that Keynes's economic thinking was greatly influenced by developments in economics.

Keynes began to draw up the plan for the *General Theory* in the autumn of 1932 and had virtually completed the book by 1934. While he was writing, his thoughts seem to have been dwelling on the progress of the British economy. Having been affected relatively mildly by the Depression, the British economy actually went through rapid recovery and economic growth between 1932 and 1935. We can therefore say that the *General Theory* is based on pre-1932 experience.

Before mid-1932, moreover, Keynes had been analysing the economy in terms of the *Treatise* theory. We can therefore conclude that the shift from the *Treatise* to the *General Theory* was brought about not so much by the economic changes in the period 1929–1932 as by his internal grappling with economic theory, prompted by the criticism of his fellow economists. In other words, the object which Keynes set about analysing in both the *Treatise* and the *General Theory* was the British economy in the 1920s.

This is further confirmed by another consideration. Unlike the *Treatise*, the *General Theory* dealt only with a closed system. It concentrated on theory, and made no attempt to apply it.[33] All this suggests that Keynes was making a thorough re-examination of the *Treatise* theory with the aim of forging a new theory for analysis of the United Kingdom's high unemployment in the 1920s. This is not to deny that the Depression stimulated and promoted the evolution of Keynes's economic thinking. What we question is the view that the *General Theory* was primarily a response to the Depression. The myth might have appeared after 1936, boosted by the New Deal and the rapid spread of the Keynesian Revolution.

We have seen similar revolutions in economics: (i) the Smithian Revolution under the influence of the Physiocrats' speculation rather than being prompted by the Industrial Revolution;[34] (ii) the Marginal Revolution, which was brought about by autonomous intellectual development within economics rather than the economic developments at the time.

In September 1938 Keynes read his paper, 'My Early Beliefs',[35] which contains his reflections on the path his convictions had taken. Around 1903 Keynes accepted Moore's 'Religion', which esteems 'passionate states of contemplation and communion', and logicalness, while rejecting Moore's 'Morals', consisting in Benthamite calculus and the duty of the individual to obey general rules because he believed in the rationality of human nature. As the years went by and 1914 loomed up, said Keynes, he grew increasingly sceptical of the rationality of human nature and attached greater importance to emotions, paying attention to convention and rule. This scepticism made him diffident of excessive individualism. As of 1938, still believing in Moore's Religion, Keynes nevertheless thought it rather narrow, and upheld the individual's duty to obey general rules, criticising Benthamism as 'the worm which has been gnawing at the insides of modern civilisation' (*JMK*.10, p. 445).[36]

V   The Second World War

In July 1940 the Chancellor of the Exchequer's Consultative Council was established. Keynes agreed to become a member, which meant deep involvement in a range of important assignments. They can be classified in three types.

1   External war finance. He played a key role in, for example, the Anglo-American Mutual Aid Agreement[37] (February 1942), and the Anglo-American Financial Agreement (December 1945).
2   The shaping of the postwar world economic order. His most celebrated achievement was the 'International Clearing Union',[38] followed by his proposals on commercial policy, the reparations problem, the relief-reconstruction problem, the commodity problem and so forth. Keynes himself, as chief British representative, proposed and entered into negotiations with America.
3   The formation of the postwar domestic order. Keynes was particularly involved in the problems of employment and social security.

On the issue of employment policy,[39] conflict arose between the 'Economic Section' (Meade, Stone, Robbins) supported by Keynes, and the Treasury,[40] represented by Hopkins, Eady and Henderson. The conflictive points were: (i) the estimate of postwar national income; (ii) the cause of unemployment; (iii) the theoretical framework; (iv) policy stance. Keynes's view as articulated in the *General Theory* got through to the government, and bore fruit as *The White Paper on Employment Policy* (Ministry of Reconstruction, 1944).[41]

As for social security policy, Keynes was instrumental in the drafting of the *Beveridge Report*.[42] Here Keynes and the Economic Section applied simple Keynesian economics.[43]

Within the British Empire his authority and influence stood secure. On the wider, international front, however, he suffered setbacks, particularly in relation to the United States. With Britain militarily and economically exhausted, and American relief taking on such proportions, Keynes's plans in the international sphere were foiled.

It was in his last testimony, shortly before his death, in 'Political and Military Expenditure Overseas' (*JMK*.27, pp. 465–481), that Keynes pointed out the risk implicit in the United Kingdom's assuming the benevolence of the Big Powers, while in 'Random Reflections from a Visit to USA' (pp. 482–487) he expressed confidence in the international competitiveness of British industries.

In 1944 Keynes represented the government at the seminal Bretton Woods International Monetary Conference. In March 1946 he travelled to America to attend the founding sessions of the IMF and the World Bank. Immediately on his return home he died of heart disease.

Let us conclude this chapter with a look at his will (14 February 1941). Keynes instructed the executers and trustees (Geoffrey and Richard Kahn) that (i) his collected books, pictures and manuscripts be deposited at King's College; (ii) his private letters be handed over to Geoffrey; (iii) his manuscripts and letters be handed over to Kahn; (iv) £1,000 be paid to Geoffrey, £1,000 to Kahn, £1,000 plus annuity to Grant, £32,000 to his nephews and nieces, £150 as annuity to Mrs Stephens (his secretary), and the remaining income from the trust fund to Lydia.

What strikes us is the fact that Duncan Grant receives mention in Article 2, with Keynes's earnest wish that his portrait painted by Duncan in the summer of 1908 be kept with special care, while his wife Lydia only appears in Article 10.

4   From the *Tract* to the *Treatise*

Keynes was, at one and the same time, a theoretical and applied economist. Spurred on in his endeavours by upheaval in the real economy, and influenced by the new developments in economics, he tackled analysis of the real economy. *A Tract on Monetary Reform* (December 1923. Hereafter the *Tract* or *TMR*) and *A Treatise on Money* (October 1930. Hereafter the *Treatise* or *TM*. *TM*.1 indicates Vol.1 while *TM*.2 indicates Vol.2) were his major achievements in the 1920s.

Our main concern here is how (and why) Keynes transformed his theory from the *Tract* into the *Treatise*. We will analyse his development around this period, locating when the crucial points occurred and considering why he changed theory. Few serious investigations have been attempted[1] given the paucity of relevant manuscripts.

In Sections I and II the frameworks of the *Tract* and the *Treatise* are outlined respectively, followed by a comparison between the two in Section III. Addressing Keynes's vision which anticipated the *Treatise* in Section IV, we examine the intermediate process in Section V. In Section VI we consider why Keynes changed his theory.

I   *A Tract on Monetary Reform*

The *Tract* stresses the stability of the value of money and the role of the central bank in creating this stability. It also argues that if each country could stabilise its currency value, foreign exchange would also be stabilised, and the Gold Standard would become more of a hindrance than a help.

The *Tract* begins by arguing that changes in the value of money have harmful effects on society. Inflation redistributes wealth in a way that penalises the investing class, with the result that 'inflation [destroys] the atmosphere of confidence [as]...a condition of the willingness to save' (*TMR*, p. 29). Deflation leads to impoverishment of both the wage-earning and the business classes, by inducing the latter to restrict production and employment.

Keynes then goes on to deal with the changes in the value of money caused by printing money – a form of taxation. He warns that this might destroy the monetary system by affecting the public's use of money, recommending a capital levy.

1   *The fundamental equation*

Keynes puts forward the theory of the domestic value of money, advocating a monetary policy to attain a stable price level. His 'fundamental equation' – a Marshall-Pigou type quantity theory,[2] is

$$n = p \, (k + rk')$$

where n denotes cash in circulation, p the price of a consumption unit, k the consumption units equivalent to what the public desire to keep in cash, k' the consumption units equivalent to the public's bank deposits, and r the cash reserve rate of the banks.

The crux here is that 'the price level $[p]$...is the resultant of [bankers' and depositors'] decisions and is measured by the ratio of the...[cash in circulation] $[n]$ to that of the real balances created $[k + rk']$' (*TM.1*, p. 201. Hereafter brackets in quotations are mine).

On this basis he argues as follows. The duty of the monetary authority is to keep the price level stable. Both n and r are under its control, while k and k' depend on the wealth of the community and its habits – 'fixed by its estimation of the extra convenience of having more cash in hand as compared with the advantages to be got from spending the cash...' (*TMR*, p. 64).

Price stability can be attained (i) by stabilising k and k' directly; or (ii) by manipulating n and r in such a way that the fluctuations of k and k' are cancelled.

Although the bank rate influences k' and k to a degree, Keynes doubts 'whether bank rate...is always a powerful enough instrument' (*TMR*, p. 68); instead, he chooses (ii).[3]

Based on the equation, he distinguishes three kinds of inflation/deflation: cash inflation/deflation (an increase/decrease in n); credit inflation/deflation (a decrease/increase in r); and real balances inflation/deflation (a decrease/increase in k and k').

Keynes criticises the quantity theory that a change in n influences p only. In the long run this may be true, but what matters occurs in the short run. The quantity theory, he says, should be revised in such a way that changes in n also influence k, r and k'.

2   *The purchasing power parity theory*

Keynes then considers the 'purchasing power parity theory' accounting for the foreign exchange:[4]

> ...the essence of the...theory [lies] in its regarding internal purchasing power as being...a more trustworthy indicator of a currency's value than the market rates of exchange.

> (*TMR*, p. 71)

He stresses the internal purchasing power rather than foreign exchange in maintaining the stability of a currency's value. On this basis Keynes develops his policy views:

(i) A devaluation policy offers the possibility of 'stabilising the value of the currency somewhere near its present value' (*TMR*, p. 117);
(ii) When the stability of the internal price level is incompatible with that of its foreign price level, the former should have priority;
(iii) Restoration of the Gold Standard would threaten the stability of the internal price level, while it would attain foreign exchange stability only if all other countries would accept it.

II   *A Treatise on Money*

The *Treatise* was published after 'seven years off and on'. Our understanding is that its core is composed of 'Keynes's own theory' and 'Wicksellian theory', both of which are dynamic and monetary.[5] (Four bank rate theories and three versions of the quantity theory seen in the *Treatise* have already been treated in Section II(1) of Chapter 2.)

1   *The core*

In our view, the most significant feature of the *Treatise* theory is the coexistence of a Wicksellian theory and 'Keynes's own theory'. Allow me to repeat, for the sake of convenience, what was explained in Section II(1) of Chapter 2.

We designated the monetary economic tradition stemming from Wicksell and developed by several economists as the 'Wicksell's influences'. The *Treatise* belongs to the Wicksell's influences.[6] Putting the market rate of interest together with the natural rate at its centre, distinguishing between investment and saving, and accepting 'Wicksell's three conditions of monetary equilibrium', the *Treatise* explains fluctuations of prices and output in both dynamic and monetary terms with stability of the price level as an objective. Keynes's Wicksellian theory (the second fundamental equation) plays an important role in Volume 2 of the *Treatise*.

At the same time, Keynes develops his 'own theory' (to be fully explained in Section I(1) of Chapter 5). It consists of two parts, one of which addresses the determination of variables relating to consumption goods and investment goods in 'each period' (Mechanisms 1 and 2, respectively). Mechanism 1 is, in substance, equal to the 'first fundamental equation', which is theoretically more important than the 'second' (see Section II(1) of Chapter 5).

The other part concerns the determination of variables between one period and the next (Mechanism 3). This is formulated in such a way that, if entrepreneurs make a profit (take a loss) in the current period, they expand (contract) output in the next.

'Keynes's own theory' can be expressed as a dynamic process composed of Mechanisms 1 and 2 working through Mechanism 3.

2   *Policy view*

The *Treatise* emphasises the bank (or discount) rate policy manipulated by the central bank. The policy can make the value of investment move in one direction while savings move in the other until profit disappears, and stability of price levels and level of output is achieved.

> ...the governor of the whole system is the rate of discount. ...the only factor...subject to...the central authority.../[T]he control of prices is exercised...through the control of the rate of investment. [O]ur fundamental equation has shown that, if the rate of investment can be influenced at will, then this can be brought in as a balancing factor to affect in any required degree...the price level of output as a whole.
>
> (*TM*.2, p. 189)

The 'fundamental equation' should be the second fundamental equation.

III   Comparison

Let us now draw some comparisons between the two books.

1   The most conspicuous difference between the two texts lies in the position of the rate of interest. In the *Tract* it plays a marginal role, in the *Treatise* a central role.
2   The *Tract*'s fundamental equation does not depart far from the quantity theory of money while the *Treatise*'s fundamental equations decidedly part company with it.
3   In the *Tract* public finance is discussed only in relation to the procurement of fiscal funds through inflation induced by printing money. The *Treatise* expresses the view that a deficit budget may be necessary in periods of depression.
4   In the *Tract* there is only one price level. In the *Treatise* there are two.
5   In the *Tract* the whole quantity of savings is assumed to be invested, while in the *Treatise* investment and savings are distinguished.
6   In the *Tract* unemployment is dealt with only in connection with deflation, but how it relates to the fundamental equation is unclear. In the *Treatise* unemployment is dealt with more consistently.

At the theoretical level the difference between the two is greater than that between the *Treatise* and the *General Theory* (see Section III(1) of Chapter 13 of the present book).

IV   The *Treatise* vision

When did Keynes come to see the real economy in terms of the *Treatise* vision? By 'vision' we mean the basic representation of the economy upon which an elaborate theory is constructed. In any case, the vision is clearly recognisable in Keynes as a commentator on economic issues as from 1924 on.[7]

Immediately after the *Tract* we find him writing articles that no longer depend on the *Tract*, but which conceive of the economy in terms of the rate of interest and the distinction between investment and saving. This emerged even while Keynes, as a theorist, was entangled in the *Tract* theory.

The first sign we find of the change is in 'Free Trade' (*The Nation and Athenaeum* [hereafter *NA*], 24 November and 1 December 1923), where Keynes analyses the economy in terms of investment, saving, foreign investment, the rate of interest and unemployment.[8] In 'Does Employment Need a Drastic Remedy?' (*NA*, 24 May 1924), he insists that the government should use subsidies to divert savings from foreign investment to home investment, and that it should spend the sinking fund on domestic capital construction. Similarly, in 'A Drastic Remedy for Unemployment' (*NA*, 7 July 1924), he argues that a high rate of interest abroad causes a drain on domestic saving in the form of foreign investment, and that this in turn results in insufficient domestic investment, leading to unemployment and BP disequilibrium. Domestic investment and government subsidies are presented as second best given the difficulty of lowering the internal rate of interest. He repeated the same argument in 'Some Tests for Loans to Foreign and Colonial Governments' (*NA*, 17 January 1925), 'Our Monetary Policy' (*The Financial News*, 18 August 1925), and 'The Autumn Prospects for Sterling' (*NA*, 23 October 1926).

V Examination through primary material

In this section we examine Keynes's development from the *Tract* to the *Treatise*. Following a zigzag path, he continually rewrote his manuscripts, introducing new ideas. Various Tables of Contents (hereafter the TOC or the TOCs), a few manuscript fragments, several pieces of correspondence and the Macmillan Committee evidence survive.

1 *The* Tract *theory*

How long did Keynes maintain the *Tract* theory? The evidence leads us to conclude that he did so until the TOC [27.4.26] (which indicates the TOC dated 25 April 1926).

A *The fundamental equation*

The TOC [14.7.24] (Tm/3/2/6–7 [a paging system adopted in Keynes Papers, Reel 28]; *JMK*.13, pp. 15–16), entitled 'The Standard of Value', is the earliest of the TOCs.[9] We see terminology such as cash (m), the price level (p), the purchasing powers (k and k'), and the relation of credit to cash (r).

In the TOC [9.10.24] (Tm/3/2/8–10; *JMK*.13, pp. 16–18), 'The Monetary Standard', noteworthy is the heading of chapter 4, 'Prices Regarded as the Ratio of the Supply of Money Credit to the Supply of Real Credit', which the TOCs [30.11.24][10] (Tm/3/2/12; *JMK*.13, p. 18) and [21.3.25] (Tm/3/2/13–5; *JMK*.13, p. 27) also contain, and which the TOC [6.4.25] (Tm/3/2/16–7; *JMK*.13, pp. 28–29) contains in a similar form, but crosses out. The supply of money credit would correspond to *n*, and the supply of real credit to *k* plus *rk'*, so that the price level p as the ratio of the two would correspond to $n/(k + rk')$ in the *Tract* equation. This idea is related to chapter 2, 'The Law or Equation of Money Recapitulated'. These TOCs essentially belong to the *Tract* theory.[11]

In the November 1924 manuscript, 'A Summary of the Author's Theory' (Tm/3/2/63–70; *JMK*.13, pp. 19–22), two sets of conclusions are drawn. One is an argument concerning the stability of the price level, similar to that found in the *Tract* and apparently related to chapter 4 of the TOC [9.10.24]:

> I shall argue in this book ... that the general price level [*p*] can be stabilised by giving the [BOE] a control over the volume of bank-money created [*n*], ... , and by using this control to cause the volume of bank-money to vary in the same proportion as that in which the volume of real balances [*k* and *k'*] varies.
> (Tm/3/2/69–70; *JMK*.13, p. 21)

The other deals with the trade cycle theory, where circulating capital is emphasised. Judging from the absence of circulating capital from the TOC [9.10.24], the term seems to be first introduced here. Moreover, the absence of working capital suggests that this may have been written prior to the TOC [30.11.24], in which working capital is stressed, and before the manuscript for chapter 4, 'Working Capital in Slumps and Booms' (Tm/3/2/72–5; *JMK*.13, pp. 22–24).

The phrase 'the fundamental equations of money' appears for the first time in the TOC [6.4.25]. Here we find expressions like 'the determination of price by the ratio of the supply of money-credit to the supply of real credit' and 'the velocity of circulation' (both of them crossed out). We also see the phrase, 'the fundamental equation of money', in the TOCs [13.6.25] (Tm/3/2/18–20; *JMK*.13, pp. 41–42) and [30.6.25] (Tm/3/2/21; *JMK*.13, pp. 42–43).

Noteworthy in the TOCs from [9.10.24] to [13.6.25] is the stress on 'money credit' and 'real credit'. In the Keynes–Robertson correspondence in May 1925 (Tm/1/2/9–31), Keynes investigates the factors determining the volume of money credit and that of real credit, and distinguishes price fluctuations initiated by changes in money credit (inflation/deflation) from those initiated by changes in real credits (boom/slump). These correspond, respectively, to cash inflation/ deflation and real balances inflation/deflation in the *Tract*. The same investigation is seen in the TOCs [30.6.25] and [27.4.26], which have the terms 'bank money' and 'purchasing power'.

Judging from the above, we might suppose that he proceeded along the *Tract* theory until the TOC [27.4.26] (Tm/3/2/22; *JMK*.13, pp. 43–44).

B　The bank rate

Keynes shows interest in the bank rate (or discount rate): we see the title heading, 'the influence of bank rate on prices' in the TOC [14.7.24] and the phrase 'bank rate' in the TOCs [9.10.24] and [30.11.24], followed by 'the part played by the rate of discount' in the TOCs [21.3.25] and [6.4.25], and 'the *modus operandi* of bank rate' in the TOCs from [30.6.25] on.

This might not be an entirely new element, however, for these TOCs are argued on the *Tract* equation.

2   New elements

In the above-mentioned TOCs we find new elements leading to the *Treatise*.

A   Working capital

Working capital is emphasised from the TOC [30.11.24] on. It is argued in the manuscript, 'A Summary of the Author's Theory' (November 1924), which is closely related to chapter 3, 'Fluctuations in the Demand for Working Capital in Relation to the Trade Cycle' of the TOC [30.11.24].[12] In a slump, neither the recovery of business sentiment nor the expenditure of public money raised by taxation alone can suffice to bring about a rapid increase in employment.

> only through the replenishment of working capital, by new savings becoming ... available in liquid form, the position can be restored.
> (Tm/3/2/72; *JMK*.13, p. 23)

He believes that fixed capital might be an obstacle to employment by depriving working capital of current savings, thus opposing 'the expenditure, on the production of *fixed* capital, of public money ... raised by borrowing' (Tm/3/2/72; *JMK*.13, p. 23).[13]

B   The bearishness function

Although the bearishness function plays an important role in the *Treatise*, it is very difficult to find any direct traces of it. Savings deposits (semantically preceded by 'investment deposits' in the TOCs from [30.6.25] to [2.6.27], which are related to that function), appear for the first time in the TOC estimated to have been written between September 1927 and September 1928 (Tm/3/2/33). However, not even the TOC [2.8.29] reveals any section corresponding to 'the price level of new investment goods' (*TM*.1, pp. 127–131).

Concerning an investment price theory, we have a fragment (December 1929. Tm/1/2/7–8; *JMK*.13, pp. 119–120), where the price of new investment goods, P', is 'determined by degree of capital inflation which depends on rate of interest and bull-bear sentiment', while the 'price of old capital [P''] determined by rate of interest and by expectations of future prices'. He then states that 'P' will be dragged up and down by P'''.

3   *An international monetary standard*

The TOCs from July 1924 through April 1925 show Keynes's preoccupation with an international monetary standard, which suggests he was motivated by the Gold Standard controversy.

He remained a vociferous critic of the return to the Gold Standard. In the *Tract* he opposed it, mentioning points (ii) and (iii) in Section I(2) above. In Keynes (1925)[14] he warned that return to the Gold Standard at the old parity (which meant 10 per cent appreciation) together with tight monetary policy would bring harm to the British economy. What he favoured was a *uniform* reduction of wages by agreement. (See Section III of Chapter 3 of the present book.)

The TOC [14.7.24], 'The Standard of Value', includes an examination of managed and automatic currency systems, the automatic and the managed Gold Standard, and the controlling authority's instruments and objectives. In the TOC [9.10.24] entitled 'The Monetary Standard', 18 of the 23 chapters deal with ideal standards, including an important argument relating to chapter 38 of the *Treatise*, 'Problems of Supernational Management', where the requirements of a standard, 'short-period adjustability to the fluctuations of real balances and credit', and 'long-period stability of intrinsic value' are pointed out. He mentions, moreover, the tabular standard as an alternative intrinsic value standard.

However, as he proceeds to the TOCs [21.3.25] and [6.4.25], entitled 'The Theory of Money with Reference to the Determination of the Principle of an Ideal Standard', Keynes increasingly concentrates on the theories of credit money and the credit cycle.

The change of the title from 'The Monetary Standard' (October 1924) to 'The Theory of Money with Reference to the Determination of the Principle of an Ideal Standard'(early 1925) suggests that his interest was moving from a monetary standard to the theory of money. In the TOC [21.3.25], one of the nineteen chapters deals with the monetary standard, while the rest address working capital, money credit, real credit and price fluctuations.

In fact, from the second half of 1925 up to the TOC [31.8.26] (Tm/3/2/27; *JMK*.13, pp. 45–46), the title 'The Theory of Money and Credit' seems to have been related to the United Kingdom's return to the Gold Standard.

4   *Activities in the late 1920s*

Throughout the late 1920s Keynes was involved in Liberal Party policy-making and was one of the principal contributors to *Britain's Industrial Future* (1928). His commitment also extended to participation in government committees, including the Macmillan Committee. He played a major role in drafting the Committee's final report (*Macmillan Report*, 1931) which included the following recommendations: an increase in the level of employment should be pursued through public investment and import controls, while considerable difficulty would be involved in increasing the level of employment with a cut in money wages. (See Section III of Chapter 3 of the present book.)

5   *The development of the fundamental equation(s)*

The most effective method of theoretically distinguishing the *Tract* from the *Treatise* is to track how the 'fundamental equation(s)' are dealt with.

A   *The transaction approach*

What was described in the TOCs [26.5.26] (Tm/3/2/23; *JMK*.13, p. 44), [6.8.26] (Tm/3/2/26; *JMK*.13, p. 45) and [31.8.26] (Tm/3/2/28) as 'the fundamental equation of price'[15] first took the form of 'the fundamental equations of price' in the TOC [23.5.27] (Tm/3/2/31; *JMK*.13, p. 47). What characterises them is that the equation(s) are developed along Irving Fisher's Transaction Approach,[16] for the elements of the 'fundamental equation' are the velocity of circulation, the proportion of investment deposits, the volume of total deposits, the volume of transactions etc. This is true of 'the fundamental equations', which are enumerated as 'the first and second' equations, in the TOC [2.6.27] (Tm/3/2/32; *JMK*.13, pp. 47–48) and [22.9.27] (*JMK*.13, pp. 48–50). These TOCs are entitled 'A Treatise on Money').

Fisher's formulation is

$$MV + M'V' = PT$$

where M denotes the quantity of money, V its velocity of circulation, M' bank deposits, V' their velocity of circulation.

The equation shows that if M and M' are, say, doubled (M' is assumed to hold a definite relation to M), then P is doubled provided that V, V' and T remain unchanged.[17]

Simultaneously, however, Keynes maintains the *Tract* theory. We find headings such as 'cash balances and real balances', 'price level as the factor which brings decisions of bankers and depositors into harmony' (Tm/3/2/23; 26; 32: *JMK*.13, pp. 44, 45, 48).

B   *The embryo of the fundamental equations of the* Treatise

There survive three TOCs from September 1927 to September 1928 that signal sea change in Keynes's thinking from the Transaction Approach to the idea leading to the *Treatise*.[18]

Let us call the first two, estimated to have been written between September 1927 and September 1928[19] (Tm/3/2/29–30 and 33–36),[20] TOC(1) and TOC(2).

TOC(1)[21] contains headings such as 'the flow of consumers' income', 'withholding of consumption and of sales', 'quantity of money versus flow of income', and 'the fundamental equations', although we do not find savings and investment. TOC(2) contains headings such as 'quantity of money versus flow of income', 'the fundamental equations for the purchasing power of money', 'the relation of the price-level to the rate of earnings and to the rate of employment', and 'savings and investment', showing that Keynes was beginning to turn his attention to the elements comprising the *Treatise*'s fundamental equations.

In TOC(2) we first encounter the chapter, 'Alternative forms of the Fundamental Equation', which contains three types – the 'Real Balances' quantity equation, the 'Cambridge' quantity equation, and the 'Fisher' quantity equation (Tm/3/2/36) – indicating that he is still influenced by Fisher. It is interesting to compare it with the TOCs [6.10.28] (Tm/3/2/39–45; *JMK*.13, pp. 78–82) and [2.8.29] (Tm/3/2/46–55; *JMK*.13, pp. 113–117), which contain a section on the relationship between the Fisher equation and his fundamental equation (Tm/3/2/41; Tm/3/2/48).

TOC(2) is also noteworthy for the first appearance of a distinction between savings and investment, which is related to the chapter, 'Fluctuations in the Rate of Investment', followed by the TOCs [4.9.28] (Tm/3/2/37–38)[22] [6.10.28] and [2.8.29]. In the TOC [2.8.29], we see expressions such as 'by restoring equilibrium between saving and investment', 'by stimulating savings', and 'by changing the channels of investment' (Tm/3/2/52; *JMK*.13, p. 116). These corroborate our argument that Keynes slowly adopted the distinction between investment and saving.

The third TOC [4.9.28] includes headings such as 'the fundamental equation' and 'digression on savings and investment'.

The TOC [6.10.28] contains headings such as 'quantity of money versus flow of income', 'the fundamental equation for the purchasing power of money' (which should indicate 'the fundamental equation in terms of monetary factors'), 'digression on savings and investment', and 'earnings and profits'.[23] The TOC [2.8.29], which has headings such as 'flow of income versus quantity of money', 'the relation of the price level to the rate of earnings and to profits', 'the rate of employment', and 'earnings and profits' (Tm/3/2/48; all are crossed out), is noteworthy, for Keynes distinguishes between the fundamental equation 'for the purchasing power of money' and the one 'in terms of monetary factors', which might suggest two ways of expressing the price level of the consumption goods.

All the TOCs from [6.10.28] onwards place the main emphasis on the fundamental equation in terms of monetary factors.[24] While this indicates that the Transaction Approach is still dominant, we see the direction turning towards the equations of the *Treatise*. In this respect the year 1928 is crucial.

C   *Thereafter*

Keynes's Michaelmas lectures of 1929 were delivered along the lines set out in the galley for the TOC [2.8.29].

In his letter to Keynes (29 September 1929, Tm/1/2/42[25]), Kahn wrote that

> ... the modification in the treatment of the Fundamental Equations that you have now introduced ... carry, ... big advantages.

Kahn must be referring to 'the modification' of the fundamental equation 'for the purchasing power of money' (Tm/3/2/48; *JMK*.13, p. 114), as appears to be corroborated by his letter to Keynes (17 December):

> I...feel that a few simple equations involving the elements of savings and profits that are devoted to the banking system... and to new investment, would make things much clearer.
>
> (*JMK*.13, p. 121)

We also have Robertson's letter to Keynes (5 December) in which Keynes seems to refer to the role played by profits, an increase in investment, a rise in prices etc., which indicates something like the first fundamental equation:

> ...I find a certain indeterminacy about the role of profits. They first appear as a result...of the rise of P: then, ...in connection with bank-rate, as a motive-force towards the excess of investment which raises P....
>
> (Tm/1/2/34–35; *JMK*.13, pp. 118–119)

Thus, the first fundamental equation possibly came into being, in some form or another, after the TOC (2.8.29).

The preface dated 1 September 1929 (Tm/3/2/56–60)[26] is worth noting for comparison with the *Treatise* preface. In the latter Keynes declares, 'In Books III and IV... I propose a novel means of approach to the fundamental problems of monetary theory' (*TM*.1, p. xvii), while in the former he expressed his view less clearly: 'as the point of the book lies... more in its cumulative effect than in any particular part of it.... the central theory of the book is to be found in chapters 9 [the fundamental equation], 10 [digression on savings and investment] and 16 [the genesis of the price level], ...' (Tm/3/2/56).

The best source for Keynes's theoretical situation in early 1930 is the evidence he offered in February–March 1930 in the Macmillan Committee (*JMK*.20, pp. 38–157).

In his considerations on the fundamental equations (though these terms are not used) Keynes discusses the first and second fundamental equations in broad terms, with the TM supply function behind the scenes (see *JMK*.20, pp. 74–75).

However, it is also clear from Keynes's letter to Kahn (18 March 1930. *JMK*.13, pp. 125–126) that the fundamental equations had yet to be established.

> ... I...[cannot] arrive at any simple formula connecting the change in the value of investment with the amount of saving which goes on through the banking system...
>
> (*JMK*.13, pp. 125–126)

Subsequently, he revised the chapter on the fundamental equations, which is confirmed by his letter to Hawtrey (18 July 1930).

> ...I have been drastically re-writing the chapter which deals with the fundamental equations. This looks a great deal more different from the old version.... [I]t brings out much more definitely what is in my mind.
>
> (Tm/1/2/171. *JMK*.13, p. 135)

6   *Robertson's influences*

Keynes had ongoing discussions with Robertson regarding Robertson (1926)[27] in the making. Initially, as his 28 May 1925 letter[28] to Robertson (Tm/1/2/18–20. *JMK*.13, pp. 34–36) shows, Keynes objected to a 'distinction between hoarding and forced effective abort lacking' and the idea of the power of inflation to bring unused resources into use. In his 10 November 1925 letter (*JMK*.13, pp. 40–41), however, Keynes essentially agreed with Robertson's revised ideas (see *JMK*.13, p. 40).

The object of Robertson (1926) was 'to interweave with the... "non-monetary" argument of (Robertson, 1915) a discussion of the relation between saving [lacking], credit creation and capital growth' (Robertson, 1949, pp. vii–viii). Credit-creation by the banking system plays an important role in the procurement of real capital (required for the increase of production) by entrepreneurs, which in turn induces a rise in the price level.

It was not until two years later that a distinction between investment and saving began to make its appearance in Keynes. Moreover, Keynes dealt with 'savings and investment' in the TOCs [4.9.28] (Tm/3/2/37), [6.10.28] (Tm/3/2/41; *JMK*.13, 79) and [2.8.29] (Tm/3/2/48; *JMK*.13, p. 114) only as a 'Digression'.

The TOC [2.8.29] is the last of the TOCs, consisting of thirty-two chapters in the form of one volume with only chapter 23 surviving.

We recognize Robertson's two influences in chapter 23, 'The Part Played by the Banking System' (*JMK*.13, pp. 83–113).

The first concerns the stability of prices.[29] Accepting Robertson's idea that '[t]he aim of monetary policy should surely be...to permit [price increase]... necessary to...appropriate alterations in output' (Robertson, 1949, p. 39), Keynes came to think that the right way to achieve price stability

> must be sought...in the discovery of some means to meet the fluctuating demands for...credit without causing those reactions on the stability of the price level.
>
> (*JMK*.13, p. 90)

The second point concerns forced saving. Keynes considers 'methods of adjusting the supply of working capital by means of banking policy'. One of the methods is the use of credit inflation, which induces forced saving. He was prepared to allow employment and output to increase at the expense of price stability (see *JMK*.13, p .104).

These points are recognisable in the TOCs [6.10.28] and [2.8.29], which include the headings, 'the "justification" of credit inflation' and 'by forced transfers [or transferences] of purchasing power from "unproductive" consumers'.

Thereafter, however, these phrases no longer found any place in his writings. The divergence between Keynes and Robertson widened.[30]

7   *The final stage*

Keynes wrote to Harcourt (26 September 1928) that 'I have devoted the whole of this summer to [the *Treatise*]...four-fifths...is...finished' (Tm/1/3/91; *JMK*.13, p. 51). He planned to publish a one-volume book in May 1929.

Of the proofing process there survives only the first galley for chapters 30 and 31, with '16 July 1929' and '27 July 1929' stamped on them respectively. Keynes then changed the arrangement of the book, and wrote to Harcourt (28 August and 25 September 1929, respectively):

> the rewriting...will prove a great improvement.
>
> (Tm/1/3/103; *JMK*.13, p. 117)

> I have...decided to make it a two volume book and am hopeful that the sheets will be ready for dispatch to you by the end of this year....
>
> (Tm/1/3/107)[31]

Keynes wrote to Harcourt on 18 February 1930:

> Since [25 September] I have been working on the book continuously. But the labour of revision and rearrangement in two-volume form has proved very heavy, and...the end is not yet. At the moment, I have finished the revision of the first volume and about half of the second volume....next Easter vacation will see the completion of the book.
>
> (Tm/1/3/109)[32]

From the third galley of the *Treatise*, there survive only chapters 21 and 25, on which '4 March' and '28 May 1930' are respectively stamped.[33]

It was now Hawtrey who appeared as a critic. On 23 April 1930 (Tm/1/2/84–5; *JMK*.13, pp. 13–22) Keynes sent Hawtrey a batch of the proofs, followed by 'a good batch of Volume II; though unfortunately this still does not include Chapter 30...' (24 June. Tm/1/2/89).[34]

Hawtrey responded to Keynes with long critical notes[35] (7 and 9 July, Tm/1/2/94–151 and Tm/1/2/152–166 respectively),[36] representing the most important source on Keynes's state of development at the end of April: we see the formulation of the second fundamental equation[37] as well as the TM supply function and the natural rate of interest (Tm/1/2/146–147; Tm/1/2/137):

> The sequence here assumed is first a fall of prices, and then a contraction of output. With that assumption the unemployment inevitably appears as consequential upon the excess of saving over investment, for [the excess] is merely the fall of prices (relative to costs).
>
> (Tm/1/2/107)

> Mr Keynes' formula...does not recognise the possibility of a reduction of output being directly caused by a contraction of demand.
>
> (Tm/1/2/106)

> [W]hile a windfall loss...produces a tendency to a reduction of output, this has not been...a contributory cause of actual...unemployment.
>
> (Tm/1/2/116)

We know the progress as of 30 June in a letter to R. & R. Clark;

> I could let you have the proofs of the whole of Vol. I and of the first 144 pages of Vol. II, finally marked for press, the greater part of them immediately and the rest within a few days.... The further corrections are by no means extensive.
>
> (Tm/1/3/1139)

On 18 July Keynes wrote to Harcourt:

> [T]he book is now at last really reaching its final conclusion. Almost the whole of [the book] is now in type, and I am sending off sheets marked for press every few days... .
>
> (Tm/1/3/115)[38]

On 14 September Keynes wrote to his mother:[39]

> This evening...I have finished my book. It has occupied me seven years off and on...Artistically it is a failure. I have changed my mind too much during the course.
>
> (*JMK*.13, p. 176)

VI Conjectural conclusion

We must now address our unanswered question: why did Keynes change his theory?

1   Keynes went on working out his theory along the *Tract* theory until around April 1926, when he abandoned the 'fundamental equation' of the *Tract*. What made him change his mind? One reason might be that Keynes was becoming aware of the importance of the bank rate and movements in investment and saving. This is substantiated by his series of topical articles, starting from 24 November 1923. He might have thought that the *Tract* equation could not treat the interest rate.

2   He then continued to adopt the Transaction Approach up until September 1927. Awareness of the importance of the bank rate and movements in investment and saving did not mean that Keynes tried to construct his theory in terms of investment and saving. Being unsure of it theoretically, he may have sought a new possibility in Fisher's Transaction Approach.

3   Keynes might have again recognised the importance of the bank rate and movements in investment and saving. This could have something to do with Robertson's (and Wicksell's) theoretical influence in terms of the distinction between investment and saving, and a dynamic analysis. Possibly Keynes became dissatisfied with the Transaction Approach, and sought a new direction.

4   The three TOCs between September 1927 and September 1928 point the way towards the *Treatise*'s fundamental equations. They might well have constituted a breakthrough on the way to the *Treatise*. Keynes's dissatisfaction with the Transaction Approach was due to its incapability of dealing with the dynamic problem. He wanted to deal with the movement of the price level in a more explicit and quantitative way. Evidence of this endeavour is recognisable in the TOCs. Unable to find a definite solution, however, he was in no position to abandon the Transaction Approach.

5   By the end of April, the second fundamental equation, the TM supply function and the natural rate of interest made their appearance. The first fundamental equation possibly appeared around August 1929. However, he revised the chapter on the fundamental equations. We also see that the key elements for the *Treatise* theory emerged at a very late stage.

6   We cannot draw a clear line on the way from the *Tract* to the *Treatise*, for whatever stage we focus on, we find old and new ideas jostling side by side – sometimes ambiguously – in Keynes's theoretical progress.

5   The *Treatise*

The main purpose of this chapter is to elucidate the theoretical structure of the *Treatise* as clearly as possible. If we adhere to the famous 'fundamental equations', the theoretical structure of the *Treatise* will become unclear.[1] What we need to do is to clarify the theoretical structure from the basic assumptions which lie behind the fundamental equations.[2]

Keynes's critique of earlier views (four bank rate theories and three versions of the quantity theory) seen in the *Treatise* were treated in Section II(1) of Chapter 2. Concerning on several Wicksellian theories, the similarities and differences were touched on in Section II(4) of Chapter 2.

In Section I, we will put forward a concrete formulation of the theoretical structure of the *Treatise*, while in Section II we go on to examine two problems; the dual determination of the price level of investment goods, and the overestimation of the fundamental equations. In Section III we will consider certain elements which are vitally important to an understanding of Keynes's theoretical development.

It should be noted that in this chapter our main concern is to construct 'Keynes's own theory' while the other elements seen in the *Treatise* will be briefly dealt with.

I   The theoretical structure

In order to clarify the theoretical structure of the *Treatise*, we will first, under the heading 'Assumptions', extract the basic assumptions which are adopted, and then, under the heading 'Mechanism', go on to state the theoretical structure which is founded upon the basic assumptions.

1   *The basic theoretical structure*

A   *Assumptions*

Let us begin with the assumptions that are related to the production of goods.

(Assumption 1)
> Goods are classified in two groups; consumption goods and investment goods. The output of each good is determined at the beginning of the current period on the basis of the amount of profit which was made in the previous period.[3]

(Assumption 2)
>   Units of quantities of goods are defined in such a way that each unit has the
>   same cost of production.[4]

Assumption 2 implies that the average cost curve of each group of goods is infinitely elastic; that is, the average cost of each group of goods is constant. Assumption 1 means that the output of each group of goods thus measured, is determined at the beginning of the current period on the basis of the amount of the profit which was made in the previous period and that it does not change during the current period. As we shall see below, the output is assumed to be completely sold in the current period.

(Assumption 3)
>   The production cost of each group of goods is determined at the beginning
>   of the current period.

This assumption can be derived from Assumption 1 and Assumption 2. The production cost is defined as the unit cost multiplied by the volume of output.

(Assumption 4)
>   The production cost is paid as the earnings of the factors of production at the
>   beginning of the current period.

(Assumption 5)
>   Some part of the earnings is spent on consumption goods while the rest
>   are saved.[5]

We turn next to the assumptions related to the price level of investment goods. The most important point here is that the price level of investment goods is determined in the capital stock market.

(Assumption 6)
>   The output of investment goods is small as compared with capital stock
>   which has been accumulated for a long period. Therefore the price level of
>   investment goods will be determined in the capital stock market.[6]

On this assumption Keynes discusses the determination of the price level of investment goods in two ways. One is related to the stock market.

(Assumption 7)
>   Investment goods are additions to capital stock.[7] Capital stock is in a one-to-one
>   relation to securities. Therefore the price level of investment goods is
>   determined on the stock market.

In order to understand the determination of the price level of investment goods in the stock market, we need to examine the assumptions which are related to the financial structure of the *Treatise.*

(Assumption 8)

> Money is defined as including not only state money and bank money, but also short-term bonds and long-term bonds. Each bears its own rate of interest. Against 'money' stand equities.[8]

Let us see how this assumption differs from that of the *General Theory*. In the *Treatise*, the concept of the rate of interest is close to the conventional concept of the rate of interest. It does not follow the lines of 'the theory of liquidity preference'. In the *General Theory*, Keynes regards the rate of interest as a reward for parting with liquidity and compares money, which yields no interest, with bonds which do yield interest. In the *Treatise*, Keynes compares money, which includes bonds and yields interest, with equities.

If we incorporate Assumption 8, Assumption 7 means that

(Assumption 9)

> The public make a portfolio selection between money and equities.

In the *Treatise*, a portfolio selection is emphasised between money, which yields interest, and equities which are in a one-to-one relation to capital goods. On the other hand, in the *General Theory* both equities and capital stock are taken out of the system. A portfolio selection is considered as the relation between money, which yields no interest, and bonds, on the basis of the concept of 'liquidity preference'.

(Assumption 10)

> The rate of interest is a policy variable. The money supply changes as the rate of interest changes.[9]

This assumption contrasts with the assumption in the *General Theory*, to the effect that the money supply is regarded as a policy variable, and that the rate of interest is supposed to change as the money supply changes.

The other formulation concerning the determination of the price level of investment goods runs thus:

(Assumption 11)

> The demand price of capital goods (and therefore that of investment goods) can be obtained by discounting the prospective yields by the rate of interest.[10] It is realised as the market price of capital stock (and therefore that of investment goods). If the rate of interest rises, then the demand price of capital stock goes down and investment expenditure decreases.[11]

We will consider the relation between the two investment price theories in 2(C) of Section 2.

B   *The market mechanism – 'Keynes's own theory'*

The market mechanism in the *Treatise* is composed of two parts, one concerned with the determination of variables in 'each period', the other with the determination between one period and the next.

Let us begin with the former. This can be constructed on the basis of the assumptions which we set out in (A).

In the case of the consumption goods sector, the determination in each period is constructed on the basis of Assumption 1 to Assumption 5.

(Mechanism 1)

> The production cost and the volume of supply, are determined at the beginning of the current period. Once the expenditure on consumption goods is determined mechanically on the basis of the earnings, it is automatically realised as the sale proceeds of consumption goods, and both the price level and the profit are simultaneously determined.

This mechanism is simple but unclear. It is simple in the sense that (i) the output is supposed to be realised according to the entrepreneurs' plan, and the sale proceeds are taken to be realised at the consumers' will; (ii) profit is ascertained in consequence of this.

It is unclear, because it is not explained how the expenditure on consumption goods (the sale proceeds) is determined.

In the case of the investment goods sector, the determination of variables in each period is constructed on the basis of Assumptions 1 to 4 and Assumptions 6 to 11.

(Mechanism 2)

> The production cost and the volume of supply is determined at the beginning of the current period. The price level of investment goods is determined in the capital stock market. As a result of the above, profit is ascertained.

Let us turn now to the determination between one period and the next, which is summed up thus:

(Mechanism 3)

> Entrepreneurs behave in such a way that they expand (contract) output in the next period, according as they make a profit (a loss) in the current period.[12]

This mechanism suggests that Keynes deals with the relation between profit and output in terms of a one-period time lag. We will refer to it as the 'TM supply function'. It is peculiar to the *Treatise* and can be formulated:

$$\Delta R = f_1 (Q_1 <t>)$$
$$\Delta C = f_2 (Q_2 <t>)$$

(where R stands for the output of consumption goods, C the output of investment goods, Δ an increment, Q_1 the profit of consumption goods, Q_2 the profit of investment goods, $<t>$ time t).

The TM supply function occupies an important place in Keynes's theoretical development from the *Treatise* to the *General Theory*.[13]

The theoretical structure of the *Treatise* emerging from the above argument can be delineated as the dynamic process of Mechanisms 1 and 2 through the TM supply function. In each period, the price level of consumption goods and that of investment goods is determined by, respectively, Mechanism 1 and Mechanism 2.[14] The profits thus ascertained determine the output in the next period through the TM supply functions.

The next period then starts in the same way. The price level of consumption goods and of investment goods is determined, respectively, by Mechanism 1 and Mechanism 2. The output is then determined through the two TM supply functions.

This dynamic process composed of Mechanisms 1 and 2 through Mechanism 3 is 'Keynes's own theory'.

2   *The other theoretical characteristics*

A   *The investment theory*

In the *Treatise*, the value of current investment (or the expenditure on investment) is ascertained as the product of the price level determined by Mechanism 2, and the volume of output produced depending upon the profit realised in the previous period. The profit realised in the investment goods sector in the current period determines the level of output of investment goods in the next period through the TM supply function.

Capital, in the *Treatise*, is composed of fixed capital, working capital, and liquid capital. Investment is understood as an addition to capital. Investment theory in the *Treatise*, explained above, deals mainly with investment for fixed capital, investment for both working capital and liquid capital playing a secondary role in the basic theoretical structure. Keynes defines working capital as the aggregate of goods which are involved in the course of production, manufacturing and retailing, and are required in order to avoid the risks of interruption in the productive process.[15] He states that the volume of working capital is measured as 'employment $\times$ 1/2 $\times$ length of process $\times$ rate of wages' under simplifying conditions.[16] As we will see in (d), working capital plays an important role in the second phase of the credit cycle.[17] As for liquid capital, he argues that possession is avoided in the present economic system because the cost of keeping it is very high.[18]

B   *The theory of money*

Let us further examine the theory of money which appeared in Assumptions 8 to 10. In the *Treatise*, money is defined as savings deposits. In the case of the borrowing and lending of money for short periods (firms issue short-term bonds which are discounted at banks), the Bank Rate is applied to savings deposits. In the case of the borrowing and lending of money for long periods (firms issue long-term bonds which are discounted at banks), the bond rate is applied to savings deposits.[19] However, the *Treatise* contains no rigorous discussion of the markets for short-term and long-term bonds, nor are bonds dealt with as items the public choose to have in their portfolio; it is the portfolio selection between savings deposits that yield interest and equities that Keynes brings the focus on. The core of the theory of money in the *Treatise* lies in the relation between the portfolio selection behaviour of the public and the behaviour of the banking system. As a result of this, the price level of investment goods (which is also the price of capital goods) is determined.

> If we assume that banking habits and practices are unchanged, the requirements of the cash deposits are mainly determined by the magnitude of the earnings bill ... and the requirements of the savings deposits are mainly determined by the bearishness of the public's disposition taken in conjunction with the price level of securities. ... [O]nly those combinations of the rate of earnings, the volume of output and the price level of securities are feasible which lead to the aggregate requirements of money being equal to the given total.
>
> (*TM*.1, p. 132)

This is virtually the prototype of the theory of liquidity preference in the *General Theory*. Substitute liquidity preference due to the transaction-motive and the precautionary-motive for the requirements of the cash deposits, substitute liquidity preference due to the speculative motive for the requirements of savings deposits, and substitute the price level of securities for the rate of interest – and what we are left with is the theory of liquidity preference itself.

> ... the stability of purchasing power and of output requires that the total deposits should be allowed to rise and fall *pari passu* with any changes in the volume of the savings deposits; ... the terms of lending should be adjusted ... so as to balance the effect of bullish or bearish sentiment in the financial markets on the rate of new investment.
>
> (*TM*.1, p. 228)

Evidently, Keynes sees the banking system exercising two powers here; (i) the power to adjust total deposits to the changes in the volume of the savings deposits and (ii) the power to adjust the financial market (the stock market) through the manipulation of the rate of interest (the terms of lending).

C   The consumption theory

The consumption theory in the *Treatise* is found in Mechanism 1. The price level of consumption goods is considered to be determined by dividing the value of aggregate earnings over saving, by the volume of output of consumption goods which was produced on the basis of the realised profit in the previous period. Therefore the argument in terms of earnings and saving is developed as determining the price level of consumption goods, and has no direct influence upon the volume of consumption goods.[20]

Keynes considers the relation between earnings and saving to be stable.[21] The role of this relationship is held to lie in bringing about a collapse in the second phase of the credit cycle.

> ...if...[the primary phase] is caused by an increased production of consumption goods, ...the supply of such goods coming on to the market will be increased fully in proportion to earnings. Thus there will no longer be any occasion for the higher price level, and prices will drop back to their former figures.
>
> (*TM*.1, p. 259)

Behind this passage lies the supposition that savings rise faster than earnings.[22]

D   The theory of a credit cycle

In the *Treatise* Keynes depicts the normal course of the credit cycle as follows.[23] Suppose that something (such as a new invention or a return of business confidence) happens to increase the attractiveness of investment. The price level of investment goods then rises, and the output increases in the next period. As a result of this, the level of employment increases and expenditure on consumption increases. Therefore the price level of consumption goods rises, and the output in the next period increases. Thus the behaviour of firms of increasing output under the condition of high profit causes a rise in money wages. In this process, the volume of working capital, which is calculated as 'employment $\times$ 1/2 $\times$ length of process $\times$ rate of wages', also increases, so that business continues to pick up at an accelerated rate (the decrease in liquid capital will, it is argued, prove surprisingly small).

The turning point in the boom occurs as the result of the accumulation of several causes: (i) the evaporation of the attractions of new investment; (ii) the faltering of financial expectation (as bearishness prevails the requirements of financial circulation increase); (iii) the fall in the price level of consumption goods (this is due to the stagnation of expenditure on consumption as compared with an increase in the output of consumption goods) and (iv) the growing inability of the banking system to keep pace with the increasing requirements of the industrial circulation to begin with, and then of the financial circulation (this brings about a rise in the rate of interest).

Subsequently the economy tends to decline for the following reasons: (i) a fall in the price level of consumption goods drives away the entrepreneurs whose production costs are high; (ii) financial sentiment becomes bearish and (iii) an increase in the requirements of the industrial circulation, which occurs in the upward phase of a cycle, brings about a rise in the rate of interest which finally retards investment.

The fall in the price level in this period is held to prove fairly large. Soon a cut in production and wages follows, together with a decrease in working capital, so that business deteriorates rapidly (on this occasion, liquid capital increases, but the increase will, it is argued, prove surprisingly small).

Having fallen to the bottom of a cycle, the economy moves into the ascending phase once again due to the following causes: (i) the price level of consumption goods stops falling, and begins to rise. This follows from the fact that the degree of decrease in expenditure on consumption is smaller than that of the decrease in output; (ii) the liquid capital increases.

Together with the restored attractiveness of new investment, these factors exert a pick-up effect on the economy.

In this section we have been looking into the theoretical structure of the *Treatise*.

II Two problems

There are two major problems in the theoretical structure of the *Treatise*. One is the value of the fundamental equations, the other a matter of 'three dualities'. We will discuss them in turn.

1 *The value of the fundamental equations*

One problem in the theoretical structure of the *Treatise* is that not only Keynes but, with him, many interpreters, too, overestimate the fundamental equations.[24] As we have already seen, it is possible to explain the market mechanism developed in the *Treatise*, without the fundamental equations. Keynes's explanation of the market mechanism is not clear because he eschews explicit exposition, and assigns the task of explaining it to the fundamental equations. Moreover, certain dubious assumptions are used in the theoretical structure of the *Treatise*. Let us take a look at these assumptions, after which we will discuss in what way the fundamental equations are overestimated.

A *The choice of units*

As we saw in Assumption 2, in the *Treatise* a quantity unit is defined as having the same production cost.[25] This definition has the following implications. First, it implies that in order to measure the same kind of goods consistently, Keynes presupposes the production condition in which the cost per unit is constant irrespective of the level of output. Otherwise it might happen that the same quantity of goods be differently measured. Second, it implies that the quantity ratio between different kinds of goods is also constant because Keynes measures different kinds of goods on the basis of the same cost. For instance, one kilogram of meat is equal to two bushels of wheat. Third, it implies that this quantity unit is uniformly applicable to both investment goods and consumption goods.

Next we turn to the price level, which is classified in two groups: the price level of consumption goods, and the price level of investment goods. This is in contrast with the case of the quantity unit used as a unit common to all goods. Keynes first homogenises the 'heterogeneity of goods' (multiple goods) by adopting a quantity unit. He then goes on to introduce the concept of the price levels of consumption goods and investment goods, taking into consideration the difference between the market mechanism which rules consumption goods and that which rules investment goods. Apparently, these two price levels do not seem to be 'passive macro variables',[26] and the problem of indexing many goods would appear to be avoided by adopting Keynes's own quantity unit.

In fact, however, these price levels are very arbitrary. In the above example, the price of one kilogram of meat is equal to the price of two bushels of wheat, and both are equal to the price level of consumption goods by definition. As a result, arbitrary aggregation becomes possible.

As we shall see in Assumption 12 below, the price level of output as a whole is defined as the average price per quantity unit. It can be thus defined because a quantity unit, and the two price levels defined above, are presupposed.

As we saw above, Keynes's choice of a quantity unit confines the *Treatise* to analysis by means of 'passive macro variables'. Consequently, given the division of goods into consumption and investment goods, the price levels are also subject to the same limitation as the quantity unit.

B   Derivation of the fundamental equations

Whenever mention is made of the fundamental equations as major components of the theoretical structure of the *Treatise*, two things are presupposed: (i) the profit of the consumption goods sector is the difference between the investment cost and saving (in the case of the first fundamental equation); and (ii) profit in the whole economy is the difference between investment expenditure and saving (in the case of the second fundamental equation).

How is it that these profits can be expressed in such a way, making reference to the cost of investment (or the expenditure on investment) and saving? Here let us examine the derivation process of the fundamental equations that is actually developed in the *Treatise*, adding an explanation from the standpoint of the present chapter.

We begin with the first fundamental equation.

$$PR = E - S \tag{1}$$

(where P stands for the price level of consumption goods, R the volume of output of consumption goods, E the earnings, S the saving).

Equation (1) determines P.[27] R is given due to Assumption 1, and E is given due to Assumptions 3 and 4, at the beginning of the current period. If S is determined by Assumption 5, then P is determined.

$$E - S = (E/O)(R + C) - S \tag{2}$$

(where C stands for the volume of output of investment goods, O the total output of goods).

Equation (2) is a definition equation. This holds because Assumptions 1 and 2 are adopted.

$$(E/O)(R + C) - S = (E/O)R + I' - S \tag{3}$$

(where I' stands for the production cost of investment goods).

Assumption 2 is vitally important for equation (3) to hold good. From equations (1) to (3), equation (4) is derived.

$$PR - (E/O)R = I' - S \tag{4}$$

The left-hand side represents the sale proceeds of consumption goods minus the production cost of consumption goods. This is by definition, the profit of consumption goods Q_1. Therefore we get equation (5).

$$Q_1 = I' - S \tag{5}$$

Rearranging equation (4), we get equation (6) – the 'first fundamental equation'.

$$P = (E/O) + (I' - S)/R \tag{6}$$

In the derivation of this equation, Assumption 2 is vitally important.
Let us turn to the second fundamental equation.

$$\Pi = (PR + P'C)/O \tag{7}$$

(where Π stands for the price level of output as a whole and P' the price level of investment goods).

Equation (7) is Assumption 12 itself below.

(Assumption 12)
   The price level of output as a whole is defined as an average cost per quantity unit.[28]

$$\Pi = (PR + P'C)/O = ((E - S) + I)/O \tag{8}$$

In the derivation of equation (8), we make use of equation (1) and the definition equation $P'C = I$ (where I is the sale proceeds of investment goods).

From equation (8) we obtain equation (9).

$$\Pi O - E = I - S \tag{9}$$

The left-hand side represents the difference between the total sale proceeds and the total production cost, which is the total profit Q. Therefore,

$$Q = I - S \tag{10}$$

Rearranging equation (10), we get equation (11) – the 'second fundamental equation'.

$$\Pi = (E/O) + (I - S)/O \tag{11}$$

C   The overestimation of the fundamental equations

We now will consider what is to be deemed crucially important in the formulation of the fundamental equations.

In the case of the first fundamental equation, equation (1) alone matters. Earnings are the sum of the production cost in two sectors (I' and J). Therefore equation (1) becomes:

$$PR = J + I' - S \tag{12}$$
$$PR - J = I' - S \tag{13}$$

The left-hand side represents the profit of the consumption goods sector Q_1, so that equation (5) is obtainable.

In the case of the second fundamental equation, equation (1) also matters. Denote the total sale proceeds as T, the sale proceeds of consumption goods F and those of investment goods I, and we get equation (14).

$$T = F + I \tag{14}$$

Equation (1) can be transformed into $F = E - S$. By substituting this in equation (14), we get

$$T - E = I - S \tag{15}$$

The left-hand side is by definition the profit as a whole, Q. Therefore we get equation (10).

From the above argument, it is clear that equation (1) is decisively influential in both cases. As far as profits are concerned, equation (1) alone matters. In order to get the first fundamental equation, moreover, the above assumptions of a quantity unit, the price level of consumption goods, and the price level of investment goods are required, while Assumption 12 is needed in order to arrive at the second fundamental equation.

A typical argument about the fundamental equations runs as follows; suppose that the market rate of interest is set lower than the natural rate of interest by the monetary authority. In this situation the value of investment I increases while saving S decreases, so that the price level rises and the profit increases ... .[29]

Examining this argument, we shall try to bring some light to bear on the overestimation or the mysteriousness of the fundamental equations. Suppose that the market rate of interest is set lower than the natural rate by the monetary authority. Then I increases because P' rises due to Assumption 11. On the other hand, S decreases because the incentive to the public to save is supposed to decrease due to a fall in the market rate of interest. A decrease in S means an increase in the expenditure on consumption goods. This brings about a rise in P and an increase in Q_1. Looking at the increase in the profit Q_1 from the standpoint of $I' - S$, we can say that this occurs because S decreases and I' remains constant. Needless to say, the rise in P' will increase Q_2. Q increases because Q_1 and Q_2 increase. Π also rises through Assumption 12.

From the above argument, it is clear that the analysis in terms of the fundamental equations, in which the cost of investment (or the value of investment) and saving play an essential role, is not necessarily required.[30] We can rather describe the *Treatise* theory more clearly by means of Mechanisms 1, 2 and 3.

2 *Three dualities*

By 'duality' we suggest the existence of alternative, not always compatible, analyses of particular issues. There are three dualities that draw our attention, the first of which rests on the other two.

A *Duality of the theoretical framework*

In the *Treatise* there co-exist a Wicksellian theory and Keynes's own theory.

The Wicksellian theory – This is recognisable from the following features:

1 Explanation of the fluctuations of the price level in terms of a relative.
2 Relation between the natural rate of interest and the money rate of interest.
3 Stress on a bank rate policy for stabilizing the price level.
4 Acceptance of an equivalence between Wicksell's three conditions for monetary equilibrium.

The principal grounds on which Keynes regards his theory as belonging to the Wicksellian stream, however, lie not in any of these features but in his adoption of the idea that the bank rate influences investment and saving. This idea is used to provide a mechanism in which economic stability can be attained by means of a bank rate policy.

Keynes's own theory – This is the theory expressed as the dynamic process of Mechanisms 1 and 2 working through Mechanism 3.

B   *Duality of the determination of the price level of consumption goods*

In determination here, either (i) a theory dependent on earnings, or (ii) a theory dependent on the rate of interest is used.

C   *Duality of the determination of the price level of investment goods*[31]

The investment theory to which we referred in Assumptions 7 to 9, finds expression in the following passage; we shall call it 'Investment Price Theory (1)'.

> The price level of investments as a whole [capital goods] and hence of new investments [investment goods], is that price level at which the desire of the public to hold savings deposits is equal to the amount of savings deposits which the banking system is willing and able to create.
>
> (*TM*.1, p. 129)

The investment theory to which we referred in Assumption 11 emerges from the following passage; we will call it 'Investment Price Theory (2)'.

> ...the value of capital goods depends on the rate of interest at which the prospective income from them is capitalised. That is to say, the higher (e.g.) the rate of interest, the lower, other things being equal, will be the value of capital goods. Therefore, if the rate of interest rises, P' [the price level of investment goods] will tend to fall....
>
> (*TM*.1, p. 139)

According to Investment Price Theory (1), so long as the banking system adjusts the supply of savings deposits in such a way that the public be satisfied with possession of them, the price level of investment goods will not change.[32] This theory supposes that the public make their portfolio selection between money, which yields a rate of interest (saving deposits), and equities, while the banking system has sufficient capacity to cope with the public through the function of supplying money and dealing in equities.

In the *Treatise*, the rate of interest is considered to be a policy variable. And in the above argument, an endogenous variable is the price of equities. That is, this theory states that the price of equities is determined by the supply-demand relation of equities, and that the banking system can influence the supply-demand relation not only directly through dealings in equities but also indirectly through a change in the rate of interest. As a result, it is the volume of the money supply[33] and the price of equities that change.

According to Investment Price Theory (2), the price level of investment goods is determined by prospective yields (or prospective income) and the rate of interest. The rate of interest is a policy variable. Therefore, as long as the prospective yields are constant, the price level of investment goods also remains constant. This theory supposes that the price level of investment goods is determined by the activities of those who demand investment goods.

Taking the above arguments into consideration, it will be clear that the two theories are logically inconsistent. If the rate of interest and the prospective yields are constant, then the price level of investment goods on the basis of Investment Price Theory (2) remains invariable. On the other hand, on the basis of Investment Price Theory (1) the price level of investment goods can change considerably if the banking system is willing to deal in equities. Therefore there is no guarantee that the price level of investment goods, which is determined on the basis of Investment Price Theory (1), will become equal to that which is determined on the basis of Investment Price Theory (2). If there were no logical inconsistency between the two theories, then a theory bridging the gap between them would have to be forged. However, no such attempt seems to have been made in the *Treatise*.

Suppose that the price level of investment goods based on Investment Price Theory (2) is higher than that based on Investment Price Theory (1). In this case, those who prefer equities to savings deposits will increase in number, attracted by the prospect of higher rate of return.[34] As a consequence, the price of equities may be expected to climb steadily higher due to increased demand for them, until they reach the same price level as investment goods based on Investment Price Theory (2). However, according to Investment Price Theory (1), as the price of equities can remain unchanged throughout the banking system's dealings in them, no such equalisation need necessarily come about. There is no doubt that the two theories remain logically inconsistent.[35]

These two dualities of theory ((B) and (C)) appear to have led Keynes to drift – unconsciously, as it were – between his own theory and the Wicksellian theory. In his own theory, the theory of the price level of consumption goods based on earnings and Investment Price Theory (1) are used, while in the Wicksellian theory it is the theory of the price level of consumption goods based on the rate of interest and Investment Price Theory (2) that find application.

III   The key concepts

A key element in the study of Keynes's theoretical development is the TM supply function. For a few year after the *Treatise* Keynes stressed the TM supply function. By abandoning it he was able to move from the *Treatise* world into the *General Theory* world. Here we will examine two concepts: profit and the TM supply function.

1   *Profit*

The first point to make here is that profit in the *Treatise* means excess profit.[36] See the following passage.

> ... the difference between the actual remuneration of the entrepreneurs, arrived at by deducting from the sale proceeds [T] their outgoings (a), (c), and (d) above and (b) their normal remuneration, is, ... the profits [P] (*TM*.1, p. 112. (a) means salaries and wages paid to employees, (c) interest on capital, (d) regular monopoly gains, rents and the like).

If we use symbols, this means

$$\{T - [(a) + (c) + (d)]\} - (b) = P$$

The portion within braces represents the 'actual remuneration' (the realised profit), while 'normal remuneration' refers to normal profit. Thus,

The realised profit − the normal profit = P

Therefore P stands for the excess profit.

Another formulation of excess profit is as follows: (i) the profit in the consumption goods sector, Q_1, is equal to the difference between the cost of production of investment goods I' and savings S; and (ii) profit as a whole Q is equal to the difference between the sale proceeds of investment goods I and savings S.

As we saw in Section 2(I(B)), these formulae hold good because of Assumption 5. For an understanding of the characteristics and limitations of the formulae of the excess profit in the *Treatise*, we need to bear this point in mind.

Keynes stressed excess profits because he thought that the excess profits of entrepreneurs are the driving force of the economy.

> ... profits (or losses) having once come into existence become, ... (... this will be the main topic of several succeeding chapters), a cause of what subsequently ensues; indeed, the mainspring of changes in the existing economic system.
>
> (*TM*.1, p. 126)

2   *The TM supply function*

The function produces two important implications. First, it is a concept representing the supply side. Second, it is a dynamic concept determining the volume of output in the next period based on the realised profits in the current. This accords with the fact that after the abandonment of the function, Keynes adopts a method of determining quantities and prices simultaneously.

6   After the *Treatise*

Having published the *Treatise*, Keynes continued to maintain the position advanced in the book for some time, defending 'his own theory' against criticisms levelled at it from various sides.

How did Keynes go about maintaining the *Treatise* theory, and for how long? When, in other words, did this state of affairs end (and a new situation towards the *General Theory* begin)? This is an issue of decisive importance.

We determine the period concerned[1] as spanning between October 1930 and October 1932. The most noteworthy feature is Keynes's stress on the TM supply function; the fundamental equations are seldom mentioned. This will be the focus of our attention in this chapter and the next.

The chapter proceeds as follows: (1) Hawtrey's criticism; (2) the sources from June 1931 to early 1932; (3) a manuscript consisting of four chapters (*JMK*.13, pp. 381–396. Hereafter we will call it 'The Monetary Theory of Production' manuscript or the MTP manuscript, named after the title of the first chapter). (4) criticism of the 'Cambridge Circus'; and (5) two 1932 tables of contents.

I   Hawtrey's criticism

1   *Hawtrey's economics*

Hawtrey's trade cycle theory originates in Hawtrey (1913). It is a cumulative process theory of the banker-dealer connection based on two lags: the lag in the rate of interest behind change in rising or falling prices, and the lag in the demand for currency behind change in credit.

Hawtrey (1919) makes use of his concepts of 'consumers' income' and 'consumers' outlay' (the theory presented here is a revised version of Hawtrey (1913)).[2]

Then we have Hawtrey (1928; 1932, chapter III) to consider. Let us explain his theory by starting with the key concepts:

> The total of the incomes which people ... have to spend I call the consumers' income; the total which they do spend I call the consumers' outlay.
>
> (Hawtrey, 1928, p. 83)

He finds the essence of the trade cycle in the variations of 'effective demand' (the consumers' outlay), and the cause of the variations in the movement of bank credit.[3]

The trade cycle takes place in the transitional period during which the consumers' income and outlay show divergence. If the banks judge that the level of their reserves relatively to the amount of credit money is lower (higher) than is appropriate, they then proceed to raise (lower) the rate of interest. In turn the dealers holding stock of commodities and standing between manufacturers and consumers accordingly contract (expand) their bank credit and decrease (or increase) their orders to the manufacturers, who produce less (more) and reduce (increase) employment.

A contraction (expansion) of bank credit induces a return of currency to the banks (release of currency from the banks) and a decrease (increase) in consumers' income, which in turn brings about a decrease (increase) in consumers' outlay. A decrease (increase) in consumers' outlay brings about an accumulation of unsold stocks, so that dealers give fewer orders to producers, who in turn reduce their production and employment. Production then decreases and unemployment increases, which induces a decrease (increase) in consumers' income. During this process prices and profits fall (rise), followed – with a lag – by wages.

The process has a tendency to accelerate. That is, the divergence between consumers' income and consumers' outlay becomes wider and wider with the help of the above-mentioned lags.

Eventually the banks notice that the reserves/the amount of credit money is higher (lower) than is appropriate, and so they lower (raise) the rate of interest.

Thus Hawtrey concludes that trade depressions is due to deficiencies in consumers' outlay owing to credit squeezes.

2   *Hawtrey's criticism*

Hawtrey testified before the Macmillan Committee on 10 and 11 April 1930, and submitted three papers to the Committee.

In Section V(7) of Chapter 4 we referred to Hawtrey's criticism of the *Treatise* proofs. Hawtrey, questioning the TM supply function, emphasised 'present demand' based on the consumers' 'income' and 'outlay'. He also stressed the role which the adjustment of goods in stock plays, attributing unemployment to a contraction of demand.

3   *Keynes's response*

Keynes responded to Hawtrey (28 November 1930),[4] which shows just how much the TM supply function occupied his mind.

First, Keynes is of the opinion that realised profits influence anticipated profits.

> I have laid too much stress on realised profits in respect of the production period just ended as influencing anticipated profits in respect of the production just beginning . . . .

> (*JMK*.13, p. 145)

Second, he explains that because 'how much reduction of output' is not a monetary problem, it is not dealt with in detail.

> The question *how much* reduction of output is caused, ... by a ... fall of price[5]..., is ... not strictly a monetary problem. I have not attempted to deal with it in ... [the *Treatise*], though I have done a good deal of work at it.
> (*JMK*.13, p. 145. Hereafter brackets in quotations are mine)

Third, he feels the need to link monetary theory to the theory of short-period supply.

> I am not dealing with the complete set of causes ... determin[ing] volume of output. ... If I were to write the book again, I should probably attempt to probe further into [making the 'theory of short-period supply' and 'monetary theory' run together]; ... I have gone no further than that anticipated windfall loss or profit affects the output of entrepreneurs. ...
> (*JMK*.13, pp. 145–146)

Hawtrey's theory anticipates the *General Theory* although it is not a theory of employment or income, but one of income–outlay repercussion induced by bank credit. Hawtrey's criticism of the *Treatise*'s fundamental equations and his stress on the importance of effective demand seem to have contributed to weaning Keynes from the *Treatise* framework, and to setting off – after some hesitation – in the direction of the *General Theory*.[6]

II   June 1931 to early 1932

1   *June 1931*

In June 1931 Keynes delivered the lectures,[7] 'An Economic Analysis of Unemployment'[8] in Chicago (*JMK*.13, pp. 343–367). Here he discussed a trade cycle, emphasising the TM supply function:

> [W]hen ... the value of current investment is less than the savings ..., the receipts of the entrepreneurs will be less than their costs, so that they make a loss. That is ... the clue to the scientific explanation of booms and slumps. ...
> (*JMK*.13, p. 353)

> A given deficiency of investment causes a given decline of profit [which] ... causes a given decline of output.
> (*JMK*.13, pp. 355–356)

In these lectures Keynes argued that the economy is inclined to proceed cumulatively, and might reach 'a kind of spurious equilibrium'[9] (*JMK*.13, p. 356).

In the face of the Great Depression, he emphasised the importance of reviving investment:

> The cure of unemployment involves improving business profits [, which] can come about only by an improvement in new investment relative to saving.
> *(JMK*.13, p. 362)

To increase investment, he argues, the solution is to lower the long-term rate of interest.[10] To this end Keynes suggests three ways, although he believes in the effect of the short-term on the long-term rate:

1   to increase the quantity of liquid assets;
2   to diminish the attractions of liquid assets by lowering the rate of interest;
3   to increase the attractions of non-liquid assets.

He also mentions three lines of approach for the Great Depression, attaching great value to (iii):

(i)   restoration of confidence to lender and borrower;
(ii) new construction programmes under the auspices of the public authorities;
(iii) a reduction in the long-term rate of interest.

He then questions the practicality of (ii), fully accepting it theoretically.

Together with the lectures, we also have Keynes's contributions to the Round Table on 'Unemployment as a World Problem' *(JMK*.13, pp. 367–373). In one noteworthy instance he proposed:

> [L]et us consider the totality of industries. You have over a short period something of the nature of a supply curve which tells you that for a given level of prime profit there will be a given level of output... so if you have a supply curve..., you could only increase... output by increasing [aggregate] prime profit.
> *(JMK*.13, p. 368)

> [Y]ou can get a supply curve for industry as a whole in which the quantity of output is unequivocally related to the aggregate excess receipts over prime costs....
> *(JMK*.13, p. 372)

These observations attest to Keynes's view that the quantity of output for the whole industry is related to profit.[11]

2   *20 September 1931 and two manuscripts*

In his letter to Kahn (20 September 1931. *JMK*.13, pp. 373–375),[12] Keynes argues the possibility of underemployment equilibrium, which now makes its first appearance:

> [I]f, starting with equilibrium, an increase of I makes Q positive, O increases and S increases but Q/O gradually diminishes. If Q/O reaches zero before O reaches maximum, we have 'long-period unemployment', i.e. an equilibrium

position short of full employment. Similarly if a decrease of I decreases Q, O decreases and S decreases....

(JMK.13, pp. 374–375)

Behind this statement lie an idea that 'profit is equal to $I - S$' and the TM supply function. And, based on the TM supply function, a state of equilibrium, 'long-period unemployment', is explained in which employment stands at a level between zero and full. This might be the starting point for the idea found in *GT*, p. 254 – 'we oscillate...round an intermediate position'.

For the same period we also have the manuscripts, 'Why Are the Equations for Consumption-Goods and Investment-Goods Asymmetrical?'[13] (hereafter the 'Why' manuscript) and 'The Determination of Price'[14] (hereafter the 'Determination' manuscript).

In the 'Why' manuscript, which may be related to chapter 1, 'The Differential of Consumption-goods and Capital-goods' (Book III, 'The Determination of Price') of 'Table 1' (see Section V(2) below), Keynes tries to explain, in response to Robertson's criticism, why the equation determining the price of consumption goods is asymmetrical with that determining the price of investment goods.

Keynes's main argument is that given E, Q, and M, P_1 depends on the difference between saving and investment, or on the propensity to save defined as $S = \varphi(E, Q, P_1, P_2)$ while P_2 depends on the propensity to hoard defined as $M = \psi(H, P_2)$ (where E denotes the earnings, Q profit, M money supply, P_1 and P_2 the price levels of consumption goods, and investment goods respectively, S saving and H hoarding).

Dealing with P_1, he comes to the first fundamental equation of the *Treatise*.

Equalling the flow of money directed towards [consumption-goods] with the product of the price and quantity of such goods we have

$$E - S = \cdots = R \cdot P_1$$

It is this equation which I re-analyse in my *Treatise* into the form

$$P_1 = E/O + (I' - S)/R$$

(GTE/1/28)

With regard to P_2, he develops the following argument:

[W]e can equal the flow of new money...against the product of the quantity and the price of [investment goods] coming into the market....

Thus $S + Q + dM = CP_2 - (A_3 + B_3) P_2$

...We can...deduce from this

$$P_2 = -dM/(A_3 + B_3) \ [= \psi' \ (M)]$$

(GTE/1/33–34 [a paging system
adopted in Keynes Papers])

(C denotes the quantity of investment goods, A_3 the release of consumption goods by the banks, B_3 the release of investment goods by the banks.)

Here Keynes explains how the price of investment goods is determined in relation to money supply. He also uses the term, 'bull–bear position', which shows that he has not dropped the bearishness function.

The 'Determination' manuscript is very similar in content to the 'Why' manuscript. It explains how the price level of consumption-goods is determined, and then goes on to see how the price level of capital-goods is determined, emphasising the difference between the two.

A significant difference from the 'Why' manuscript is, however, to be seen in the presence of the supply schedules, which make their first appearance here.

> Let $P_1 = f_1(A_1)$ and $P_2 = f_2(A_2)$ be the supply schedules of the two types of goods in the sense that A_1 and A_2 will be the quantity of each marketed for money ... in response to prices P_1 and P_2.
>
> (GTE/5/469)

($A_1 = O_1 + \Delta B_1$ and $A_2 = O_2 + \Delta B_2$. O_i and ΔB_i respectively denote output, and the change in the stock of goods i [$i = 1, 2$] held by the public, where goods 1 are consumption goods and goods 2 capital goods.)

Keynes explains the price level of the consumption-goods based on the first fundamental equation of the *Treatise*, arguing that it depends on the 'saving propensity'. With respect to the 'saving propensity', S, Keynes argues as follows:

> S will depend, apart from fundamental changes in popular psychology, on O, the community's real income, on Q [profit] as determining the distribution of the real income and on P_1 itself relatively both to P_1 and to P_2.
>
> (GTE/5/474)

This anticipates the propensity to save in the *General Theory*.

Keynes explains the price level of the capital-goods based on the 'curve of bearishness' or 'hoarding propensity'. His argument runs thus:

> $P_2 = \Delta M / \Delta B_2 = \Phi(M)$
>
> where M is the total stock of money and $\Phi(M)$ what I have called the curve of bearishness, *i.e.* $\Phi(M)$ is the price for capital-goods at which ... the public desire to hold an amount of money M rather than ... to increase by purchase ... their holdings B_2 of capital-goods.
>
> (GTE/5/473)

Both manuscripts probably precede the MTP manuscript, for they adopt the same line as the *Treatise* on the bearishness function, and on the determination of the price levels of consumption and investment goods. In the MTP manuscript, as will be seen below, we see the embryo of the liquidity preference theory, while in the two manuscripts money is treated solely in relation to the price level of capital-goods, without referring to the rate of interest.

However, the two manuscripts may have been written immediately after the MTP manuscript, for the 'supply schedule', defined as the function of the price, appeared in the 'Determination' manuscript, and the 'propensity to save' in the two manuscripts.

III   'The Monetary Theory of Production' manuscript

This manuscript is probably preceded in time by the preface to the Japanese edition of the *Treatise* (5 April 1932. *TM*.1, pp. xx–xxvii) which states the determination of the price level of capital goods in terms of 'bearishness' ('the propensity to hoard') but contains neither the determination of the rate of interest nor the term 'liquidity preference', whereas the MTP manuscript reveals the seeds of the liquidity preference theory.

Let us review the main points of the manuscript, and then assess it in terms of Keynes's theoretical development.

1   *The short-period analysis*

In the MTP manuscript, the fluctuations of the economy and the possibility it faces of cumulative deterioration are analysed using the TM supply function.

A   The TM supply function[15]

The following passage clearly demonstrates the importance that Keynes attaches to the TM supply function:

> The essence of the monetary theory of production... can be expressed quite briefly, starting from the equation
>
> $$\Delta Q = \Delta I - \Delta S,$$
>
> ...
> or
> $$\Delta Q = \Delta D - \Delta E$$
>
> where Q stands for profit, I for investment, S for saving,..., and D for disbursement. ...
> ... entrepreneurs tend to increase their output according as their profit is increasing. Thus we are led to... the vital generalisation that increases in the volume of output... depend upon the changes in disbursement relatively to earnings $[E]$... or in investment relatively to savings.... Throughout this Book we shall be engaged in developing [it].
>
> (*JMK*. 13, p. 381)

The MTP manuscript assumes an economy in which the total volume of output, fixed at the beginning of each period, is sold in that period. This is related to the TM supply function, in the context of which both investment I and spending F are taken to be the proceeds realised as a result of the total volume of output being sold. The intrinsic logic of this function is developed as follows.[16]

The quantitative effect on output of a given decrease $-\Delta Q$... will depend on: (i) the margin between each entrepreneur's receipts and his variable costs...; (ii) the distribution of the total reduction $-\Delta Q$ between different entrepreneurs; and (iii) the duration of the period of diminished profit relatively to the durability of his fixed capital...

As a net result of... [the existence of firms in which the initial (i) is insufficient, the inequality of (ii) and the prolongation of (iii)], it is... reasonable to expect that a point will be reached at which there is some elasticity of supply in response to diminished profit, the initial reduction in entrepreneurs' profit aggravating itself until, having reached an amount $-\Delta Q$, it causes a reduction $-\Delta O$... and a reduction $-\Delta E$...

(*JMK*.13, pp. 382–383)

From this we can gather that Keynes regards the TM supply function as a useful analytical tool operating with some time lag.

B   *The possibility of cumulative deterioration*

Using profit and the TM supply functions as pivotal concepts, Keynes argues that the economy might deteriorate cumulatively:

an initial movement $-\Delta Q$ is likely to aggravate itself. For the reduction in entrepreneurs' profit will have a tendency to retard new capital development in respect both of value and volume...; and at the same time it may stimulate economy by diminishing both the expenditure of entrepreneurs whose incomes are reduced and also the expenditure of other consumers.... the initial decline in disbursement is likely to generate... a further decline in disbursement....

(*JMK*.13, pp. 382–383)

Here Keynes argues that a reduction in profit generates a further decline in disbursement, which in turn generates a further decline in profit, so that the deterioration becomes self-reinforcing. Behind this argument lies the idea that the volume of production of both investment goods and consumption goods is determined by the TM supply function.

He also discusses the case in which the economy deteriorates cumulatively even if the extent of the decline in profit remains the same as before:

Let us... assume that... the amount of disbursement declines by about the same amount as the decline in earnings.... [T]he deficiency in the profit of entrepreneurs as a whole will remain exactly the same in absolute amount as it was before. But it will be spread over a smaller number of units of production, as a result of a certain number having fallen out of production. Consequently the average loss will be greater than it was, with the result that the next most vulnerable section of entrepreneurs now falls out of production....

Thus if we can imagine the entrepreneurs ranged in a continuous series according to what percentage reduction in their receipts impels them to close down production,...a very small diminution $-\Delta Q$ in the total receipts of entrepreneurs might...gradually close down one after another....

(JMK.13, pp. 384–385)

Thus Keynes argues that the economy in which a decline in disbursement initially generates a decline in profit can enter upon a process of cumulative deterioration, due either to a falling off in profit or to an increase in the average loss as a result of a decrease in the number of units of production.

2 The long-period equilibrium

How long does the economy continue to deteriorate cumulatively? Is there a possibility that it may reach a long-period state of equilibrium? Keynes answers the latter question in the affirmative.

In the MTP manuscript he emphasises the relation between spending (consumption expenditure) and earnings (income). This relation is similar to that in the *Treatise*, and not directly connected with *GT*'s consumption function. The following is to be read in this context:

> [I]t is natural to expect that, as the earnings of the public decline, a point will eventually be reached at which the decline in total expenditure...will cease to be so great as the decline in [earnings].

(JMK.13, p. 386)

Here 'total expenditure' does not mean disbursement but consumption: the passage implies that the marginal propensity to consume (in terms of the *General Theory*) increases as earnings increase.

In the *Treatise*, the relation between spending and earnings is a factor causing a collapse in the credit cycle while in the MTP manuscript it is regarded as warranting a kind of long-period equilibrium after a series of short-period equilibria. What the two share is the idea that spending does not influence the production of consumption goods, but determines their price level, and that the profit from consumption goods determines their volume of production in the next period.

Keynes argues that the long-period equilibrium thus attained is characterised as a state of underemployment:

> [P]rovided that spending always increases less than earnings increase...any level of output is a position of stable equilibrium. For any increase of output will bring in a retarding factor, since ΔS will be positive and consequently I being assumed constant, ΔQ will be negative....

(JMK.13, p. 387)

Here it is regarded as an important condition for stable equilibrium that the rate of the change in spending be smaller than that in earnings. Equilibrium generally brings about a state of underemployment equilibrium.[17]

> [T]here is no presumption...that the equilibrium output will be anywhere near the optimum output. The essence of the above process is that the real income of the community has to be forced down to a level at which the rate of saving is not so excessive relatively to investment at the current rate of interest as to produce a crescendo of business losses....
>
> (*JMK*.13, p. 387)

3   *The relation of investment to the level of output*

The MTP manuscript stresses the role of investment in determining the level of output, and of the government in promoting investment. However, it is no easy task:

> If the relation between individual spending and earnings-profits is] determined by...habit..., then the level of output...depends on the policy of the authorities as affecting the amount of investment.... [W]hen the output of the community increases...a critical point comes when...we cease to be able to increase investment at an adequate pace, with the result that forces come into operation which prevent a further increase of output.
>
> (*JMK*.13, p. 388)

We need to consider the relation between the short-period analysis applying the TM supply function and the proposition that the level of output depends on investment. Keynes seems to be saying that if investment increases in the initial period, then output will continue to increase over a period of time, resulting in an increase in output at a new long-period equilibrium. When he says 'the level of output...the amount of investment', he is stressing the influence that both investment and the investment policy of the authorities have on the level of output at a long-period equilibrium.

Keynes also says that 'output will finally settle down to a position of equilibrium which is stable, so long as no extraneous influence interposes to change the value of Γ' (*JMK*.13, p. 388). He may seem here to express reliance on an automatic mechanism driving the economy towards long-period equilibrium, but actually this is not the case. Having serious doubts about any such mechanism, he stresses the importance of a low interest rate policy for attaining optimum output (see *JMK*.13, p. 396).

As for the relation between monetary policy and long-period equilibrium, Keynes explains it in the lecture draft for 14 November 1932 (see Section II of Chapter 7).

4   *The origin of the liquidity preference theory*

The *Treatise* stresses a portfolio selection between money as bearing interest, and equities. Contrastingly, the *General Theory* stresses a portfolio selection between money as bearing no interest, and debts – the liquidity preference.[18]

In the MTP manuscript we see the liquidity preference making its first appearance.

> [A]s output and prices decline, the proportion of the stock of money to income will...tend to increase. This growing relative abundance of money will, unless the general desire for liquidity relatively to income is capable of increasing without limit, lead...to a decline in the rate of interest.
>
> (*JMK*.13, p. 395)

This may be read in terms of the *General Theory* as follows:

1   A decrease in the demand for money due to the transactions motive makes money relatively abundant;
2   The abundance of money causes a decline in the rate of interest, unless the liquidity preference due to the speculative motive is infinitely elastic.

Here the MTP manuscript abandons two of the ideas in the *Treatise*: (i) The price level of investment goods is determined in the financial market dealing with savings deposits and equities;[19] (ii) The rate of interest is a policy variable.

In short, the role of the financial market switches from determining the price level of investment goods to determining the rate of interest. The rate of interest thus determined is expected to influence investment, which in turn influences the level of output through the TM supply function.

This change represents an enormous transformation in monetary theory. From the viewpoint of Keynes's theoretical development, however, it is nothing like the change in the theory of the commodity market, for it does not undermine the grounds for the MTP manuscript which is argued within the *Treatise* framework.

5   *The place of the MTP manuscript*[20]

We are now in a position to evaluate the place of the MTP manuscript[21] in the development from the *Treatise* to the *General Theory*.

1   Its fundamental framework belongs to the *Treatise* theory, for it maintains (i) profit and the TM supply function as determining the level of output, (ii) the relation, similar to Mechanism 1, between consumption and earnings which determines the price level of consumption goods, and (iii) the value of investment, determined in the same way as in Mechanism 2.
2   The basic theoretical structure is put forward as the dynamic process of Mechanisms 1 and 2 working through the TM supply function (Wicksellian theory no longer used).
3   The TM supply function and profit are discussed in detail. This is of special significance.[22]
4   The liquidity preference theory appears for the first time.
5   The three features of the MTP manuscript – (i) the possibility of cumulative deterioration, (ii) underemployment equilibrium, and (iii) the role of investment

and its fragility – can be traced back (on (i) and the first half of (iii)) to the *Treatise*,[23] and (on (ii) and the second half of (iii)) to the Chicago lectures, 'An Economic Analysis of Unemployment' (see Section II(1) above).[24]

The MTP manuscript describes the fluctuations of the economy using the TM supply function. It also describes long-period equilibrium as the economy reaching through a series of short-period equilibria, and thereby attempts to analyse short-period disequilibrium and long-period equilibrium in tandem. This was to come in for criticism from the 'Cambridge Circus' – criticism which, although he resisted it for some time, was eventually to prompt a great transformation in Keynes's thinking.

IV   The 'Cambridge Circus' criticism: May 1932

Immediately after the publication of the *Treatise*, several economists, including Kahn, Sraffa, Meade, and Austin and Joan Robinson, formed a group – the 'Cambridge Circus' (January–May 1931) – to study it. The members attended Keynes's lecture of 2 May and responded with a 'Manifesto', to which Keynes replied.[25]

1   *The 2 May 1932 lecture*

We can reconstruct Keynes's lecture from some surviving fragments, probably, his preparatory notes (*JMK*.29, pp. 39–42). The picture that emerges is substantially similar to the MTP manuscript, for the proposition, 'the volume of output and employment depends predominantly on the amount of investment', is emphasised in terms of the TM supply function.

The argument begins by making two assumptions: (i) ΔO and $\Delta E'$ have the same sign; and (ii) $\Delta E' - \Delta F$ and $\Delta E'$ have the same sign, where O denotes the volume of output, E' earnings plus profit, F spending, and ΔX an increment in X.

On these assumptions Keynes attempts to establish a positive relation between the volume of output and that of investment.

He then goes on to examine the case in which this relation does not hold. By looking closely into his procedure we can understand the relation between the positive output/investment relation and the TM supply function:

> If..., whenever there was an increase in investment, there should also be such an increase in rates of earnings that the increase in aggregate earnings on the basis of the old output was greater than the increase in investment, and if earners were to save these increased earnings whilst entrepreneurs maintained their expenditure at their previous level, then every increase in investment would be associated with a decrease in profit and therefore in output./Thus we are left with the remarkable generalisation that ... anything which increases the [volume of investment] will increase the [volume of output].
>
> (*JMK*.29, p. 40)

Keynes argues for this relation in the context of 'generalisations of far-reaching practical importance' (*JMK*.29, p. 40), stressing $\Delta Q = \Delta I + \Delta F - \Delta E$, which appeared in the MTP manuscript.

The key to a proper understanding of the lecture lies in Keynes's attempt to link the positive output/investment relation with the TM supply function. His analysis centres on the short-period process.

2   The Cambridge Circus

The lecture drew criticism from the Circus – the 'Manifesto' by Kahn and the Robinsons (*JMK*.29, pp. 42–45), which, arguing that Keynes's procedure for the proposition 'an increase in investment (I) brings about an increase in the volume of output (O)' lacks generality, proposes an alternative way of proving it:

> The problem seems... to be susceptible to treatment by the method of Supply and Demand. For the truth of the proposition..., the two following conditions appear to us to be sufficient... :
>
> (a) An increase in I will lead...to a rise in the demand for consumption goods,....
> (b) The conditions of supply of consumption goods are not affected by a change in I.
>
> When these conditions are fulfilled, an increase in I will lead to a rise in the demand curve for consumption goods without raising the supply curve, and so must lead to an increase of output of consumption goods, and...to an increase in total output.
>
> (*JMK*.29, pp. 43–44)

Keynes put forward the proposition in terms of the TM supply function, while the Circus did so in the framework constructed by Kahn (1931),[26] disregarding the function. The Circus's position is very clear in Joan Robinson's letter to Keynes:

> You begin by increasing I. Now...tell me...how much increase in output does this ΔI entail. Then I will tell you for any set of conditions of supply of consumption goods what increase in E would be necessary to prevent O from increasing....
>
> I consider our method more general than yours. ...yours only works when ΔQ and ΔO have the same sign. Ours is designed to overcome that limitation.
>
> (*JMK*.29, p. 47)

The Circus's argument was based on two considerations: (i) the elasticities of supply in capital and consumption goods industries; and (ii) the influence of an increase in investment on the demand for consumption goods.

On 8 May Keynes discussed the whole matter with Kahn and Joan Robinson. The next day he wrote a letter to Robinson, revealing some doubt about his own argument, while having no less doubt about Robinson's:

> [W]hich is the best of two alternative exegetical methods [?]...your way would be much more...cumbersome....I lack...sufficient evidence...to induce me to scrap all my present half-forged weapons.
>
> (*JMK*.13, p. 378)

The 'two alternative exegetical methods' are: (a) the credit cycle theory by way of the TM supply function; (b) the multiplier theory, including the method of supply and demand. The point is unmistakably the supply function.[27]

Robinson replied to Keynes on 10 May.[28]

> Then the supply price for each output is (on your view) the average prime cost + the profit per unit just sufficient to retain the marginal entrepreneurs....
> [L]ike the rest of us you have had your faith in supply curves shaken by [Sraffa]. But what he attacks are just the one-by-one supply curves that you regard as legitimate. His objections do not apply to the supply curve of output....[29]
>
> (*JMK*.13, p. 378)

The first sentence can be taken to mean that profit per unit is defined as the difference between the (supply) price as determined in the period, and the (average) prime cost as determined at the beginning of the period.

Let us now see how the quotation continues. First, Robinson suggests that Keynes deems a supply curve, in the ordinary sense, to be useful for the analysis of an individual firm or an individual industry, while Sraffa rejects this.

Second, the supply curve of output (of the economy as a whole) lies outside Sraffa's theory. Here Robinson's reference is to Sraffa (1926), of epoch-making importance for the imperfect competition revolution. Sraffa maintains that increasing returns are applicable to the industry in the narrower range:

> [T]he more nearly [an industry] includes...only those undertakings which produce a given type of consumable commodity – the greater will be the probability that the forces which make for increasing returns will predominate... [if the more nearly [an industry] includes all the undertakings,... decreasing returns will predominate].
>
> (Sraffa, 1926, p. 538)

Thus the 'supply curve of output' works under diminishing returns, while the 'one-by-one supply curves' under increasing returns.[30] Robinson seems to have this in mind.

If we understand Robinson's comments aright, it follows that she fails to recognise that (i) Keynes considers the TM supply function useful for analysis not only of the economy as a whole, but also of an individual industry; (ii) Keynes had never used the 'supply curve in the ordinary sense'.

Indeed, Keynes stressed the TM supply function in a letter to Robinson (12 May):

> [A]n increment in aggregate profit can reasonably be expected to produce an increment of aggregate output – which is … what I have said.
> …. even when one is dealing with separate industries, … my supply curve is one which relates output and profit.
>
> (*JMK*.13, p. 380)

By the end of 1932, however, he came to accept the Circus criticisms. He abandoned the TM supply function and adopted 'the method of Supply and Demand' – the lines of Kahn and Robinson.[31]

V   Two tables of contents (1932)

In this section we deal with two sets of material indispensable for a proper understanding of Keynes's theoretical development.

1   *Keynes and Kitoh*

In the preface to the Japanese edition of the *Treatise* (5 April 1932), Keynes announced his intention 'to publish a short book of a purely theoretical character, extending and correcting the theoretical basis … in Books III and IV …' (Tm/1/3/255). Kitoh, the translator, asked Keynes about the progress of the book (30 June. Tm/1/3/270). Keynes replied that '… [it] is … still many months off' (20 July. Tm/1/3/271). On 18 September he remarked to his mother: 'I have written nearly a third of my new book on monetary theory' (*JMK*.13, p. 380).

When Kitoh repeated his enquiry Keynes (20 October 1933. Tm/1/3/273) replied: '… [My book] may possibly be published some time next year' (9 November. Tm/1/3/272), followed by a letter saying that 'I am hard at work on my further book on the Pure Theory of Money …. But it will be some months more before … printing' (22 June 1934. Tm/1/3/274).

2   *Two tables of contents*

We have two tables of contents for 1932 (*JMK*.29, pp. 49–50. Hereafter 'Table 1' and 'Table 2'). It is a pity that the two tables contain nothing of the relevant text, but they nevertheless offer evidence for filling out the picture we are piecing together.

As we shall see, the work to which Keynes referred in his letters of 1932 both to Kitoh (20 July), and to his mother (18 September) is probably related to a third (missing) table of contents.

A Table 1

The table of contents entitled 'The Monetary Theory of Production' has several noteworthy points:

1 Chapters 1–4 (of Book I) may argue disbursement, profit, earnings and output in the same way as the MTP manuscript in terms of the equation $\Delta Q = \Delta I + \Delta F - \Delta E = \Delta D - \Delta E$;
2 Chapter 2, 'The Relation of Profit to Output' (of Book I) may point to the TM supply function;
3 Chapter 6, 'Generalisations' (of Book I) may argue the 'vital generalisation' in the MTP manuscript;
4 Chapter 7, 'Historical Retrospect' (of Book I) may be related to a note, 'Historical Retrospect' (*JMK*.13, pp. 406–407);
5 Chapter 1, 'The Differential of Consumption-Goods and Capital-Goods' (of Book II) may be related to the 'Why' manuscript;
6 Chapter 2, 'The Meaning and Consequences of "Bearishness"' (of Book III) may suggest the *Treatise* theory of money.

B Table 2

The untitled table of contents, whose main chapters are almost the same as in the Table 1, shows the following features:

1 Chapter 20, 'The Factors Determining Liquidity Preference' (of Book III) may propose the liquidity preference theory;
2 Chapters 23–27 (of Book IV) bear titles regarding economic policy. No such chapters re-appear thereafter.

C Chronological order

Let us consider the chronological order of this material. Obviously Table 1, referring to 'bearishness', precedes Table 2, referring to 'liquidity preference'.

The MTP manuscript was probably written based on the basis of a third table of contents following these two tables of contents, as indeed is suggested:

1 by the chapter titles of the MTP manuscript, which have no corresponding titles in the two tables of contents;
2 by the fact that the MTP manuscript contains the seeds of the liquidity preference theory.

However, this is not to deny that Tables 1 and 2 are closely related to the MTP manuscript.

VI Conclusion

This chapter has examined how and for how long Keynes maintained the *Treatise* theory after its publication, and has shed some new light on this problem. The following three points are worth noting.

A clarification of how Keynes tried to defend and extend his own theory developed in the Treatise – Through the Chicago lectures, and the Round Table (June 1931) we saw how Keynes emphasised the TM supply function in his analysis. We also argued that the MTP manuscript analyses the fluctuations of the economy and its possibility of cumulative deterioration by means of the TM supply function, and describes a long-period equilibrium as a point reaching after a series of short-period equilibria. Moreover, we saw that the MTP manuscript stresses the role of investment in determining the level of output, and of the government in promoting investment, and contains the seeds of liquidity preference.

The significance of two criticisms of the Treatise – The first criticism came from Hawtrey in 1930, who, questioning the TM supply function, emphasised effective demand. Hawtrey criticised Keynes's theory from the standpoint of his own theory, which to some extent anticipates the *General Theory*, while Keynes reveals his state of mind concerning the TM supply function, feeling the need to link monetary theory to the theory of short-period supply.

The second came from the Cambridge Circus, which, questioning the TM supply function, proposed an alternative in terms of Kahn (1931). Around May 1932 there was a controversy over the credit cycle theory between Keynes and the Cambridge Circus.

By the end of 1932, however, he had come to accept the Circus criticisms.[32] He abandoned the TM supply function and adopted 'the method of Supply and Demand'.

The 'Why' and the 'Determination' manuscripts — We have also examined the 'Why' and the 'Determination' manuscripts probably written prior to the MTP manuscript. Both argue that the price level of consumption goods is determined by Mechanism 1, the price level of investment goods by Mechanism 2. In this respect they are in line with the *Treatise* theory. However, they also contain the beginnings of the propensity to save, and the 'Why' manuscript has the 'supply schedule' as a relation between price and output appearing for the first time. These indicate some change towards the *General Theory*.

From these crucial developments we ascertained a time span between October 1930 and October 1932. Exactly why October 1932 should mark the end of the period will be clarified in the next chapter.

7   The turning point

Towards the end of 1932 Keynes reached a turning point in the development of his economic theorising – a turning point from the world of the *Treatise* to that of the *General Theory*. Our investigation of this seminal event is based on two main sources: the manuscript with the heading, 'The Parameters of a Monetary Economy' (*JMK*.13, pp. 397–405. Hereafter the 'PME manuscript'),[1] probably written in October or November, and Keynes's Michaelmas lectures.

By 'turning point' we do not mean Keynes's formulation of the theory explaining the level of employment, but rather his construction, in the PMT Manuscript, of a new model in which (i) the prices and volumes of output are determined in the same period (using the 'general state of time preference' as a key concept), and (ii) the TM supply function to all intents and purposes loses its role. In other words, Keynes was for the first time using equilibrium of investment and saving to analyse the short period; hitherto he had used it as a 'norm' for the long period.

In the PME Manuscript Keynes developed three other important concepts: the 'fundamental psychological law' (though he rejected an idea which later led to the consumption function of the *General Theory*); the theory of liquidity preference; and the 'first postulate of the classical economics'. Thus, while still retaining some elements which belong to the *Treatise* world, he nonetheless moved decisively into that of the *General Theory*.

In Sections I and II we examine, respectively, the PME Manuscript and Keynes's lectures. In Section III we discuss Kahn's contribution to Keynes's turning point. In Section IV we discuss to what degree Keynes was influenced by Malthus around November 1932.

I   'The Parameters of a Monetary Economy' manuscript

In this section we examine the PME manuscript (*JMK*.13, pp. 397–405). We begin by discussing three ideas introduced for the first time, which signpost the 'turning point' towards the *General Theory*. We then go on to point out that the PME Manuscript is, nevertheless, still incomplete on several points.

1   *Progressive ideas*

A   *The concept of 'complex'*

In the PME manuscript Keynes utilises the concept of 'complex', rejecting that of 'index'. In the case of assets, for example, this results in a vector of prices instead of an index of the prices of individual assets. The latter differs from the former in that it is obtained on the basis of the prices of individual assets through some formula representing the price level as a whole. Methodologically, the 'complex' concept represents the starting point on the road to the *General Theory*.[2]

> [W]e are here interpreting P_2, not as the *average* price of assets..., but as the complex of prices of assets. For, since the supply schedules of different industries will not be the same, the same average price may lead to a different volume of investment if it is differently made up.
>
> (*JMK*.13, p. 399)[3]

Two points come to mind reading this: Keynes's great expertise in the index problem, typically shown in 'The Method of Index Numbers' (1909; *JMK*.11, chapter 2) and Volume 2 of the *Treatise*, and the fact that the *General Theory* adopts 'two fundamental units of quantity' (*GT*, p. 41).

B A new formula for a system of commodity markets

A new model put forward in the manuscript marks a breakthrough that would lead to the *General Theory*. Here Keynes adopts an idea similar, in certain respects, to the multiplier theory and formulates a supply schedule as a function of a complex of prices.

The model is described by

$$P_2 = B(\rho) \tag{1}$$

$$I' = C(P_2) \tag{2}$$

$$I = P_2 \times I' \tag{3}$$

$$P_1 = G(I, H) \tag{4}$$

$$R = H(P_1) \tag{5}$$

where ρ denotes the complex of interest rates, P_1 and P_2 the price complex of consumables and that of capital assets, B the complex of expected quasi-rents, I' the current volume of investment, H and C the supply schedule of investment goods and that of consumables, I the value of investment, G the general state of time preference, and R the output of consumables.

The model runs as follows. Given the complex of interest rates, the price complex of capital assets is determined by equation (1). Once we have this, the volume of investment is determined by equation (2). The value of investment is determined by equation (3). From this and equation (5), the price complex of consumables and the output of consumables are determined by equation (4).

Let us examine each equation. Equation (1) is a theory determining the price level of capital assets by their prospective yields and the rate of interest. The price complex of the total stock of assets is assumed to regulate that of currently produced assets.[4]

In fact, equation (1) is virtually the 'demand price of the investment' of the *General Theory* (*GT*, p. 137). The time series of quasi-rents which a capital asset is expected to yield (the 'prospective yield' in the *General Theory*) is compared with the 'present value of a debt which would have an interest yield year by year' (*JMK*.13, p. 398).

Moreover, distinction is made between the mechanism determining the rate of interest and the method of valuing assets. In this connection, Keynes refers to 'the failure of the attempt to avoid [the] circularity which makes Marshall's treatment of the rate of interest unsatisfactory'[5] (*JMK*.13, p. 400). Incidentally, no reference is made to anything like the 'supply price of the investment' of the *General Theory*.

Keynes defines two supply schedules as functions of the price complex.[6] Although the PME manuscript provides no evidence of what they look like, on the evidence of the seventh lecture of 21 November (see Section 2 below) they might possibly be the same as the 'first postulate of the classical economics' in the *General Theory*. In these schedules, the volumes of output in both sectors depend on the prices in the current period. This is his first attempt to use the first postulate, although up to 'the Second Manuscript of 1933' (see the next chapter) he hesitates to use it.[7]

Equation (4) deals with consumption:

> When we ... deduce from the general state of time preference, ..., what part of the community's aggregate income will be spent and what part will be reserved, we are soon in difficulties. For the amount of total expenditure responds immediately to the amount of total income, whilst, for the community as a whole, the amount of total income depends ... directly and immediately on the amount of total expenditure. We ... must approach our goal ... by a different route.
>
> (*JMK*.13, p. 400)

Interestingly, Keynes appears to reject an idea which later leads to the consumption function. The 'different route' should be a theory to the effect that the price level of consumables is determined where investment becomes equal to saving:

> [S]ince the amount of money reserved by the public out of their incomes must always be exactly equal to the amount of current investment, the level of prices ... has to rise to a point at which the amount of money which the public desire to reserve [saving], having regard to the general state of time preference, *is* equal to the amount of current investment.
>
> (*JMK*.13, p. 401)

That is,

$$P_1 = G(I) \tag{4'}$$

Equation (4) is a revised version of equation (4)':

> Hence we must bring in the supply schedule ... of consumables, namely $R = H(P_1)...$, and re-write our equation for P_1 as $P_1 = G(I, H)$.
>
> (*JMK*.13, p. 403)

Thus, given the supply schedule, the price level (and output) of consumables is determined in such a way that investment becomes equal to saving. This equality[8] is crucial, for it means a shift from a theory of investment–saving deviation to that of investment–saving equilibrium, which gave him a chance to change his model building.[9]

In order to complete the model, Keynes put forward the equation for the complex of interest rates:

$$\rho = A(M) \tag{6}$$

where A denotes the state of liquidity preference and M the quantity of money.

> [T]he rate of interest has to move until the amount of money which the public desire to hold, having regard to their liquidity preferences, is equal to the amount of money which the banking system is creating.
>
> (*JMK*.13, pp. 400–401)

Keynes argues that liquidity preference determines the rate of interest – the first appearance of this concept apart from the embryo in the MTP Manuscript. Expressions such as 'a debt which would have an interest' (*JMK*.13, p. 398), and 'the price of debts (i.e. the rate of interest)' (*JMK*.13, p. 405), indicate that he conceives of money and debts on equal terms (in the *Treatise* money was compared with assets and debts together). Notwithstanding the difference in the commodity market mechanism, however, both the MTP and the PME manuscripts share the view that the role of the rate of interest is confined to determination of the price complex of capital assets (and investment goods).

The system (1)–(6), which we will call 'Model 1', has six endogenous variables, so it can be solved. Equation (4) is the most important, for equilibrium of investment and saving is used to determine the price complex of consumables in the current period. The mechanism by which the values of investment and consumption are determined is also worth noting. Their prices and volumes of output are determined simultaneously without the TM supply functions. The following passage dealing with consumption should be read with this in mind:

> The simplest condition for stable equilibrium is that when aggregate income changes, the change in aggregate expenditure should be the same in direction but smaller in absolute amount.[10]
>
> (*JMK*.13, p. 401)

'Aggregate expenditure' refers to consumption expenditure, while 'condition' connotes a stability condition for P_1 and can be understood as a version of the 'fundamental psychological law' – the first appearance, albeit relating to the stability of P_1.

To sum up, Model 1 contributes to the *General Theory* with regard to:

1   the supply schedule based on the first postulate;
2   the equality of investment and saving;
3   the value of investment, the general state of time preference, and the supply schedule of consumables as factors determining the mechanism of the consumption goods sector;
4   the theory of liquidity preference.

Point (3) is similar to the multiplier theory of the *General Theory* in which, given the value of investment, the prices and quantities of consumables are determined by the propensity to consume and the supply schedule of consumables.[11]

C   *The variables in a system of simultaneous equations and their causal relations*

In the PME manuscript Keynes consciously builds his theory as a system of simultaneous equations. However, the following passage is very instructive, for he attaches importance to the causal relations as well:

> These parameters... are not entirely independent of one another and the schedules expressing them should be stated... in the form of simultaneous equations. But for purposes of analysis they are as distinct from one another as economic factors ever are.
>
> (*JMK*.13, p. 405)

It is crucial to grasp Keynes's conception of the causal relations, for it reveals his position concerning the relation between his model and the real world, and illuminates his policy outlook.

He stresses the capacity of the monetary authority to adjust the rate of interest so that the economy might attain an optimum level of output. Although we started our discussion with the commodity markets, our contention is that the money market plays a crucial role in the PME manuscript.

The following is from '9 The Parameters of a Monetary Economy' – the same approach as the *General Theory*:

> Let us imagine that we have been asked to explain what consequences will result to prices, output and incomes if the monetary authority decides to increase the quantity of money by a given amount. ... [T]o lay down the general principles on which questions of this kind can be answered is the object of the monetary theory of production.
>
> (*JMK*.13, pp. 396–397)

We attach importance to the PME manuscript for the following reasons. Keynes abandons a dynamic model using the TM supply function, introducing the theory of investment–saving equilibrium. Moreover, Model 1 offers a key to understanding the *General Theory*, prices and the 'supply side' being clearly explicated here.

Table 7.1 From the *Treatise* to 'The Parameters of a Monetary Economy' manuscript

Period		October 1930	June 1931	May 1932	Mid-1932	End of 1932
Material		(a)	(b)(c)	(d)(e)	(f)	(g)
Commo-dity market	Supply side	TM supply function				*Supply schedule (the first postulate of the classical economics)
	Demand side	Determination of the price level of consumption goods				*General state of time preference
		Two types of Investment Price Theory		Abandonment of Investment Price Theory (1)		Revised Investment Price Theory (2)
	Equili-brium	Assumption to the effect that the total volume of output, fixed at the beginning of the period, is sold out in that period				*Simultaneous determination of quantities and prices *Equilibrium of investment and saving (determination of the price level of consumption goods)
	Profit	profit = investment – saving or disbursement – earnings				
Money market		Bearishness function (Investment Price Theory (1))		*Liquidity preference (rate of interest)		
Others						*Heterogeneity of goods (complex) *Simultaneous equations system

Notes

1 * indicates a new idea.

2 a: The *Treatise*.

   b: 'An Economic Analysis of Unemployment'.

   c: Unemployment as a World Problem.

   d: Robinson's letter to Keynes (10 May).

   e: Keynes's letter to Robinson (12 May).

   f: 'The Monetary Theory of Production' manuscript.

   g: 'The Parameters of a Monetary Economy' manuscript.

The PME manuscript has in general been either ignored or undervalued. For example, Patinkin (1982, pp. 21–23), who makes no reference to it in Patinkin (1976; 1993), regards it as another product in the *Treatise* mould, while Amadeo (1989), Hession (1984, chapter 12) and Moggridge (1992, chapter 21) make no reference to it.

Even the scholars who stress the importance of the PME manuscript such as Vicarelli (1984), Hishiyama (1993), Kojima (1997) and Okada (1997), seem to fall short of grasping its true significance. Asano (1987), having detected certain progressive elements in it, argues that Keynes still adheres to the *Treatise* theory.

2   *The incompleteness*

Thus we attach great importance to the PME manuscript as the turning point. However, it is in fact theoretically incomplete on three points.

First, notwithstanding Model 1, Keynes still clings to the TM supply function:

> [To...assume] that the supply schedules of assets and consumables are dependent on the prices of the articles produced would be reasonable for a single industry...[but]...not reasonable for industry as a whole,...it is more nearly accurate to think of the supply schedule as relating output to profit.
>
> (*JMK*.13, p. 403)

He then puts forward a model with equations (2) and (5) replaced with (2)' and (5)' respectively:

$$P_2 = B(\rho) \tag{1}$$

$$I' = C'(Q_2) \tag{2'}$$

$$I = P_2 \times I' \tag{3}$$

$$P_1 = G(I, H') \tag{4'}$$

$$R = H'(Q_1) \tag{5'}$$

$$\rho = A(M) \tag{6}$$

where Q_1 denotes profit of the consumption goods industry, Q_2 profit of the capital goods industry, C' and H' a supply function defined as a function of profit in the capital goods industry and the consumption goods industry respectively.

This system, which we will call 'Model 2', is virtually the same as the model in '9 The Parameters of a Monetary Economy' (*JMK*.13, pp. 396–397).

As far as the rate of interest and the price complex of capital assets are concerned, Model 2 does not differ from Model 1. The profit per unit of output in the capital goods industry, q_2, is determined as the difference between the price complex of capital assets P_2 and their cost w, which is assumed to be constant. Then, I' is determined by equation (2)' and $Q_2 = q_2 \times I'$. Considering $Q_1 = q_1 \times R$, where q_1 denotes the profit per unit of output in the consumption goods industry, equation (5)' can be taken as exhibiting the relation of q_1 to R. Let us express this as $R = h(q_1)$. Together with $P_1 = q_1 + w$ and $R = h(q_1)$, equation (4)' determines q_1, P_1 and R.

The problem with Model 2 lies in equations (2)' and (5)'. They are not the TM supply functions, although Keynes takes them to be so. Even here profit plays no dynamic role, and the volumes of output are determined in the current period.

Second, Keynes advances the theory that, given the rate of interest, the prices of capital assets are determined by expected quasi-rents (which we call 'Revised Investment Price Theory (2)'), which means that the marginal efficiency of capital has yet to appear.

Third, Model 1 fails to provide an argument in terms of macro-variables such as the aggregate supply and demand functions in *GT*'s chapter 3. It was not until 1933 that he developed such an argument.[12]

We might be tempted to regard the PME manuscript as still belonging to the *Treatise* world, considering that (i) Keynes still clings to the TM supply function, (ii) Models 1 and 2 deal with the price levels only, and (iii) the liquidity preference theory is not the same as in the *General Theory*.

However, to regard it in this way would be to overlook its importance. In either Model both the price levels and the volumes of output are determined in the current period in which profit plays no role. In Model 1, above all, the price level of the consumables is determined in such a way that investment becomes equal to saving.

The main arguments discussed from Chapter 5 up to this Section are visualised in Table 7.1.

II   The 1932 Michaelmas lectures

Further important material indicating the turning point is to be found in the 1932 Michaelmas lectures, for which we have notes taken by Bryce, Cairncross and Tarshis,[13] as well as the lecture drafts for 10 October and 14 November (*JMK*.13, pp. 50–57).

Before examining the lectures, let us briefly see how they have since been evaluated. Clarke (1988; 1998, pp. 93 and 95) sees the inception of the *General Theory* occurring at the end of 1932. In Clarke (1988; 1998, pp. 96–97), however, reference goes up to the third lecture, while Clarke (1988; 1998, chapter 4) pays no attention to Model 1 in the seventh lecture. Skidelsky (1992, pp. 459–466) deals with the lectures as showing 'the embryo of the *General Theory*' or 'the main building blocks of a theory of output'. Although he does not refer to Model 2, and Model 1 cannot be taken as a theory of effective demand, Skidelsky's evaluation is close to ours.

On the other hand, Milgate (1983, p. 195), who does not mention Model 1, regards the lectures as orthodox marginalist thought. Patinkin (Patinkin and Leith eds 1978, p. 14) and Dimand (1988) maintain that the lectures are within the *Treatise* framework. Dimand (1988, pp. 153–155), without distinguishing Model 1 from Model 2, judges that 'windfall profits or losses, investment minus saving, are at the centre of the analysis of the Michaelmas 1932 lectures . . ., just as in the *Treatise*'.

So let us now examine the lectures.

In the first lecture Keynes argues that in the monetary theory of production the real-world economy is treated in terms of the monetary economy, whereas economic theory had so far analysed only a 'neutral money' economy. Here he puts forward an employment theory, albeit not very clearly. He argues that, in the monetary economy, 'the short-period supply price of labour is nearer horizontal' (*JMK*.29, p. 51), and proceeds to consider the case in which the short-period disturbance occurs due to 'a change in demand as a whole relatively to supply as a whole due to deficient disbursement' (*JMK*.29, p. 53). These ideas might be the origins of *GT*'s chapter 2. Keynes aims at analysing the situation in which deficient disbursement leads to losses for entrepreneurs and a decrease in employment.

In the second and third lectures Keynes develops an argument to the effect that total income is equal to aggregate disbursement:

$$\text{Total Income} = E + Q = \text{Aggregate Disbursement}$$

where E is earnings and Q windfall profits.

Incomes of individuals continue to change until total income equals aggregate disbursement, and entrepreneurs continue to revise the scale of their production unless Q is zero. Thus equilibrium is attained when Q is zero. Keynes then analyses the causal sequence induced by insufficient disbursement.

The idea that changes in output depend on changes in the difference between disbursement and earnings is similar to the TM supply function in the MTP Manuscript, suggesting that the lectures at this stage were influenced by it.

Aggregate disbursement is composed of the amount of investment, I, and the expenditure on consumables, F. From this, together with the above equation:

$$Q = I - S$$

where $S \ (= E - F)$ is voluntary saving.

This is followed by some interesting discussion regarding voluntary saving:

> [W]hatever spending the public and entrepreneurs adopt, the amount of surplus remains always the same and equals the amount of investment. What will be changed will be the price of consumables. If we hold I as given, what S determines is the price level [of consumables]. Or increased saving permits [the] same investment at a lower price level.
>
> (Rymes [Tarshis], 1988, p. 113 [A paging system adopted by Rymes. The note taken by Tarshi. See Section I(f) of Bibliography.])

This argument is used in the equation $P_1 = G \ (I, H)$, and possibly opens the way to the 'time preference' in the seventh lecture. Despite some ambiguities in relation to investment, saving, and profit, Keynes seems to be thinking of both the short and the long periods.[14]

The fourth lecture deals with the theory of liquidity preference, the fifth with the theory of investment. Here Keynes discusses both topics in the context of the MTP manuscript theory.

Keynes develops his theory as follows:

> The rate of interest measures the return in terms of money ... in exchange for parting with the control of that money for a stated time for a debt.... [It is] the rate of exchange between money and debts.
>
> (Rymes [Tarshis], 1988, p. 115)

> [The] rate of interest is fixed with the policies of the bank and the preferences of the people for keeping control of their money.
>
> (Rymes [Bryce], 1988, p. A28)

Given M as the amount of money, A the state of liquidity preference and ρ the rate of interest, then

$$\rho = A(M)$$

It generally has a negative slope.[15] Keynes also touches on something like the 'liquidity trap'[16] and flight from the currency.

A fragment from the lecture draft for the sixth lecture runs:

> The rate of earnings will fall, and output will fall.... Consequently the demand for money in the active circulation will fall, which ... affects the state of liquidity preference so that ... a lowering ... of the rate of interest [occurs] ... given quantity of money.
>
> (*JMK*.29, p. 56)

In the fifth lecture Keynes first argues that the value of capital assets is the present value obtained by discounting the stream of expected quasi-rents at the current rate of interest. He then argues that investment takes place if the price of an asset exceeds its current cost of production, so that 'the volume of investment is determined by [the streams of] prospective quasi-rents, ... [the] rate of interest and [the] cost of production' (Rymes [Bryce], 1988, p. A32). This idea is not to be found in the *Treatise*.

In the sixth and seventh lectures Keynes proposes the 'astronomical structure' and the 'mechanical structure' models.

The former has two versions, depending on an assumption concerning a supply function. The first version is the same as Model 1, while the second has a supply function expressed in terms of profits, and is the same as Model 2 except for an 'earnings reaction' function.

However, the second version is unsatisfactory, in that: (i) $Q_1 = Q_2 = 0$ occurs because saving is supposed to be equal to investment in the equation $P_1 = G(I, H)$; (ii) it is unclear how I', P_1 and R are determined in this model; (iii) the role of the supply functions is unclear.

Keynes proposes Model 1, followed by Model 2, preferring the latter to the former. Finally, he refers to the 'mechanical structure':

$$\Delta Q = \Delta I - \Delta S = \Delta D - \Delta E$$

When disbursement, D, increases faster than earnings, E, first profits increase, and then output. That is, whether output increases or not depends upon whether investment increases faster than saving. Here something like the TM supply function plays a central role, so that the amount of investment is not necessarily equal to that of saving. In the draft for the sixth lecture, moreover, Keynes discusses the trade cycle and underemployment equilibrium within the MTP manuscript framework.

What emerges here is that Keynes is wavering between the *Treatise* world (Model 2 [albeit superficially] and the 'mechanical structure') and the *General Theory* world (Model 1).

However, Keynes's state of mind is one thing, his true state of development another: (i) the supply function in Model 2 is not the TM supply function and Model 2 fails to fulfil its intended role; (ii) Model 1 includes new ideas contributing towards the *General Theory*, and should be taken seriously. We can say that his economic theorising goes through a transition, which is why we regard both the PME manuscript and the 1932 lectures as constituting the *turning point*.

In his final lecture, Keynes examines the views of earlier economists which might support his theory. This naturally leads to *GT*'s chapter 23.[17]

He also outlines an embryonic argument leading to chapters 19 and 21 of *GT*:

> [L]abour is essentially the standard of value – the level of wages determines prices... explanat[ion] of prices was to be found in effective demand – raising incomes raising prices, etc.
>
> (Rymes [Tarshis], 1988, p. 128)

The term 'effective demand' makes its first appearance, and is argued in relation to Malthus, who makes his first appearance in the notes by Cairncross (Rymes, 1988, p. D22) and Bryce (Rymes, 1988, p. A51).[18]

Keynes concludes the lectures with stating that the normal tendency is for saving to exceed investment by far, so that loss of profits and unemployment ensue.

We find Keynes wavering between the *Treatise* world and the *General Theory* world. Here the idea of the TM supply function as from the *Treatise* and the ideas leading to the *General Theory* coexist in a confusing way. We would stress, however, that what matters is not Model 2 but Model 1.

III   Kahn's contribution

Why did Keynes change the way of constructing his economic model at this particular time? What and who drove him to do so?

There is no simple answer to the question, but the 'Cambridge Circus' merits some consideration.[19,20]

The controversy between the two can be summarised as follows. Keynes put forward the credit cycle theory by way of the TM supply function, while the Circus did so by way of the multiplier theory and the method of supply and demand based on Kahn (1931).

The point of contention is the supply function. By the end of 1932, however, Keynes had accepted the Circus criticisms. This transformation provides a very good reason to look into Kahn (1972 [1931], pp. 1–27). Dating from 1930, this particular article by Kahn is discussed here because the idea was not incorporated into Keynes's own theory until 1933.

Looking back in 1971, Kahn recalled:

> I circulated a very early version to the members of the Committee of Economists...in September 1930. [It]...was revised and considerably expanded as a result of discussions with Colin Clark..., and with James Meade and others in Cambridge.
>
> (Kahn, 1972, p. vii)

As for Kahn's influences, we would suggest two points.

The first is that we now see the supply–demand analysis developed.[21] The following passage should be read bearing in mind the Cambridge Circus criticisms, which we examined in Section IV of Chapter 6:

> The price-level and output of home-produced consumption-goods, ...are determined by the conditions of supply and demand. If the conditions of supply can be regarded as fixed, both the price-level and the output are determined by the demand; .... The volume of employment [and output]... in...consumption-goods [sector] and the price-level of home-produced consumption-goods are uniquely correlated.
>
> (Kahn, 1972, pp. 5–6)

It was when Keynes accepted the first postulate in mid-1933[22] that he adopted this idea.

The second point is that the multiplier theory is developed as a concrete formula.[23] The original idea goes back to Lloyd George's pledge (April 1924), and was developed within the Liberal Party with Keynes as a key figure.[24]

Criticising the 'Treasury View',[25] Keynes-Henderson (May 1929; *JMK*.9, pp. 86–125) argue that a national development policy can increase the number employed, not only directly but also indirectly, and that this brings about a cumulative effect on production activity.

Kahn (1931) fleshed out to this idea with consideration of how much employment would be generated by an increase in employment in the investment goods sector. In the memorandum (21 September 1930. *JMK*.13, pp. 178–200), helped by the multiplier theory, Keynes advocated government home investment schemes:

> Mr Kahn has produced an argument...for supposing that...in Great Britain a given amount of primary employment gives rise to an approximately equal amount of secondary employment.
>
> (*JMK*.13, 188)

Again, he used the theory as an indicator assessing the excess of saving over investment within the *Treatise* framework:

> [W]e may assess the existing excess of saving over investment at £187,500,000 per annum. [We assume]... our abnormal unemployment at 1,500,000 and the output corresponding to the employment of a man for a year at £250.
>
> (*JMK*.13, p. 188. The multiplier is 2)

In the Draft Report (6 October 1930. *JMK*.20, pp. 437–443), Keynes explained the multiplier theory:

> Apart from the primary employment..., there is...a further source of secondary employment,...For the newly employed men and others whose receipts are increased as a result of the new investment may spend these receipts...on increasing their own consumption, with the effect of increasing employment in...producing consumption goods [industries]; and those engaged in these consumption industries will also have more to spend; and so the ripple of increased demand will spread over the whole pool of employment.
>
> (*JMK*.20, p. 439)

However, Keynes did not put the multiplier theory at the centre of his system until 1933, as is attested by the fact that:

1   In the seventh of the 1933 Michaelmas lectures he argues for the multiplier theory;
2   In the third table of contents (December 1933. See Section II of Chapter 8) he entitles chapter 16 with the term 'Multiplier'.[26]

To sum up, the method of supply and demand and the multiplier theory were eventually adopted. By the end of 1932 Keynes's adoption of the former is evident in the PME manuscript and the Michaelmas lectures, although he still sticks to the TM supply function. As for the multiplier theory, however, Keynes did not incorporate it into his theory.

IV   Malthus and Keynes

To what extent did Keynes's reading of Malthus's pamphlet and his letters to Ricardo around November 1932 influence his theoretical development? This has been a source of recent controversy.

Malthus's theory, as developed in *Principles of Political Economy* (1820, chapter 7, section III), can be summarised as follows:

1   The capitalists determine how much to save based on the profits in the preceding period. In the current period, saving thus determined is used as the

fund for employing labourers. The labourers thus employed productively contribute to an increase in output.

2   The capitalists spend the excess of the profits over saving. The labourers spend all their wages. The landlords spend all the rent.
3   Prices and the profits are determined in relation to the commodities produced and the demand for them. The monetary demand for commodities is directed to the commodities produced. Malthus named the price thus determined 'effective demand'. On the basis of the ensuing profits the capitalists determine how much to save. The process returns to (1).

We will call his theory thus interpreted 'Malthus's general theory'.

Our answer to the question of Malthus's influence, then, can be summed up as follows: Malthus's general theory is a predecessor of the *Treatise* theory as constituted by the first fundamental equation plus the TM supply function rather than that of the *General* Theory, although there are some points on which Malthus influenced Keynes.

Keynes's paper, 'Thomas Robert Malthus', dates from 1922, but it was not until around November 1932 that Keynes discussed Malthus with regard to the theory of unemployment and effective demand. The text is reproduced as *JMK*.10, chapter 12, and an editorial note points out that Keynes added two elements:

(i)   an evaluation of *An Investigation of the Cause of the Present High Price of Provision* (Malthus, 1800) in which the concept of 'effective demand' is to be found (*JMK*.10, pp. 87–91);
(ii)   a discussion of Malthus's letters to Ricardo in which Malthus's general theory is put forward (*JMK*.10, pp. 94–100).

Concerning (i), Keynes notes the concept of 'effective demand' as determining prices and profits. He finds that in Malthus's argument the price level is determined by the marginal principle given that the volume of output is fixed and the demand is supported by the people's ability to pay. Keynes recognises here 'the beginning of systematic economic thinking'.

The significance of Keynes's remarks on Malthus's pamphlet can be understood as follows:

1   In the Second Manuscript of 1933 (see Section I of Chapter 8) Keynes adopts the marginal principle in the form of the first postulate of classical economics.
2   In the First Manuscript of 1933 (see Section I of Chapter 8) Keynes develops the model composed of equations (1)–(4).
3   Keynes does not use the term 'effective demand' in the same sense as Malthus does. Even in the Third Manuscript written in December 1933 (see Chapter 8) he uses it, rather, to indicate the 'pseudo-TM supply function mk2' (see Section I(2) of Chapter 8).

Thus we may therefore reasonably conclude that the direct influence of Malthus upon Keynes's thinking was rather limited.

In connection with (ii), Keynes quotes several passages (see *JMK*.10, pp. 98–100) suggesting a special case of Malthus's general theory. They indicate that Keynes adhered to the TM supply function.

It may have been through study of Malthus's pamphlets and letters that Keynes was stimulated to note deficiency in demand as the cause of unemployment. This influence seems to be reflected in equations (3) and (4) of the First Manuscript.

V   Conclusion

Our considerations show that the PME manuscript and the 1932 Michaelmas lectures occupy a crucial place in Keynes's theoretical development. Model 1 is decisive. Although he still clings to the TM supply function idea, the PME manuscript marks a turning point.

Why did Keynes change his way of constructing his economic model at this point in time? Before the PME manuscript, Keynes's model was constructed in such a way that only when the volume of output in the initial period was given could the volumes of output in the succeeding periods be determined – a restriction that he must surely have been dissatisfied with. Around May 1932, Keynes's view was criticised by the Cambridge Circus, the central figure of which was Kahn. This criticism was to prompt him to change his theory after a period of time. The central problem lay in how to deal with a supply function. He abandoned the TM supply function, adopted the first postulate, and constructed Model 1.

Thus we regard the PME Manuscript and the Michaelmas lectures of 1932 as constituting a turning point. So far they have been largely ignored or misinterpreted. This may have something to do with the failure to appreciate the role played by the TM supply function subsequent to the *Treatise*.

8   Searching for a new theory of employment

We saw in Chapter 7 that by the end of 1932 Keynes had not only proposed a simultaneous equations system, which we called 'Model 1', that took the equality of investment and saving for granted, but had also adopted the liquidity preference theory, the fundamental psychological law, a theory similar to the multiplier theory, and the first postulate (though he retained doubts about the last of these).

To what extent, then, did he succeed, in 1933, in putting together the *General Theory*'s account of how the level of employment is determined? This is the question that we now address.

The chapter is structured thus: in Section I we examine three manuscripts of 1933 except for the tables of contents, which we discuss in Section II.

I   Three manuscripts[1]

The manuscripts we shall be looking into here are: 'The Monetary Theory of Employment' (*JMK*.29, pp. 62–66. Hereafter the First Manuscript); 'The General Theory of Employment' (*JMK*.29, pp. 63, 66–73, 87–92, 95–102. Hereafter the Second Manuscript); and the manuscript with the same title as the Second Manuscript (*JMK*.29, pp. 76–101 and *JMK*.13, pp. 421–422. Hereafter the Third Manuscript). The three tables of contents are, for the sake of convenience, dealt with in Section II.

1   *The First Manuscript*

The First Manuscript is composed of part of Chapter 6, 'A Summary of the Argument So Far', and is assigned to the 'First Table' (see Section II). Two points are particularly noteworthy:[2] the system of equations leading to the *GT*'s chapter 3, and the 'accounting period'.

A   *The system of equations*[3]

Keynes argues:

> Thus the amount of employment will be determined by a set of simultaneous equations which relate together employment (*N*), prospective investment (*I*)

and prospective consumption (C), ... :

$$N = f_1(Q) \tag{1}$$
$$E = f_2(N) \tag{2}$$
$$C = f_3(D) \tag{3}$$
$$D = E + Q = I + C \tag{4}^4$$

where f_1 ... may be called the Supply Function, f_2 the Cost Function, and f_3 depends on the propensity to save ....

If ... we suppose the entrepreneur firms to know ... f_1, ... f_2, ... f_3 and ... I, then ... N which they will offer will be determinate. (*JMK*.29, p. 65. E denotes earnings, Q expected 'excess profit').

a   THE COMPONENTS

Equation (1) differs from the TM supply function as follows (in each case reference is first to equation (1), then to the TM supply function):

1   Q and N belong to the same period: Q belongs to the current period and N [in fact the volume of output] to the next;
2   N is determined by the system of equations: N [in fact the volume of output] by a single equation;
3   Q and N are variables: Q and an increment in output are variables;
4   Q is expected by entrepreneurs: Q is realised.

Keynes, however, tends to regard the two as playing a similar role, for he takes the view that entrepreneurs determine the level of output (and of employment) based on profit:[5]

> The aggregate amount of employment offered will depend ... on the amount by which the sale proceeds of output ... are expected to exceed their variable cost.
>
> (*JMK*.29, p. 64)

Keynes seems to think that equation (1) works for the determination of the level of employment in the same way as equations $I' = C'(Q_2)$ and $R = H'(Q_1)$ do in 'Model 2' of the PME manuscript (*JMK*.13, p. 403).[6] This, however, is not the case, for Q and N in equation (1) belong to the same period:

> ... we are basing our conclusions about employment on the proper criterion, ... whether the result of spending money on employment and of selling the output is expected to result in a larger net sum of money at the end of the accounting period than if the money had been retained.
>
> (*JMK*.29, p. 66)

Keynes compares the 'proper criterion' with 'other criteria':

> Other criteria, such as the relation between the real output which a given
> employment will yield and the disutility ... of that employment [the second
> postulate], or the relation between the real wages of a given employment and
> the amount of its marginal output [the first postulate] ... are not appropriate
> to the actual nature of business decisions ... .

$$(JMK.29, \text{ p. } 66)$$

Thus, rejecting the two postulates,[7] Keynes retains the idea that entrepreneurs
determine the level of output based on profit. Given the difference from the TM
supply function, and yet the perceived continuity, let us call equation (1) the
'pseudo-TM supply function'.

Equation (2) may be interpreted as $E = W \cdot N$ (W denotes the money wage.
See Section I (2(B))).

Equation (3) is the consumption function formulated for the first time.[8]

Equation (4) may look like the equations $\Delta Q = \Delta D - \Delta E$ or
$\Delta Q = \Delta I + \Delta F - \Delta E$ of the MTP manuscript. However, it is not so much an equation determining profit as one equalising supply and demand.[9]

Given I, the system determines the level of employment.[10]

b   THE POSITION OF THE SYSTEM

Let us review the position of this system in the light of Keynes's development.

1   The First Manuscript maintains the idea that equilibrium of investment and
    saving determines the amount of employment, so that equation (4) follows
    equation (4) of the PMT manuscript.
2   In the *Treatise* profit and prices are simultaneously determined, while the volume
    of output changes with one time lag. In the MTP manuscript a time lag between
    profit and the volume of output is assumed, without reference to prices. In the
    PME manuscript prices, the volume of output, and profit are simultaneously
    determined. In the First Manuscript, the level of employment (the volume of
    output) and profit are simultaneously determined without reference to prices.[11]
3   The TM supply function virtually disappears in the First Manuscript,
    although a version of $I' = C'(Q_2)$ and $R = H'(Q_1)$ of 'Model 2' of the PME
    manuscript is retained. However, it does not work in the way he intends.
4   The 'aggregate demand function', $D = f(N) = X(N) + D_2$, where $X(N)$ is the
    expected volume of consumption and D_2 the expected volume of investment, of
    the *General Theory* is fundamentally the same as the equation obtainable from
    equations (3) and (4),

$$D = f_3(D) + I,$$

The following, on the other hand, can be derived from equations (1) and (2):

$$E + Q = f_2(N) + f_1^{-1}(N) = H(N)$$

where f_1^{-1} is an inverse function of f_1.

The function $H(N)$ describes entrepreneurs' economic activities corresponding to the 'aggregate supply function', $Z = f(N)$, of the *General Theory*. Strictly speaking, it is not the same because of rejection of the first postulate. Moreover, the system does not have a single concept such as $H(N)$. Thus we have some difficulty in establishing a link, and yet the system might well be the first precursor of *GT*'s chapter 3.

B   *The 'accounting period'*

The First Manuscript defines the accounting period as the span of time during which capital equipment remains constant, and analyses the economy in terms of it. It corresponds to the Marshallian short run, and Keynes might implicitly have used this in Model 1 of the PME manuscript.

Two points in particular are worth noting here.

First, while seemingly static, his analysis is dynamic. The values of the variables determined in the system belong to the current period. Given the renewed values of the exogenous variables, the values of the variables in the next are determined in the same way. In each period 'a snapshot' is taken, and the economy's dynamic process is depicted as a series of snapshots:[12]

> The commencement of the next accounting period will find the firms... [with] a different capital equipment, modified... by wastage and obsolescence... and the new investment.... [A]t any given time the productive processes... are decided in relation to the then existing capital equipment.... [W]e have transcended the awkward distinction between the long and the short period.
>
> (*JMK*.29, pp. 65–66)

Second, the First Manuscript assigns the role of connecting the current period with the next to capital equipment, while the manuscripts up to the MTP manuscript to the TM supply function. Hitherto he had not shown any particular interest in capital equipment, but now, with the accounting period, he had the opportunity to reconsider capital and investment.

2   *The Second Manuscript*

This manuscript consists of three fragments: one with no heading, and two respectively bearing the headings 'Some Fundamental Equations', and 'Definitions and Concepts Relating to Capital'. According to Moggridge (see *JMK*.29, p. 66), they belong to chapters 1, 5 and 8, respectively, of the 'Second Table' (see Section II below).

In the Second Manuscript, Keynes emphasises the accounting period. He also uses equation (4) and the equation $E = W \cdot N$ – a variant of equation (2). Thus the Second Manuscript stands on essentially the same ground as the First.

The features not recognisable in the First Manuscript are

1   a function similar to, but a little different from, the pseudo-TM supply function;
2   suggestion of the stability of the system;
3   acceptance of the first postulate;
4   heterogeneity of goods;
5   two kinds of period concept.

(1) and (2) are theoretically important and related to chapter 3 of the *General Theory*. The others are methodologically important: (3) is related to chapter 2, (4) to chapter 4 and (5) to chapter 5, of the *General Theory*.

A   The 'pseudo-TM supply function mk2'

What characterises the Second Manuscript is a function[13] resembling the pseudo-TM supply function. This would seem to be obtained by differentiating equation (1). However, this is not the case, for it is excluded from the system determining the level of employment, and relates to a stability condition. Let us call it the 'pseudo-TM supply function mk2'.

We need to note a change in the definition of profit. In the *Treatise* profit was defined as exclusive of normal profit, but profit here includes it:

> ... the excess of earnings over consumption corresponds to ... Saving (S) in [the *Treatise*]. It is not identically the same concept, since it does not include the normal return to capital equipment ...
>
> (*JMK*.29, p. 69)[14]

Along with this, the concept 'economising' appears, referring to 'the excess of earnings over consumption', while saving means 'income minus consumption'.

In the *Treatise*, earnings include normal profit, and consumption is assumed to be effected out of earnings. Saving is the difference between earnings and consumption.

Contrastingly, 'profit' in the Second Manuscript is composed of normal and excess profit. It comprises income together with earnings. Consumption is assumed to be effected out of income.[15]

Nevertheless, the idea that entrepreneurs determine the level of output (and the level of employment) based on profit is retained:

> ... ΔN [an increment of employment] and ΔQ [an increment of quasi-rent or profit] have the same sign. Further, since $\Delta Q = \Delta I - \Delta S'$ [I is investment; S' economising], ...
>
> (*JMK*.29, p. 70)[16]

> ... the fluctuations of aggregate quasi-rent ... lead to fluctuations in employment.
>
> (*JMK*.29, p. 71)

Thus the concept relating profit to the level of employment might correspond to $N = f_1(Q)$ in the First Manuscript. As the following quotation shows, however, profit and the level of employment are considered to change within the same accounting period.

> Our first fundamental proposition, namely
>
> N and Q have the same sign, can then be expressed: – the quantity of employment and the expectation of quasi-rent during the employment [accounting] period increase and decrease together.
>
> (*JMK*.29, p. 76)

B A suggestion for the stability of the system

The Second Manuscript does not contain the system of equations (1)–(4). However, we know that it stands on the same ground as the First Manuscript. Considering this and the role of equation (1), Keynes possibly used the pseudo-TM supply function mk2 similarly. If so, contrary to Keynes's intention it would not work for determining the level of employment.

Therefore something like the following solution would be required: the pseudo-TM supply function mk2 could be separated from the system for determining the level of employment and used for the stability condition.

An argument for the stability of the system might then be suggested in terms of the pseudo-TM supply function mk2:

> fluctuations in employment will primarily depend on fluctuations in aggregate expenditure relatively to aggregate costs. This is the essential feature of an entrepreneur economy.
>
> (*JMK*.29, p. 91)

This proposition indicates the stability of the system, since adjustment is assumed to be made within each employment period. The pseudo-TM supply function mk2 might be interpreted as adjusting the system.

However, Keynes develops his analysis ambiguously as he deals with normal and excess profit. This, together with a change in the definition of profit and in the absence of systematic analysis, makes it difficult to reconstruct the original model. Nevertheless, confining changes to a minimum, we might formulate the 'pseudo-TM supply function mk2' as follows:

$$Q_i = I + C - (E + Q_n) \tag{7}$$

$$\Delta N = \psi(Q_i) \tag{8}$$

$$\psi'(Q_i) > 0 \tag{9}$$

$$\psi(0) = 0 \tag{10}$$

(where I denotes investment, C consumption, E variable costs, Q_n normal profit, Q_i excess profit, N employment, and $\psi(\cdot)$ the pseudo-TM supply function mk2).

In equation (7), Q_i is defined as the difference between aggregate expenditure, $I + C$, and aggregate costs, $E + Q_n$ (Keynes in fact regards E only as aggregate costs).

Equation (8) is the entrepreneurs' behavioural function (actually Keynes uses the sum of normal and excess profit, and uses the total level of employment).[17] As excess profit increases, increase in the level of employment accelerates (equation (9)), whereas when excess profit falls to zero, increase in the level of employment comes to a halt (equation (10)).

The stability conditions for the system are:

If $N < N^*$, then $I + C > E + Q_n$

If $N > N^*$, then $I + C < E + Q_n$

(where N^* is the equilibrium level of employment).

If we call the function relating the difference between aggregate expenditure and aggregate costs to the level of employment the 'excess demand price function', the stability condition is that the excess demand price is a decreasing function of the level of employment (equilibrium is attained at the point where excess profit is zero):

$$d\{(I + C) - (E + Q_n)\}/dN < 0 \qquad (11)$$

To complete the model, we need a system for determining the level of employment. This can be expressed as

$$I + C = E + Q_n \qquad (12)$$
$$D = I + C \qquad (13)$$
$$E = W \cdot N \qquad (14)$$
$$C = f_3(D) \qquad (15)$$
$$Q_n = \bar{Q}_n \qquad (16)$$

In the Second Manuscript, the 'fundamental equation' is formulated as

$$Y = E + Q = C + I = D$$

(where Y denotes income, E earnings, Q quasi-rents, and D disbursement).

The Second Manuscript has equation (14). Equation (15) is verbally expressed. With regard to equation (16), we read that ' "normal" [return] is constant for a given capital equipment' (*JMK*.29, p. 69). Excess profit is excluded from the right-hand side of equation (12), and is defined as the difference between $I + C$ and $E + Q_n$. So defined, it becomes zero at the equilibrium point. Thus, given W, Q_n and I, the level of employment is determined.[18]

C   The first postulate[19]

Keynes accepts this postulate for the first time.

> [T]he value of the marginal product is equal to its variable cost....
>
> *(JMK.*29, p. 72)[20]

D   The heterogeneity of goods

In the Second Manuscript this is emphasised:

> ...the concept of an average price per unit of output...raises precisely the same difficulties as to a quantitative measure of a non-homogeneous complex, as does the measurement of real output itself....
>
> I find it, however, a matter of considerable intellectual satisfaction that these partly insoluble difficulties of quantitative description do not arise in our causal analysis, which is strictly logical...and is subject, in practice, not to essentially insoluble difficulties....
>
> *(JMK.*29, p. 73)

Keynes, well-versed in the index problem, tries to avoid the ambiguities of the general price level and output as a whole, finding units appropriate for the theory of employment. *GT*, chapter 4, section II originates from this, apart from the concept of 'complex' in the PME manuscript.

E   Two kinds of period concept

In the Second Manuscript two kinds of period concept are compared: the 'production' ('investment') period and the 'accounting' ('employment') period:

> The first forecast [covering the investment period] is that which...[an entrepreneur] has to make when he decides to spend money on setting up a capital equipment... The second forecast [covering the accounting period] is when, being in possession of a capital equipment, he decides how much variable cost to incur in working it....
>
> *(JMK.*29, pp. 73–74)

This argument is the origin of *GT*'s chapter 5. The first and second forecasts correspond to the short- and long-term expectations respectively.

Keynes emphasises the accounting period because 'all decisions to employ labour depend on expectations covering this period *(JMK.*29, p. 74). This corresponds to *GT*, pp. 50–51 where he stresses that the volume of employment is 'determined by the producer's short-term expectations'.

He also stresses the importance of distinguishing the accounting period from the investment period, for failure to do so causes confusion:

> [The investor's] forecast relates to the hire which he expects to get during each accounting period until the goods are worn out.... It leads...to a great confusion to...regard the whole period from the first employment of labour until the goods are finally worn out as constituting a single period of production.... its appearance of logical completeness is illusory....
>
> (*JMK*.29, p. 75)

Keynes criticises Hayek's (1931) theory in which consumer goods and intermediate products differ only in production stage.[21]

F The second postulate

The Second Manuscript rejects this postulate along with the argument of the First:

> [According to] the Classical Theory..., given the amount of capital equipment and the supply schedule of labour in terms of output, the volume of output and hence the ratio of aggregate quasi-rent [Q] to the price of output [P] tends to be constant...[This]...must...[follow] from the second postulate. Output will be pushed to the point at which the utility of the marginal product is equal to the disutility of the marginal employment...only when we waive [it]...[,]...[Q/P] can be supposed to fluctuate....
>
> (*JMK*.29, pp. 70–71)

This can read as follows. If the postulate is accepted, the economy reaches full employment. Applying this to the equation $O = NW/P + Q/P$ − a variant of the equation in the Second Manuscript (see *JMK*.29, p. 71) − , given O and NW/P, Q/P is kept constant. Unless Q/P fluctuates, output (and employment) are unable to fluctuate.

Besides these, the Second Manuscript contains various other points of considerable significance, including:

1 stress on fiscal policy (first appearance in Keynes's manuscripts) and low interest rate policy;
2 support of a protectionist policy;
3 Keynes's persistent theme[22] based on equations (7)–(10), that unless effective demand increases, entrepreneurs cannot protect themselves from losses either by increasing the volume of output,[23] or by reducing money wages;[24]
4 the definitions of some concepts, leading to an argument in *GT*, chapter 6, section II.

3 The Third Manuscript

The Third Manuscript (December 1933) has chapter 2, 'A Difference between a Cooperative Economy and an Entrepreneur Economy', and chapter 3,

'The Characteristics of an Entrepreneur Economy', both being assigned to the Third Table of Contents.

This text is largely similar to the Second Manuscript. We focus on 'effective demand' and the 'entrepreneur economy'. The argument for effective demand corroborates our interpretation of the stability of the system.

A   Effective demand

The Third Manuscript develops an argument based on the pseudo-TM supply function mk2, focusing on 'effective demand'.[25] Although the term first appears in the Second Manuscript (*JMK*.29, p. 97), the argument for effective demand appears here. The definition differs from that in the *General Theory*.

> Effective Demand may be defined by reference to the expected excess of sale proceeds over variable cost... [It]fluctuates if this excess fluctuates, being deficient [excessive] if it falls short of [exceeds] some normal figure... [I]n an entrepreneur economy the fluctuations of effective demand may be the dominating factor in determining the volume of employment.
>
> (*JMK*.29, p. 80)

Comparison is made between sale proceeds and variable cost. The difference is defined as 'profit' in the 1933 three manuscripts. By subtracting 'some normal figure [profit]', 'excess profit' is obtained.[26] The phrase 'it falls short of some normal figure' refers to excess loss. Effective demand is defined in relation to excess profit, moving in the same direction.

If we take into consideration that '[an entrepreneur] will increase his output if by so doing he expects to increase his money profit' (*JMK*.29, p. 82), the passage can read: if excess profit is negative [positive], effective demand is deficient [more than sufficient], so entrepreneurs will reduce [increase] the volume of output (and the level of employment); if excess profit is zero, effective demand is in equilibrium, so entrepreneurs will keep the volume of output constant.

Here Keynes does not argue how the level of employment is determined, but discusses its stability condition.

In the Third Manuscript effective demand is discussed solely in terms of sale proceeds and variable costs, which suggests that Keynes is only using a concept representing the aggregate demand side.

Keynes criticises Say's Law, presenting an alternative proposition:

> ...the classical economists have taught that supply creates its own demand;...For [that] proposition, I shall substitute the proposition that expenditure creates its own income....
>
> (*JMK*.29, pp. 80–81)

These, together with a quotation from Marshall (1879), form the starting point for *GT*, chapter 2, section VI.

In the Third Manuscript, Keynes endorses Marx's view, quoting from McCracken (1933):

> The nature of production in the actual world is not... a case of $C - M - C'$ ... the attitude of business... is a case of $M - C - M'$.
>
> (*JMK*.29, p. 81)

Keynes divides the economists advocating this view between those asserting 'the inevitable excess of M'' (e.g. Marx) and those asserting 'the inevitable excess of M' (e.g. Hobson) (*JMK*.29, 82). This is closely related to *GT*, chapters 3, section III and chapter 23, section VII.

B   The 'entrepreneur economy'

Keynes regards 'fluctuations of effective demand' as the essence of an entrepreneur economy (see *JMK*.29, p. 85).

He examines the relationship between the entrepreneur economy and 'money':

> [A]nything in terms of which the factors of production contract to be remunerated, which is not and cannot be a part of current output and is capable of being used otherwise than to purchase current output, is, in a sense, money. If so,... the use of money is a necessary condition for fluctuations in effective demand.
>
> (*JMK*.29, p. 86)

Money defined as something used as a means of payment and of storing wealth is a necessary condition for the fluctuations in effective demand. Although money alone does not cause the fluctuations, no economic fluctuations would occur but for money.

In the monetary system, argues Keynes, deficient effective demand occurs more frequently than the opposite:

> [T]he money... will 'keep' more readily than the output....
>
> (*JMK*.29, p. 86)

Keynes notes the difference in property between goods and money. This, although only 'carrying cost' is mentioned, leads to *GT*'s chapter 17:

> [I]t is a characteristic of finished goods,... that they incur substantial carrying charges for storage, risk and deterioration, so that they are yielding a negative return...; where such expenses are reduced to a minimum... in the case of money.
>
> (*JMK*.29, p. 86)

C   Shortcomings of 'classical economics'

The Third Manuscript criticises the classical theory of employment and of interest.

The level of employment in a co-operative economy is determined in accordance with the second postulate, but classical economics erroneously assumes that the postulate is applicable to the existing economy.

Keynes also attacks Fisher and Marshall's interest theory, in particular the 'real rate of interest',[27] arguing that the idea that fluctuations of prices cause those in the level of employment is, practically and theoretically, an error. Effective demand is again stressed:

> [I]t is not the prospect of rising prices as such which stimulates employment, but the prospect of an increased margin between sale proceeds and variable costs [an increase in effective demand].
>
> (*JMK*.29, p. 85)

4   *An evaluation of the three manuscripts*

A   *The essential points*

The fundamental elements can be summed up thus:[28]

1   In the First Manuscript, under the concept of 'accounting period' the system determining the level of employment appears for the first time, using the consumption function and all the variables in terms of expected values.
2   In the Second and Third manuscripts, the stability conditions are argued in terms of aggregate expenditure over variable costs.

Point (1) is important, for it leads to *GT*'s chapter 3. As far as point (2) is concerned, the stability conditions are not taken into consideration as such.

B   *Several inconsistencies*

The three manuscripts are flawed by four inconsistencies.

1   Keynes tends to regard the relation between the commodity market analysis in the *Treatise* and in the *General Theory* as continuous.

This has to do with the fact that Keynes unconsciously transformed the TM supply function into, first, the pseudo-TM supply function, and then the pseudo-TM supply function mk2.

This inclination is to be found in the argument of the Second Manuscript (*JMK*.29, pp. 71–73), which might indicate a reversion to the *Treatise* world. Surprisingly enough, it appears in *GT*, pp. 77–78. This comes partly from his unconscious adherence to the idea of the TM supply function.

Nevertheless, the argument in the Second and Third manuscripts can be properly understood only if the function concerned is interpreted as the pseudo-TM supply function mk2.

2   In the First Manuscript, equation (1) is in an awkward position, for it contributes to determining the level of employment while it is also treated as if it is the TM supply function.
3   In the Second and Third manuscripts, normal returns are considered to be constant, while the maximising behaviour of entrepreneurs is acknowledged.
4   In the three manuscripts there exists no concept representing the aggregate supply side.

C   Two clues

From our investigations[29] two clues for the interpretation of *GT*'s chapter 3 can be gleaned.

First, a Marshallian framework is adopted from the First Manuscript onwards. It is reflected in

1   an equilibrium analysis by means of the demand and the supply functions (although the supply side is unclear);
2   the stability condition;
3   the period concept.

Second, Keynes probably thinks that 'windfall profit' becomes zero at the equilibrium point determined in *GT*'s chapter 3.

II   Comparison of the 1933 three tables of contents

Keynes produced three tables of contents in 1933:

1   'The Monetary Theory of Employment' (17 chapters. *JMK*.29, pp. 62–63. Hereafter the First Table);
2   'The General Theory of Employment' (17 chapters. *JMK*.29, p. 63. Hereafter the Second Table);
3   'The General Theory of Employment', dated December 1933 (21 chapters with two excurses. *JMK*.13, pp. 421–422. Hereafter the Third Table).

1   The First Table

In chapters 3 and 4, disbursement, economising and saving might have been defined as expounded in Section I above.

In chapter 5, the consumption function might have been expressed as equation (3).

Chapter 6 is important because some fragments survive in which the system of determining the level of employment appears for the first time.

Chapters 7 and 9 might have dealt with the liquidity preference theory, and Chapter 10 with the liquidity trap.

Chapter 13, 'The Relation between Real Wages and Employment', may have had to do with Keynes's criticism of Pigou (1933)[30] (see *JMK*.13, p. 312).

Chapter 14 may have argued the influence exerted on the amount of employment by changes in the distribution of aggregate quasi-rent, and equation (1) in detail:

> The aggregate amount of employment offered will depend... on the amount [of quasi-rent] ... — [albeit] ... the nature of the distribution of the aggregate expectation of quasi-rent between different firms will probably affect the volume of employment, since the supply and cost functions... of different firms are not uniform.
>
> (*JMK*.29, p. 64)

Chapter 15 might have argued the multiplier theory for the first time among manuscripts. Keynes developed the multiplier theory in Keynes (March 1933. *JMK*.9, pp. 335–366), so the First Table might have been written before it.

Chapter 16, 'The Theory of Prices', may have been related to the argument at *JMK*.29, pp. 71– 73.

Chapter 17 may have foreshadowed *GT*'s chapter 23.

2   *The Second Table*

The only differences from the First Table are found in Book I.

Chapter 2, 'The Characteristics of an Entrepreneur Economy', deals primarily with the proposition that changes in employment depend mainly on changes in aggregate expenditure relative to aggregate costs.

Chapter 5, 'Fundamental Equations' deals with the equations $Y = E + Q = C + I = D$ and $Q = D - E = I - (E - C)$.

Chapter 8 addresses the accounting period.

3   *The Third Table*

The Third Table comes closer to the contents of the *General Theory* than the First and Second Tables.

Chapter 1, 'The Postulates of the Classical Economics', establishes the argument of the *General Theory*.

The remarkable features of the Third Table are found in Book II, which comprises 'Quasi-rent', 'Income', 'Disbursement', and 'Saving'. Given that Keynes stresses the 'Essential Feature', the definitions of quasi-rent, income, disbursement and saving might have been the same as those in the Second Table.

Chapter 8, 'The Propensity of Spend', chapter 10, 'The Problem of the Rate of Interest', and chapter 11, 'The Concept of Liquidity Preference as Determining the Rate of Interest', might have established the arguments of the *General Theory*.

Chapter 12, 'The Nature of Capital', chapter 13, 'The Conditions of Stability' and chapter 14, 'The General Theory of Employment', are new, but with no surviving text.

Chapter 12 might have been related either to *GT*'s chapter 8 or chapter 16 – possibly the former, judging from the fact that the table of contents of 'The General Theory' in 1934 (*JMK*.13, pp. 423–424) has no chapter corresponding to chapter 12.

Chapters 13 and 14 might have developed an argument explained, respectively, in Section I (2(B)) and in Section I (1(A)).

Chapter 15, 'The Supply Function', is particularly interesting. The function might have been equation (1) of the First Manuscript rather than the first postulate. There are two reasons for this: (i) Chapter 3, 'The Characteristics of an Entrepreneur Economy', deals with the 'Essential Feature' (moreover, there is no concept corresponding to the aggregate supply function of the *General Theory*); (ii) quasi-rent is treated as an independent chapter.

Chapter 16 uses the term 'Multiplier' for the first time.

Chapter 18, 'The Equations of Price', may have been related to the argument in *JMK*.29, pp. 71–73.

Excursus II uses the term 'Marginal Efficiency of Capital' for the first time. The sense in which it is used differs from that in the *General Theory*.

Our examination of the three tables of contents yields some important information on Keynes's state of development as of December 1933.

(i) Keynes maintains either the pseudo-TM supply function or the pseudo-TM supply function mk2 for determination of the level of employment or the stability condition.

(ii) Because of (i), Keynes does not come to develop a concept representing the supply side of the economy as a whole.

For the sake of convenience we defer our conclusion to this chapter, combining it with the conclusion to Chapter 9.

9 Establishment of the investment and consumption theories

In this chapter we focus on the period from the autumn of 1933 to the middle of 1934. During this period, what would later become *GT*'s consumption theory was effectively completed and what was to emerge as *GT*'s investment theory was improved in crucial respects.

Our investigation proceeds as follows. First we examine Keynes's lectures for the Michaelmas term of 1933. Second, we examine two manuscripts, which we shall refer to as 'The First Undated Manuscript' (*JMK*.29, pp. 102–111) and 'The Second Undated Manuscript' (*JMK*.29, pp. 111–120). Although neither of these manuscripts can be dated exactly, both appear to have been written between the end of 1933 and the beginning of 1934.

I The 1933 Michaelmas lectures

The remarkable feature of the 1933 lectures[1] (16 October[2]–4 December) is that the theoretical framework comes close to that of the *General Theory*.[3]

In the fifth lecture (11 November) Keynes states that income and price levels are determined in such a way that $Y = C + I$ (or $I = S$), which is the essential feature of the monetary system (Y is income, C consumption, I investment and S saving).

In the sixth lecture (20 November) the 'normal psychological law' makes its first appearance. Keynes then argues that, given the state of expectation and the propensities to consume and invest, a set of values for Y and C is obtained which satisfy $Y = C + I$, criticising the classical theory of interest. In order to increase income some change must be made either in the state of expectation, or in the propensity to consume or the amount of investment. It was not until this lecture that determination of income was proposed in terms of $Y = C + I$.

His new model appears more concretely in the eighth lecture (4 December):

$$M = A(W, \rho) \tag{1}$$

$$Y = C + I \tag{2}$$

$$C = \varphi_1(W, Y) \tag{3}$$

$$I = \varphi_2(W, \rho) \tag{4}$$

where M is the quantity of money, A the state of liquidity preference, W the state of 'news', and ρ the rate of interest.

Y is given by

$$Y = \varphi_1(W, Y) + \varphi_2(W, \rho)$$

Equation (1) shows that the rate of interest is determined by the equality of the quantity of money and the state of liquidity preference.[4] This is essentially the same as equation (6) of the PME manuscript. Keynes explains it as follows: the income, business, precautionary motives depend on the business cycle, the facility of overdrawing and the rate of deposit interest while the speculative motive depends on the state of bearishness.[5]

Equation (4) – the Investment Function – shows that, given the rate of interest, the value of investment is determined. This might belong partly to 'Investment Price Theory (2)' and partly to a theory to the effect that investment is a function of the cost of production, the rate of interest and the streams of prospective quasi-rents (see the fifth lecture of Michaelmas term of 1932 [Section II of Chapter 7]). Then, in the Third Table of Contents of 1933, the concept of the 'marginal efficiency of capital' makes its appearance. Keynes seems to have distinguished it from the rate of interest from 'The Second Undated Manuscript' onward, though the definition here differs from that found in the *General Theory* (*JMK*.29, pp. 111–120; see Section II (2)).

Equation (3) – the Consumption Function – and equation (2) – the aggregate demand function – are akin to equations (3) and (4) respectively of the First Manuscript of 1933. They share in common that given I, either the level of employment (in the First Manuscript) or the level of income (in the last lecture) is determined.

As for consumption, in the fifth lecture Keynes regards it as a function of income and 'windfall appreciation' ($C = f(Y, A)$) where A is windfall appreciation, while in the sixth it is seen as a function of income alone ($C = f(Y)$).

The significant difference between the model in the lectures and that of the First Manuscript is: (i) in the former the pseudo-TM supply function is not used and quasi-rent plays no role in determining the level of income; (ii) in the latter that function is used and quasi-rent plays a role in determining the level of income.

In the eighth lecture Keynes advances 'a better analysis' (Rymes [Fallgatter], 1988, p. G34) for determining the level of employment:[6]

$$M = A(W, \rho) \tag{1}$$

$$N_1 = f_1(N) \tag{2}$$

$$N_2 = f_2(\rho) \tag{3}$$

$$N = f_1(N) + f_2(\rho)^7 \tag{4}$$

where N is the amount of employment as a whole, N_1 that in the consumption goods sector, and N_2 that in the capital goods sector.

The fundamental factors for determining the level of employment are the state of confidence, the propensity to consume, the state of liquidity preference, and the quantity of money. This is called 'The General Law of Employment' (Rymes [Fallgatter] 1988, p. G35), in contrast to 'The Particular Law of Employment' of classical economics, which tells us what national income will be at full employment.

The two models are constructed in such a way that their endogenous variables are simultaneously determined. This construction is in tandem with the following developments:

1   Acceptance of the 'first postulate'.
2   Adoption of the marginal propensity to consume and the multiplier theory.
3   Reference to the 'fundamental psychological law'.

Besides the above, we also see several elements making their first appearance in these lectures[8] and apparently anticipating various aspects of the *General Theory*, namely:

1   Acceptance of the first postulate and rejection of the second;
2   A 'choice of units' in terms of money value and employment;
3   Reference to short-period and long-period expectations.

In contrast to these, the following two points do not differ fundamentally from the corresponding points in the lectures of 1932:

1   The theory of investment. The value of capital in stock is supposed to regulate the price of new capital goods, because the flow of new goods is small compared to the quantity in stock. The volume of investment is a function of the current cost of production, the rate of interest, and the streams of prospective quasi-rents.
2   Liquidity preference determines the rate of interest.

Nevertheless, while advancing these innovations, Keynes still adheres, in the fifth and sixth lectures, to the argument, which is found in the Second Manuscript of 1933, that ΔQ, ΔO, ΔN have the same sign, using relations such as $\Delta Q = \Delta I - \Delta S'$ (S', correspondent to 'saving' in the *Treatise*, is called the 'amount of economizing').

It is not clear how this discourse is connected with the main argument in which income (or the volume of employment) is determined by $Y = C + I$. It seems to suggest a stability condition, but this role is entrusted to the 'fundamental psychological law'. The connection is indeed complex. At any rate, the role of quasi-rents re-defined here as an inducement in terms of short-period expectations recedes into the background, falling back from the relatively prominent position it held in 1932.

II   The two undated manuscripts

Let us try to ascertain a bit more precisely the periods in which these manuscripts were composed. As the first postulate is adopted in 'The First Undated Manuscript' (see *JMK*.29, p. 108), we may assume that it was written after the First Manuscript of 1933.[9] Keynes uses the 'propensity to save' in the tables of contents of the First Manuscript and the Second Manuscript, but changes it into the 'propensity to spend' in the table of contents of the Third Manuscript of 1933. This suggests that 'The First Undated Manuscript', in which the term 'propensity to consume' appears for the first time, was not written earlier than the Second Manuscript and the Third Manuscript.

Consideration of these facts together with our discussion in Section 1 suggests the possibility that 'The First Undated Manuscript' was written at the end of 1933, for he develops the multiplier theory (the central theme of 'The First Undated Manuscript') in the seventh lecture. 'The First Undated Manuscript' is probably closely related to chapter 16, 'The Multiplier', of the Third Manuscript.

'The Second Undated Manuscript' must have been written immediately after the last lecture, to judge by the fact that an analysis by means of the marginal efficiency of capital (the key concept of 'The Second Undated Manuscript') is discussed here but is absent from his lecture, while the table of contents of the Third Manuscript (December 1933) contains Excursus II, 'The Marginal Efficiency of Capital'.

This manuscript was written before 'The General Theory' (to be examined in the next chapter), in which the concept of the marginal efficiency of capital is similar to that of the *General Theory*. Moreover, the marginal efficiency of capital and the rate of interest in Marshall's *Principles of Economics*, both of which appear as chapter titles in the table of contents of the Third Manuscript, are discussed in 'The Second Undated Manuscript'.

Putting these findings together, we may say that 'The Second Undated Manuscript' and the Third Manuscript were probably written around the same time.

1 *'The First Undated Manuscript'*

Four points are to be noted in particular here (*JMK*.29, pp. 102–111).

The first point is that Keynes puts forward the fundamental psychological law, develops the theory of underemployment equilibrium based upon it, and essentially establishes *GT*'s consumption theory:

> Thus, it is a necessary condition of equilibrium that, when aggregate income falls, the aggregate expenditure on consumption should fall by a lesser amount than the fall of income. That this condition is fulfilled in practice is, however, in accordance with what our knowledge of popular psychology leads us to expect; and the fact that a point of equilibrium is reached in experience when incomes fall is confirmation of the validity of this expectation.
>
> (*JMK*.29, p. 103)

This passage should be understood with the following points in mind.

1   Neither the fundamental psychological law nor the theory of underemployment
    equilibrium based upon it appear in the three 1933 manuscripts. In relation
    to stability, there is no reference to the consumption function, though the
    function itself appears in the First Manuscript. The argument which suggests
    the stability of underemployment equilibrium in the Second and Third
    Manuscripts centres on the quasi-TM supply function mk2.
2   The argument about the relation between income and consumption here
    departs from the line that had been developed so far. The earlier argument
    concerned the determination of the price level of consumption goods, whereas
    the new one deals with the determination of the level of employment.
3   The idea expressed here leads to the argument developed in 'The General
    Theory' (see *JMK*.13, pp. 445–446).

The second point is that this is the first manuscript in which the multiplier
theory is clearly stated. Keynes handled the multiplier theory cautiously. He
finally put it at the centre of his theoretical system in mid-1933.

The first indication was the title, 'The Magnitude of Changes in Employment
Relatively to Changes in Investment', of chapter 15 in the table of contents of the
First Manuscript, followed by the title, 'The Multiplier', of chapter 16 in the table
of contents of the Third Manuscript.

'The First Undated Manuscript' is thus seen to follow after the Third Manuscript:

> If the increase of real investment is ΔO_2, the increase of real consumption
> will be $(k-1)\,\Delta O_2$ where k is the multiplier... and depends on the propensity
> to consume.
>
> (*JMK*.29, p. 110)

The third point is that the prices and the volume of output for consumption
goods are determined in such a way that supply becomes equal to demand:

> The extent to which output will rise as a concomitant of a given increase of
> investment, will depend on what proportion of an increment of real income
> the public's propensity to save... leads them to choose not to consume. The
> extent to which prices will rise, given the extent to which output will rise, will
> depend on the shape of the supply function....
>
> [Normally]... the increase in output will be greater than the increase in
> investment; and... there will be some rise in prices.
>
> Thus the normal concomitants of an increase of real investment will be
>
> (1) an increase of real consumption;
> (2) an increase of Q due to higher prices;
> (3) an increase of economising.
>
> (*JMK*.29, pp. 109–110)

The 'supply function' here is the usual supply schedule in which output increases as prices rise. Keynes assumes decreasing returns in the short run (see *JMK*.29, p. 110), and accepts the first postulate (see *JMK*.29, p. 108).

In the passage quoted above Keynes explains how an increase in real investment influences the performance of the consumption goods sector. How much the public decides to consume (the demand for consumption goods) and the supply function of the consumption goods sector together determine real consumption and the price of consumption goods (see *JMK*.29, p. 103).

This argument can be extended as follows.

On the one hand, expenditure on consumption goods is determined as a consequence of the multiplier process. This point is explicitly made in Keynes (March 1933):

> At each stage there is...a certain proportion of leakage. At each stage a certain proportion of the increased income is not passed on in increased employment. Some part will be saved by the recipient.
>
> (*JMK*.9, p. 340)

> We might assume that at least 70 per cent of the increased income will be spent and not more than 30 per cent saved.
>
> On these assumptions the first repercussion will be 49 per cent... of the primary effect,...; the second repercussion will be one-half of the first repercussion,... and so on. Thus the multiplier is 2.... The amount of time which it takes for current income to be spent will separate each repercussion from the next one. But it will be seen that seven-eighths of the total effects come from the primary expenditure and the first two repercussions, so that the time-lags involved are not unduly serious.
>
> (*JMK*.9, p. 343)

The expenditure on consumption goods in the quotation is equal to 'the primary expenditure and the first two repercussions'.

On the other hand, the function of each industry relating output to sale proceeds can be derived from the supply function.

The actual consumption and the prices of consumption goods are determined by the interaction between the expenditure and the supply function.

This extension of the argument is reasonable. The expenditure is the value which is directed towards some quantity of output. Therefore, in order to make the multiplier theory logically consistent, the [usual] supply function needs to be adjusted to have the sale proceeds as the vertical axis. The resulting market mechanism of the consumption goods sector is virtually the same as that developed in the *General Theory*.[10]

The three features evidenced above are concerned with either the consumption function or the multiplier theory. Here we should pay attention to 'quasi-rent'.

Although *prima facie* the concept of quasi-rent in 'The First Undated Manuscript' seems to be the same as that in the three manuscripts of 1933, on closer examination we see that Keynes has in fact modified the role it plays.

Quasi-rent is here considered exclusively in relation to the supply function and plays a passive role in analysis, while in the three manuscripts it is related to fluctuations in employment or the stability condition and plays an active role

> Given the supply function, there is no method of increasing employment in a degree corresponding to an increase $k\Delta Q$ in output, without bringing about an increment ΔQ of quasi-rent. ΔQ is merely a reflection of the fact that industry is operating in the short period subject to diminishing returns, so that employment can only improve with an increase in profits.
>
> (*JMK*.29, pp. 110–111)

Here Keynes argues that higher prices necessarily bring about an increase in quasi-rent and that how much quasi-rent increases depends on the form of the supply function. This argument is related to the observation in Keynes (1933):

> Higher prices will mean higher profits, with the result that, more of the increased income being profit and less of it being wages, more of it will be saved.
>
> (*JMK*.9, p. 108)

Profit and quasi-rent are interchangeable. Quasi-rent is considered to be directed towards the demand for consumption goods. Therefore, although 'The First Undated Manuscript' uses the same argument (to the effect that 'quasi-rent is the excess of the sale proceeds of output over its variable cost' (*JMK*.29, p. 108) and $P \cdot O = Q + E$ where P is the price of output, O output, Q quasi-rent, and E the variable cost (see *JMK*.9, p. 108)) as set out in the three 1933 manuscripts, they are qualitatively different.

The definition of 'economising' used in 'The First Undated Manuscript' also differs from that in 'The Second Manuscript': In the latter economising is defined as earnings (which do not include normal profit) minus consumption, and saving as income minus consumption; in the former economising is defined as an 'increase of voluntary saving' (*JMK*.9, p. 108) where voluntary saving is the same as in the *Treatise* (see *JMK*.9, p. 108).

The difference between quasi-rent in the 1933 manuscripts and the version in 'The First Undated Manuscript' is so subtle that there is a danger of overlooking it. Nevertheless, it is very important to recognise this difference (though Keynes himself may have overlooked it), for in 'The First Undated Manuscript' the role of profit either as determining the volume of output or in relation to the stability condition has ultimately been lost.

We have seen that 'The First Undated Manuscript' is related to chapter 16 of the Third Manuscript. However, seeing that quasi-rent here does not fit in with the argument presented in chapter 3 of the Third Manuscript, we must recognise the distance, slight though it may be, between 'The First Undated Manuscript' and chapter 16.

We are now in a good position to review Keynes's development.

On the one hand, the three 1933 manuscripts are seen to lead to *GT*'s chapter 3, 'The Principle of Effective Demand', in the sense that the system of equations determining the level of employment was there advanced for the first time.

The argument which centres around the pseudo-TM supply function or the pseudo-TM supply function mk2 concerns the stability condition, although Keynes might have thought of it as an extension of the *Treatise*. However, the argument concerning stability thereafter disappears. This is related to the change in the role of quasi-rent in 'The First Undated Manuscript'.

On the other hand, the main feature of 'The First Undated Manuscript' is a presentation of the multiplier theory. This leads directly to *GT*'s multiplier theory.

To sum up, the two lines of reasoning flow into the *General Theory*. The former sees Keynes still groping towards a new theory, the latter in the act of forging it.

The fourth point is that we now know how Keynes conceives of his investment theory. He does not hold that the price of investment goods is determined by equilibrium between investment and saving, for he considers that an increase in investment necessarily brings about an equal increase in saving. Keynes rebuffs Robertson's criticism of his (Keynes') argument concerning the peculiarity of consumption goods as compared with investment goods:

> If and when investment has increased, even so there will exist no reason why the price of investment goods should rise, since the supply of investment goods will have increased in value as a result of the new investment by exactly the same amount as the demand for them has increased as represented by the increased aggregate saving....The price of investment goods must be governed...by some other factor.
>
> (*JMK*.29, pp. 104–105)

As we have seen, Keynes abandoned 'Investment Price Theory (1)' in the MTP manuscript and adopted 'Revised Investment Price Theory (2)' in the PME manuscript (see p. 95 of the present book). The investment theory of 'The First Undated Manuscript' is basically similar to 'Revised Investment Price Theory (2)', to which Keynes referred in the Michaelmas term of 1933, observing that

> the act of individual saving will in itself diminish quasi-rent, so that, if it has been anticipated..., it will, unless it is offset by a fall in the rate of interest... diminish the motive towards increasing capital equipment, so that new investment...will be diminished.
>
> (*JMK*. 29, p. 106)

2 'The Second Undated Manuscript'

This manuscript (*JMK*.29, pp. 111–120) is the fragment headed '5. Quasi-Rent and the Marginal Efficiency of Capital'. We can here detect a new development in the theory of investment, moving towards the theory of investment of the

General Theory. Although the *GT* investment theory itself appears in 'The General Theory', the 'marginal efficiency of capital' is here for the first time defined as independent of the rate of interest:

> This conclusion serves to bring out... the essential independence of the rate of interest as a factor in the economic situation, and the hopelessness in a non-stationary system of attempting to derive it, even in conditions of fullest monetary equilibrium, from the marginal efficiency of capital.
>
> *(JMK.29*, p. 115)

The *General Theory* contains two investment theories:[11]

1   The volume of investment is determined in such a way that the marginal efficiency of capital is equal to the rate of interest (let us call it 'Investment Theory (1)'):
2   The volume of investment is determined in such a way that the demand price is equal to the supply price (let us call it 'Investment Theory (2)').

Investment Theory (1) is traceable to the passage in 'The Second Undated Manuscript':

> [T]he tendency in full equilibrium is for equality between the rate of interest on a debt, the amortisation of which will be spread over the same period as the life of the asset, and the prospective marginal efficiency of the asset year by year during its life.
>
> *(JMK.29*, p. 115)

Investment Theory (2) is traceable to the passage in 'The Second Undated Manuscript':

> Let p_r be the cost of production at time r
>
> k_r m.e.c.''
>
> q_r profit''
>
> d_r present value of £1 deferred r years.
>
> Then $S\ (p_r \cdot k_r + q_r)d_r$ is the present value of an equity assuming all the relevant quantities are known...
>
> The volume of development [investment] at any time will depend on the relation between the money-value of each category of capital goods arrived at in this way and its current cost of production.
>
> *(JMK.29*, p. 114)

The marginal efficiency of capital, k_r, is a 'prospective normal rate of profit', while profit, q_r, excess profit. Then $(p_r \cdot k_r + q_r)$, called 'prospective quasi-rent', is the prospective profit which a capital asset earns year-by-year during its life.[12]

This corresponds to *GT*'s 'prospective yields'. If we denote the rate of interest by i, d_r becomes $1/(1+i)^r$, so that the present value of a capital asset, $\Sigma(p_r \cdot k_r + q_r)d_r$, corresponds to *GT*'s 'demand price of the investment' of and the cost of production of a capital asset corresponds to *GT*'s 'supply price of the investment'.[13]

The 'marginal efficiency of capital' in 'The Second Undated Manuscript', unlike the version in the *General Theory*, is defined as follows:

> [M]arginal efficiency of capital (or m.e.c.) is the equilibrium concept about which quasi-rent oscillates, quasi-rent being, so to speak, the short-period version of m.e.c.
>
> (*JMK*.29, p. 113)

This means that if the economy is in equilibrium, profit, q_r, is zero, normal profit is $p_r \cdot k_r$, and quasi-rent $(p_r \cdot k_r + q_r)$ fluctuates around normal profit as q_r is not zero. Quasi-rent is defined as follows:

> The quasi-rent of an asset in any period is the money value of the services it renders, or money income derived from it, in that period. The prospective quasi-rent is the anticipated series of such annuities during the life of the asset.
>
> (*JMK*.29, p. 111)

Note that the 'quasi-rent' here has nothing to do with the quasi-rent we have thus far discussed. The role of the rate of interest in 'The Second Undated Manuscript' differs from that in the manuscripts examined hitherto. That liquidity preference determines the rate of interest was mentioned in the MTP manuscript. Even thereafter, however, Keynes continued to use the rate of interest to obtain the price level of capital goods by discounting their prospective yields. With regard to the determination of the volume of investment goods, the 'supply schedule' was introduced in the PME manuscript. In 'The Second Undated Manuscript', however, the rate of interest together with the marginal efficiency of capital determines the prices and volume of investment goods simultaneously.

Structurally, 'The Second Undated Manuscript' is composed of four sections. Section I, which treats quasi-rent and the marginal efficiency of capital and refers to Marshall's treatment of the subject, is the basis of *GT*'s pp. 135–140, albeit not quite the same. Section III, which treats capital, leads to some parts (*JMK*.13, pp. 453–455) of 'The General Theory', and finally leads to section II of chapter 16, 'Sundry Observations on the Nature of Capital', of the *General Theory*.

III Conclusion

In Chapters 8 and 9 we examined Keynes's theoretical development in 1933. The main question was, to what degree did Keynes succeed, in 1933, in light of the *General Theory*, in establishing the theory explaining how the level of employment is determined? The majority of scholars have concluded that by 1933 Keynes had

Table 9.1 The situation in 1933–1934

Period		1933	1933	December 1933	The End of 1933 to the First Half of 1934	
Material		First Manuscript	Second Manuscript	Third Manuscript	First Undated Manuscript	Second Undated Manuscript
Commodity market	Supply side	*Supply function (pseudo-TM Supply function) *Cost function *Two postulates of classical economics and their rejection	*Acceptance of the first postulate of the classical economics			
	Demand side	*Formulation of the propensity to save (the consumption function)			*Establishment of the fundamental psychological law	
	Equilibrium	*Simultaneous equation system determining the level of employment	*Examination of stability condition (pseudo-TM supply function mk2)		*Simultaneous and supply-demand conception of prices and the volume of output in the consumption goods sector	*Determination of investment by an equilibrium of demand price and supply price *Determination of investment by an equilibrium of the marginal efficiency of capital (different from that in the General Theory) and the rate of interest
	Profit		*Profit is defined as the sum of excess profit and normal profit	*Effective demand is defined as the excess proceeds over variable costs		
Money market						*Change in the position of the rate of interest in the investment theory
Others		*Accounting period *Expression in terms of expectations			*Development of the multiplier theory	

Note
An item flagged with an asterisk indicates a new idea.

established the core for the *General Theory*. While this conclusion is basically correct, it can only be accepted with the following qualifications.

In Chapter 8 two concepts were emphasised: the pseudo-TM supply function and the pseudo-TM supply function mk2. We use the prefix 'pseudo' because the functions, in substance, differ from the TM supply function, while we retain the phrase 'TM supply function' because Keynes tends to regard them as continuous.

The three manuscripts of 1933 constitute the origins of chapter 3 of the *General Theory*. They discuss both an equilibrium condition for the level of employment and its stability condition, although no concept corresponding to *GT*'s aggregate supply function makes any appearance.

In the First Manuscript Keynes put forward for the first time a system determining the level of employment. This was a breakthrough.

Keynes's way of formulating the system, however, suffered from certain insufficiencies. Although we interpreted it as describing the stability condition for the equilibrium level of employment, the argument in terms of the pseudo-TM supply function mk2 remained unclear. Among other things, the argument in the Third Manuscript which stresses effective demand lacks clarity, because it is still developed in terms of the sale proceeds and variable cost. In fact, throughout the three manuscripts, no concept corresponding to *GT*'s aggregate supply function makes any appearance. As will be seen below, moreover, the concept of 'effective demand' is to undergo several changes before reaching the *General Theory*. The arguments to be seen in the Second and Third Manuscripts disappeared thereafter. This has very much to do with the fact that the role played by profit was to change drastically, as is clear from 'The First Undated Manuscript'.

These ambiguous points in Keynes's argument show that he is in a state of feeling his way towards a new employment theory.

With the above qualifications, we can say that the end of 1933 saw Keynes making a great advance towards the *General Theory*. Bringing together the various arguments found in the scattered fragments we can confirm that Keynes had by now established the following: the system determining the level of employment; the consumption function; the fundamental psychological law; the liquidity preference theory as determining the rate of interest; the marginal efficiency of capital (albeit not yet that of the *General Theory*); and the multiplier theory.

The main arguments discussed in Chapters 8 and 9 are visualised in Table 9.1.

10 The eve of the *General Theory*

As we saw in the preceding chapter, by the end of 1933 Keynes had already developed the theoretical system explaining the level of employment, as well as the consumption function, the fundamental psychological law, the theory of liquidity preference, the concept of the marginal efficiency of capital, and the multiplier theory. In this chapter, we examine the great advances he made in these areas in 1934 towards the formulations we find in the *General Theory*.

To explore these developments we look first at two manuscripts: (i) a typescript entitled 'The General Theory of Employment, Interest and Money', written probably in the spring of 1934 (*JMK*.13, pp. 423–456; hereafter 'The General Theory') (Section I); and (ii) a revised version of chapters 8 and 9 of this, written in the summer of 1934 (*JMK*.13, pp. 471–484; hereafter 'The Summer Manuscript') (Section II). In Section III we will look at the Michaelmas lecture of 1934, which were delivered on the basis of a manuscript we will refer to as Galley 1(I) (see Section III of Chapter 11).

Although Keynes had put forward the system determining the level of employment, it remained incomplete. This incompleteness emerged very clearly in the examination we made of the system of equations in the First Manuscript of 1933 and the argument by means of 'effective demand' in the Third Manuscript of 1933. In 'The General Theory' Keynes proposes a new model to explain how the level of employment is determined, but, as we shall see, his argument still lacks precision. This is also true of the Summer Manuscript. It is very important to bear in mind that in the area of employment theory, Keynes's endeavours to explain coherently the workings of the economy were to continue right up to the *General Theory*, and that in this area, even the *General Theory* itself still lacks precision.

The *General Theory* was an epoch-making work which revolutionised macroeconomics by providing a system explaining how the level of employment is determined. The book's theoretical inconsistencies do not undermine this achievement, but they do call for close attention.

By early 1934 Keynes's thinking had gone far beyond the world of the *Treatise* and had plunged deep into that of the *General Theory*. Thus our attention will naturally focus on the relations of the manuscripts to the *General Theory*, rather than on their relations to the *Treatise*. This tendency will become progressively more pronounced as we approach the *General Theory* itself.

I 'The General Theory'

Of the 27 chapters (divided into five 'books') listed in the table of contents of this manuscript, only chapters 6 to 12 survive. Chapter 12, 'The State of Long-Term Expectation (or Confidence)', has not only almost the same title as chapter 12 of the *General Theory*, but is also 'the final printed version with very few changes'.[1]

The manuscript has two features particularly relevant to our concern here: (i) the way in which the concept of 'effective demand' and the theory of employment are discussed; (ii) the way consumption theory and investment theory are argued out. Point (i) is full of ambiguities, reflecting the struggle Keynes was going through in his search for a new theory of employment, while point (ii) is very similar to the argumentation in the *General Theory*. This is the most salient characteristic of 'The General Theory'.

As we saw in the preceding two chapters, ambiguities in the concept of 'effective demand' and in the theory of employment were to be seen in the three 1933 manuscripts, while establishment of the consumption and investment theories was a noteworthy feature of the two undated manuscripts. Taken together, they constitute a forerunner of 'The General Theory'.

However, our manuscript is the first to include all the above-mentioned elements (the concept of 'effective demand' and the theory of employment, with their ambiguities, the consumption theory, and the investment theory), and was to have some influence on the formation of the theoretical structure of the *General Theory*.[2]

Here we will examine chapters 6–11, focusing on three points: (i) the ambiguities in the concept of 'effective demand' and the inconsistency of the employment theory; (ii) the consumption theory; and (iii) the investment theory. We then touch on some other fundamental concepts.

1 *Effective demand and an employment theory*

Let us begin with chapter 6, 'Effective Demand and Income', and chapter 9, 'The Functions Relating Employment, Consumption and Investment', which are concerned with the sphere with which *GT*, chapter 3, 'The Principle of Effective Demand' deals.

They are interesting on two counts. First, they show the state of development of Keynes's employment theory. Here we need to pay attention to the ambiguity in the concept of 'effective demand'. Second, the employment theory contains the same sort of inconsistencies as the *General Theory* in respect of the relations[3] between the first postulate and the employment function, and between the arguments of chapters 6 and 9.

A *Effective demand*

In 'The *General Theory*', 'effective demand' is defined as the 'present value of the expected sale proceeds' (*JMK*.13, p. 425). This is different from the version presented in the Third Manuscript of 1933, where it was defined 'by reference to the expected excess of sale proceeds over variable cost'. Also differing from the definition in the Third Manuscript, moreover, effective demand does not seem to be related to the stability of the equilibrium level of employment.

We first examine the relations between, and definitions of, some key concepts in 'The General Theory', including effective demand, income, and quasi-rent, and then show that the effective demand in this manuscript partially corresponds to the 'aggregate supply price' concept of the *General Theory*.

> [We shall] call the actual sale proceeds income and the present value of the expected sale proceeds effective demand.[4]...and it is the effective demand which is the incentive to the employment of equipment and labour. The difference between the two we shall call entrepreneur's windfall – profit or loss,...;
>
> The following notation will be used.
>
> Y for Income
>
> D for effective demand
>
> F for entrepreneur's windfall [here, not F_u but F is used]
>
> These expressions are in terms of money. Income and effective demand in terms of the wage unit will be written Y_w and D_w.
>
> The quasi-rent (Q) from a given output of finished goods we have already defined...as being the excess of the expected sale proceeds of the goods over their prime cost (NW) [N denotes employment, and W the money wage]. Thus...$D = Q + NW$
>
> (*JMK*.13, pp. 425–426)

From this, the following equations can be extracted:

$$F_u = Y - D \tag{1}$$
$$D = Q + NW \tag{2}$$

Two characteristics are to be noted. First, quasi-rent, which is the difference between D and the prime cost (NW), means normal profit. This can be proved as follows. From these equations we obtain:

$$Y - NW = F_u + Q \tag{3}$$

The left-hand side is the actual sale proceeds minus the prime cost, so that it represents the realised profit, while F_u is windfall profit. Therefore Q is normal profit. Second, as shown in equation (1), excess profit (or windfall profit) is defined as the difference between the actual sale proceeds and the expected sale proceeds.

These two points are not found in the formulations in the three 1933 manuscripts. In those manuscripts, the difference between the expected sale proceeds and the prime cost (the sum of normal profit and excess profit) was defined as effective demand, and quasi-rent, Q, was defined as including excess profit.

Thus effective demand D is equal to the sum of normal profit ($= Q$) and the prime cost, so that it corresponds, in terms of the *General Theory*, to the 'aggregate supply price' rather than the 'aggregate demand price'.

Thus the argument centring around effective demand in 'The General Theory' differs from that in the three 1933 manuscripts, not only in definition, but also in theory. Moreover, as we will see later, this argument needs to be considered in connection with the fact that chapters 6 and 9 of 'The *General Theory*' are theoretically inconsistent.

B   The employment theory

Prior to 'The General Theory' Keynes did not explicitly adopt the method of supply–demand equilibrium.[5] The *Treatise* envisions a world in which the TM supply function plays a dynamic role and the price level of consumption goods is determined by the demand side, given the volume of output supplied. It is only in Investment Price Theory (1) that the method of supply–demand equilibrium is adopted.

In the PME manuscript this method is adopted only in the liquidity preference theory. In the area of the commodity market, it appeared for the first time in the First Manuscript of 1933. Thereafter, Keynes progressively came to adopt a supply–demand equilibrium approach.

However, there are certain ambiguities in the way he uses it. This is typically seen in the argument concerning the 'employment function'.

a   THE EMPLOYMENT FUNCTION

The employment function, which makes its first appearance in 'The General Theory', is conceived as follows:

> $D_w = F(N)$ is the employment function, where an effective demand equal to D_w leads to N units of labour being employed.
>
> *(JMK.*13, p. 440)

Preceding this is Keynes's explanation of its inverse function.

> The above [the first postulate] is, of course, subject to the qualification that different classes of enterprise do not... respond equally... to equal changes in the effective demand for their product, since they are not all working under the same conditions of supply. Thus the same aggregate effective demand may correspond to different levels of employment according to the way in which it is distributed between different classes of enterprise. This will be

a matter for subsequent discussion.... But at the present stage of the argument I shall . . . assume that all firms have similar employment functions, so that aggregate employment is a simple function of the aggregate effective demand measured in terms of the wage unit.

(*JMK*.13, pp. 427–428)

On the one hand the employment function seems to be (i) a supply concept, and on the other (ii) an equilibrium concept.

We have two reasons for point (i).

First, Keynes puts forward the employment function in relation to the first postulate of classical economics, and, moreover, with the assumption that 'all firms have similar employment functions', he considers that 'aggregate employment is a simple function of the aggregate effective demand'. This suggests that he understands the employment function as a supply concept in the whole economy, as well as in the individual firm or industry.[6]

Second, as we saw in (A) above, he puts forward 'effective demand' *D* as, in the terminology of the *General Theory*, the aggregate supply price, and as will be shown in (b) below, in the equation determining the level of employment, Keynes puts the employment function on the left-hand side, placing the sum of the propensity to spend and the propensity to invest on the right.

But the employment function seems to be an equilibrium concept as well. Keynes tries to obtain aggregate employment given the distribution ratio of aggregate effective demand between industries.[7] When he refers to 'the effective demand for their product', he seems to be using it as representing the demand side, for he argues in such a way as to have it determining the level of employment in each industry together with the 'conditions of supply' (the first postulate). Therefore, the effective demand in each industry is not only a demand concept but also an equilibrium concept. The employment function is obtained by aggregating, on the one hand, the effective demand in each industry, and, on the other, the level of employment in each industry. Therefore, the employment function shows a functional relation between the aggregate effective demand (an equilibrium value) and the aggregate employment (an equilibrium level).

Looking at the employment function from a different angle, it is, as it were, merely a signal indicating the level of employment which corresponds to the aggregate effective demand, for the aggregate effective demand depends on the implicit and arbitrary assumption that its distribution between industries is given. 'The aggregate effective demand' per se has to be determined by some other mechanism.

Our argument that the employment function has the appearance of an equilibrium concept may be explained as follows:

$$Z_w = F(N) \tag{4}$$

$$D_w = Z_w \tag{5}$$

Suppose that equation (4) shows some concept representing the supply side, while D_w represents the demand side. Then equation (5) equilibrates supply with demand.[8] From these we obtain:

$$D_w = F(N) \tag{6}$$

Therefore, we can suppose that equation (6) (the employment function) indicates an equilibrium of commodity markets.

The duality characterising the employment function emerges in the *General Theory*.

b   THE EMPLOYMENT FUNCTION IN RELATION TO THE DETERMINATION
OF THE LEVEL OF EMPLOYMENT

In 'The General Theory', determination of the level of employment is conceptualised as follows:

Both C_w and I_w are to be interpreted ... as the expected rates of consumption and investment. Hence it follows that $D_w = C_w + I_w$. Thus the level of employment, given the propensities to spend and to invest, is given by the value of N which satisfies the equation[9]

$$F(N) = f_1(N, r, E) + f_2(N, r, E)$$

(*JMK*.13, pp. 441–442; r denotes the rate of interest, E the state of long-term expectation, f_1 the propensity to spend [or consume], and f_2 the propensity to invest).

The employment function here represents the supply side, and does not depend on profit. This is in marked contrast with the position in the First Manuscript of 1933 (where the system determining the level of employment was first developed), in which the 'supply function' (the pseudo-TM supply function) is formulated as a function of profit. Keynes's affirmative attitude towards the first postulate and the change from the pseudo-TM supply function to the employment function might well be closely related.

On the other hand, the employment function here is in substance the same as the employment function[10] of the *General Theory*, except that the former is the inverse of the latter. We can interpret both as equilibrium concepts. In the *General Theory*, the employment function is measured in wage units and defined as the inverse of the aggregate supply function $Z = f(N)$, which corresponds to equation (4). However, the actual argument proceeds by means of an equation similar to equation (6); that is, not $N = F^-(Z_w)$, but $N = F^-(D_w) \cdot D_w$ in the *General Theory* is effective demand which is defined as the value of the aggregate demand price at the point where the aggregate demand function intersects the aggregate supply function. Again we are faced with the ambiguous nature of the employment function.

C   *The first postulate*

In the Second Manuscript of 1933,[11] Keynes accepted for the first time the first postulate and rejected the second. He maintained this view thereafter.

The relation between profit and the first postulate in 'The General Theory' is worth noting. Normal profit Q contributes, together with the first postulate, to determination of the level of employment. However, so far as the extant sources are concerned, we find no discussion of windfall profit (F_u), nor of the stability conditions for the level of employment, as distinct from 'The Second Manuscript' and the Third Manuscript of 1933. Thus Keynes's emphasis on the maximisation of quasi-rent in the first postulate comes to the foreground:

> Under normal assumptions of competition etc. the condition of maximum quasi-rent will be satisfied by a volume of employment such that the prime cost of the marginal employment will be equal to the expected sale proceeds of the resulting increment of product. ...
>
> Furthermore, in the normal case we must assume decreasing returns for a given capital equipment.
>
> (*JMK*.13, p. 426)

The notion of the 'condition of maximum quasi-rent [normal profit]' might indicate some development in Keynes's theory. In the Second Manuscript and the Third Manuscript, despite acceptance of the first postulate, Keynes assumed 'normal profit' to be constant, and did not incorporate the idea of profit-maximising entrepreneurs[12] into his system. Consequently, the first postulate was incompatible with the main theoretical system. In 'The General Theory', on the other hand, Keynes repeatedly emphasises maximisation of quasi-rent,[13] and confines profit to quasi-rent.

D   *Two theoretical difficulties*

There are two elements in particular that do not sit happily in 'The General Theory': (i) the relation between the first postulate and the employment function is unclear; (ii) the relation between the argument of chapter 6 and that of chapter 9 is unclear.

The same kind of theoretical inconsistency persists in the *General Theory*: between the consumption theory of Book III and the investment theory of Book IV, on the one hand, and chapter 3, 'The Principle of Effective Demand', on the other.

a   THE FIRST POSTULATE AND THE EMPLOYMENT FUNCTION

The relation between the first postulate and the theory determining the level of employment is taken up seriously for the first time in 'The General Theory'. In the First Manuscript, the supply side was represented by the sum of the cost function and the inverse of the 'supply function'. Here the supply side is represented by the employment function, which is connected with the first postulate. Keynes states:

> the employment function tends to approximate to a straight line drawn at a constant angle, which ... would be in the neighbourhood of 45°, between the axes of the quantity of employment and the effective demand measured in wage units.
>
> > (*JMK*.13, p. 446)

We can begin by expressing the first postulate as follows:

$$\Delta O/\Delta N = W/P \tag{7}$$

where O denotes the level of output, P the price, and ΔX an increment in X.

From equation (7):

$$\Delta(P \cdot O/W) = \Delta N \tag{8}$$

And using the definition equation $P \cdot O = D$, we obtain:

$$\Delta D_w/\Delta N = 1 \tag{9}$$

This means that the slope of the employment function $D_w = F(N)$ is 1.

However, this method does not run through 'The General Theory'. The employment function presupposes a certain distribution of aggregate effective demand between different classes of firms, and the industry as a whole is divided into two sectors. Consequently, the first postulate cannot be directly connected with the employment function.[14]

b   THE ARGUMENTS OF CHAPTERS 6 AND 9

In chapter 6 the entrepreneur's windfall profit is defined as the difference between income and effective demand, while in chapter 9 income Y finds no place in the equation which determines the level of employment:

$$F(N) = f_1(N, r, E) + f_2(N, r, E)$$

Certainly, effective demand D $[D_w = F(N)]$ can be determined with this equation. However, it is not clear how the windfall profit is determined or how it is considered to work. No concept corresponding to the pseudo-TM supply function mk2 of the Second Manuscript appears here. If the arguments were susceptible to being interpreted along lines similar to our interpretation of the Second Manuscript, we could resolve the inconsistency between chapters 6 and 9. The definitions of normal profit and windfall profit in

'The General Theory' differ from those in the three 1933 manuscripts, and we can conclude that the equation $F_u = Y - D$ corresponds to our equation (7) in Chapter 8. Moreover, we presume that 'The General Theory' is devoid of anything like Chapter 8's equation (8) (the pseudo-TM supply function mk2),[15] though we cannot completely rule out the possibility of its appearance in the missing part.

Thus we can understand the arguments of chapters 6 and 9 in a manner which makes them consistent by considering that Keynes puts forward the stability of the equilibrium level of employment in chapter 6, and the determination of the equilibrium level of employment in chapter 9. If so, the three 1933 manuscripts might lead, by way of these two chapters of 'The General Theory', to chapter 3 of the *General Theory*.

2   *The consumption theory*

The consumption theory in 'The General Theory' adopts that of 'The First Undated Manuscript'. It deals with both the 'subjective' and the 'objective' factors, and possesses the same theoretical framework as the consumption theory of the *General Theory* (chapters 8 and 9). It is discussed mainly in chapter 10, 'The Propensity to Spend'.

A   *The subjective factors*

Concerning the subjective factors, the argument here is, in style, very similar to that of the *General Theory*. It is therefore fairly safe to suppose that in the missing pages Keynes would have referred to items corresponding to the sixth, seventh and eighth – namely, '(vi) To secure a masse de manoeuvre to carry out speculative or business projects; (vii) To bequeath a fortune; (viii) To satisfy pure miserliness' – in the *General Theory* (p. 108), and the first, second and third of the four saving motives of governments and firms: '(i) The motive of enterprise ... (ii) The motive of liquidity ... and (iii) The motive of improvement ...' (pp. 108–109).

In section IV of chapter 8, 'Investment and Saving', of 'The General Theory', Keynes almost completes an argument to the effect that 'financial provision' for the future becomes an obstacle to employment. Keynes treats the financial provision in such a way that it is added to the subjective factors.

This section is succeeded by sections I–III of chapter 8, 'Investment and Saving', of 'The Summer Manuscript' (see Section II below), into which Keynes incorporated Colin Clark's statistical data for the British economy. This is further developed in chapter 9, 'The Meaning of Investment', of 'Galley 1' (see Chapter 11), and finally leads to *GT*, chapter 8, section IV (which mainly deals with the financial provision). In 'The General Theory', Keynes treats the financial provision in such a way that it is added to the subjective factors, although he ceases to do so after 'Galley 1(I)' (see Chapter 11).

B   The objective factors

The objective factors also appear for the first time in 'The General Theory'. The discussion here corresponds to *GT*'s chapter 8, sections II and III, but there are some notable differences.

In 'The General Theory' Keynes lists the following: (a) the quantity of employment as determining the aggregate current rate of real income; (b) the rate of interest; and (c) the state of 'confidence' or long-term expectation (*JMK*.13, p. 444).

In the *General Theory* the following are given: (i) a change in the wage-unit; (ii) a change in the difference between income and net income; (iii) windfall changes in capital-values not allowed for in calculating net income; (iv) changes in the rate of time-discounting; (v) changes in fiscal policy; and (vi) changes in expectations of the relation between the present and the future level of income.

Items (b) and (iv) are very similar in style, while (c) and (iii) share something in common, in that both take into account the influence which changes in capital-values have upon consumption.

In 'The General Theory' the quantity of employment is regarded as the most important, and is referred to at the point where the consumption function is considered in relation to the fundamental psychological law, whereas in the *General Theory* it is not regarded as an objective factor at all. So far as the other factors are concerned, there is no similarity between the two texts.

The above argument must be understood in the following context: as far as the consumption theory is concerned, the theoretical framework in 'The General Theory' is the same as that in the *General Theory*. Among the factors which determine the propensity to spend (consume), Keynes defines those factors which do not change in the short period to be the 'subjective' factors, and those which do change in the short period as the 'objective' factors. He also puts forward the consumption function in relation to the fundamental psychological law. Compared with these similarities, the differences between 'The General Theory' and the *General Theory* in the items named as objective factors are of only secondary importance.

3   *The investment theory*

In 'The General Theory' Keynes improves on the investment theory of 'The Second Undated Manuscript' and formulates the theory that would be enshrined in the *General Theory*.

For a start, the marginal efficiency of capital here is virtually the same as in the *General Theory*:[16]

> Given this series of annuities [the prospective yields]... there is some rate of interest on the basis of which the present value of the series of annuities will be equal to the supply price of the investment. The rate thus arrived at we may call the marginal yield (or efficiency) of capital.

> (*JMK*.13, p. 453)

Second, what we call Investment Theory (1) of the *General Theory* is put forward:

> [N]ew investment will be pushed to the point beyond which the marginal yield of capital would fall short of the current rate of interest.
>
> (*JMK*.13, p. 453)

Third, what we call Investment Theory (2)[17] of the *General Theory* is also put forward:

> The series Q_r, which can be called the prospective yield of the investment, depends on the state of long-term expectation E; whilst the series d_r [the present value of £1 deferred r years] is given by the rate of interest. The two together determine the schedule of effective demand for investment; and, finally, the supply from this for investment goods fixes the amount of employment which will be actually directed towards investment corresponding to any given effective demand.
>
> (*JMK*.13, p. 452)

Here the demand schedule for investment to be used in Investment Theory (1) of the *General Theory* appears in the area belonging to Investment Theory (2). In the passage quoted, Keynes argues that the schedule of effective demand for investment is determined by the prospective yield of the investment and the rate of interest, and argues that the schedule of effective demand for investment and the 'supply' determine the amount of employment which is directed toward investment, though it is not clear what the coordinate axes on which that schedule is measured are, nor how it relates to the 'supply'.

4   *Some other fundamental concepts*

In chapter 8 of 'The General Theory' Keynes examines some fundamental concepts, centring his attention on '(gross) investment' and '(gross) saving'.[18] This part of the discussion is the predecessor of chapter 8, 'Investment and Saving', of 'The Summer Manuscript' and 'The Pre-First Proof Typescript' (see Chapter 11), which are the origins of chapter 6, 'The Definition of Income, Saving and Investment', and sections I–III of chapter 7, 'The Meaning of Saving and Investment Further Considered', of the *General Theory*.[19]

II 'The Summer Manuscript'

Keynes sailed to America on 9 May 1934 to participate[20] in a ceremony at Columbia University, staying there until 8 June.

He resumed work on the *General Theory* immediately after his return to England. The texts of five chapters written in this period survive.

Chapter 8, 'Investment and Saving', and chapter 9, 'The Functions Relating Employment to the Independent Variables of the System', are revisions (centring on 'effective demand' and the employment theory), respectively, of chapters 8 and 9 of 'The General Theory' (*JMK*.13, pp. 471–485).

The other three are chapter 5, 'The Units of Quantity', chapter 4, 'Expectation', and chapter 11, 'The Propensity to Invest', and the 'first versions of what were to become chapters 4, 5 and 11 [respectively]' (*JMK*.13, p. 471) of the *General Theory*. The last three are in fact close to the *General Theory*, and we shall therefore defer discussion of them until the next chapter.

1   *Effective demand*

The viewpoint seen in 'The General Theory' which stresses gross investment and gross saving as the fundamental quantities in economic analysis is here seen as well. The appearance of the concept of 'user cost' renders the relations between various concepts in this manuscript different from those in 'The General Theory'. The concept of user cost here is, rather, akin to depreciation, and differs from the concept that appears in the *General Theory*:

> Effective demand ... is gross of user cost, being equal to the gross proceeds of current output, i.e. to consumption plus investment plus the user cost of current output.
>
> (*JMK*.13, p. 472)

> [The entrepreneurs] sell their output for $C + I + U$ [C denotes consumption, I investment, and U user cost] ... Their own return Q is the excess of these sale proceeds over E, their outgoings to the other factors of production. Thus $C + I + U = E + Q$ ....
>
> Their aggregate income Y is made up of the income of the earners E and the income of the entrepreneurs $Q - U$; and they [the public] spend their income on current consumption C or retain it as savings S for the acquisition of capital assets .... Thus $E + Q - U = Y = C + S$[21]
>
> (*JMK*.13, pp. 477–478)

Two points are worth noting here.

First, effective demand is defined as the user cost plus income. Income here is treated as not a gross but a net concept. Effective demand here corresponds to 'income' in 'The General Theory', which is regarded as a gross concept.

Second, gross profit disappears in 'The Summer Manuscript'. In 'The General Theory', excess profit (entrepreneur's windfall profit) appeared explicitly. However, in 'The Summer Manuscript', profit (Q) is defined as including user cost, and the sum total of excess profit and normal profit equal the difference between profit and user cost.

The argument about effective demand and income in 'The Summer Manuscript' shows that Keynes has yet to find a new theory in this area, and the change in the definition of profit leads us to reconfirm that profit ceases to play the role it had previously held in his thinking.

Let us summarise the formulation in 'The Summer Manuscript':

$$Y = C + I \tag{10}$$

$$Y = C + S \tag{11}$$

$$Y = E + (Q - U) \tag{12}$$

where Y denotes (net) income and I (net) investment.

2   The employment theory

In 'The Summer Manuscript', the system determining the volume of employment is revised as follows:

i $N_1 = F_1(C_w)$ and $N_2 = F_2(I_w)$ are the employment functions for consumption and investment goods respectively, where effective demands C_w and I_w for the two classes of goods lead to volumes of employment N_1 and N_2, respectively on producing them.

ii $C_w = Q_1(N, r, e)$ is the propensity to spend, where an aggregate employment N, a rate of interest r, and a marginal efficiency of capital e lead to an effective demand C_w for consumption goods.

iii $I_w = Q_2(N, r, e)$ is the propensity to invest, where N, r and e lead to an effective demand I_w for investment goods.

Since $N = N_1 + N_2$, the volume of employment N will be determined by the equation

$$N = F_1\{Q_1(N, r, e)\} + F_2\{Q_2(N, r, e)\}$$

(JMK. 13, p. 483)

Four points are worth noting here.

First, the employment function is expressed as the inverse function of 'the employment function' in 'The General Theory'.

Second, the propensity to spend and the propensity to invest are directly substituted for the employment function. This shows that the employment function is used as both a supply and an equilibrium concept. As far as this point is concerned, the formulation here is in contrast with that in 'The General Theory' which seems to represent the supply side. It would appear that Keynes unwittingly uses the employment function as representing a supply concept in some cases, and an equilibrium concept in others. This ambiguity continues up to, and is apparent in, the *General Theory*.

Third, the equation determining the volume of employment is derived from the constraint equation on employment, $N = N_1 + N_2$. This differs from the case of 'The General Theory', in which the equation determining the volume of employment is based on supply–demand equilibrium. In the *General Theory* the equation, $N = N_1 + N_2$, is not used for determining the volume of employment, but only in relation to the additivity of the individual employment functions,[22] while the idea used in 'The General Theory' is adopted as the equation determining the volume of employment.

Fourth, the relation between the definitions of certain concepts and the equation determining the volume of employment is not completely clear. Although, for example, in the equation determining the volume of employment $N = F_1\{Q_1(N, r, e)\} + F_2\{Q_2(N, r, e)\}$, C_w and I_w play important roles, it is not clear how this is related to effective demand $Y + U$, to which Keynes attaches importance in the equation $Y + U = C + I + U$.

3   Connections between 'The Summer Manuscript' and 'The General Theory' (1934)

In addition to the points discussed above, there are some passages in 'The Summer Manuscript' which are directly related to certain passages in the *General Theory*. Section III and part of section I of chapter 8, 'Investment and Saving', are linked to section IV of chapter 8, 'The Propensity to Consume: I. The Objective Factors', of the *General Theory*. Section IV of chapter 8, in which Keynes criticises the theory of forced saving[23] advocated by Hayek and others, is linked to section IV of chapter 7, 'The Meaning of Saving and Investment Further Considered', of the *General Theory*, via section II of chapter 8, 'The Meaning of Saving', of Galley 1(I) which is to be dealt with in the next chapter.

III   The 1934 Michaelmas lectures

Keynes started the proofreading of the *General Theory* at about the same time he began his lecture course for 1934.[24] The galley of the first three chapters of Galley 1(I) was ready on October 10. He began the lectures based on them. He subsequently sent chapters 4 to 11 and 12 to 19 in manuscript to the publishers. The galleys of these are estimated to have come out between early December in 1934 and mid-January 1935.

The Michaelmas lectures for 1934,[25] entitled 'The General Theory of Unemployment', are identical to those for 1933 in the most important respect – they advance a model in which income (or the level of employment) is determined within a single period (the endogenous variables are determined simultaneously).

In the lectures for 1934 Keynes puts forward his model under the label 'Theory of Effective Demand', which runs as follows:

The 'effective demand function' $D = f(N)$ relates the number of men employed, N, to the expected sales of their output ($=$ effective demand), D. The level of employment is determined at the point at which the effective demand function intersects the 'employment' (or supply) function $D' = F(N)$, which relates N to the sum which will just make it worthwhile to employ N men, or the supply price D'. Effective demand is the sum of what people are prepared to spend on current consumption, D_1, and what firms are prepared to set aside for investment, D_2.

The consumption function is defined as $D_1 = f_1(N_1)$ (N_1 is the number of men employed in the consumption goods sector needed to meet the consumption resulting from real income). Furthermore, we have the equation $N_1 = f(N)$ (where $0 < \Delta N_1 / \Delta N < 1$).

The investment function is represented as $D_2 = f_2(N_2)$. This means that N_2 (the number employed in the investment goods sector) will be increased up to the point at which the marginal efficiency of capital becomes equal to the rate of interest.

To sum up, the system can be expressed as follows:

$$F(N) = f_1(N_1) + f_2(N_2) \tag{1}$$

$$N_1 = f(N) \tag{2}$$

Keynes then argues that given $f_2(N_2)$, N and N_1 are determined (though in this case $N = N_1 + N_2$ is not necessarily satisfied). The level of employment thus determined is not guaranteed to be full employment.

Keynes expresses the above ideas clearly as follows:

> [W]hen the propensity to invest will absorb the output of N_2 men, eq[uilibriu]m requires that agg[regate] employment should be N where N is such that, with [the] existing psych[ological] prop[ensity] to consume, this vol[ume] of employment will lead to an am[ount] of cons[umption] that will absorb the labour [of] $(N - N_2)$ men.[26]
>
> (Rymes [Bryce], p. C10)

> [G]iven [the] propensity funct[ions] there is only one level of employment will be consistent.... There is a level of I which leads to full employment but no reason why it should always exist.... That is, [the] marginal efficiency of capital, the rate of interest, and the propensity to consume will give us all.
>
> (Rymes [Tarshis], p. K5)

The argument is almost identical in content to that of *GT*'s chapter 3.

The point on which the 1934 lectures differ from the 1933 lectures is that we no longer find any argument in terms of the TM supply function (moreover, the concept of quasi-rents, Q, is dealt with as a 'realised' concept).

Besides this, the novelties we meet with here are:[27]

1   The argument presented in *GT*'s chapters 4–6, which can be traced back to the lectures of 1933, approaches completion here. Above all, the concept of 'user cost', which is the same in content as that in the *General Theory*, makes its first appearance, playing a central role in dealing with the relations among various concepts.
2   Quasi-rents are defined in relation to realised profits.
3   The 'objective' factors influencing the propensity to consume make their first appearance.

4   The 'marginal efficiency of capital' makes its first appearance, and the theory of investment is constructed in flow terms.

5   The speculative motive is made clearly dependent upon the rate of interest (in the lectures of 1933, the income, business, and precautionary motives were made dependent upon the rate of interest, while the speculative motive was made dependent upon the state of bearishness).

IV   Conclusion

In this chapter we have examined Keynes's developmental state in 1934 through 'The General Theory', 'The Summer Manuscript' and his Michaelmas lectures in 1934.

'The General Theory' is the manuscript which succeeded the three 1933 manuscripts and two undated manuscripts (see Section II of Chapter 9), and was to form the theoretical backbone of the *General Theory*.

First, 'The General Theory' possesses the same theoretical framework as the consumption theory of the *General Theory*. It deals with the subjective factors and the objective factors. The subjective factors are almost the same as those in the *General Theory*, but the objective factors which appear for the first time in 'The General Theory' are, to some degree, different from those in the *General Theory*.

Second, 'The General Theory' has an improved version of an investment theory which is to be enshrined in the *General Theory*. The marginal efficiency of capital here is virtually the same as that in the *General Theory*.

So far, so good. We see a clear improvement there.

The following is, however, quite different. In 'The General Theory' as well as 'The Summer Manuscript' Keynes puts forward new models to explain how the level of employment is determined, but his argument still lacks precision. Concerning 'The General Theory' we pointed out the ambiguities in the concept of 'effective demand' and the inconsistency of the employment theory (esp. the relation between the first postulate and the employment function and the relation between the argument of chapter 6 and that of chapter 9). In this respect, Keynes's endeavours to explain the workings coherently were to continue right up to the *General Theory*, even here falling somewhat short of the requisite precision.

The Michaelmas term lectures of 1934 are identical to those of 1933 in that they advance a model in which income (or the level of employment) is determined within a single period. The difference is that no argument in terms of the TM supply function is to be seen. We also pointed out five new features which were not to be found in the 1933 lectures.

11 The proofing process (I)

From 'The Pre-First Proof Typescript' (Summer 1934) to 'Galley 1(III)' (June–July 1935)

I Introduction

Keynes had constructed many of the major components of the *General Theory* (including the theory of liquidity preference, the marginal efficiency of capital, the fundamental psychological law, and the multiplier) before the time of 'The General Theory'. However, in terms of style it is in 'The General Theory' that we first find material that was actually incorporated into the *General Theory*. For example, chapter 12, 'The State of Long-Term Expectation (or Confidence)', of 'The General Theory' was very much the prototype for chapter 12, 'The State of Long-Term Expectation', of the *General Theory*. Similarly, chapter 10, 'The Propensity to Spend', of 'The General Theory' is the precursor of chapter 8, 'The Propensity to Consume: I. The Objective Factors', and chapter 9, 'The Propensity to Consume: II. The Subjective Factors', of the *General Theory*.

As mentioned in Section V of Chapter 6, Keynes remarked in his letter to Kitoh of 22 June 1934 that 'it will be some months more before I am ready for printing'. This should be considered in relation to the fact that he had completed almost all the text outlined in the table of contents of 'The General Theory' by March 1934, went to the United States in May and came home in June, as we saw in Section II of Chapter 10. Our purpose in this and the next chapter will be to illuminate in chronological order the succeeding phases of the proofing process leading up to publication of the *General Theory*.

During the eighteen months or so from summer 1934 to February 1936, Keynes submitted the manuscript to his publisher in instalments, and revised the galley proofs several times. In fact, he continued to modify the expression of his ideas all through this period right up to publication.

Reconstructing the proofing process brings revealing light to bear on the gestation of the *General Theory*. There are two main reasons for this. First, Keynes adopted the somewhat unusual procedure of handing in his manuscript piecemeal rather than in one go, rewriting constantly as he went along. Retracing this process gives us considerable insight into the significant changes he introduced along the way. In this context it should be remembered that although the consumption theory, the investment theory, and the theory of liquidity preference had all virtually reached their final forms by spring 1934, the theory of effective demand and the definitions of some fundamental concepts – such as user cost – had yet to be finalised. Second, Keynes sent the corrected galley proofs to several close colleagues for their reactions. The correspondence this generated highlights the differences between Keynes's theory and the theories of these colleagues very clearly, as well as the features they had in common. The picture is somewhat complicated, however, because the debates concerning points of disagreement Keynes had with Robertson and Hawtrey had begun prior to the *Treatise* and continued into the period of the *General Theory*, with no clear line of demarcation between the discussions of the one book and those of the other.

In this chapter we will examine the developmental process of the *General Theory* from 'The Pre-First Proof Typescript' (summer 1934) up to Galley 1(III) (to be explained below. June–July 1935). It is worth noting the following points in advance. First, the First Galley (or Galley 1), which is composed of Galley 1(I), Galley 1(II) and Galley 1(III) (to be explained below), is the most telling of the galleys for our purpose. There are two reasons for this: (i) the galley is written in line with the Galley Table of Contents (to be called the 'TOC' below), which leads us to suppose that the First Galley laid the foundations for succeeding galleys; (ii) by examining the appendix to Volume 14 of *JMK*, entitled 'Variorum of Drafts of the *General Theory*' (*JMK*. 14, pp. 351–512; hereafter referred to as 'The Variorum'), we can confirm that in the Second and Third Galleys (or Galley 2 and Galley 3. To be explained below) Keynes for the most part made only formal revisions, though there were a few exceptions to this. It will therefore be convenient for us to deal with these when we come to discuss Galley 1.

Second, we need to compare and contrast the developments in this particular set of galleys not only with Keynes's economic-theoretical development prior to their production, but also with the theory presented in the corresponding parts of the *General Theory*. For the first set of comparisons we focus on the new ideas each set of galleys contains. For the second set of comparisons, in addition to the new ideas found in each set of galleys, we will also examine more formal aspects of the text, such as the degree of completion, as this will assist us in clarifying in concrete terms the degree to which Keynes changed and did not change his theory in the process.

In Section II we will examine 'The Pre-first Proof Typescript', and in Sections III–VIII we will go on to examine Galley 1, Galley 2 and Galley 3. The material which follows will be, for the sake of convenience, examined in the next chapter.

II 'The Pre-First Proof Typescript'

A typescript named 'The Pre-First Proof Typescript' (hereafter 'The Typescript') was written in the summer of 1934. It can be divided into two parts.

The first part consists of chapter 4, 'The Choice of Units', chapter 5, 'Expectation as Determining Output and Employment',[1] and chapter 9, 'The Marginal Efficiency of Capital'. They are identical to chapters 4, 5 and 11 of the *General Theory*, respectively, in both form and title.

The second is chapter 6, 'The Meaning of Income'. It differs considerably in form from the corresponding part of the *General Theory*. After some changes in Galley 1(I), small formal changes ensued until the Third Galley, and in 'The Great Revision' (to be explained in Section I of Chapter 12) it was revised in form.

That summer Kahn helped Keynes. In early September Keynes wrote to Daniel Macmillan, his publisher: 'I am now fairly well on with my forthcoming [book]… My provisional title is The *General Theory* of Employment, Interest and Money.'[2]

Here we will examine 'The Typescript'. The employment function and the definitions of some fundamental concepts merit particular attention.

1   *The employment function*

The following quotation, which deals with the employment function, represents the origin of *GT*, chapter 4, section IV, although different in substance:

> We can substitute for the supply function what we shall call the employment function. The employment function for a given firm (and similarly for a given industry or for industry as a whole) is given by $N = F(D_w)$, where D_w is the sale proceeds in terms of wage units, the expectation of which will induce a level of employment N. Similarly we can write $(D_w/N) = Q(N)$, which relates the money proceeds per wage unit to the quantity of employment, so that if N men produce an output O, $(D_w/O) = Q(O)$ is the ordinary supply curve.
>
> (*JMK*.14, p. 387)

Keynes's intention might have been as follows. The employment function $N = F(D_w)$ can be reformulated as

$$D_w = f(N) \tag{1}$$

By dividing equation (1) by N, we obtain the equation:

$$D_w/N = f(N)/N = Q(N) \tag{2}$$

Let us express the production function as

$$O = g(N) \tag{3}$$

Then, from equations (2) and (3) the following equation can be obtained:

$$D_w/O = N \cdot Q(N)/O = g^{-1}(O) \cdot Q\,(g^{-1}(O))/O = Q'(O)^3 \tag{4}$$

Keynes calls this the 'ordinary supply curve'. Here he seems to be considering the inverse of the employment function.

On the one hand, the employment function is a supply concept, for it is considered to be a substitute for the 'supply function'. On the other, it is of the same type as the employment function in 'The Summer Manuscript'. Therefore, $N = F(D_w)$ may also be considered an equilibrium concept.

So much can be verified with two considerations.

First, Keynes frequently changed the employment function formulation: (i) in 'The General Theory' as $D_w = F(N)$; (ii) in 'The Summer Manuscript', 'The Typescript' and Galley 1(I) as its inverse function; (iii) in Galleys 2 and 3 as $D_w = F(N)$; and (iv) in the *General Theory* as its inverse function.

Second, the role which the aggregate supply function plays in the *General Theory* was assumed by the employment function, denoted by either D_w or D, until the *General Theory*, in which D is replaced by Z (aggregate supply price), while D now denotes effective demand. This likewise indicates that both the employment function and the aggregate supply function have the attributes of an equilibrium concept as well as those of a supply concept. Thus, there is some apparent difficulty in deriving the 'ordinary supply curve' from the employment function.

Compared with this difficulty, the derivation of 'the ordinary supply curve' is of little importance. Suffice it to point out that

1   unlike the other galleys, Galley 1(I) does not use the production function;
2   from Galley 1(I) up to the *General Theory* the 'ordinary supply curve' describes a relation between the level of employment and the price level, so that it is not a supply curve in the ordinary sense.

2   *Some fundamental concepts*

Keynes discusses fundamental concepts such as income, investment, saving and effective demand in chapter 6.

This chapter, taking over chapter 8, 'Investment and Saving', of 'The General Theory' and 'The Summer Manuscript', forms the basis for fundamental concepts in the period from 'The Typescript' to Galley 3.

In Galley 1(I) Keynes inserts chapter 7, 'The Definitions of Quasi-Rent, Saving and Investment'. The material is utilised somewhat dispersively in *GT*, chapter 6, 'The Definition of Income, Saving and Investment'. We will therefore defer discussion of fundamental concepts until Section I of Chapter 12, simply observing here that chapter 6 of 'The Typescript' is more relevant to chapter 6 of the *General Theory* than the galleys from Galley 1(I) to Galley 3.

III   Galleys 1, 2 and 3

After 'The Typescript' came a set of galleys, which we will call Galley 1, 2 and 3 (see Table 11.1).

1   Three galleys have the same table of contents, which we will call the 'TOC'.[4]
2   Galley 2 is a revised version of Galley 1 while Galley 3 revises Galley 2. In each galley, only part of the material specified in the TOC was written. Moreover, Galley 2 rewrites only parts of Galley 1, while Galley 3 rewrites only parts of Galley 2. Consequently, some sections of the text remained at either Galley 1 or 2 stage until September 1935.

3   The text of Galley 1 was, of course, written first, but it appeared in various periods: (i) early December – mid-January 1935 (Galley 1(I)); (ii) March–May 1935 (Galley 1(II)); (iii) June–July 1935 (Galley 1(III)), so parts of Galley 1 postdate Galley 2.

4   Galley 1(I) laid the foundations for succeeding galleys;

5   On the evidence of 'The Variorum' we see that in Galleys 2 and 3 Keynes made only formal revisions.

6   Although chapter 17, 'The Psychological and Social Incentives to Liquidity', and chapter 19, 'The Essential Properties of Interest and Money' of Galley 1 have not survived, we have confirmation that they existed in Robertson's letter to Keynes (3 February 1935).[5]

We will compare these sets of galleys with both the preceding developments and the *General Theory*.

IV   Galley 1(I) (chapters 1–19)

On 7 September 1934 Keynes announced his publication programme to the Macmillan Co. and by 13 September 1934 he had sent off the first three chapters (i.e. Book I), the titles of which are the same as those of the corresponding chapters in the *General Theory* (although chapter 3, 'The Principle of Effective Demand', differs in substance). The galley of these chapters came out in October.

Table 11.1 The proofing process

Ch. of TOC	Galley 1 (I)* [TOC]		Galley 2 [TOC]	Galley 1(II) [TOC]	Galley 3 [TOC]	Galley 1 (III) [TOC]
1			H (the end of January 1935)			
2–3		R	(the end of January 1935)		H (June 1935)	
4–6						
7–14			H (the end of April 1935)			
15–19						
20–25				H**		
26–28						(June–July 1935)

Notes

1 R: the galleys sent to Robertson; H: the galleys sent to Harrod , Hawtrey, Kahn and J. Robinson.

2 The dates in parentheses indicate the period in which the galleys concerned came out.

3 * The period between early December 1934 and mid-January 1935.

   ** The period from March 1935 on. Chapters 21–24 with the date of 7–17 May 1935.

Keynes delivered his Michaelmas lectures based on this galley together with the manuscript for chapters 4–14.

That Keynes felt this manuscript needed revising is revealed in two letters to Kahn (18 and 27 September):[6]

> I ... have found out one or two interesting novelties. ... I've solved the riddle of how to define Income in some sort of a net sense .... The deduction from the gross sales proceeds of the output of a given equipment necessary to yield income is that part of the quasi-rent ... necessary to induce the entrepreneur not to leave his equipment idle. ... the sacrifice involved in using the equipment as compared with postponing its use ....

> I am getting towards the end of the re-writing which you led me into and will show you the new way for dealing with net income in detail next term.

These progress reports relate to chapter 6, 'The Meaning of Income', which treats user cost, and chapter 7, 'The Definitions of Quasi-Rent, Saving and Investment', of the TOC.

Keynes sent the publisher, first, chapters 4–11, and, second, chapters 12–19 (which respectively correspond to chapters 4–9 and chapters 11–17 of the *General Theory*). Their galleys probably appeared between early December 1934 and mid-January 1935. They mark the virtual birth of the *General Theory*. Keynes sent to Robertson[7] chapters 1–19, which we call 'Galley 1(I)'.

Let us examine Galley 1(I). It can be divided into two parts: chapters 10 and 11 for consumption, and chapters 14–19 for the rate of interest (the chapters to which we refer below, unless otherwise noted, are those in the TOC).

1 *Consumption*

Chapter 10, 'The Propensity to Spend' covers the area of *GT*, chapter 8, sections II and III.

Section III, which discusses the fundamental psychological law, shows hardly any change from Galley 1(I)[8] onward.

However, Section II differs considerably from Galley 1(I). 'The General Theory' had identified the objective factors as

1 the quantity of employment as determining the aggregate current rate of real income;
2 the rate of interest;
3 the state of long-term expectation.

Galley 1(I) deletes (1), keeping (2) and (3). It discusses (1) separately, using income rather than the quantity of employment[9] (the *General Theory* added an argument justifying this substitution).[10]

Item (2) is kept in 'The General Theory', and is included in *GT*'s fourth objective factor, 'changes in the rate of time-discounting'.[11] Item (3) is also

retained in 'The General Theory', and is incorporated to some extent in
GT's third objective factor, 'windfall changes in capital-values not allowed for in
calculating net income'.

Chapter 11 corresponds to *GT*'s chapter 9, 'The Propensity to Consume: II. The
Subjective Factors'. 'The General Theory' had regarded financial provision as
a subjective factor, but neither Galley 1(I) nor the *General Theory* followed
this line.

The argument concerning the influence of distribution on the propensity to
consume restates that of 'The General Theory', namely that the employment
function becomes a 45° straight line. The *General Theory* drops it and takes
income distribution as given.

Concerning 'negative saving', Galley 1(I) adds negative saving by firms and
'unemployment relief financed by borrowing' together with the purchase of
annuities and death duties in 'The General Theory'. The *General Theory* refers
only to 'unemployment relief financed by borrowing'.

Besides these changes, chapter 11 is essentially the same as *GT*'s chapter 9.

As far as chapters 10 and 11 are concerned, there is no discernible difference
between Galley 1(I) and Galley 2, aside from minor changes in wording.

2   *The rate of interest*

Chapter 14, 'The General Theory of the Rate of Interest' is nearly identical to
GT's chapter 13, in which the core of the theory of interest is articulated.
In other words, Galley 1(I) brings the liquidity preference theory to its final
form. Only small revisions are made to chapter 14 between Galley 1(I) and
Galley 2.

The same is true of chapter 18, 'Sundry Observations on the Nature of Capital',
which corresponds to *GT*'s chapter 16 (the same title) (Section II is traceable to
'The Second Undated Manuscript' and 'The Typescript').

Neither chapter 17, 'The Psychological and Social Incentives to Liquidity',
nor chapter 19, 'The Essential Properties of Interest and Money'[12]
(corresponding respectively to *GT*, chapter 15, 'The Psychological and
Business Incentives to Liquidity', and chapter 17 (the same title)) are extant.
However, we have Keynes's letter to Kahn (15 January 1935),[13] and Robertson's
letter to Keynes (3 February)[14] attesting to them. The letter to Kahn indicates
that Keynes rewrote 90 per cent of these chapters (see Section V below).
Certainly chapters 17 and 19 of Galley 2 are almost identical to *GT*'s
chapters 15 and 17.

Chapter 15, 'The Classical Theory of the Rate of Interest', and chapter 16,
'Notes on the Rate of Interest in Marshall's *Principles of Economics*, Ricardo's
Principles of Political Economy, and Elsewhere' correspond, respectively, to
General Theory, chapter 14 (the same title), and its Appendix (the same title,
replacing 'Notes' with 'Appendix').

The differences between Galley 1(I) and Galley 2 are of very little account.

In 'The Great Revision' (to be explained in Chapter 12), however, both chapters were considerably rewritten, as is confirmed by

1 Keynes's letter to Kahn (27 August)[15], in which he is thinking of completely rewriting the chapters on the theory of interest;
2 the fact that among the chapters on the theory of interest, Keynes rewrote these two chapters only.

Keynes rewrote these two chapters under the impetus following on discussion with Harrod.[16]

General Theory's chapter 14 consists of 11 pages, of which 7 pages (pp. 177–183) were completely rewritten. Nevertheless, there is no difference of argument between Galley 1(I) and the *General Theory*. In both versions he argues that the classical theory of interest assumes full employment, so that when income changes, the theory can no longer account for the actual rate of interest.[17]

A similar relationship is discernible between *GT*'s appendix to chapter 14 and chapter 16 of Galley 1(I).[18] Keynes completely rewrote four and a half (out of about seven and a half) pages of the appendix discussing Marshall-Pigou's theory of interest (section I). Yet when chapter 16 of Galley 1(I) and the relevant passages in *GT*'s chapter 14 are compared, no changes appear to have been made to the argument:

> The perplexity which I find in Marshall's account ... is fundamentally due ... to the incursion of the concept 'interest', which belongs to a monetary economy, into a treatise which takes no account of money.
>
> (*GT*, p. 189 and *JMK*.14, p. 484)

> Professor Pigou ... leads us (in his *Economics of Welfare*) to infer that the unit of waiting is the same as the unit of current investment and that the reward of waiting is quasi-rent, and practically never mentions interest, – which is as it should be.
>
> (*GT*, p. 190 and *JMK*.14, p. 484)

The theme is common to *GT*'s appendix to chapter 14 and to Galley 1(I)'s chapter 16, apart from two formal points of difference:

1 Galley 1(I) argues that Marshall does not clearly distinguish quasi-rent as a return on assets from interest as a return on money,[19] while the *General Theory* eliminates this part;
2 Keynes's criticism of Pigou's theory of interest is more extensively developed in the *General Theory*, using Pigou (1927; 1933).[20]

Galley 1(I) also has chapters 6–9 (Book II, 'Definitions and Ideas'), and chapters 2–3 (Book I, 'Introduction'), which will be examined in the next chapter.

V   Galley 2

The revision of Galley 1(I), that is Galley 2 is particularly interesting from our point of view on account of the fact that chapter 17, 'The Psychological and Social Incentives to Liquidity', and chapter 19, 'The Essential Properties of Interest and Money', which correspond to *GT*'s chapters 15 and 17, respectively, are both extant. Judging from the fact that the second galleys for chapters 1–6 were ready on 29 January 1935, it would seem that some of Galley 1(I) must have been revised and returned to the publisher by the end of 1934. The remaining part of Galley 1(I) would then have been revised by the end of January 1935, as is confirmed by the letter Keynes wrote to Kahn on 15 January,[21] in which he says:

> I have done two more chapters for you.... [T]hey cover the ground of the philosophical chapter, ninety per cent re-written...concerning the fundamental characteristics of interest...considerably remodelled.

This would appear to relate to chapter 18, 'Philosophical Considerations on the Essential Properties of Capital, Interest and Money', of 'The General Theory', suggesting that Keynes reworked this as chapter 18, 'Sundry Observations on the Nature of Capital', and chapter 19, 'The Essential Properties of Interest and Money'. In response, the publisher returned the remainder of Galley 2, that is chapters 7–19, to Keynes towards the end of April 1935.

VI   Galley 1(II) (chapters 20–25)

Galley 1(II) consists of chapters 20–25 which exist only in the First Galley: these chapters appear in neither Galley 2 nor Galley 3. They correspond to chapters 18, 20, 10, 19, 21 and 22 of the *General Theory* respectively.

Two pieces of evidence suggest that Keynes probably sent this off to the publisher after the end of March 1935.

First, he announced in his letter to Kahn of 26 March 1935:

> I have now finished a full-dress critique of the Prof. [Pigou] to go in as an appendix to the chapter on changes in money wages.
>
> *(JMK*.13, p. 525)

This would indicate that he had already finished writing 'Appendix on Professor Pigou's *Theory of Unemployment* to chapter 23, "Changes in Money Wages"', which corresponds to 'Appendix on Prof. Pigou's Theory of Unemployment' to chapter 19, 'Changes in Money Wages', of the *General Theory*.

Second, this manuscript was sent off for comment to several other economists in June 1935. From these we deduce that Keynes received the galley in May 1935.

Galley 1(II) represents the final version of the parts of the *General Theory* to which it corresponds.

Chapter 22, 'The Marginal Propensity to Consume and the Multiplier', becomes *GT*'s chapter 10 (same title); chapter 20, 'The Equilibrium of the Economic

System', becomes *GT*'s chapter 18, 'The General Theory of Employment Re-stated'; chapter 21, 'The Employment Function', becomes *GT*'s chapter 20 (same title); chapter 23, 'Changes in Money-Wages', becomes *GT*'s chapter 19 (same title); and chapter 24, 'The Theory of Prices' becomes *GT*'s chapter 21 (same title). Chapter 25, 'Notes on the Trade Cycle', does not survive.

The original idea of chapter 22 is traceable to 'The First Undated Manuscript', and that of chapter 21 to 'The General Theory' and 'The Summer Manuscript'.

As will be explained in the next chapter, chapter 3, 'The Principle of Effective Demand', of Galley 1(I) defined the employment function as $D' = F(N)$ (D' denotes 'the supply price' in the sense of an expectation of sale proceeds), N the volume of employment). However, chapter 21 of Galley 1(II) defines it as $N = F(D)$[22] (where D denotes effective demand).

Then, in 'The Great Revision', Keynes sets about clearing up the confusion by calling the employment function of Galley 1(I) the 'aggregate supply function', and that of Galley 1(II) the employment function.[23] He also brings in the concept of the 'aggregate demand function' for the first time, and re-defines effective demand as exclusive of 'user cost'.

From this development we can infer that the employment function, $N = F(D_w)$, of the *General Theory* is a function of the equilibrium value, D_w (effective demand in terms of wage units). This can be verified by examining the theoretical structure of the *General Theory* directly, which we do in Chapter 13 of the present book.

Chapter 23 of Galley 1(II) is traceable to

1   Keynes's attack on Pigou (1933) in September 1933, and the controversy with Robertson;[24]
2   his first lecture of the 1933 Michaelmas Term;
3   the letter to Kahn (26 March 1935) to the effect that he has finished writing an appendix for Pigou's book.[25]

Aside from chapters 21–23, we find no precursors to Galley 1(II).

We see no difference in content between Galley 1(II) and the corresponding parts of the *General Theory*. The only exception[26] is section II of chapter 20, which summarises the argument in the preceding chapters. It was considerably rewritten, probably, in 'The Great Revision'.

VII   Galley 3

Galley 3 (June) comprises chapters 2–6, which correspond to *GT*'s chapters 2–5 and part of chapter 6.

In early June Keynes sent to Harrod, Hawtrey, Kahn and Joan Robinson:

1   Chapter 1 of Galley 2;
2   Chapters 7–19 of Galley 2, which correspond to some of chapter 6, chapter 7, section I–IV of chapter 8, chapters 9–14, appendix to chapter 14 and chapters 15–17, of the *General Theory*;
3   Chapters 20–25 of Galley 1(II).

To sum up, what they received was chapters 1–25 of the TOC, corresponding to *GT*'s chapters 1–22.

According to Keynes's letter to Daniel Macmillan (31 July):[27]

1   He sent the final pages of Galley 3 to the printer;
2   He expected the book to appear in November.

VIII   Galley 1(III) (chapters 26–28)

Galley 1(III) contains three chapters of the TOC. Although the galley is not extant, the chapter titles are known to us:

1   Chapter 26, 'Notes on Mercantilism and the Usury Laws';
2   Chapter 27, 'Notes on the History of the Notion of "Effective Demand" ', and
3   Chapter 28, 'Is an Individualist Economy Capable of Providing Full Employment?'[28]

Chapters 26 and 27 together would correspond to *GT*, chapter 23, 'Notes on Mercantilism, the Usury Laws, Stamped Money and Theories of Under-Consumption'[29] while chapter 28 corresponds to *GT*, chapter 24, 'Concluding Notes on the Social Philosophy towards Which the *General* Theory Might Lead'.

Keynes's letter to J. Robinson (3 September) indicates that they were sent to her, and were still written along the TOC:

> I now have ... the last three chapters.... The last two chapters are completely unrevised. Roy [Harrod] strongly objects to chapter 26 as a tendentious attempt to glorify imbeciles.... I have been occupied for several weeks in somewhat re-writing Book I and completely re-writing Book II. In the case of Book II practically not a word of the version you have read has been left standing. ... I have somewhat modified my definition of user cost.
>
> (*JMK*.13, pp. 650–651)

On the evidence of this letter together with the galleys he sent to some fellow-economists in June 1935 and his letter to Daniel Macmillan (11 September),[30] Keynes's work on these chapters and their appearance in galley form would have taken place between June and July.

Together with chapter 25 these constitute Book VI, 'Short Notes on Some Applications of the General Theory'.

As far as the tables of contents are concerned, these can be traced back to the following:

1   Chapter 17, 'Historical Notes', of the First Manuscript of 1933;
2   Chapter 21, 'Notes on the Trade Cycle' and chapter 22, 'Notes on the History of Cognate Ideas', of the Third Manuscript of 1933;
3   Chapter 25, 'Notes on Mercantilism, the Balance of Trade and Foreign Investment', chapter 26, 'Is an Individualist Economy Capable of Providing

Full Employment?', and chapter 27, 'Notes on the History of Similar Ideas', of 'The General Theory'.

That Keynes must have produced these chapters in June or July 1935 is confirmed by the letters to his mother (9 August)[31] and to Harrod (17 August). At this point there are three observations to be made.

First, in his letter to Harrod, Keynes writes:

> Chapter 26 is too long.... In chapter 27 the emphasis hasn't worked out as I intended....
>
> (*JMK*.13, p. 542)

Possibly Keynes transferred the substance of chapter 26 to the sections of *GT*'s chapter 23: sections I–IV (on Mercantilism); section V (on the Usury Laws); section VI (on the theory of Gesell); (together with the substance of chapter 27) section VII (on theories of under-consumption).

Second, we know the origins of some of the ideas in *GT*'s chapter 23. The starting point should be 'Historical Retrospect' (1932)[32] (which could be connected with chapter 17, 'Historical Notes', of the First Manuscript), which is in favour of

1 mercantilist and protectionist policies as increasing foreign investment by improving the balance of trade;
2 anti-usury laws and principles of cheap-money policies as increasing home investment by lowering the rate of interest;
3 expenditure as being a thing in itself 'good for trade' by diminishing the excess of saving over investment.[33]

'Historical Retrospect' is close to the MTP manuscript in its basic tenor. Also, we have a note concerning Keynes's 1932 spring lectures[34] which refers to 'Mercantilism and Protection'. Keynes also discusses the seeds of his ideas in his 1932 Michaelmas lecture.

In *GT*, chapter 23, section III Keynes quotes, from Hecksher (1935), several points advocated by various mercantilist authors as precedents for some of his ideas in the *General Theory*, which are

1 scepticism about the policy of laissez-faire;
2 the theory of liquidity preference;
3 the need to distinguish between the rate of interest and the marginal efficiency of capital.

Keynes's extensive quotation of Hecksher's text reflects its recent availability in English. Keynes had an interesting observation to make on Hecksher and his own position:

> Prof. Heckscher is himself an adherent... of the classical theory and much less sympathetic to the mercantilist theories than I am. Thus there is no risk that his choice of quotations has been biased....
>
> (*GT*, p. 341, fn.1)

In *GT*, chapter 23, section VII Keynes discusses under-consumption theories. Although his line of argument on Malthus can be traced back to 1922, he did not refer to the relation between unemployment and effective demand until 1933.

Here Keynes also discusses in detail Mummery-Hobson (1898), which must date from July 1935, for, writing to Kahn (30 July), he states:

> the book Hobson helped him [Mummery] to write, *The Physiology of Industry*, is a wonderful work. I am giving a full account of it.... .
>
> (*JMK*.13, p. 634)

Third, from the letter to his mother (9 August) we are given to understand that Keynes commenced on chapter 28 in August 1935.[35] Furthermore, according to the letter to Robinson (3 September),[36] the chapter had by that time been finished. We can infer that chapter 28 became the basis of *GT*'s chapter 24.

Thus far we have examined all the chapters of the TOC, with the exception of chapters 2, 3 and 6–9, which we examine in the next chapter. That is to say, we have completed our examination of the latest-written of the chapters listed prior to 'The Great Revision' in Table 11.1.

12   The proofing process (II)

'The Great Revision' and the 1935 Michaelmas lectures

Our examination in Chapter 11 of the galleys from 'The Typescript' (summer 1934) to Galley 1(III) (June–July 1935) omitted consideration of chapters 2, 3 and 6–9 of what we call the TOC. The main reason for this is that these chapters changed considerably after Galley 1(III).

Here there are some particularly relevant points to be taken into account: (i) As of June–July Keynes had chapter 1 of Galley (2), chapters 2–6 of Galley (3), chapters 7–19 of Galley (2), chapters 20–25 of Galley 1(II) and chapters 26–28 of Galley 1(III) with him as the latest version (all the chapters belong to the TOC); (ii) There exists no galley after Galley 1(III); (iii) We have several sources of information on how Keynes changed in the period between August 1936 and February 1936 (the publication of the *General Theory*).

Therefore, we are forced to reconstruct Keynes's developmental process in the last phase by using item (iii).

What characterises August–October is the fact that Keynes altered chapters 3 and 6–9 considerably (chapter 2 is an exception), which, of course, involved a great deal of rearrangement and brought about a change from the TOC to *GT*'s table of contents. We will call this activity 'The Great Revision': it is dealt with in Section I. Here we will bring the developmental process from 'The General Theory' to the *General Theory* into focus.

For October–December, the relevant material is in the Michaelmas lectures, which will be examined in Section II.

I   'The Great Revision'

Keynes continued to revise the galley even after Galley 1(III), as attested by the following evidence.

In his letter to Harrod (17 August 1935) he wrote: 'Here are the last two chapters of my book. ...But chapter 26 is too long, ... In chapter 27 the emphasis hasn't worked out' (*JMK*. 13, p. 542. The TOC has 28 chapters, while the *General Theory* has 24 chapters).

From Keynes's letter to Robinson (3 September 1935) we learn that he had spent several weeks rewriting Book I (chapters 1–3) and Book II (chapters 4–9). And in his letter to Hawtrey (4 September 1935)[1] he announces: 'I have... completed my re-writing of the first three books, namely chapters 1–11'

(*JMK*. 13, p. 576. The TOC ends Book III with chapter 11, while the *General Theory* ends it with chapter 10). In his letter to Harrod (10 September 1935), we read: 'I shall be here from September 22 . . . up to the end of the month. . . . by then I shall have finished re-writing the chapters dealing with rate of interest' (*JMK*.13, p. 559). This might be chapters 15 and 16; it bears fruit in *GT*, chapter 14, 'The Classical Theory of the Rate of Interest'.

We know, moreover, from Hawtrey's detailed comments, and Keynes's response (1 October), that Keynes had also embarked on rewriting chapters 15 and 16 of Book IV (which has chapters 12–19).

On 10 October Keynes sent a letter to Robertson saying: 'I am now practically finished, and am sending my galleys to the printers to be paged' (*JMK*.13, pp. 523–524). This means that Keynes had drawn up the table of contents of the *General Theory*.

All these activities come within what we call 'The Great Revision'. In these activities Keynes carried out his rewriting (among others, chapters 2–3, 6–10, 15 and 16) along the TOC, but his activity soon accompanied the decomposition and realignment of the chapters concerned, which means that the product of 'The Great Revision' is virtually the text of the *General Theory*.

Due to the paucity of our sources, however, we do not even know when precisely Keynes compiled the table of contents of the *General Theory*. He revised the chapters concerned so greatly that he might have felt the need to rearrange them and draw up a new table of contents.

It might have been in September–October that Keynes rearranged the whole galley in line with the table of contents of the *General Theory*. What remains as a fact is that Hawtrey, in his letter to Keynes dated 19 December 1935, made comments on the proofs which are based on the table of contents of the *General Theory*, for we find such a passage as 'Own-rates of interest. A renewed study of chapter 17 leads me . . .' (*JMK*.13, p. 625. *GT*'s chapter 17 deals with own-rates of interest while it is chapter 19 of the TOC that does so). Judging from this, we may reasonably suppose that the galley based on the table of contents of the *General Theory* reached Keynes in November.

Let us now examine chapters 6–9 of Book II, 'Definitions and Ideas', and chapters 2–3 of Book I, 'Introduction'.

1   Chapters 6–9

Book II of the TOC consists of chapters 4–9, of which chapters 4 and 5 were finalised in 'The Typescript'.

A   Chapters 6 and 7 – some fundamental concepts

a   REVISIONS TO THE FORMAL STRUCTURE

There are two points worth noting about the revisions – in terms of formal structure – to chapter 6, 'The Meaning of Income', and chapter 7, 'The Definitions of Quasi-Rent, Saving and Investment'.

First, the two chapters are at the completion stage, not only in terms of contents but also at the level of style, as far as the text in the TOC is concerned. Chapter 6,[2] the revised version of chapter 6, 'The Definition of Income', of 'The Typescript', is slightly revised yet further in Galley 2 and Galley 3, and chapter 7[3] is slightly revised in Galley 2.

Second, rewriting these chapters became Keynes's main preoccupation in August.

Chapter 6, consisting of five sections, was revised from Galley 3 to the *General Theory* as follows:

1 Part of section I (*JMK*.14, pp. 401–402) becomes the corresponding passage (pp. 52–53) in *GT*, chapter 6, 'The definition of Income, Saving and Investment', section I, 'Income';
2 Part of Section II (*JMK*.14, pp. 401–402) becomes the corresponding passage (pp. 67–68) in *GT*, appendix to chapter 6, section I;
3 Section III remains unchanged in terms of style, but is restructured to form *GT*, appendix to chapter 6, 'Appendix on User Cost', sections II, III and IV;
4 Sections IV and V do not appear in the *General Theory*. Section IV dealt with the calculation of income in extreme cases, such as that of 'a product prepared long beforehand [which] necessarily yields up its fruits now and is incapable of being stored up for a later date' (*JMK*.14, p. 413), and 'that part of the wastage of any piece of equipment which occurs by the mere passage of time and irrespective of whether it is used or not' (*JMK*.14, p. 414). Section V stressed the need to define income, saving and investment consistently.

Chapter 7, consisting of three sections, is revised from Galley 2 to the *General Theory* as follows:

1 Section I, which deals with quasi-rent, is dropped in the *General Theory*;
2 Some of the arguments in sections II and III dealing with fundamental concepts in relation to long- and short-period expectation as well as the actual result and also in relation to user cost, correspond to *GT*, pp. 60–64, which are almost identical with *GT*, chapter 6, section II, 'Saving and Investment';
3 *GT*, chapter 6, section I, 'Income' (pp. 54–60), in which user cost and supplementary cost are discussed, was largely rewritten at this time.

With respect to the *General Theory* the above changes can be summarised as follows:

1 Keynes wrote *GT*'s chapter 6, taking up the contents of sections II and III of chapter 7 of Galley 2 and those of sections I and II of chapter 6 of Galley 3 and reworking them considerably;
2 Keynes wrote *GT*, appendix to chapter 6, following the contents of section III of chapter 6 of Galley 3.

b   THEORETICAL AND CONCEPTUAL REVISIONS

Chapter 6 (Galley 3) and chapter 7 (Galley 2) contain the core discussion, in terms of the TOC, of the definitions of fundamental concepts such as income, investment and saving. These chapters are closely related to *GT*'s chapter 6, which contains the core of the argument concerning fundamental concepts.

Let us see how Keynes changed the definitions of such fundamental concepts in order to arrive at the final form. This task can be opportunely addressed by comparing 'The Typescript' with the manuscripts written before and after it, as well as comparing Galley 1(I) with *GT*'s chapter 6.

c   'THE TYPESCRIPT' AND THE IMMEDIATELY PRECEDING AND
    SUCCESSIVE MANUSCRIPTS

The definitions of fundamental concepts adopted in the *General Theory* can be traced back to those in 'The General Theory'. Let us look at how Keynes changed the definitions as he proceeded from 'The General Theory', through 'The Typescript', to Galley 3.

The most important characteristics these manuscripts have in common are as follows:

1   Income is defined as the realised value of, and effective demand as the expected value of the sale proceeds;
2   Income differs from effective demand, even if the difference between the realised value and the expected value of the sale proceeds is disregarded.

'The General Theory' (1934) – We have already seen the formulations in Chapter 10, Section I. Income (Y) is defined as larger than effective demand (D) by the amount of windfall profit (F), while effective demand is defined as the sum total of the quasi-rent (Q, meaning normal profit) and the prime cost (E).

These formulations are peculiar to 'The General Theory'; in particular, the definition of windfall profit (excess profit) makes no further appearance subsequently.

The relation between investment I, saving S and consumption C is also peculiar[4] to 'The General Theory'. Effective demand is composed of consumption and investment. Income is equal to consumption and saving. By using the definition of windfall profit we can obtain

$$F = S - I \tag{1}$$

As from the PME manuscript Keynes stood by the notion of investment–saving equilibrium. Equation (1), however, appears as a consequence of his argument, though he does not state it explicitly in 'The General Theory'.

Keynes stresses that investment and saving should be construed as 'gross' concepts. Gross investment is defined as inclusive of new investment, replacements, and repairs, while gross saving is defined as inclusive of sinking funds.[5]

'*The Summer Manuscript*' – In Chapter 10, Section II, we have already seen the formulations (the notation follows 'The General Theory', except where indicated). The most significant differences between 'The Summer Manuscript' and 'The General Theory' in the definitions are that in 'The Summer Manuscript':

1   windfall profit disappears;
2   user cost, U_s, is considered to be the difference between effective demand and income;
3   income equals the sum of consumption and investment.

Keynes defines the difference between effective demand (D) and the prime cost (E) as the return to the entrepreneurs, Q_{s1}. The income of the entrepreneurs Q_{s2}, defined as the difference between Q_{s1} and U_s corresponds to quasi-rent in 'The General Theory'. (Subscript 's' indicates 'The Summer Manuscript'.)

In 'The Summer Manuscript' the fundamental concepts are defined in nearly the same way as in Galley 1(I). In both cases Keynes treats those concepts that include user cost as 'gross' concepts, and stresses that effective demand can be defined as a gross concept. It is hard to tell exactly how Keynes defines user cost. However, given the reference Keynes makes here to 'the user cost of the initial stock of capital goods' (*JMK*.13, p. 472), and, moreover, given the fact that he explicitly adopts user cost in the definition of investment although it makes no appearance in 'The General Theory', we can safely say that this is a new concept.[6]

'*The Typescript*' – Keynes deals with the definitions of fundamental concepts in chapter 6, 'The Definition of Income'. The title does not appear in the table of contents of 'The General Theory'. This chapter corresponds to chapter 6, 'The Meaning of Income', in the TOCs from Galley 1(I) to Galley 3. That is, after some revision, this chapter becomes chapter 6 of Galley 1(I)[7]. Unfortunately the parts in 'The Typescript' which correspond to chapter 7, 'The Definitions of Quasi-Rent, Saving and Investment' of Galley 1(I), in which the interrelation between the concepts concerned are discussed, are not extant. However, on the basis of material reproduced in *JMK*.14, pp. 398–418, we may express the interrelation as conceived in 'The Typescript', as follows:[8]

$$Y = A - U_p \qquad (2)$$

$$U_p = S_p - E \qquad (3)$$

$$Q_{p1} = A - E \qquad (4)$$

$$Q_{p2} = Q_{p1} - U_p \qquad (5)$$

where A is gross sales proceeds, U_p user cost, S_p the supply price, E the prime cost, Q_{p1} quasi-rent, and Q_{p2} net quasi-rent. Subscript 'p' indicates 'The Typescript'. (Note: In 'The Typescript' the argument is not couched in symbols. For the sake of convenience we use them.)

As in Galley 1(I), we might assume that the firm is completely integrated. It should also be noted that 'the cost spent on the maintenance and improvement of the initial capital equipment', B, which is important in the Galley 1(I), is yet to appear.

Since the definitions of fundamental concepts in 'The Summer Manuscript' are for the most part closely carried over to Galley 1(I), and since 'The Typescript' was written in between, we can safely say that the definitions in 'The Typescript' for the most part closely reflect 'The Summer Manuscript'. (One exception is equation (3), which defines user cost. This makes no appearance in 'The Summer Manuscript'). In that case, equation (2) becomes the same as equation $D = Y + U_s$, provided the definition of user cost is the same in 'The Typescript' and Galley 1(I). Then, gross sales proceeds, A, becomes equal to effective demand, D, and the equivalence $Q_{p1} = Q_{s1}$ is obtained from equations (4) and equation $Q_{s1} = D - E$. Moreover, $Q_{p2} = Q_{s2}$ is obtained from equations (5) and equation $Q_{s2} = Q_{s1} - U_s$.

In 'The Typescript', the term 'user cost' is defined as 'the loss in the prospective value of a plant due to using it as compared with not using it',[9] so we can conclude that the definition of user cost is established in 'The Typescript'. The supply price, S_p, is defined as 'the lowest price which the owner of the equipment will accept for its output rather than lay it up'.[10] By transforming equation (3) into the following, we find that the supply price is, by definition, the sum total of the user cost and the prime cost:

$$S_p = U_p + E \qquad (6)$$

In Galley 1(I) and the *General Theory*, for Keynes's definitions of fundamental concepts, we need to attend to how the concept of 'user cost' is defined.

In chapter 6, there is no difference in content between Galley 1(I) and Galley 3. In chapter 7, the same is true with respect to Galley 1(I) and Galley 2. We will examine chapter 6 of Galley 3 and chapter 7 of Galley 2 below. It should cause no confusion even if we term them collectively as Galley 1(I).

Let us begin with the differences in fundamental assumptions between Galley 1(I) and the *General Theory*:

1   In Galley 1(I) firms are fully integrated, but not in the *General Theory*;[11]
2   In Galley 1(I), but not in the *General Theory*, Keynes uses 'B' to denote the cost of the maintenance and improvement of the initial capital equipment. As we shall see, this is a vital point which determines the differences in the definitions of some fundamental concepts.

With respect to (1), the *General Theory* denotes a certain sum paid on purchasing finished output from other entrepreneurs by A_1. In Galley 1(I), therefore, $A_1 = 0$ (for the sake of comparison we will assume that $A_1 = 0$ below).

The notation in the *General Theory* is as follows:

A: the sale proceeds of finished output either to consumers or to other entrepreneurs. Assuming $A_1 = 0$, A equals the value of consumption.

G: the actual value of capital equipment at the end of the period. In Galley 1(I) this is denoted by C.

G': the greatest value of capital equipment at the end of the period which would have been maintained had it not been used for production. In Galley 1(I) this is denoted by C'.

B': the cost which must be incurred to maintain the value of capital equipment at G'.

User cost – This is the opportunity cost of capital equipment which current production requires. We will denote the user cost in Galley 1(I) by U_1 and that in the *General Theory* with U_2. Thus

$$U_1 = (C' - B') - (C - B) \tag{7}$$

$$U_2 = (G' - B') - (G - A_1) \tag{8}$$

where B denotes the cost of the maintenance and improvement of the initial capital equipment.

With $A_1 = 0$, equation (7) becomes

$$U_1 = (G' - B') - (G - B) \tag{9}$$

Equation (8) becomes

$$U_2 = (G' - B') - G \tag{10}$$

The difference lies in B. The expenditure on capital equipment installed in the current period accounts for most of B, so that $G - B$ is the value of capital equipment which contributed to current production at the end of the period. We now know that U_1 is the opportunity cost of the capital equipment which contributed to the current production. On the other hand, U_2 is defined in such a way that the expenditure on capital equipment installed in the current period is deducted from it. Therefore, it is inappropriate for the definition of user cost. (The definition of user cost in Galley 1(I) seems to be more appropriate than that in the *General Theory*.)

From equations (9) and (10) we obtain

$$U_2 = U_1 - B \tag{11}$$

If U_1 is a more appropriate conception of user cost than U_2, then Keynes makes an extra deduction of B from U_1.

Income – Income as conceived in Galley 1(I), which is denoted by Y_1, is defined by

$$Y_1 = A + B - U_1 \tag{12}$$

Income as conceived in the *General Theory* is defined by the following equation, if we denote it with Y_2:

$$Y_2 = A - U_2 \tag{13}$$

By making use of equation (11), we obtain

$$Y_1 - Y_2 = B - U_1 + U_2 = 0$$

Thus Y_1 equals Y_2.

Consumption, investment and saving – Consumption is equal to A in the system with $A_1 = 0$. Saving is defined as the excess of income over consumption in both the integrated and non-integrated cases. The definitions of consumption and income are the same in both cases, so that the definition of saving is also the same.

In the definition of investment, however, there is some difference between the two. Let us denote the conception of investment in Galley 1(I) I with I_1, and that in the *General Theory* with I_2. Then we have

$$I_1 = Y - A + U_1 \tag{14}$$
$$I_2 = Y - A \tag{15}$$

From these we obtain

$$I_1 = I_2 + U_1 \tag{16}$$

Thus I_1 is larger than I_2 by U_1. By making use of equation (12), equation (14) becomes:

$$I_1 = B \tag{17}$$

That is, the cost of maintenance and improvement of the initial capital equipment equals investment Galley 1(I). Keynes refers to the difference between I_1 and U_1 as 'net investment'. Let us denote this with I_{1n}. Then

$$I_{1n} = I_1 - U_1 \tag{18}$$

From equations (9), (17) and (18) we obtain

$$I_{1n} = G - (G' - B') \tag{19}$$

This is the definition of investment in the *General Theory* (see *GT*, p. 55). On the one hand, in Galley 1(I) 'gross' ('net') concepts are defined as inclusive (exclusive) of user cost, U_1, while on the other hand, in the *General Theory*, 'gross' ('net') concepts are defined as inclusive (exclusive) of the supplementary cost, V

(which is defined as the 'depreciation of the equipment which is involuntary but not unexpected' (*GT*, p. 56)). Thus net investment, I_{1n}, in Galley 1(I) corresponds to gross investment in the *General Theory*, while net investment in the *General Theory* can be expressed as $I_{1n} - V$.

The factors of production – In Galley 1(I) the prime cost, which we denote with E_1, is composed of the amount spent on finished goods (the main constituent of which is labour-cost[12]), and B (the main constituent of which is the labour-cost required for production of investment goods within firms).[13] Thus the prime cost equals the amount of money which the fully integrated firm pays for both the investment goods which are produced and retained within the firm and the finished output. It does not contain U_1 and equals the factor cost, F, of the *General Theory*:

$$E_1 = F \tag{20}$$

In the *General Theory*, prime cost, which we will denote with E_2, is defined as the sum of the factor cost and the user cost:[14]

$$E_2 = F + U_2 \tag{21}$$

The profit of entrepreneurs, as understood in Galley 1(I), which we will denote as P_1, equals the income of entrepreneurs as understood in the *General Theory*, which we will denote as P_2. This can be shown as follows. P_1 and P_2 are respectively defined by

$$P_1 = A + B - U_1 - E_1 \tag{22}$$

$$P_2 = A - E_2 \tag{23}$$

From these we obtain:

$$P_1 - P_2 = B - U_1 - E_1 + E_2 \tag{24}$$

If we make use of the equation $B - U_1 = -U_2$ (derived from equation (11)), as well as equations (20) and (21), then equation (24) gives us:

$$P_1 - P_2 = -U_2 - F + (F + U_2) = 0 \tag{25}$$

The concept of 'quasi-rent' in Galley 1(I) is dropped in the *General Theory*. In Galley 1(I) Keynes distinguishes three kinds of time elements in variables: the actual value, short-period expectation and long-period expectation. He uses (') to indicate the short-period expectation, and (") the long-period expectation.

In the case of quasi-rent, its actual value is called 'profit', while its long-period expectation is termed 'prospective yields'. The term 'quasi-rent' is retained for its short-period expectation, and is formulated as

$$Q = P' + U_1' \tag{26}$$

where Q denotes 'quasi-rent'.

Effective demand – The definition of 'effective demand' in the *General Theory* differs from that in Galley 1(I), though the definition of 'income' is the same. In Galley 1(I) effective demand includes user cost, U_1, but in the *General Theory* it does not include user cost, U_2. If we denote effective demand in Galley 1(I) with D_1 and that in the *General Theory* with D_2, then we have:

$$D_1 = Y' + U_1'$$ (27)

$$D_2 = Y'$$ (28)

where Y denotes income.

In Galley 1(I) Keynes explains the concept of effective demand as follows:

> ... in contradistinction to income, effective demand is reckoned gross of user cost, so that $D = Y' + U'$. It is essential to reckon effective demand gross, since it is the gross value of output which absorbs spending power.
>
> (*JMK*.14, p. 422)

In the *General Theory* effective demand is defined as the 'aggregate income which the entrepreneurs expect to receive, inclusive of the incomes which they will hand on to the other factors of production' (*GT*, p. 55).

From equations (27) and (28) we obtain

$$D_1 = D_2 + U_1'$$ (29)

In Galley 1(I) Keynes argues that effective demand is important because it contains user cost, and distinguishes the concepts inclusive of user cost (such as quasi-rent and gross investment) from those exclusive of it (such as income, profit and saving). In the *General Theory* he defines effective demand, investment, income, profit and saving as exclusive of user cost, and does not use quasi-rent. This suggests that the role of user cost recedes somewhat in the *General Theory*.

B   *Chapters 8 and 9*

Chapter 8, 'The Meaning of Saving', of Galley 1(I) corresponds to *GT*, chapter 7, 'The Meaning of Saving and Investment, Further Considered'. Chapter 9, 'The Meaning of Investment', of Galley 1(I) corresponds to *GT*, chapter 8, 'The Propensity to Consume: I. The Objective Factors'. Overall, there is less change in the proofing here than in the case of chapters 6 and 7.

a   CHAPTER 8

This chapter is extant in Galley 1(I) form and in Galley 2 form. Each version consists of three sections. Section II of Galley 1(I) version, which criticises Hayek's theory of forced saving, derives directly from section VI of chapter 8, 'Investment and Saving', of 'The Summer Manuscript'. In Galley 2 Keynes adds to this only a supplementary explanation to the effect that net investment necessarily equals saving, and that the theory of forced saving is an inappropriate application of Bentham's theory to the state of underemployment. In Galley 2 Keynes rewrites his account of how a change in the quantity of money brings about a change in saving through a change in distribution,[15] but the content of the theory is unaltered.

In terms of formal arrangement, the transformation from chapter 8 of Galley 2 to *GT*'s chapter 7, which has five sections, is considerable. In the *General Theory* Keynes adds section I (which states that the difference in terminology lies in the difference in the definitions of investment and income) and section II (in which he defines investment, and criticises Hawtrey's definition of investment as exclusive of liquid capital, as well as the Austrian School's idea of capital formation and capital consumption).

GT, chapter 7, section III corresponds to parts of section I of chapter 8 of Galley 2.[16] There is no difference in content between the two. *GT*, chapter 7, section IV is virtually the same as section II of Galley 2. On the other hand, *GT*, chapter 7, section V was compiled out of several parts of chapter 8 of Galley 2 (*JMK*.14, pp. 428–429, 432–433 and 434–436), plus some new passages (*GT*, pp. 82–83) which discuss the relation between the granting of bank credit and the theory of investment–saving equilibrium.

b   CHAPTER 9

In chapter 9, 'The Meaning of Investment', Keynes argues that 'financial provision', by functioning as saving, decreases net investment and causes stagnation. This argument is already complete in both contents and even form in section IV of chapter 8, 'Investment and Saving', of 'The General Theory'.

Chapter 9 survives in Galley 1(I) and Galley 2. The only difference lies in the point that in Galley 2 Keynes adds Kuznets' data of gross capital formation in the United States. This is an addition to discussion of Clark's study in the United Kingdom in Galley 1(I). Chapter 9 of Galley 2 is incorporated into *GT*'s chapter 8, section IV.

2   *The introductory chapters*

The three chapters of Book I, 'Introduction', are chapter 1, 'The General Theory', chapter 2, 'The Postulates of the Classical Economics' and chapter 3, 'The Principle of Effective Demand'. (They are reproduced in *JMK*.14, pp. 351–352, 352–359 and 359–379 respectively.) Chapter 1 is almost identical to *GT*'s chapter 1.

A   *Chapter 2*

Chapter 2 exists in the galleys from Galley 1(I) to Galley 3. Apart from a few slight changes of expression, there is no difference between them. In 'The Great Revision', moreover, there is no change in substance, although there are some stylistic changes.

GT's chapter 2 has seven sections. In sections I and II, Keynes adds 'a decrease in the marginal disutility of labour' to the list of the means of increasing employment available to classical economics (*GT*, p. 7). Apart from this, we see some minor revisions of style and wording.

In section III Keynes states that the struggle over money-wages does not determine the level of real wages. The section is the same in content as the corresponding part (*JMK*.14, pp. 363–365) of Galley 1(I), albeit with some stylistic changes.

Section IV, which deals with involuntary unemployment, is the same in content as the corresponding parts (*JMK*.14, pp. 366–369) of Galley 1(I) although, again, there are some stylistic changes. The only real difference is that in Galley 1(I) Keynes discusses involuntary unemployment from the point of view of the supply side of labour only, while in the *General Theory* he also discusses it from the point of view of the demand side for labour. The argument in section V of the *General Theory*, which discusses the implications of accepting the first postulate and rejecting the second, was formerly included in section IV of Galley 1(I).

The argument in section VI, in which Keynes states that Say's Law underlies the entire classical theory, formerly 'appeared in an abbreviated form' (*JMK*.14, p. 368) as Section I of Chapter 3 Galley 1(I). In the *General Theory* Keynes adds a quotation from Mill to illustrate the classical economists' belief in Say's Law.

Section VII refers to three assumptions, namely

1   The real wage equals the marginal disutility of the existing employment;
2   There exists no involuntary unemployment; and
3   Say's Law, on which the classical theory depends, was newly written for the *General Theory*. It is absent from Galley 1(I).

B   Chapter 3 – employment function

The galleys from Galley 1(I) to Galley 3 for chapter 3 are extant, and share an important passage (*JMK*.14, pp. 370–371), which can be formulated as follows (this formulation is the same as that in the second of his 1934 Michaelmas lectures):

$$D = f(N) \tag{30}$$

$$D' = F(N) \tag{31}$$

$$D = D' \tag{32}$$

where D denotes effective demand, $F(\cdot)$ the state of effective demand, D' the supply price, and $F(\cdot)$ the employment function.

The level of employment is determined by these equations. This formulation is basically the same as in the *General Theory*, except for the terminology. In the *General Theory* equation (30) is called the 'aggregate demand function', equation (31) the 'aggregate supply function', D the 'aggregate demand price', D' the 'aggregate supply price', and the value of D at the level of employment determined by equation (32) 'effective demand'.

Let us compare this formulation with the formulations in 'The General Theory', 'The Summer Manuscript', and 'The Typescript'. As we have seen, the employment function in the three manuscripts was used not only as a supply concept but also as an equilibrium concept. This duality is absent from chapter 3 (*JMK*.14, pp. 369–378) of the galleys from Galley 1(I) up to and including Galley 3, in which the function $D = f(N)$ is treated as representing the demand side, and the function of $D' = F(N)$ as representing the supply side. However, in the *General Theory* the duality reappears, and characterises its theoretical structure.

In the galleys from Galley 1(I) to Galley 3, Keynes argues that income as a realised value differs from effective demand as an expected value by the amount of user cost. As we saw above, effective demand is vital in determining the level of employment because it includes user cost. Moreover, user cost is important for the definitions of concepts such as investment, saving and profit. In equations (30) to (32), D and D' include user cost.

When we say that equations (30) to (32) are the formulation used in the *General Theory* it is with the proviso that in the *General Theory* the definitions of effective demand, investment, income, profit and saving have been changed in such a way that user cost is not included. In the *General Theory* Keynes explains the reason for this change as follows: 'since user cost is obviously dependent both on the degree of integration of industry and on the extent to which entrepreneurs buy from one another, there can be no definition of the aggregate sums paid by purchasers, inclusive of user cost, which is independent of these factors' (*GT*, p. 24, fn. 2).

II   The 1935 Michaelmas lectures

After 'The Great Revision' how did Keynes proceed to work on producing the *General Theory*? Did he make no further changes, or did he, rather, make certain substantial changes? We must now address these questions. The lecture notes taken by Lorie Tarshis in the Michaelmas Term of 1935 (14 October– 2 December) are the only material for this.[17]

The lectures were not delivered exactly in accordance with the final text of the *General Theory*, which indicates that Keynes rewrote the galleys during and even after the lectures.

In the Michaelmas lectures of 1935 the theory of employment is formulated in terms of the aggregate supply and the aggregate demand functions (the time span here is confined to the short period in which capital equipment and the technology of production are given).

$$Z = \psi(N) \tag{1}$$
$$D = f(N) \tag{2}$$
$$\psi(N) = f(N) \tag{3}$$

Equation (1) is the aggregate supply function. This relates the volume of employment to the sale proceeds, the expectations of which induce entrepreneurs to employ the corresponding volume of employment (Z is the cost of production of the volume of output of N men).

Equation (2) is the aggregate demand function. This relates the aggregate demand entrepreneurs expect to encounter for their output to the number of men they employ. The volume of employment is determined at the intersection between the two functions.

The aggregate demand, D, is composed of the demand for consumption, D_1, and that for investment, D_2. When employment increases, both aggregate real income and aggregate consumption increase, but the latter does not increase as greatly as the former. This is expressed by the function $D_1 = X(N)$. Demand for investment is expressed by the function $I = D_2 = F(N)$. It follows that $\psi(N) - X(N) = I$, so that N depends on ψ, X and D_2.

The theory of investment here has two characteristics:

1   The discussion of the marginal efficiency of capital here is not so close to the treatment in the *General Theory* as was the discussion of it in the lectures of 1934.
2   With regard to the theory of liquidity preference, in the sixth lecture (18 November) the precautionary motive is dependent on the rate of interest, while in the seventh (25 November) it is made to depend on income.

Besides these, the following points also deserve mention:

1   The objective factors make their first appearance so far as the lectures are concerned. However, the list here differs somewhat from that in the *General Theory*. The salient differences are that in the *General Theory* changes in the wage-unit are added and changes in the rate of interest are replaced by changes in the rate of time-discounting.
2   The qualified items which are listed in the calculation of the multiplier are not always the same as those in the *General Theory*.
3   The discussion of 'the relation between a change in the money wage and effective demand' differs from that in *GT*'s chapter 19 in terms of the order and number of items listed.
4   As the means of curing unemployment in the case where the two classical postulates hold good, 'improvement in organization' is added, though 'improvement in foresight' is not still mentioned.
5   The definitions of various concepts, including user cost, attain the final forms found in the *General Theory*.
6   Keynes invokes a number of problems for the quantity theory of money which remain insoluble even if many conditions necessary to make the theory hold good are added. The problems mentioned are virtually the same as those discussed in the *General Theory*.

In his letter to Macmillan (9 January 1936) Keynes writes: 'I now have the exact sise of the book for the leaflet, namely, xii plus 403'.[18]

After 19 January or thereabouts, the *General Theory* was out of his hands. It was published on 4 February.

Two tables are given here. One is Table 12.1 which shows how each chapter of the *General Theory* was developed. The other is Table 12.2 from which we can get the whole view of Keynes's Michaelmas lectures in 1932–1935.

Table 12.1 The process of development of the chapters of the *General Theory*

Book	Chapter	The process of development
Book I Introduc- tion	1 The General Theory	· Finalised in Galley1(I) in substance and form.
	2 The Postulates of the Classical Economics	· The idea begins as early as the Second Manuscript of 1933 or the Michaelmas lectures of 1933. · Effectively completed in Galley1(I).
	3 The Principle of Effective Demand	· The idea first occurs as early as the First Manuscript of 1933 or the Michaelmas lectures of 1933. · Various changes up to Galley1(I) or the Michaelmas lectures of 1934 and 1935.
Book II Definitions and Ideas	4 The Choice of Units	· The idea first occurs as early as the Michaelmas lectures of 1933. · Completed in form in 'The Typescript'.
	5 Expectation as Determining Output and Employment	· The idea first occurs as early as the Michaelmas lectures of 1933. · Effectively completed in 'The Typescript'.
	6 The Definition of Income, Saving and Investment	· The idea first occurs as early as the Michaelmas lecture of 1933. · The original form first appears in 'The Typescript'. · Has a corresponding part in Galley1(I). · Undergoes alteration in 'The Great Revision'.
	Appendix on User Cost	· The idea first occurs as early as 'The Summer Manu-script' or the Michaelmas lectures of 1933. · Has a corresponding part in Galley1(I). · Undergoes alteration in 'The Great Revision'.
	7 The Meaning of Saving and Investment Further Considered	· Has a corresponding part in Galley1(I). · Undergoes alteration in 'The Great Revision'.
Book III The Propensity to Consume	8 The Propensity to Consume: I. The Objective Factors	· Has a corresponding part in 'The General Theory'. · Undergoes alteration in 'The Great Revision'.
	9 The Propensity to Consume: II. The Subjective Factors	· Has a corresponding part in 'The General Theory'. · Finalised in substance in 'The General Theory'. · Completed in form in Galley1(I).
	10 The Marginal Propensity to Consume and the Multiplier	· The idea first occurs as early as the Michaelmas lectures of 1933. · Finalised in substance in 'The First Undated Manu-script'. · Finalised in form in Galley1(II).
Book IV The Induce-ment to Invest	11 The Marginal Efficiency of Capital	· The idea first occurs as early as 'The Second Undated Manuscript' or the Michaelmas lectures of 1934. · Completed in substance and form in 'The Typescript'.
	12 The State of Long-Term Expectation	· The idea (volatility and irrationality of expected quasi-rents) first occurs as early as the Michaelmas lectures of 1933. · Completed in substance and form in 'The Pre-First Proof Index Version' (in 'The General Theory').

	13 The Gene Theory of the Rate of Interest	· The idea first occurs as early as the MTP Manuscript. · Finalised in Galley1(I).
	14 The Classic Theory of the Rate of Interest	· The idea first occurs as early as the Michaelmas lectures of 1932. · Finalised in substance in Galley1(I). · Undergoes alteration in 'The Great Revision'.
	Appendix on the Rate of Interest in Marshall's *Principles of Economics*, Ricardo's *Principles of Politcal Economy*, and Elsewhere	· The idea first occurs as early as the Michaelmas lectures of 1932 or the Third Manuscript of 1933. · Undergoes alteration in 'The Great Revision'.
	15 The Psychological and Business Incentives to Liquidity	· The idea first occurs as early as the Michaelmas lectures of 1933. · Finalised in substance in Galley 1(I). · Finalised in form in Galley 2.
	16 Sundry Observations on the Nature of Capital	· Has a corresponding part in 'The Second Undated Manuscript' and 'The Typescript'. · Finalised in substance and form in Galley 1(I).
	17 The Essential Properties of Interest and Money	· Finalised in Galley 2.
	18 The General Theory of Employment Re-Stated	· Has a corresponding part in 'The General Theory' and 'The Summer Manuscript'. · Finalised in substance and form in Galley1(II).
Book V Money Wages and Prices	19 Changes in Money-Wages	· Finalised in substance and form in Galley 1(II).
	Appendix on Prof. Pigou's *Theory of Unemployment*	· The idea first occurs as early as the Michaelmas lectures of 1933.
	20 The Employment Function	· The idea first occurs as early as 'The General Theory'or 'The Summer Manuscript'. · Finalised in substance and form in Galley 1(II).
	21 The Theory of Prices	· Finalised in substance and form in Galley 1(II).
Book VI Short Notes Sugges-ted by the General Theory	22 Notes on the Trade Cycle	· (Probably) finalised in Galley 1(II).
	23 Notes on Mercantilism, the Usury Laws, Stamped Money and Theories of Under-Consumption	· The idea first occurs as early as the Michaelmas lectures of 1932. · Has a corresponding part in the First Galley.
	24 Concluding Notes on the Social Philosophy towards Which the *General Theory* Might Lead	· Has a corresponding part in Galley 1(III).

Table 12.2 Michaelmas lectures: 1932–1935

	1932	1933	1934	1935
Supply side	· Supply function as a function of price	· Acceptance of the first postulate of the classical economics		
Demand side	· State of time preference · Investment defined as a function of the rate of interest and the streams of prospective quasi-rent	· Effective demand = expenditure – income · Fundamental psychological law	· Subjective factors · The marginal efficiency of capital · Investment determined at the point at which the marginal efficiency of capital equals the rate of interest	· Objective factors
Equili-brium	· Simultaneous determination of quantities and prices · Equilibrium of investment and saving (determination of the price level of consumption goods)	· Disbursement = Income · Determination of the level of income (or employment) by means of $Y = C + I$ (or $I = S$)	· The theory of effective demand in which the level of employment is determined at the point where effective demand function intersects the employment function (or supply function)	· Theory of the determination of volume of employment by means of the aggregate supply function and the aggregate demand function
Profit	· Profit = investment – saving or disbursement earnings	· Quasi-rent defined as the inducement in terms of short-period expectations	· Quasi-rent defined as the realised returns	
Money market	· A basic skeleton of the theory of liquidity preference theory: $\rho = A(M)$	· Analysis of motives for liquidity prefer-ence (income, business, and precautionary motives – business cycle, overdraft facilities and the rate of interest: speculative motive – the state of bearishness)	· Analysis of motives for liquidity prefer-ence: transaction motive–current operations; a store-of wealth motive – the rate of interest	· Analysis of motive for liqui-dity preference · Sixth lecture: transaction motive – (in the short run) the volume of busi-ness and prices, (in the long run) changes in bank-ing habits; pre-cautionary and speculative motives – the rate of interest · Seventh lecture: the same as the *General Theory*
Others	· Simultaneous Equations system ('Model 1' of the astronomical structure)	· Rejection of the second postulate of the classical economics · Choice of units– in terms of money and employment · Short-period and long-period expectations · The multiplier	· User cost · Four perplexities	· User cost · Supplementary cost · First appear-ance of material corresponding to chapters 16, 17,19 and 21 of the *General Theory*

III   Conclusion

In Chapters 11 and 12 we set ourselves two main objectives: (i) to show how Keynes carried out the proofing process, and (ii) to separate out its main features.
Concerning (i) the following points emerge from our analysis:

1   Galley 1(I) represents the most considerable revision work carried out on the topics covered in the TOC. Galley 2 and Galley 3 represent stylistic revisions of Galley 1(I).
2   Galley 1(I) is composed of chapters 1–19.[19] The chapters except for chapters 4, 5, 12 and 13 were completed in Galley 1(I) both in contents and at the stylistic level, as far as the TOC is concerned.
3   The largest change after Galley 1(III) occurred in 'The Great Revision'. The definitions of some fundamental concepts changed due to both the change in the definition of 'user cost' and a change in its treatment.
4   In the Michaelmas lectures (18 November) the precautionary motive is dependent on the rate of interest.

In the case of (ii) our main concern was: What kind of significance do changes or struggles detected in the latter half stage hold for our understanding of Keynes's theory?
Here there are two major changes to point out, one concerning the 'employment function', the other having to do with fundamental concepts.

Employment function – In 'The General Theory', 'The Summer Manuscript' and 'The Typescript', the employment function was used as both a supply concept and an equilibrium one. This duality disappears in Galley 1(I) up to and including Galley 3. However, in the General Theory it reappears, and overshadows its theoretical structure.

Some fundamental concepts – We can summarise the relation between the definitions of fundamental concepts in Galley 1(I) and in the *General Theory* as follows:

1   The difference in effective demand, investment and prime cost in definition depends on whether they include user cost (Galley 1(I)) or not (the *General Theory*);
2   The definitions of income, profit and saving are the same;
3   The equation $U_2 = U_1 - B$ is vital to the relation.

13 The *General Theory*

The monetary economics of underemployment equilibrium

We have now finished tracing Keynes's theoretical development from the *Tract* to the *General Theory*. We have examined not only the important documents per se at each stage, but also them in relation to both the preceding and succeeding stages. We have yet, however, to consider the *General Theory* itself. It is to this task that we now turn.

We proceed as follows. In Section I we consider Keynes's critique and defence of the economics developed up to his own time. Then in Section II we shall present our analysis of the *General Theory* characterised as the Monetary Economics of Underemployment Equilibrium. In Section III we shall examine the essentials of the Keynesian Revolution, touching on the relation between the *Treatise* and the *General Theory*.

I Views on earlier economists

How does Keynes as the author of the *General Theory* understand, critically or otherwise, the science of economics as it had developed up to his own time?

1 Criticism

Let us begin with Keynes's criticism, which is levelled at two schools – the 'classical' and the 'neoclassical', to use the terms of his peculiar designations. By the 'classical school' Keynes means Ricardo and his followers, including J.S. Mill, Marshall, Edgeworth and Pigou, while the latter embraces a group of economists we referred to as 'Wicksell's influences' (see *GT*, pp. 177, 183, and Chapter 2 of the present book), the most influential stream of economics in the interwar period.

A Classical economics

Keynes criticises classical economics[1] on two points – (i) classical dichotomy; (ii) the theory of interest rate.

Point (i) appears in *GT*, pp. 292–293, where Keynes criticises classical economics as putting forward two price theories (a microeconomic theory and the quantity theory), while making no attempt to connect them.[2] He insists that the determination of prices should be incorporated into an employment theory as monetary economics.

Keynes's dissatisfaction has two consequences, one being his attack on the quantity theory (see chapter 21, section III). He begins by introducing several simplifying assumptions necessary for the quantity theory to hold good, and then argues that in reality the theory of prices must allow for 'possible complications' (*GT*, p. 296).

The other consequence is an attack on the classical school's employment theory (see chapter 2 and chapter 19, section I), which is in fact more significant than his criticism of the quantity theory. He criticises it because it assumes full employment or Say's Law. The unemployment dealt with in classical theory is confined to the 'frictional' and 'voluntary' varieties, but what really matters is 'involuntary unemployment'.

The classical theory, according to Keynes, proposes that the volume of employment is determined by the first (the demand schedule for employment) and second postulates (the supply schedule) of the classical economics (see *GT*, p. 6).

Keynes criticises this view, rejecting the second postulate for two reasons. One regards the actual behaviour of labourers. Even if prices rise, he says, workers will not withdraw their offers to work so long as money wages remain unaltered. The other reason is that the classical school, he argues, wrongly holds that if money wages are reduced, a reduction in real wages will follow. Keynes disputes this, arguing that classical economics erroneously applies the argument concerning an individual industry to industry as a whole (see *GT*, p. 259).

An important point we must bear in mind here is that Keynes contends that real wages are determined by certain other forces, and his criticism here comes from his stance stressing the interdependence within the economic system, as his criticism of the quantity theory does.

Point (ii) is presented mainly in chapter 14[3] and its appendix, where his criticism of the classical theory is fourfold, for: (i) it overlooks the fact that a change in the level of investment changes income; (ii) it overlooks the simultaneous determination of income and the rate of interest (see *GT*, pp. 183–184); (iii) it falls into a kind of 'dichotomy', meaning by this that it uses two theories of interest – one [$I = S$] in the theory of value, one [an increase in M reduces i] in the theory of money (which does not mean the quantity theory) – without any bridge between the two (see *GT*, pp. 182–183); (iv) it is not monetary economics equipped with dealing with the rate of interest (see *GT*, pp. 189–190).

B   *Wicksell's influences*

Let us turn to Keynes's criticism of 'Neoclassical Economics' (or Wicksell's influences).

Different from the *Treatise*, Wicksell's influences are seen as having strayed along the wrong track.[4] This is seen most explicitly in chapter 7, the main theme of which is that the idea of a divergence between saving and investment is fundamentally erroneous, owing to neglect of the fact that transactions are always two-sided. Keynes repeatedly stresses the need to allow for the interdependent manner in which the economy as a whole works, and argues that saving must necessarily equal investment (see *GT*, pp. 84–85).

In this connection Keynes criticises two related ideas: (i) the idea that credit creation by the banking system makes investment possible without any corresponding saving (again the 'interdependence' is stressed); (ii) the theory of forced saving (this will, after all, be defined on full-employment. Note that Keynes had criticised it in the *Treatise*).

Keynes further criticises Wicksell's 'natural rate of interest' concept, denying its value (see *GT*, p. 243) and doubts the value of the 'general price level' concept per se, arguing that it is unnecessary for his theoretical analysis (see *GT*, p. 39).

The above considerations demonstrate that Wicksell's three conditions of monetary equilibrium which Keynes recognised in the *Treatise* are completely rejected in the *General Theory*.

Moreover, he is critical even of the idea of taking a cumulative view of the economy, favouring an understanding of the economy along interactive lines.

Let us now turn to two views shared by other Wicksellians, but which came in for criticism from Keynes from the *Treatise* on. The first is the theory of roundabout production (see chapter 16, section II). His dissatisfaction is closely related to his rejection of the concept of capital adopted in this theory. His own theory of capital is the 'scarcity theory' (see *GT*, pp. 213, 215). The second view he rejects is the theory of interest adopted by Mises and Hayek, in which the rate of interest is defined as the relative price level of consumption to capital goods. He argues that it confounds 'the marginal efficiency of capital with the rate of interest' (*GT*, p. 193).

It should be noted that Keynes treats the *Treatise* tolerantly in comparison with the works of the other Wicksellians, for he tends to regard the relationship between the *Treatise* and the *General Theory* as continuous to a degree that we cannot accept. This is particularly true of his discussion of the idea of equality of saving and investment (see *GT*, p. 77) and his claim of effective demand in the *Treatise* (see *GT*, p. 78).

All this might have something to do with the fact that Keynes was so intent on wrenching himself away from Wicksell's influences.[5]

2   *Defence*

Keynes defends certain preceding theories then condemned as heretical by the orthodox economists, finding in them anticipations of some ideas of the *General Theory*. The relevant discussion is to be found mostly in chapter 23.

In sections I–VI, the major themes are money and the rate of interest as an inducement to investment.

In sections I–V Mercantilism is defended and praised, mainly in the context of his liquidity preference theory. Keynes argues, drawing on Hecksher (1935), that the Mercantilists knew the liquidity-preference theory (see *GT*, pp. 341–344), distinguished the rate of interest from the marginal efficiency of capital, and regarded 'the scarcity of money as causes of unemployment' (*GT*, p. 346).

In section VI Keynes expressed a very high opinion of Gesell's monetary theory, stating that Gesell distinguished between the rate of interest and the marginal efficiency of capital, and grasped the essence of the rate of interest, but did not work out the notion of liquidity-preference (see *GT*, p. 356).

The other clutch of theories supported by Keynes relate to consumption. In section VII, he examines theories which ascribe weakness in the economy to under-consumption, making reference to the works of Mandeville,[6] Malthus, and (Mummery and) Hobson[7] (we saw Keynes's view of Malthusian theory in Section IV of Chapter 7 of the present book).

II   The monetary economics of underemployment equilibrium

In this section we examine the theoretical structure of the *General Theory*, which can be characterised as the monetary economics of underemployment equilibrium. First, we shall delineate the central themes, and then bring the theoretical model into focus.

1   *The central themes*

There are three central themes we can identify as running through the *General Theory*: (i) contrasting potentialities; (ii) monetary economics; (iii) underemployment equilibrium; (iv) equilibrium and interrelation.

A   *Contrasting potentialities*

Keynes sees the market economy as possessing two contrasting potentialities:[8] stability, certainty and simplicity; instability, uncertainty and complexity. His fundamental perception of the market economy can be summarised as follows:

> The market society is stable in the sense that it can remain in 'underemployment equilibrium', but if it goes beyond certain constraints, it becomes unstable.

Stability, certainty and simplicity – Keynes argues that the market economy is equipped with several built-in stabilisers, so that it has an inherent tendency to converge to equilibrium. It does not, however, reach an optimum (or full-employment) level, but rather stays at underemployment level. This is a normal state of the market economy if left to itself. He mentions other stabilisers, such as the 'convention' used in connection with the state of long-term expectation, and the 'existence of a variety of opinions about what is uncertain'.

Based on this 'optimistic' vision, he constructs a theoretical model in which the level of employment is determined where the aggregate demand function intersects the aggregate supply function, incorporating the multiplier theory. The model is constructed in a simple and straightforward way, providing the foundations upon which Keynes presents his economic policy proposals for attaining full-employment.[9]

Instability, uncertainty and complexity – At the same time, however, Keynes repeatedly argues that the stability towards which the market economy tends cannot set in unless some conditions are met; failing these, the market economy is doomed to instability. In this respect we are faced with a structure built on fragile foundations, reflecting the uncertainty and complexity to be observed in the market economy.[10]

Keynes argues that the working of the market economy depends on various psychological and expectation factors such as short-term expectations, long-term expectations (the marginal efficiency of capital [the precariousness of the foundations upon which prospective yields are estimated, and that of the 'convention'[11]] and the nature of the stock market [the danger of 'speculation' overwhelming 'enterprise']), liquidity preference, and user cost. He also refers to 'the instability due to the characteristic of human nature that a large proportion of our positive activities depend on spontaneous optimism' (*GT*, p. 161).

The other element making the market economy unstable is its vulnerability to large changes in some exogenous variables. Keynes is concerned, above all, about any large changes in the quantity of money or in money-wages, for they can bring about great changes in expectations. This is why he counsels a modest monetary policy, and not a radical one. Furthermore, he repeatedly argues that the market economy works in a complex and interactive way. Thus he urges that some of the destabilising factors be got rid of, for example, by making the stock market less accessible, introducing government management of investment, and issuing 'stamped money'.

In using his own model to analyse the economy, Keynes repeatedly warns us to remember that what is being contemplated is only a simplification of the real world, and that if the real world were to be depicted with greater veracity it could be done only through the use of an interactive–descriptive method going far beyond the powers of any mathematical technique.

Keynes seems confident that the possibility that the market economy will be undermined through the falling away of the above-mentioned conditions is remote, and that an economy stuck in underemployment equilibrium could be cured with policies such as national capital works programmes and low interest rate policies.

B Monetary economics

Keynes puts forward his theory of underemployment equilibrium as monetary economics, as distinct from the real economics to which 'classical economics' belongs. He argues that the monetary economy in which we live can only be analysed within a framework of monetary economics. Let us look at this from his fundamental idea and the place of money in Keynes's monetary economics.

Keynes's fundamental idea – This is expounded in chapter 21, I, where he presents two new ways of dividing up economics. One is a division 'between the theory of the individual industry or firm and of the rewards and the distribution between different uses of a given quantity of resources on the one hand, and the theory of output and employment as a whole on the other hand' (*GT*, p. 293). The other is a division 'between the theory of stationary equilibrium and the theory of shifting equilibrium – meaning by the latter the theory of a system in which changing views about the future are capable of influencing the present situation' (*GT*, p. 293).

In both cases, the criterion of division hinges on money. Indeed, when dealing with the determination of the level of output and employment as a whole in the real world we must consider the role played by money. This is what Keynes means by monetary economics.

Keynes argues that monetary economics in his sense should remain 'a theory of value and distribution, not a separate "theory of money" ' (*GT*, p. 294).

The place of money – The above considerations show that Keynes's monetary economics aims at analysing an economy in which money plays an essential role. It is not surprising, then, that Keynes allocates a lot of room to discussion of the rate of interest (see chapters 13, 14, 15, 17, 23 and 24).

Apart from his liquidity preference theory, Keynes, in chapter 17,[12] develops a theory of 'own-rates of interest'. This is an account of why the behaviour of money becomes an obstacle to full employment.

Keynes sets this problem in an economy in which there exist many types of capital assets. Because capital assets are used over long periods, they have their own 'spot' and 'future' markets, which produce their 'own-rates of interest', defined as $q - c + l$, where q is the yield, c the carrying cost, and l the liquidity-premium. Keynes then points out an essential difference between money and all the other assets (see *GT*, p. 227), and describes how an economy in which various types of capital assets exist will reach a new state of equilibrium at which they are newly produced (see *GT*, p. 228).

Keynes argues that because the money-rate of interest 'declines most slowly as the stock of assets in general increases', investment in other capital assets cannot help but stop at the level at which their own rates of interest become equal to the money-rate of interest. The money-rate of interest dominates, and is responsible for underemployment equilibrium. This brings out a principle which underlies the liquidity preference theory developed in chapters 13 and 15. Keynes states this principle from viewpoints relating to two properties of money. One is the demand side, which has something to do with 'liquidity trap'. The other is the supply side: both its 'elasticity of production' and its 'elasticity of substitution' are zero, so that the supply of money is fixed. Keynes consistently assumes the exogeneity of the money supply, a move he justifies on the basis of these properties.

C   Underemployment equilibrium[13]

The central message of the *General Theory* is that, left to itself, the market economy will remain in underemployment equilibrium (see *GT*, pp. 249–250). Underemployment equilibrium is characterised by four features: involuntary unemployment, equilibrium, stability, and fluctuation. Let us see what these terms imply.

Involuntary unemployment – Keynes's chief concern is to work out how the volume of employment is determined. In the monetary economy, argues he, the volume of employment usually persists at a level of less than full employment, insisting that the remaining unemployment should be involuntary (see *GT*, p. 15).

Equilibrium[14] – Keynes uses an equilibrium analysis, concentrating on how the economy would reach equilibrium in terms of employment (or output) and prices.

The main elements comprising the theoretical structure of the *General Theory* are argued in terms of equilibrium:

1   The volume of employment is determined where the aggregate demand function intersects the aggregate supply function;
2   The rate of interest is determined where the liquidity preference function intersects the quantity of money;
3   Investment is determined where the schedule of the marginal efficiency of capital is equal to the rate of interest;
4   The investment multiplier shows an equilibrium value of an increased income which results from an increase in investment.

Keynes addresses the relation between these main elements with two considerations in mind. On the one hand there is the need to emphasise the interactions between the elements and the repercussions they have on one another (see *GT*, p. 249, and chapter 21, section IV), while on the other hand there is, at the same time, the need for simplicity (see *GT*, pp. 249, 299).

To be noted here in addition to the above points are his arguments regarding 'a number of positions of long-period equilibrium corresponding to different conceivable interest policies on the part of the monetary authority' (*GT*, p. 191) and the equilibrium between the 'own rates of interest' of different types of assets (see *GT*, p. 227).

Stability – In chapter 18, section III Keynes argues that the market economy is equipped with several built-in stabilisers:

1   The marginal propensity to consume lies between zero and one (*GT*, p. 98);
2   Moderate changes in the prospective yield of capital or in the rate of interest will not cause great changes in the rate of investment (see *GT*, pp. 239, 271, 304, 336);
3   When the level of employment changes, the change in money wages will be modest;
4   Capital has the property that fluctuations tend to reverse the movement of the marginal efficiency of captial.

Fluctuation – To say that the economy is at underemployment equilibrium is not to say that it remains stable over periods of time. Keynes rather insists that the economy is subject to cyclical fluctuations within a modest range.

In chapter 22 he maintains that the trade cycle can be ascribed to cyclical fluctuations in the schedules of the marginal efficiency of capital. He also argues that an explanation of the time-element in the trade cycle can be found in 'the influences which govern the recovery of the marginal efficiency of capital' (*GT*, p. 317).

D   Equilibrium and interrelation

The *General Theory* is described in terms of a sort of general equilibrium analysis and the interrelations between a number of variables. Let us see what is meant by 'general' and 'interrelations'.

Distinguishing given factors, independent variables, and dependent variables, Keynes presents the model in the form of a set of simultaneous equations.

Keynes also takes into account, however, the 'interrelations' between the variables in his system which cannot be expressed in mathematical language, endeavouring to analyse a complicated and very often fragile and delicate set of interrelations which underlie the mathematical model. This concern is evident throughout the book, emerging, in particular, in chapters 21 and 19. Keynes warns the reader against the traps into which mathematical modelling of the economic system can easily fall (see *GT*, pp. 275, 297 and 305). Here again we encounter the co-existence of simplicity and complexity.

2   *The theoretical model*

In chapter 3, section II (esp. *GT*, pp. 27–29) and chapter 18, section II (esp. *GT*, p. 248) the theory of employment (or income) is succinctly stated.[15] In the former Keynes summarises the theory in terms of how an equilibrium volume of employment is determined, in the latter in terms of how a new equilibrium level of income is obtained after some change in the level of investment.[16]

Let us go on to the theoretical model.[17]

A   Assumptions

As 'our ultimate independent variables' (*GT*, p. 246) Keynes chooses the following:

1   the wage-unit (as determined by the bargains between employers and employees);
2   the quantity of money (as determined by the central bank);
3   the three fundamental psychological factors: the propensity to consume, the liquidity preference, and the schedule of the marginal efficiency of capital.

Let us examine variables (1) and (2) among them.

Keynes adopts the wage-unit not merely for convenience, but out of deep considerations.[18] This is made eloquently clear in chapter 4, where he points out that the concepts of national dividend, the stock of real capital, and the general price-level lack precision, and are not required for economic analysis (see *GT*, p. 39), arguing that we should use 'quantities of money-value and quantities of employment' (*GT*, p. 41) in dealing with the theory of employment.

Two implications are derived from this.

First, Keynes's theoretical model is constructed on the basis of the two units – quantities of money-value and quantities of employment. Now, since the wage-unit is, by nature, sticky, Keynes argues, this contributes to the stability of the economic system.

Second, Keynes uses concepts such as the quantity of output as a whole and the general level of prices within restricted contexts. He uses them in three places, all of which relate to the explanation of the quantity theory of money: (i) chapter 15, section IV; (ii) p. 285 (chapter 20); (iii) chapter 21, section VI.

The formulation of the quantity theory is of secondary importance, for his main concern is to criticise it.

Having said that, however, Keynes uses the general price level without confining to 'historical comparison'. This applies mainly to chapter 21, sections II–IV, which will be examined below.

The *General Theory* assumes the exogeneity of the money supply. The reason for this is provided in pp. 230–231. Keynes argues that, due to its low elasticity of production and low elasticity of substitution, money cannot increase other than through the monetary authority. He also stresses that these properties contribute to the stability of the economic system, so that the exogeneity is not a matter merely of theoretical taste, but of fundamental importance (see *GT*, pp. 238–239).

There are two more items that we must examine carefully: prices and the multiplicity of goods.

Prices – Keynes treats prices as endogenous variables which are flexible. His theory of prices, namely, 'the analysis of the relation between changes in the quantity of money and changes in the price-level with a view to determining the elasticity of prices in response to changes in the quantity of money' (*GT*, pp. 296–297), is mainly developed in chapter 21, sections II–IV. Now the question arises: how can Keynes's statement that the general price level is unnecessary when dealing with the level of employment in the economy as a whole be compatible with his argument here?

It can be answered as follows. First, Keynes's main model determining the level of employment is constructed without the concept of the general price level. There he uses only the price of an individual commodity, so that it is prices, and not the general price level, that appear as endogenous variables (though they do not play such crucial roles here as they do in the Walrasian system).

Second, in the argument set out in chapter 21, sections II–IV Keynes is in reality using the general price level. If, however, we look more closely into his argument here, we find that it is, in essence, based on his main model, while the 'general price level' appears only as a vague concept expressing the trend of prices.

The multiplicity of goods – The *General Theory*, right from the start, assumes the existence of many kinds of goods and capital assets. His theory of employment must not be understood as being based on aggregate concepts only. What he intends to accomplish is to construct a model of underemployment equilibrium, making use of the two fundamental units, but not overlooking the heterogeneity of goods.[19]

B   *The theoretical model – an interpretation*

Keynes constructed his employment theory based on his methodology, which suggests that a theory of employment should be expressed in terms of the two fundamental units. This position, declared in chapter 4,[20] is closely connected to Keynes's intention to analyse the economy as a whole, taking into account many kinds of goods and capital assets. His position is substantiated by the fact that he never fails to develop his argument using four kinds of aggregate supply functions (or employment functions), as well as the first postulate of the classical economics.

A great problem here is how Keynes's model ought to have been constructed, once all those factors had been taken into account. Would it have been possible for him to construct the model consistently, retaining all the elements which appear in the *General Theory*? If not, then on what criteria should we drop some of them in order to construct a consistent model, in the sense closest to Keynes's intentions?

Our starting point is that Keynes does not shy away from acknowledging the multifarious mass of goods present in the economy, while declaring his intention to make use of the two fundamental units only. Second, Keynes argues that the market economy is influenced by various expectations – short-term expectations, long-term expectations (marginal efficiency of capital, the nature of the stock market), the liquidity preference due to speculative motives, user cost and so forth – which will influence the public's attitude toward the future.

Starting from these assumptions, we shall explore how Keynes came to build his theory of employment. Addressing this task brings us up aganist a major question: how should we understand and evaluate the relationship between the micro- and macro-structures in the *General Theory*?

At this point it is opportune to set out our view of the commodity market mechanism, advancing our ideas as to how Keynes's model should be reconstructed, and on what points he is ambiguous. Let us go through our main arguments, dividing them into four areas. (The following is a summary of the arguments developed in detail in Hirai (1981).)

The first is concerned with several ambiguous aspects of the *General Theory*. The corrections and clarifications that need to be made are as follows:

(i)   The first postulate of the classical economics should be used only to describe the behaviour of an individual firm in the multiple-goods economy;
(ii) The concept of the 'marginal efficiency of capital'[21] should be taken only as expressing the demand for investment goods;
(iii) The part played by the supply side in the consumption goods sector needs to be made explicit.

Let us explain these points.

Keynes often treats the first postulate as if it could be applied at the aggregate level as well. Although he might argue its legitimacy, this step does not accord with the main thrust of his theory. In the case of the marginal efficiency of capital, in *GT*, p. 136 Keynes seems to derive it from the supply side only, which renders his investment theory ambiguous. As for the consumption theory, Keynes sometimes argues as if it pertained to the demand side only. This is not correct, however, for his true theory is developed in terms of the supply–demand analysis.

The second area concerns our version of the commodity market mechanism. Let us refer to the micro-structure with the above-described ambiguities removed as the 'purified micro-structure'.

> *Proposition 1.* The commodity market mechanism of the *General Theory* can be expressed in terms of the 'purified micro-structure' and the macro-structure expressed as the 'revised IS curve'. The 'purified micro-structure' is composed of the market mechanisms in the investment and consumption goods sectors; the 'revised IS curve' is derived from the former.

The model starts with the fundamental assumptions, after which the market mechanisms in the investment and consumption goods sectors are constructed in the form of the 'purified micro-structure', from which, finally, the 'revised IS curve' is derived.

As our endeavour is to reconstruct the theoretical structure of the *General Theory* from the fundamental assumptions, removing the inconsistencies in the original, our interpretation may be called the 'heterogeneity-expectations approach'.

The third area concerns our understanding of the commodity market mechanism as it stands in the *General Theory*.

> *Proposition 2.* The mechanism of the commodity market actually described in the *General Theory* can be expressed in terms of the 'non-purified micro-structure' and the macro-structure as described in chapter 3. The 'non-purified micro-structure' comprises the market mechanisms of the investment and the consumption goods sectors, while the macro-structure as described in chapter 3 is derived from the 'non-purified micro-structure', provided the distribution of the effective demand among different industries is given.

The model starts with the fundamental assumptions. The market mechanisms in the investment and consumption goods sectors are then constructed in the form of the 'non-purified micro-structure' (the original micro-structure in which the ambiguities remain intact). Finally, from the 'non-purified micro-structure' we derive the theoretical structure as developed in chapter 3, in which the volume of employment is determined where the aggregate supply function intersects the aggregate demand function, assuming that the distribution of the existing quantity of effective demand among various industries is fixed.

Strictly speaking, as we see below, the derivation cannot be achieved, for this assumption cuts off the connection between the micro- and macro-structures – in the *General Theory* the macro-structure is grafted onto the micro-structure in a somewhat cavalier fashion.

Through purification of the micro-structure (this relates to points (ii) and (iii) above), reworking of the analysis of the supply side (this relates to point (i)), and maintenance of the two fundamental assumptions, we can reconstruct the commodity market mechanism without making any arbitrary assumptions (Proposition 1).

The fourth area relates to certain propositions as by-products of Proposition 1.

Proposition 3. The aggregate supply and the aggregate demand functions describe one and the same micro-structure from different angles, so that both are equilibrium concepts.

We have already stated that what should really be derived from the 'purified micro-structure' is the 'revised IS curve'. Through this derivation we can demonstrate Proposition 3.

The next proposition is related to Proposition 3.

Proposition 4. Chapter 3, 'The Principle of Effective Demand', of the *General Theory* provides not so much a supply–demand equilibrium analysis as a 'pseudo-macro system'.

Concerning the consumption theory we have the following proposition.

Proposition 5. There are two, mutually inconsistent, consumption theories in the *General Theory*: The theory based on the heterogeneity-expectations approach and the 'consumption function' theory. What is required in the *General Theory* is the former.

The consumption theory based on the heterogeneity-expectations approach is as follows. The market price, the volume of production, and the volume of employment in an individual consumption goods industry are determined in such a way that the effective demand for the consumption goods, generated through the multiplier process with the income in the investment goods sector as the prime mover, meets a 'sales proceeds function' for that industry, by which is meant the relationship between the volume of employment and the sales proceeds.

The most relevant observations in this respect can be found at *GT*, pp. 115–116, 286 and 122, as well as in Keynes (1937a) and a paper presented to the American Political Economy Club on 6 June 1934 (*JMK*.13, pp. 457–468).

The consumption function theory, on the other hand, contains some flaws:

1   Its argument is intuitive – this is camouflaged with an examination of the 'objective factors' – and differs from the theoretical system based on the fundamental assumptions.

2   The consumption function is argued in a circle. In order to obtain the function, we require the functional relation between the volume of employment and consumption. For that purpose, in turn, we need to presuppose the theoretical relation between the volume of employment and income. And for this, in turn, we need to know how income should be determined (see Hirai (1981, p. 248)).

3   The heterogeneity-expectations approach is able not only to give us the consumption function as an a posteriori concept, but also to incorporate explicitly the heterogeneity of consumption goods into Keynes's system without Keynes's incompleteness – an assumption that the distribution of the amount of effective demand among different industries is fixed.

With regard to Keynes's consumption theory, moreover, two comments are worth making. One is that the consumption theory of the heterogeneity-expectations approach contains a serious flaw, in that it is not based on the behaviour of individual consumers. The other is that Keynes endeavours to connect the two theories of consumption (see *GT*, pp. 90–92).

Proposition 6. Determination of the equilibrium values. The national income and the rate of interest are determined where the 'revised IS curve' intersects the LM curve.

In our view, *GT*'s Chapter 3 should be replaced by this proposition. As we saw above, determination of the volume of employment in terms of the aggregate supply and the aggregate demand functions is impossible. They should be replaced by the 'revised IS curve', which expresses the whole real economy in terms of a functional relationship between the rate of interest and the national income.

In order for the system to be determinate we need another equation expressing a functional relationship between the two variables: that is, the LM curve, which shows the state of equilibrium in the money market.

Let us now turn to the theory of money.

We have already considered how Keynes conceived of the essential properties of money and interest. He assumes the exogeneity of the money supply because its elasticities of production and substitution are zero, and argues that money's own-rate of interest falls most slowly because of the highest liquidity-premium.

From these rather philosophical reflections, Keynes develops, in chapters 13 and 15, his own theory of money – the liquidity preference theory.[22] There the rate of interest is treated as a purely monetary phenomenon, but is argued as influencing the volume of employment and output. The rate of interest is defined as 'the reward for parting with liquidity' for a certain period, in exchange for debts. It is 'a measure of the unwillingness of those who possess money to part with their liquid control over it' (*GT*, p. 167).

Keynes goes on to inquire why the liquidity preference should exist at all. He finds two reasons. One is 'the existence of uncertainty as to the future of the rate of interest' (*GT*, p. 168). The other relates to an organised market for dealing in debts[23] (see *GT*, p. 168), which gives individuals scope to estimate the prospects differently.

Keynes formulates his theory of money as follows:

$$M = M_1 + M_2 = L_1(Y) + L_2(r)$$

where M is the total amount of money, M_1 and M_2 the amount of money held to satisfy, respectively, the transactions and precautionary motives, and the speculative motive, $L_1(\cdot)$ the liquidity preference function due to the transactions and precautionary motives – an increasing function of income Y, $L_2(\cdot)$ the liquidity preference function due to the speculative motive – a decreasing function of the rate of interest r.

There is nothing new in $L_1(Y)$. The essence rests with $L_2(r)$, for it is closely related to the speculative activities of the public. He argues that '[W]hat matters is not the absolute level of r but the degree of its divergence from what is considered a fairly safe level of r' (*GT*, p. 201).

The role of the monetary authority is stressed. On the question of a direct connection between the changes in the quantity of money and those in the rate of interest, Keynes argues that this has something to do with the fact that 'the banking system and the monetary authority are dealers in money and debts and not in assets or consumables' (*GT*, p. 205). The rate of interest is determined through interactive behaviour of the monetary authority and the public in the debts market. Keynes stresses that the degree of success of any monetary policy would depend on psychological and conventional[24] phenomena. Monetary policy should not be changed drastically, for this would run the risk of increasing the volatility of the economic system through the collapse of public confidence. Thus the monetary policy Keynes recommends is very modest.[25]

The rate of interest here is not short-term but long-term. In contrast with the view taken in the *Treatise*, Keynes regards any influence of the short-term rate of interest on the long-term as suspect.

Proposition 7. A dual (or two tier) adjustment mechanism. The rate of interest plays an essential role in adjusting the whole system, while individual prices in the investment goods sector and the multiplier process in the consumption goods sector play subsidiary roles therein. In this sense the adjustment mechanism in Keynes's system is a two tier one.

The rate of interest plays a primary role in the adjustment of the whole system, for it alone can adjust any discrepancy between the level of national income determined through the mechanism of the commodity markets and the level of national income that would bring about equilibrium in the money market. On the other hand, individual prices play a role in bringing about equilibrium in the investment goods markets, in which, given the rate of interest, is ascertained a demand curve which meets a supply curve. The multiplier process, through which purchases of consumption goods occur one after another until they converge at a certain point (the income generated in the investment goods sector being the initial impulse), plays a role in the adjustment of the consumption goods markets. Relative to the rate of interest, individual prices and the multiplier process might play minor roles. Thus the adjustment mechanism in the *General Theory* is composed of two tiers.

III   The essence of the Keynesian Revolution

Having examined the *General Theory*, we are now in a position to evaluate the Keynesian Revolution in a much broader perspective.

1   *The relation between the* Treatise *and the* General Theory

The *Treatise* has two theories – a Wicksellian theory and Keynes's own theory. It is a crucial work for a clear understanding of Keynes's theoretical development. Indeed, Keynes arrived at the *General Theory* by pondering over how his own theory in the *Treatise* should be revised. This is not to say that the *General Theory* is an improved version of the *Treatise* theory. On the contrary, the *General Theory* is an achievement completely apart from the *Treatise*.

Let us make a brief comparison between the two books.

1   In the *Treatise* the TM supply function plays an essential role in the dynamic movement of the system; the *General Theory* addresses the question of how the volume of employment is determined.
2   The *Treatise* provides no theoretical account of investment and consumption; in the *General Theory*, theories of both investment and consumption are put forward, and play important roles in determining the volume of employment.
3   Although it is true that we can find some continuity between the concepts of bearishness and liquidity preference (the view that the banking system and the public, with their psychological inclinations, behave interactively; the classification of the motives for holding money), the fact remains that the role assigned to money in the two books differs considerably.

In the *Treatise* the rate of interest is a policy variable, through which the banking system is supposed to adjust the supply of money to the public's bearishness, which plays an essential role in determining the price of equities, which in turn determines the price of investment goods; in the *General Theory* the rate of interest is supposed to be adjusted in such a way that the supply of money, which is a policy variable, meets the liquidity preference. Liquidity is also used for explaining why money stands in the way of attaining full employment. Keynes also argues money's zero elasticities of production and substitution, which is presented as the ground for accepting the exogeneity of the money supply.[26]

The question of whether the key factor in the Keynesian Revolution was the principle of effective demand or the theory of liquidity preference[27] has been much discussed. In our opinion it was the former, and indeed we have placed considerable stress on the principle of effective demand, but this is not to say that the theory of liquidity preference plays a minor role. It plays a central role together with the theory of effective demand for the determination of the volume of employment. The *General Theory* is, after all, a system of simultaneous equations. Moreover, we argue that the rate of interest plays an essential role in the adjustment of the system as a whole.

2   *The Essence of the* General Theory

The essence can be summarised as follows:

(i)   Keynes worked out, in concrete terms, a theory of how the volume of employment in the economy as a whole is determined. In a clear and detailed way, he developed a theory according to which the volume of employment is determined at the intersection of the aggregate demand function and the aggregate supply function, making use of such subsidiary concepts as the consumption function, the marginal efficiency of capital and the liquidity preference theory. This theory constitutes the most important contribution of the *General Theory*.[28]

(ii) Through his theory of employment, Keynes filled out his vision of the capitalistic economy which, if left to itself, would suffer from involuntary unemployment or underemployment equilibrium.[29]

(iii) Keynes put forward his theory of employment as a form of monetary economics in which the theory of value and distribution is integrated with the theory of money.

(iv) The *General Theory* is, at the same time, founded on the vision of a economic system haunted by 'instability, uncertainty and complexity'.

3   *The place of the* General Theory *in the history of economics*

From the late nineteenth century on, economists increasingly concentrated their attention on the phenomenon of exchange in the market, which eventually led to microeconomics in the form of Marshall's partial equilibrium theory and Walras's general equilibrium theory. The main concerns of these economists were with the problem of how resources are exchanged through the price mechanism. They assumed full employment, and accepted Say's Law. Their systems were composed of two spheres: the 'price theory' and the quantity theory. They accepted the classical dichotomy. This strand of economics is referred to as 'Catallactics'.

A new approach to economics was initiated by Wicksell at the turn of the century. Wicksell put forward the theory of cumulative process alternative to the quantity theory. A number of economists of diverse intellectual backgrounds emerged in the inter-war period to follow up Wicksell's lead – Wicksell's influences. They were united in their desire to construct a new monetary economics, criticising the quantity theory, the classical dichotomy, and Say's Law.

Keynes parted with Wicksell's influences soon after the *Treatise* was completed, and ultimately arrived at the *General Theory*. The *General Theory* is, in a nutshell, a monetary economics which demonstrates underemployment equilibrium. It was an independent achievement, and generated the Keynesian Revolution. In Hicks's phrase, Keynes established a new 'Plutology'.[30] In wider doctrinal–historical perspectives, though, both the Wicksell's influences and the *General Theory* belong to the strand of monetary economics which stands in opposition to neoclassical economics.

The *General Theory* criticised 'classical economics' for endorsing Say's Law, the classical dichotomy, and the quantity theory, overlooking the distinction that classical economics is the old 'Plutology' whereas neoclassical economics is 'Catallactics'. In short, Keynes repudiated 'classical economics' because it is real economics; he endeavoured to establish a new monetary economics.

14 Interpretations of Keynes and the development of postwar macroeconomics

The *General Theory* exerted a profound influence on both theoretical economics and economic policy-making in the postwar world. But its influence also extended well beyond these spheres to the vaster world of social philosophy with the *Beveridge Report* – the 'Keynes-Beveridge System or the Post-war Consensus' to the effect that the government should be responsible for attaining full employment through economic policy, and establishing a social security system through its partial contribution so that the people could make a stable living.

Indeed, the book's impact was so powerful that the phenomenon has come to be called the 'Keynesian Revolution'.

A preliminary point to be stressed is that, at the level of economics in the strict sense, the Keynesian Revolution came about and propagated itself embodying four essential elements.

The first element is that in the employment policy controversy in the 1940s Keynes and the Economic Section adopted a simplified Keynesian theory of the 45 degree type, and worked out various policy tools such as built-in stabilisers on the basis of it.

The second element is the fact that Keynes's theory was developed in tandem with national income accounting. Keynes himself contributed to develop systems of national accounts together with Stone and Meade as is seen in the budget problem in the 1940s.

These two elements were due to Keynes himself in his activities in the 1940s.

The third element is the fact that Keynes's theory was developed on the basis of the IS-LM model. The IS-LM model, which was formulated, immediately after the publication of the *General Theory* by Hicks, Harrod, Meade and so forth, was elevated to orthodox Keynesianism not only in the United Kingdom but also in the United States through Hansen among others.

The fourth element is the fact that Keynes's theory was developed in tandem with econometrics, although Keynes himself was very critical of it.

Putting together these four elements, it turns out that the Keynesian Revolution – a revolution in the sense that it drastically changed economic theory and economic policy – took place and proceeded in the form of elaboration of the IS-LM model in tandem with the development of the national income accounting method and econometrics. In turn, as the national income accounting system and econometrics gained increasing popularity as a tool for economic forecasting, economists paid correspondingly more attention to developing Keynes's theory both theoretically and in terms of economic policy.

In this chapter we examine three aspects of the Keynesian Revolution in economics. In Section I we look at how the *General Theory* has been interpreted. In Section II we then go on to examine how the development of Keynes's economics has been understood, while Section III outlines the development of postwar macroeconomics up to the 1970s in relation to the *General Theory*. Finally, in Section IV, we shall briefly deal with the situation of macroeconomics during the last thirty years.

I Interpretations of the *General Theory*

Epoch-making writings are doomed to be endlessly reinterpreted. Yet because each interpretation comes more or less under the influence of the economic theory and conditions then prevailing, we encounter a spectrum of interpretations so wide as to encompass incompatible readings of the text in question.

Let us first consider the interpretations of economists who in one way or another adopted Keynes's theory as the foundation of their views ('Keynesians'), followed by the interpretations of economists who developed their theories in opposition to Keynes's teachings ('Anti-Keynesians').

1 *Keynesians*

They can be divided into two categories.

First we have the 'Income-Expenditure Approach' Keynesians – the mainstream Keynesians and the mainstream macroeconomists: Hicks, Patinkin and Tobin are fairly representative figures.

The second category consists of those who adopted a critical stance towards the first. They can be subdivided into two groups – the 'Disequilibrium Approach' Keynesians and the Post-Keynesians. We shall take Leijonhufvud as representative of the former, and Davidson as representative of the latter.[1]

A *The 'Income–Expenditure Approach' Keynesians*

Hicks played a key role in getting Walras's ideas taken seriously in the Anglo-Saxon world, largely through his elaboration of the Walrasian general equilibrium theory in Hicks (1939). He also contributed to laying the foundations of the 'Income-Expenditure Approach' through his IS-LM model in Hicks (1937).

To begin with, Hicks claims that his IS-LM model provides a faithful[2] encapsulation of the *General Theory*, the main features of which are identified in Hicks (1937):

1 Keynes's theory differs from the classical theory in insisting that the demand for money depends on the rate of interest, and that saving is part and parcel of the multiplier theory. The former is the more important point.
2 It is in relation to the liquidity trap that Keynes's theory reveals its most distinctive characteristics.[3]

3   Considered as a system of equations, it is less a 'general' theory than a revised Marshallian theory.[4]

Second, Hicks sees the *General Theory* as providing an analysis of 'fixprice' markets in which, thanks to economies of scale and product standardisation, producers are in a strong position to determine prices. He holds that the *Treatise*, by contrast, analyses 'flexprice' markets in which prices are determined, through merchants' activities, by supply and demand.[5]

Third, Hicks judges the *General Theory* as lapsing from the dynamic approach that characterises the *Treatise* to a static theory, and thus tends to rate the *General Theory* rather less highly than the *Treatise*.

Finally, Hicks identifies Keynes's theory with monetary – not real – economics. Concretely, he argues that Keynes moves from concentration on the long-term rate of interest in the *Treatise* to 'fiscalism' (which is connected with the liquidity trap) in the *General Theory*.[6]

In stressing the liquidity preference theory[7] Hicks differs from Patinkin while, unlike Patinkin and Tobin, he agrees with Friedman in judging that emphasis is placed on the role of the liquidity trap.

Patinkin, who is famous for Patinkin (1965) as embodying the Neoclassical Synthesis, also pursued a doctrine-historical study of Keynes's theory.

First, Patinkin argues that the central message of the Keynesian Revolution lies in Keynes's having brought to light the decisive role played by changes in output in equalising aggregate demand and aggregate supply (or investment and saving).[8] He does not rate the liquidity preference theory so highly, although he grants that it possesses a degree of originality.[9] This view is widely shared among the Income–Expenditure Approach Keynesians except for Hicks.

Second, Patinkin argues that the *General Theory* analyses the economy which is inclined, due to its slowness of adjustment,[10] to fail to attain full-employment equilibrium, and that it thus describes a world of dynamic disequilibrium. He insists that Keynes's position in this regard is elaborately developed in chapter 19, 'Changes in Money-Wages' – the 'apex' of the *General Theory*.[11] Patinkin also insists that in the *General Theory* both prices and money wages are treated as flexible,[12] differing here from Hicks and Friedman.

Third, Patinkin judges that the *General Theory* actually applies a Marshallian and a Walrasian approach, and yet, he maintains, it could be regarded as the first practical application of the Walrasian general equilibrium theory, although Keynes himself was not aware of it.[13]

Finally, in light of the second point above,[14] Patinkin opposes the view (held by Hicks, Modigliani and Friedman) that *GT*'s underemployment equilibrium is attributable to the liquidity trap.

We owe to Tobin a very considerable contribution to the development of a portfolio selection theory and an inventory-theoretical approach towards the demand for money.

Tobin holds that the IS-LM model grasps the essence of the *General Theory*. Unlike Hicks, he also believes that it still retains its usefulness as an analytical tool. Tobin argues that the IS-LM model is usefully applicable, for it can be regarded as a discrete cross-section model within the framework of a dynamic process,[15] while Hicks tends to see the IS-LM model in a negative light, on the grounds of its being static.

Tobin argues that the LM curve is not horizontal, but upward sloping. On this he takes the same stance as Patinkin, opposing Hicks and Friedman, and for this reason Tobin objects to being labelled a 'fiscalist'.[16]

In Tobin's view, the *General Theory* takes prices and money wages to be flexible. In the IS-LM model he uses price as an endogenous variable,[17] while citing chapter 20, 'The Employment Function' as evidence for the flexibility of money wages.[18] On prices he takes the same position as Patinkin and Davidson, while the question of money wages sees him closer to Patinkin than to Davidson.

B The 'Disequilibrium Approach' Keynesians (or the Post-Walrasians)

Leijonhufvud stands along with Robert Clower as a leader of the 'Disequilibrium Approach'.[19]

To begin with, Leijonhufvud argues that in Keynes's macro-system the Marshallian ranking of prices and quantities in terms of adjustment is reversed, the basic idea being that because the adjustment speed of prices (inclusive of money wages) is slow, the economic system is adjusted through quantities (or incomes).[20]

Leijonhufvud also argues that the essence of Keynes's theory lies in the 'dual decision hypothesis', which is most explicitly found in the consumption function. Behind the scenes lies a criticism that the Walrasian general equilibrium theory is not so much a general theory as a special one.[21] Being understood as constructed on the dual decision hypothesis, Keynes's theory should be general. *Prima facie*, in stressing the consumption function, the Disequilibrium Approach might follow the same line as the Income–Expenditure Approach, but they differ in how they evaluate and treat the general equilibrium theory.

Third, Leijonhufvud sees the multiplier theory as a process through which an initial deviation is amplified through the 'consumption-income relation' – the 'deviation-amplifying feedback-loop'.[22]

Finally, Leijonhufvud argues that the 'aggregative structure' in Keynes's theory is composed of consumption goods, non-monetary assets, money, and labour services, while the Income–Expenditure Approach sees the aggregative structure as composed of goods, debts, money and labour services.[23]

C The Post-Keynesians[24]

These economists were vehemently opposed to the Income–Expenditure School, as witnessed by the 'Cambridge-Cambridge Controversy'[25] from the mid-1950s to the 1970s. Often working together with Sidney Weintraub, Paul Davidson was a key figure.

According to Davidson, the *General Theory* succeeds in providing an analysis of the economy in which we actually live. The outstanding features of this monetary economy involve uncertainty, contracts, sticky money-wages, carrying and transaction costs, and zero production- and substitution-elasticities of money.[26] Taking this approach, he maintains that the *General Theory* is utterly inconsistent with the Walrasian general equilibrium theory.[27]

Davidson further argues that in the *General Theory* money wages are assumed to be sticky, and prices flexible. The stickiness of money wages is a condition imposed by the real world, in which uncertainty prevails and production takes time,[28] while price flexibility is explicitly there, in chapter 20, 'The Employment Function', and chapter 21, 'The Theory of Prices'.[29]

In his analysis of the goods market, Davidson stresses the aggregate demand and supply functions in chapter 3, 'The Principle of Effective Demand'. He is critical of the IS-LM model which utilises a 45° line and the aggregate expenditure curve.[30]

Finally, with regard to the liquidity preference theory, Davidson emphasises the precautionary and finance motives.[31] He does not think the liquidity trap matters.[32]

D   The Neo-Ricardians[33]

They adopt the same stance as the Post-Keynesians in harshly criticising the Income–Expenditure Approach Keynesians and the neoclassical orthodoxy, but they are theoretically quite different. We will take Garegnani and Milgate (Eatwell and Milgate eds, 1983, chapters 2 and 5 respectively) as representative.

They maintain that the *General Theory* is composed of two mutually exclusive contributions:

1   a positive contribution which consists of the work on the relationship between saving and investment, the principle of effective demand and the multiplier analysis. It is revolutionary in terms of the long-period positions;
2   a negative contribution which 'would be concerned with the flaws in classical theory' and neoclassical (marginalist) capital theory.

Meanwhile they argue that the marginal efficiency of capital and the liquidity preference theory should be abandoned because they are based on the marginalist theory. They also hold that uncertainty and expectations do not play an essential role in the *General Theory*.

2   Anti-Keynesians

Up until the 1970s, postwar macroeconomics was developed by the Income-Expenditure Approach Keynesians, which is why economists doubtful of Keynes's or Keynesian theories were so earnest in criticising them, while constructing their own theories based on greater faith in the automatic adjustment mechanism of the market economy.[34]

Here we see two economists involved in particular – Pigou[35] and Friedman.

Pigou succeeded Marshall to the Chair of Political Economy at Cambridge in 1908, and was a representative of the Cambridge School. The 'classical economists' in the *General Theory* refers mainly to this school. It was in particular Pigou that Keynes singled out as the target for attack.[36]

Pigou (1950) formulates Keynes's model as follows:

$$\varphi(r) = f\{r, F(e)\} \tag{1}$$

$$\omega = m \cdot g\,(r)/F(e) \tag{2}$$

where $\varphi(\cdot)$ is the demand function of investment, $f\{\cdot\}$ the supply function of investment, $g(\cdot)$ the income-velocity of money, $F(\cdot)$ the production function measured in terms of labour-units, r the rate of interest, e the volume of employment. The money-wage ω and the quantity of money m are exogenous variables.

In this model, the number of endogenous variables (r and e) and of equations is the same, so the system is soluble.

Pigou states that equation (1), which shows a supply–demand equilibrium of investment goods, is the essence of Keynes's theory.[37] He calls $f\{\cdot\}$ the supply function of investment, and adopts 'one commodity model'.[38]

Second, Pigou understands Keynes's analysis of the money market within the framework of the quantity theory, which comes from his judgement that the liquidity preference theory is a variant of Marshall's theory.[39]

Third, Pigou sees the significance of the *General Theory* in a theoretical framework which consistently connects real and monetary factors. He calls particular attention to pp. 246–247 (in chapter 18, 'The General Theory of Employment Re-Stated'), where Keynes summarises his view that the three fundamental psychological factors, money-wages, and the volume of money determine the level of national income and employment.[40]

Friedman was unflagging in challenging the Income–Expenditure Approach with his empirical studies, establishing Monetarism as the modern version of the quantity theory.[41]

Friedman holds that in the *General Theory* both prices and money wages are assumed to be rigid.[42] He judges that the rigidity of prices is partly connected with Keynes's assumption that prices are adjusted slowly, while quantities (incomes) adjust rapidly (a reversal of Marshall's assumption), and partly comes from Keynes's neglect of the distinction between real and nominal values.

Friedman argues that the rigidity of money wages is partly attributable to money-illusion on the part of labourers, and the existence of trade unions, but principally due to the absence of the equilibrium nominal price level within the range of underemployment, which forced Keynes to construct a real-term model in which all the variables are measured in terms of wage-units.

Friedman also maintains that the demand function of money assumes the 'liquidity trap',[43] so that any change in the quantity of money is wholly absorbed by the change in income-velocity of money. Thus money does not influence the real economy. Monetary policy can influence only the income-velocity of money. Given prices and money wages, real income, consumption and investment are determined by the 'saving–investment' equation at the rate of interest at which the liquidity trap kicks in.[44]

II   Interpretations of the development of Keynes's economics

Let us now review some representative interpretations of Keynes's theoretical development.[45] Once we have done so, the place our own interpretation takes among them should become clearer.

To grasp the evolution of Keynes's thought, three stages in particular must be considered: (i) the *Treatise*; (ii) the *General Theory*; (iii) the process in between. One's understanding of points (i) and (ii) tends to influence point (iii) more than the other way round, for the former have a long history while the latter has been studied in depth only recently.

1   *Leijonhufvud*

Leijonhufvud judges that both the *General Theory* and the *Treatise* belong to the 'Wicksell Connection', defined as a saving-investment theory characterised by the 'maladjustment of the rate of interest', seeing no fundamental changes between the two (see 1968, p. 349). This is well developed in chapter 19, 'Changes in Money-Wages'.[46] In this respect Keynes's books is a variant of the Wicksell Connection approach, albeit an important one.

Leijonhufvud (1981, p. 168) sees the *Treatise* theory in terms of 'two stages' approach. The first is a theory of the nominal income determination, which corresponds to the 'fundamental equation' (an excess of saving over investment is interpreted as an excess supply of goods). The second stage deals with the division of nominal income into real income and prices.

Moreover, Leijonhufvud (1981, p. 168) argues that in the *Treatise* the market rate of interest is determined in the stock market, while the banking system, which is left outside the scheme, is supposed not to interfere with the market.

Taking into consideration Leijonhufvud's understanding of the *General Theory*, let us see his understanding of the relation between the two books. He argues that the essence of the Keynesian Revolution lies in Keynes's having advanced the 'Z theory', defined as either 'the *Treatise* plus quantity adjustment' or 'the *General Theory* minus the theory of liquidity preference'.

Departing somewhat from his original account in 1968, Leijonhufvud came to downplay the liquidity preference theory, placing instead the loanable fund theory at central stage on the grounds that it is compatible with the 'maladjustment of the rate of interest'. Leijonhufvud (1981, p. 166) argues that Wicksell's theory is developed in the form of the loanable fund theory. Both the Income–Expenditure Approach Keynesians and the Monetarists are critically assessed from this point of view.

2 *Meltzer*

Meltzer (1988) regards the *Treatise* and the *General Theory* as continuous in both theory and policy prescriptions. He argues that both books are founded on Keynes's belief, in the 1920s, that 'progress depended on investment and capital accumulation' (p. 60).

Meltzer maintains, moreover, that many ideas advanced in the *General Theory* had already appeared in the *Treatise*. He interprets the *Treatise* fundamental equations as determining the rate of interest and the price level,[47] given the level of income or output, in terms of simultaneous, general equilibrium (see p. 112). Meltzer also argues that the *Treatise* develops a static theory of prices and interest rates which can be regarded as a forerunner of the theory of interest rates and output in the *General Theory* (see p. 13).[48]

Again, Meltzer maintains that in policy measures, the *General Theory* is on the same lines as the *Treatise* (see p. 112), although he identifies some changes in Keynes's thinking between the two:

1   A change in the relative roles of output and prices. In the *Treatise* the main focus of analysis is on prices, while in the *General Theory* it comes on output and employment.
2   A shift from analysis of disequilibrium (the *Treatise*) to a static theory of equilibrium at under-employment (the *General Theory*) (see p. 113).

The main point in the *General Theory* lies in:

> the economic argument that fluctuations in output impose social costs that cannot be removed by private action. Variability imposes a premium for bearing risk or uncertainty... and holds the capital stock below the social optimum.... Keynes' main proposal follows: Let the state remove the excess burden by directing investment... The *General Theory* provided the theoretical framework that supported that [proposal].
>
> (p. 15)

Capital stock and the divergence between private and social return are the key concepts for a proper understanding of the *General Theory* (see pp. 300, 304 and 309).

In Meltzer's view, Keynes believes that 'state management or direction of investment would remove the externality... that holds the expected rate on private investment above the social rate of return' (p. 199).

3   *Dimand*

Dimand (1988) regards the relation between the two books as discontinuous.[49]

He interprets the *Treatise* as advancing a theory of how price levels are determined under full employment. His formal model deals with changes in price levels only (see p. 188). The level of output is fixed, he argues, by the full employment of available resources (see p. 26), so that the *Treatise* lacks any theory of how the levels of output and employment are determined. The principal failing of the *Treatise* is that it neither incorporates discussion of unemployment into any theory of the level of output, nor turns from price dynamics to fluctuations in output and employment (see p. 44). In his view, therefore, the *Treatise* is a failure.

Dimand formulates the *Treatise* model in the form of thirteen equations (see p. 39). He assumes the volume of output at full employment, and introduces an investment function, $I(r, Q_{-1})$, where I is the value of investment, r the rate of interest, and Q_{-1} the windfall profits in the preceding period. He also introduces an equation, $I(r, Q_{-1}) = S(r)$, where S is saving, as 'the internal equilibrium condition that there be no windfall profits or losses' (p. 39).

It is Dimand's contention that Keynes's development can be characterised as a change from price adjustment to quantity adjustment (see p. 124).

In explaining Keynes's new focus on quantity adjustment, Dimand examines in detail how the multiplier theory (together with the propensity to save) came to be established. He surmises that because Keynes remained unable to work out a formula for calculating an exact figure, he chose not to incorporate the multiplier theory into the core of his theoretical system.

4   *Amadeo*

Amadeo (1989) sees the *Treatise* as integrating two aspects of the economic mechanism – the determination of prices and that of quantities.

The first aspect concerns both the determination of prices and the emergence of windfall profits in any production period. Amadeo sees the fundamental equations as describing this, referring to the analysis as the 'historical statics method'.

The determination of quantities treats changes in production and employment in the next period, as determined by entrepreneurs based on the windfall profits realised in the preceding period. Amadeo calls this analysis the 'historical dynamics method'.[50] He regards the *Treatise* as belonging to the Post-Wicksellian stream, which, in his view, is the orthodox view containing the quantity theory as its core.

There are three other salient points in Amadeo's understanding of the *Treatise*: (i) the use of the production function (see pp. 35–36); (ii) the interpretation that a cut in money wages might bring full employment; and (iii) Keynes's alleged acceptance of the doctrine of forced saving.

Amadeo sees the relation between the *Treatise* and the *General Theory* as follows. The *Treatise* discusses the economy in terms of historical statics and dynamics, whereas the *General Theory* treats it in terms of 'equilibrium statics'. He maintains that as Keynes moved from the *Treatise* to the *General Theory*, profits and expectations had ever less importance.

Amadeo furthermore argues that the *General Theory* advances two logically distinct versions. Chapter 3 contains what he calls the 'supply version', whereas the subsequent chapters propose the 'expenditure version'. He addresses the issue of profits discussed in the *Treatise* in the inappropriate context of his analysis of *GT*'s chapter 3, interpreting them as the difference between realised income and effective demand. Based on his supply-and-expenditure-versions analysis, Amadeo sees the relation between the two books as broadly continuous, apart from the difference in analytical method.

III Keynes and postwar macroeconomics up to the 1970s

1 *Three periods*

The relation between the *General Theory* and the development of macroeconomics up to the 1970s can be conveniently divided into three periods.

The first period runs from 1936 to the end of the 1950s. During this span of time controversies arose between those who rated Keynes's theory highly and those who dismissed it.[51]

The first group of economists shared the view that the IS-LM model captures the essence of the *General Theory*. As Young (1987) documented, the IS-LM model was simultaneously formulated by Hicks, Harrod, Meade and Champernowne immediately after the publication.

This also became the central theoretical framework of American Keynesianism. It was extended in various ways by Klein, Modigliani, Tobin and others, the difference between them lying in assumptions of the functions which comprise their models. Klein (1947, pp. 90–91), who saw the multiplier theory as the core of the Keynesian Revolution, endeavoured to prove, assuming both the interest-elasticities of investment and saving to be zero, that full employment is not attainable even in the case of flexible money wages. Using a model similar to that of Klein (1947, pp. 214–215), Modigliani (1944) ascribed the cause of underemployment to the liquidity trap.

This is the 'Income–Expenditure Approach', and the economists who belong to it are simply called 'Keynesians' *tout court*. Harris (1947) is a milestone for this approach.

The second group of economists, whose leader was Pigou, ascribed unemployment to the rigidity of money wages, and argued that if money wages were to become flexible, full employment would be attained. The concept of the 'Pigou effect' emerged from this group.

The second period runs from the end of the 1950s up to the mid-1960s. The battle between the above two groups came to an end. It was the former group which became much more prevalent and carried the day. The development of econometrics ushered in an age in which almost all economists were Keynesians 'after a fashion'. This is clear from Peacock (Greenaway and Presley, 1989, pp. 4–5) and Robbins (1961). Klein (1947) was a work symbolising this period.

This is the period when Keynesian Economics swept the world in terms of economic theory and economic policy. It evolved in tandem with econometrics, although Keynes criticised Tinbergen (1939) as a pioneering work on econometrics, on the grounds that economics should be moral science and belong to a field of logics. The models were those which formulated Keynesian theory in terms of the general equilibrium framework, and they grew ever more ambitious in scale. Klein and Goldberger (1955) stands as a landmark.

Thereafter the IS-LM model has been used as a central piece in macroeconomics and economic policy as well as in the pedagogical field.

Another important economic theory is the Walrasian general equilibrium theory.[52] This theory, which had already captivated mathematical economists in the interwar Europe and was used by scholars (Lange, Taylor and so forth) who argued for the possibility of the socialistic economy in the Socialist Economic Calculation Controversy, was further elaborated in the United States as is seen in the studies on the proof of the existence of the general equilibrium solution, and on the stability condition of the solution. Representative of this field is Arrow and Debreu (1954).

The situation that developed, together with Keynesian theory as macroeconomics, the general equilibrium theory as microeconomics in the United States determined the new direction of economics – the emergence of the paradigm known as the 'Neoclassical Synthesis' (which has Keynesian economics and the Walrasian general equilibrium theory as its hard core). This advocates that the IS-LM model is applicable so long as underemployment persists, but once full employment is attained (through Keynesian monetary and fiscal policies) the economy behaves in accordance with the Walrasian system. Thus almost all economists were Keynesians as well as Walrasians.

As the Neoclassical Synthesis swept through the world, however, the concerns of economists increasingly shifted to the general equilibrium theory and the neoclassical growth theory, with the result that through the 1960s 'theoretical and exegetical interest in the *General Theory* ... declined markedly' (Leijonhufvud, 1968, p. 3).[53]

Theoretically, the Neoclassical Synthesis could not help being 'eclectic'. Keynesian economics was formulated in terms of the Walrasian general equilibrium theory. In the field of economic growth theory, the neoclassical type (Solow brand) was rated more highly than the Harrod-Domar brand. It reflected the same stance as that in which the Pareto-Optimality was highly rated in the Welfare Economics, and the Heckscher–Ohlin–Samuelson model was highly rated in international economics.

In terms of social philosophy, the Neoclassical Synthesis could not help being 'eclectic' as well. Although the main element was the 'postwar consensus', it contained elements of laissez-faire thought, which reflected the economic situation which was in sharp contrast with that in the prewar period.

Could such eclecticism[54] prove viable? Could monetary economics co-habit with real economics? This problem was, in fact, to emerge in the last thirty years.

At the same time the predominance of the Neoclassical Synthesis spelt the gradual decline of the dominant schools of economics of the interwar period. Marshallian economics was downgraded to a position, as it were, servant of Walrasian economics. The Austrian School, the Wicksell Connection, the

Quantity Theory and the Institutionalism were all but totally neglected. This phenomenon was brought about partly by the Keynesian Revolution and partly by Walrasian economics.

The third period runs from the end of the 1960s up to the 1970s. Clower and Leijonhufvud advanced and propagated an alternative interpretation of the *General Theory*, criticising the IS-LM model. This is the 'Disequilibrium Approach'. This group of economists shares the view that the *General Theory* analyses an economy in disequilibrium, in contrast to Walrasian economics which analyses an economy in equilibrium.

It should be noted that a different group of economists vehemently criticised both the IS-LM approach and the Walrasian general equilibrium theory, advancing an alternative approach based on the *General Theory*. These are the Post-Keynesians, who are also critical of the 'Disequilibrium Approach' Keynesians.

We must also mention the surge of schools which were profoundly critical of Keynesian economics as well as Keynes's economics, believing firmly in the automatic mechanism of the market economy. Monetarism led by Friedman is the foremost example.

Thus the IS-LM model has come in for criticism from both the scholars who supported Keynes's theory and those who opposed it. It should be noted, however, that even today, thirty years later, leading American economists have declared its appropriateness in terms of theory as well as pedagogy. Alternative models to the IS-LM model, which have higher applicability and simplicity, in spite of many shortcomings, have yet to be developed.

What is important in understanding the period covered is the fact that logical positivism became predominant as a methodology. Essentially, the methodology consists in clarification of presuppositions and modelling thereof as deductive system, and evaluation of the model by using it empirically. Another influence of logical positivism was to be seen in predominance of the principle that meta-physical aspects should be thoroughly excluded from economics as a science. In consequence, most economists steered clear of all questions of ideologies or value judgements. The price paid here was neglect of a wide and potentially fecund field of social philosophy, while the area of economics became narrower and more specialised than it had been in the prewar period.

Having outlined the movement of the postwar economics, let us our eyes to representative theories.

2   *Representative macroeconomics*

Let us take a look at some representative macroeconomics in the postwar period.

A   *Keynesian macroeconomics*

Here there are two kinds of Keynesian macroeconomics to consider – the Income–Expenditure Approach and the Disequilibrium Approach.

a   THE INCOME–EXPENDITURE APPROACH

Immediately after publication the *General Theory* was already exerting a revolutionary impact on macroeconomics and economic policy. However, the main influence was not so much direct as indirect through the IS-LM model. This school's approach might be divided into four versions.

The 'Real Term' version – Keynes's theory originally aimed at analysing both the commodity and money markets. 'Real Term' Keynesians, however, concentrate on the commodity market, ignoring the money market. They regard the following equation as central:

$$Y = C(Y) + I \tag{1}$$

where Y is national income, C the volume of consumption, and I the volume of investment taken as an exogenous variable. All the variables have nominal values, and the price level is assumed to be given.

The equation can be expressed by means of the familiar 45 degree line and the aggregate expenditure curve. Several factors explain why the view stressing the real aspect became prevalent, notwithstanding the fact that the *General Theory* is monetary economics: (i) the Oxford investigation in the late 1930s, which reported that investment is inelastic with respect to the rate of interest; (ii) the stress on the liquidity trap; (iii) the attention to empirical studies of the consumption function (the 'Consumption Function Controversy'); and (iv) the emphasis on the price rigidity resulting from the oligopolistic nature of the modern economy and on money wage rigidity due to trade unions.

Through the influence of these factors, concentration on the real aspect of the economy became predominant among economists in the 1950s. It is helpful to bear in mind that when Friedman attacks Keynes, it is quite often these economists that he is in fact criticising.

Taking this line, but from a dynamic point of view, Samuelson, Hicks and others advanced their 'real' trade cycle models, which became the main focus of interest for macroeconomists in the 1950s.

The 'IS-LM' version – Hicks reformulated Keynes's theory as an integrated system containing the commodity and money markets: the IS-LM model.[55] It is composed of the following equations, showing equilibrium in the commodity and money markets respectively:

$$Y = C(Y) + I(i) \tag{2}$$

$$M = L_1(Y) + L_2(i) \tag{3}$$

where i is the rate of interest, M the quantity of money, assumed to be given, L_1 the liquidity preference due to the transactions and precautionary motives, L_2 the liquidity preference due to the speculative motive. The price level is assumed to be given.

This model forms the core of the Income–Expenditure Approach. The IS curve derives from equation (2), the LM curve from equation (3). National income and the rate of interest are simultaneously determined at the point where the two curves meet.

The IS-LM model was technically elaborated[56] and widely applied in making policy prescriptions. One form of elaboration is an application of the general equilibrium theory, and another is a dynamic extension which introduces the 'government budget equation', such as Ott and Ott (1965) and Christ (1968).

The 'General Equilibrium Theory' version – As is clear from the IS-LM model, the Income–Expenditure Approach tends to reconstruct Keynes's theory within the framework of the general equilibrium theory. If the labour market is added, for example, it can be extended as follows:

$$Y = C(y) + I(i) \tag{4}$$

$$M/P = L_1(y) + L_2(i) \tag{5}$$

$$Y = Py \tag{6}$$

$$W = P \cdot df/dN \tag{7}$$

$$W = \bar{W} \tag{8}$$

$$y = f(N) \tag{9}$$

where y is real national income, W money wages, assumed to be given, and N the volume of employment. Equation (7) is the first postulate, equation (9) a production function. C, I, L_1 and L_2 are expressed in real terms.

This system is composed of six equations with six unknowns (y, i, P, Y, W, N), so a solution exists.

Modigliani (1944) is an early representative of this approach. Subsequently, economists became increasingly concerned to model Keynes's theory based on the general equilibrium theory. Patinkin, for example, presented a model of this type in the mid-1950s, in which Walras Law is assumed.

The 'Aggregate Demand–Supply Curves' version – As the 'new inflation' emerged in the United States in the late 1950s, some economists began to argue that the Keynesian theory cannot appropriately analyse inflation because it 'assumes prices as given'. Although this criticism might be applicable to the 'Real Term' version, it does not apply to the 'general equilibrium' version, for this treats the price level as an endogenous variable.

Let us consider a model. The functional relation between P and y known as the 'aggregate demand curve' can be derived from equations (4) and (5). The functional relation between P and y derived from equations (7), (8) and (9) is called the 'aggregate supply curve'. Thus the price level and real national income are simultaneously determined by the two curves.

This style of modelling reached a new peak with the Philips curve, which shows a negative correlation between the rate of change in money wages and the rate of unemployment, introduced by Samuelson and Solow in 1960. If we substitute the mark-up pricing equation and the Philips curve for equations (7) and (8) in the system of equations (4)–(9), we can then derive a new aggregate supply curve (the aggregate demand curve remains the same as before).

The following points should be mentioned: (i) this model was the theoretical backbone of the 'Incomes Policy' implemented in the 1960s; (ii) the Philips curve was later revised through the introduction of expectations; and (iii) a great controversy over the Philips curve arose between Keynesians and Monetarists.

b   THE DISEQUILIBRIUM APPROACH

This approach has two distinctive features. First, it insists that the revolutionary nature of Keynes's, as distinct from Keynesian, economics lies in its having demonstrated the 'partiality' of the Walrasian general equilibrium theory – the absence of money, and the assumption of tâtonnement, among other things – and in having established a general theory of disequilibrium[57] which includes the Walrasian theory as a special case.

Second, it argues that in Keynes's theory adjustment is made through changes in income, prices being assumed to be fixed. Keynes's theory analyses a market economy in which quantity adjustment works under a fixed price system.

Clower encapsulated these features in his 'dual decision hypothesis', reappraising the consumption function from the point of view of the behaviour of a household under conditions of excess supply of labour. In 1955 Patinkin had analysed the behaviour of a firm whose sale proceeds were restrained by the level of aggregate demand. The two analyses were integrated into a general disequilibrium theory by Barro and Grossman (1971).

Almost all the disequilibrium approach analyses presuppose fixed prices and money wages. In this regard Negishi (1974, 1979) occupies a unique position: assuming the Keynesian macro-situation, he endeavours to explain, using a kinked demand curve, why prices and money wages tends to be fixed in a perfectly competitive market in a state of disequilibrium.

B   *Neoclassical macroeconomics*

During the first period defined above, many economists continued to champion neoclassical economics, rejecting Keynes's new theory. Moreover, even in the 1960s and 1970s the neoclassical approach to economic growth, for example, was more dominant than the Keynesian approach. Furthermore, in the 1970s, Monetarism and the 'New Classical Economics' came to the fore in vigorous assault on the Income–Expenditure Approach.

For the sake of convenience, let us refer to these economists collectively as the 'neoclassical macroeconomists'. They share a strong belief in the market economy's capacity for self-adjustment. Let us first consider an orthodox static model and then the neoclassical growth theory (the dynamic model), followed by Monetarism.

a THE STATIC AND DYNAMIC MODELS

The static model – Orthodox economics responded to the challenge of the 'New Economics' initiated by Keynes in two ways.

Faced by certain systems of equations presented by Keynesians, such as equations (4)–(9) above, the first response was to reconstruct an orthodox macroeconomic theory the typical example of which runs as follows:

$$S(i) = I(i) \tag{4}'$$

$$M = kPy \tag{5}'$$

$$Y = Py \tag{6}'$$

$$W = P \cdot \mathrm{d}f/\mathrm{d}N \tag{7}'$$

$$N = g(W/P) \tag{8}'$$

$$y = f(N) \tag{9}'$$

where S is saving, (8)' the labour supply function, k the 'Marshallian k' (the rest of the notation is the same as in equations (4)–(9)).

The volume of (full) employment, N, is determined in the labour market (equations (7)' and (8)'). Real national income, y, is then determined by equation (9)'. Equation (4)' shows the state of equilibrium in the bond market, in which the rate of interest, i, is determined. Finally, the price level, P (and with it money wages, W) is determined by equation (5)', which shows the state of equilibrium in the money market. The loanable fund theory (equation (4)'), the quantity theory (equation (5)'), Say's Law, and the classical dichotomy are all to be discerned in this system.

The second response was to show that the economic system has an inherent tendency to converge to full employment. Orthodox economists endeavoured to demonstrate that this would be the case even if one accepted the Keynesian logic. Representative of these tactics is the argument based on the 'real balance effect' developed by Pigou in the late 1930s and elaborated by Patinkin in the 1950s.

The dynamic model (economic growth theory) – Keynes's theory was a short-run static theory. As from the latter half of the 1940s, many economists endeavoured to upgrade it into a long-run dynamic theory. The fruits of these efforts include the 'real' trade cycle theories, and the Keynesian economic growth theories of Harrod and Domar (the 'antinomy theory').

Then, as from the latter half of the 1950s, neoclassical economic growth theories gathered momentum. They were first advanced by Solow and Swan in 1956, followed by Solow's 'vintage model' (1960) and Uzawa's two-sector model (1961), and enjoyed their heydays in the mid-1960s.

They share the following features: (i) the assumption of full employment and a certain rate of population growth; (ii) the assumption that the entire volume of savings is realised as investment; and (iii) the assumption of the first degree of homogeneity in the production function.

Under these assumptions, the neoclassical growth theorists sought to show that the economy would eventually converge on the equilibrium growth path.

b   MONETARISM

The quantity theory of money was articulated for the first time by Hume, and was elaborated and incorporated into the classical system by Ricardo, and further into neoclassical economics by Marshall (the cash balance approach), Fisher (the transaction approach), and various others. It had thus occupied a central place in monetary theory before the Wicksell Connection and the Keynesian Revolution, the latter decisively pushing it aside. Then, in the 1970s, it was revived by Friedman under the name of Monetarism.

Monetarism has two prominent characteristics. First, it is a variation of the quantity theory. Thus although Friedman (1970, 1971) starts his argument with the IS-LM model, as he proceeds on his way he rejects the 'IS' concept, and, moreover, transforms the 'LM' concept into the following equation:

$$Y = V(i) \cdot M \tag{10}$$

where V is the velocity of circulation of money.

Furthermore, as the rate of interest, i, is assumed to be determined by the predetermined variables, it is a constant in the current period.

Based on this reasoning, and with the aid of empirical research on the so-called 'single equation approach', Friedman maintained that the velocity of circulation is stable, so that an increase (decrease) in the quantity of money will proportionately increase (decrease) the price level. From this position he advocated the non-arbitrary monetary policy known as the 'X per cent rule'.

Second, Monetarism advances the 'natural rate of unemployment' hypothesis. This was put forward by Friedman and Phelps in 1968, challenging the Philips curve advocated by the Income–Expenditure Approach. This hypothesis maintains that (i) in the short run, money illusion may occur, so that we find many Philips curves dependent on expected rates of inflation; (ii) in the long run, the economy converges to the natural rate of unemployment.

In the succeeding years heated controversy arose around the empirical validity of this hypothesis.

IV   The situation of macroeconomics during the last thirty years

The Neoclassical Synthesis collapsed in the 1970s. The main cause for this might be found in: (i) a failure in working out the situation of the actual economy; (ii) the arrival of a kind of saturation in which elaboration of theory has been exhausted and something new could no longer be hoped for.

The next three decades might be conveniently divided into two phases – dissolution within the neoclassical school in the wider sense, and the emergence of the anti-neoclassical schools.

Criticism of the 'Income–Expenditure Approach' Keynesian School was initiated by Monetarism, the leader of which was Friedman (who believed, in nature, Marshallian theory[58] and the quantity theory). Between the Keynesian School and Monetarism the controversy evolved over the Philips curve and the 'natural rate of unemployment' hypothesis. Moreover, the Keynesian School was criticised even more harshly by the 'New Classical School' (the Rational Expectations School)[59] which emerged from the academic circle that was closely related to the Monetarism.

Agreeing with Monetarism in policy matters, the New Classical School went beyond it, as is seen in the 'Policy Ineffectiveness Proposition'. It should be noted that the New Classical School does not succeed Monetarism in theory. Each approach has its own theory. The New Classical School maintains that economics as a science should start with the 'representative household' hypothesis (a sort of cardinal utility theory) and deductively[60] construct a model. A representative household is an individual who can form rational expectations in its peculiar sense of the word, provided that he or she has enough information on the macro economy.

It should be noted that the very idea of 'rational expectation' is itself a technical assumption concerning expectations. In practice, however, this type of models was not built for the sake of abstract theory, but was put forward as an alternative to Keynesian theory to explain and diagnose the actual economy, arousing a great deal of controversy in policy matters.

For example, we may mention the policy ineffectiveness hypothesis, according to which aggregate demand management policy is ineffective. This fuelled a tendency among economists and, indeed, the public at large to negate discretionary economic policy, and with it an ideology that proclaims the ineffectiveness of economic policy in general. In consequence macroeconomics seems to have nowhere. Macroeconomics which is not effectively usable in economic policy loses its charm, and many economists are tempted to concentrate their attention on building theoretically consistent models in the microeconomic dimension, going so far as to insist that macroeconomics is not wanted.[61] This could be a serious state of affairs with the point of contact between theory and the real world practically lost.

The New Classical School puts absolute trust in the working of the price mechanism (the equilibrating function) in the market economy, and advocates neo-liberalism in social philosophy. It severely criticises discretionary policy and forecast based on Keynesian econometrics (the 'Lucas Critique').

It was the first time in the history of the discipline that an economics came into vogue that takes for granted the following assumptions: full employment, Say's Law, the Pareto Optimality (expected) utility theory, an ultra-rational economic agent and Laissez-Faire.[62]

In a sense, this might be said to have incorporated only the elements which belong to microeconomics within the Neoclassical Synthesis in a new way,[63] adding to the neo-liberalistic ideology.

This phenomenon has no doubt been strengthened and sustained by the re-evaluation of liberalistic philosophers such as Hayek, Mises and Knight.[64]

It was the New Keynesian School which stood up against these movements, emphasising the imperfection in the working of the price mechanism in the market economy, and searching for the causes for various kinds of the price rigidities (e.g., 'menu cost hypothesis', 'efficiency wage hypothesis', the upward rigidity of the rates of interest[65]). Because they regard these price rigidities as the most essential elements in Keynesian economics, they call themselves the 'New Keynesians'.

In social philosophy they support discretionary economic policy.[66] In spirit they can be said to succeed the Neoclassical Synthesis.

The Income–Expenditure Approach, which was an orthodox Keynesianism, has decreased in influence under the attack of Monetarism and the Rational Expectations School. However, this does not mean the disappearance of this approach: it still exists as an effective tool of analysis,[67] and is positively evaluated, mainly, by the New Keynesians.[68] A simple and versatile theory alternative to the IS-LM model has yet to be developed in spite of various shortcomings that have been pointed out in that model.

The New Classical School, on the other hand, takes a stance which rejects Keynesian economics as well as Keynesian social philosophy, approving the microeconomic element of the Neoclassical Synthesis.

It was due to this split that brought the breakdown of the the Neoclassical Synthesis in terms of theory and social philosophy. The eclecticism was abandoned, and views were divided as to whether the price mechanism of the market society has the ability of instantaneous adjustment, or whether it possesses some kind of rigidity. This could be called the internal collapse of the Neoclassical School.

Another cause which brought about the collapse of the Neoclassical Synthesis was the movement of some groups outside it.

The Disequilibrium Approach,[69] the Post-Keynesian School and the Neo-Ricardian School – all of which are sympathetic to Keynes's theory and find Present-day relevance in the original Keynes, albeit on different grounds – have developed their own theories based on Keynes's theory, criticising both the Income–Expenditure Approach and the Walrasian general equilibrium theory.[70] In contrast with the right wing, they constructed their theories calling into question the assumptions of full employment, Say's Law, the Pareto Optimality, expected utility theory, and an ultra-rational economic agent.

Criticisms of the Neoclassical Synthesis are not confined to the circle of economists who see the foundations of their theories in Keynes's theory. Rather, a characteristic feature of this period was the criticism from a new point of view, and from those who could not assent to the vision of the right wing. The Austrian School, which had long been neglected, began to reassert itself in the form of the Neo-Austrian School. This movement was critical of Keynes's theory, and at the same time represented the resurgence and independence of the school 'encaged' in the Walrasian general equilibrium school.

Recent growing interest in Shumpeter's theory culminated in the advent of the Neo-Shumpeterians. This seems to have occurred because scholars critical of the right-wing movement of the New Classical Economics focused their attention on the dynamic theory developed in his *Theory of Economic Development* from a new perspective.

Thus economics today shows two polarisations, in contrast with the period of the Neoclassical Synthesis. Because it recognised both the Keynesian way of thinking and the general equilibrium pattern, the Neoclassical Synthesis was bound to be eclectic, and somewhat unclear in its stance. This seems to some extent to have resulted from the conviction that matters of value judgements should be excluded from the object of economics (the distinction between science and ideology). At that time, the exponents of the Neoclassical Synthesis seem to have avoided declaring its stance explicitly.

In a word economics, which seemed once to converge to one point, has shown a sharp cleavage – a split between two polarisations over the past thirty years, various groups of economists having clarified their own stance in terms of thought, ideology and value.

How should we evaluate this recent phenomenon? Should we judge it positively as diversification of economics? Or should we, rather, see it as split, stagnation, and confusion of economics? Some economists claim that economics has made revolutionary progress in recent years, while others see it has been sinking deeper into confusion. Apart from this, there is no doubt that economics has lost a great deal of credence among the authorities of economic policy as well as the public, for the ability to analyse the economy and propose economic policy based on economic theory has evidently been on the wane. On the other hand, there is a tendency for more and more scholars to concentrate their energies on mathematisation of economics and to lose contact with the actual economy. We need to reconsider basic issues, and ask ourselves to what degree this tendency should be justified.

Notes

1 The relative decline of the British economy

1 For a survey of the Industrial Revolution, see Mokyr's paper, and McCloskey's paper (in Mokyr ed., 1985). Crafts and Harley (1992), which regards it as 'a genuine industrial revolution reflected in changes in Britain's economic and social structure' (p. 705), contrasts with Clark (1986) and Jones (1991), which regard the idea of the Industrial Revolution as spurious. The 'Gentlemanly Capitalism' historians represented by Cain and Hopkins (1993 a,b) tend to downplay the significance of the Industrial Revolution in British history, pointing up the nexus of the City financiers and the aristocracy as the essence of British capitalism.
2 See Mantoux (1983, Part 2).
3 Calculated from Crafts and Harley (1992, Table A3.1).
4 Calculated from Mitchell (1988, p. 355).
5 Calculated from Mitchell (1988, p. 355).
6 See Deane and Cole (1967, Table 43).
7 See Deane and Cole (1967, Table 43).
8 See Yoshioka (1981, pp. 57–65, 77–82, 121–131).
9 In the *Tract*, Keynes characterised the nineteenth-century world as follows: (i) stable prices; (ii) the emergence of the middle class investing their savings in Consols; (iii) the stable value of gold.
10 Keynes (1919, p. 15) describes the prewar European capitalist system as depending on three unstable factors: 'the instability of an excessive population dependent for its livelihood on a complicated and artificial organisation, the psychological instability of the labouring and capitalist classes, and the instability of Europe's claim on the food supplies of the New World'.
11 The theme has recently been argued in Clarke and Trebilcock eds (1997) which is under the influence of B. Supple. Contrastingly, Cain and Hopkins (1993b, chapter 1) rejects the idea of the relative decline in the British Powers.
12 See Rostow (1960, p. 38).
13 See Ratner, Soltow and Sylla (1979, pp. 187–191).
14 See Henderson (1975).
15 See Aldcroft (1986, chapter 2, Table 2).
16 See Aldcroft (1986, chapter 3, Table 1).
17 See Kirby (1981, Table 2).
18 See Mitchell, King, MacCauley and Knauth (1921, Table 16). On this theme, Aldcroft and Richardson (1969, chapter 3) and Kirby (1981) are useful.
19 See Henderson (1975, pp. 186–198).
20 See Ratner, Soltow and Sylla (1979, chapters 12, 13 and 16).
21 This theme is pursued in Elbaum and Lazonick eds (1986). See also Hannah (1976), and Chandler and Daems eds (1980). On the low level of R & D investment in the British manufacturing, see Mowery's paper (in Elbaum and Lazonick eds, 1986).

22 See Aldcroft and Richardson (1969, chapter 5).
23 Wiener (1981), Sampson (1962) and Barnett (1972) describe the decline of the industrial spirit. For criticism of the 'Wiener thesis', see Ashworth (1981) and Collins and Robbins eds (1990). The 'Gentlemanly Capitalism' historians (e.g. Rubinstein, 1993) are also critical of the 'Wiener thesis'.
24 See Strachey (1918).
25 See Barnett (1972, chapter II). For the influences of Eaton on Keynes, see Mini (1991, chapter 2).
26 See Barnett (1972, pp. 98–106), and Wrigley's paper (in Elbaum and Lazonick, eds, 1986).
27 See Kirby (1981, Table 1).
28 See Yoshioka (1981, pp. 282–283).
29 See Rostow (1960, Table 8).
30 See Ratner, Soltow and Sylla (1979, pp. 466–467).
31 See Ratner, Soltow and Sylla (1979, p. 467).
32 See Taussig (1892, chapters 9–11).
33 See Kindleberger (1973, p. 292).
34 This went hand in hand with the emergence of great oligopolistic corporations in the British economy. See Cain and Hopkins (1993b, chapter 2).
35 See Aldcroft and Richardson (1969, p. 4).
36 Calculated from Feinstein (1972, Table 5).
37 Calculated from Kuznets (1937, Table 77). For Keynes's attitude to the New Deal, see *JMK*.21, chapter 4.
38 See Feinstein (1972, Table 57).
39 Calculated from Sayers (1976, pp. 312–313). However, the issue of securities for domestic industries dramatically increased, and to such a degree that it exceeded that of securities abroad. See Cain and Hopkins (1993b, Figure 2-1).
40 See Deane and Cole (1967, Table 12). Sayers (1976, pp. 312–313) puts the figures in the period 1925–1938 at minus 263 million pounds.
41 See Aldcroft and Richardson (1969, p. 71).
42 See Aldcroft and Richardson (1969, p. 65).
43 On the role which the 'new industries' played in the interwar British economy, controversy has persisted since the early 1960s. See Aldcroft and Richardson (1969, chapter 8) and Kirby (1981, pp. 72–75).
44 In the period 1925–1936, the difference between revenue and expenditure was on average minus 5 million pounds with 19.86 as the standard deviation and 839 million pounds as the average revenue. See Board of Trade (1938, p. 169).
45 In 1919–21 the Treasury officials held to their traditional 'knave proof' doctrine, whereas Prime Minister Lloyd George who advocated public works programmes to tackle unemployment had no sufficient argument to support his position. See Peden (1993). For the formulation of the Treasury View during 1924–1929, and its reformulation during 1929–1930, see Clarke (1988, chapter 3; chapter 7) and Peden's paper (in Corry ed., 1996).
46 The ratio of interest payments on the national bonds to the combined expenditure of the central government, the local governments and the social insurance amounted on average to 30 per cent in the period 1925–1930. See Clark (1937, pp. 140–141).
47 See Taylor (1965, pp. 206–209).
48 The following description is derived from Kindleberger (1973).
49 See Kindleberger (1973, p. 280).

2 Wicksell's influences on Keynes and his contemporaries

1 For the difference between the Wicksellian and the Walrasian general equilibrium theories, see Rogers (1989, chapter 2).

2 See Chiodi (1991, pp. 48–50). For the difference between Wicksell and Mises, see Bellofiore (1998, pp. 549–554).

3 Wicksell (1889, p. 514 in Boianovsky and Trautwein, 2001) ascribes his theory of cumulative process to Ricardo (1810). For comparison with Wicksell (1898), which does not take reference from Thornton, see Boianovsky and Trautwein (2001). The similarity to Thornton's theory was pointed out in 1916 by Davidson to Wicksell. See Laidler (1991a, p. 150).

4 See Wicksell (1936[1898], pp. 165–167).

5 See Wicksell (1936[1898], p. 135). For the discussion over it – between Wicksell, Davidson and Åkerman, see Siven (1998). Wicksell (1913) is a rejoinder to Davidson. Ahiakpor (1999) regards the TCP as retrogression. Gootzeit, M., Ebeling, R., Humphrey, T., and Aschheim, J. and Tavlas, G. oppose his view. My understanding is close to Humphrey's. We do not, however, concur with the view shared by the four that the TCP is an elaborate version of the quantity theory.

6 Wicksell (1935[1915]) does not take fluctuations in prices to occur due to a divergence between investment and saving.

7 Stressing the 'supply of deposits', Humphrey (1997) regards Wicksell as 'a bona fide quantity theorist'.

8 'The Great Depression' in the late ninetenth century saw a gradual fall in prices together with full employment. The TCP reflects this. Wicksell turned his attention to change in output and employment in the early 1920s. See Boianovsky (1998).

9 With regard to the argument that incomes determine the price level of consumption goods, Wicksell (1936[1898], p. 44) refers to the first half of Tooke's 13th proposition. This is followed by Lindahl (1939, p. 142), Myrdal (1939, p. 22) and *TM*.1, p. 122.

10 This accords with Siven's (1998, p.131) view in relation to 'excess demand or interest gap as an engine of inflation'.

11 We regard Hawtrey (1913) and Robertson (1926) as pertaining to the Wicksellian stream of thought, albeit they are not influenced by Wicksell.

12 See *TM*.1, pp. 176–177. Kahn (1984, p. 74) denies Wickell's influence.

13 Mises makes this assumption, which is emphasised as an 'ultra-Wicksellian idea' by Bellofiore (1998). For Mises' criticism of Wicksell, see Mises (1912, pp. 355–357) and Wicksell's reply (1914).

14 Keynes (1914) reviews it critically, though he evaluates Part III. He doubts that the distinction can be found in Wicksell's writings. See Keynes's letter to Ohlin, 29 April 1937 (*JMK*.14, p. 189).

15 Keynes unfailingly acknowledged Robertson, calling him 'my grandfather' (Keynes, 1937b. *JMK*.14, p. 202, n. 2). See also *JMK*.14, p. 94.

16 See *TM*.1, p. 205. We identify three types of interpretation: the *Treatise* accepts it; the *Treatise* criticises it; and the *Treatise* stands in between.

17 Laidler (1990a) appraises the *Treatise*'s portfolio selection theory and Lavington's (1921) as redeeming the defect of neoclassical monetary economics.

18 See *TM*.1, pp. 196–197. This shows why the *Treatise* regards money supply as endogenous. For exogeneity/endogeneity in Keynes's economics, see Moore (1988) and Graziani (2003).

19 Hicks (1935) identifies three theories of money: savings and investment theory, a Wicksellian natural rate theory, and the *Treatise*' bearishness function, finding the third the most interesting.

20 See Myrdal (1939, pp. 10–11).

21 See Myrdal (1939, pp. 11–12).

22 See Myrdal (1939, pp. 14–15).

23 See Myrdal (1939, pp. 16–17).

24 Wicksell (1908) stresses the importance of the price level stability. This led to a controversy with Davidson, who believed in the relation between increase in productivity and fall in the price level. Robertson's (1928, pp. 56–57) argument runs along Davidson's line.

25 See Myrdal (1939, p. 96).
26 See Myrdal (1939, p. 90). Y is not used in the original.
27 See Myrdal (1939, p. 79). In the original, c_1' and r_1' are written as c_1 and r_1, respectively.
28 See Myrdal (1939, pp. 83–84).
29 See Hayek (1931a, pp. 3–4). Mises (1912, pp. 91–92) argues that the quantity theory fails to explain variations in the value of money in terms of subjective valuation and criticises the classical dichotomy.
30 See Hayek (1931a, pp. 25–26). For the relations between Wicksell, Hayek and Mises, see Bellofiore (1998).
31 See Hayek (1931a, pp. 28–29).
32 See Hayek (1931a, pp. 50–57, 75–79).
33 In Mises and Hayek the money rate of interest is defined as the price of consumers' goods over that of producers' goods: this comes in for criticism in the *General Theory* (p. 192), as well as Hawtrey (1935).
34 For the main difference between Keynes's theory and other Wicksellian theories (Mises, Schumpeter, Hayek and Robertson), see *TM*.1, pp. xxii–xxiv.
35 For criticism of the so-called 'Z theory' from the point of view of stock equilibrium, see Cottrell and Lawlor (1991).
36 Realfonzo (1998) characterises Wicksell's influences as 'monetary theory of production' which is critical of the neoclassical theory.
37 For recent developments in relation to Wicksell's influences, see, for example, Moore (1988) and Rogers (1989).
38 See the reviews by Mehrling, Boianovsky and Trautwein, Hoover, and Laidler, and Woodford's rejoinder on the *Journal of the History of Economic Thought* (2006, No. 2).

3 The life of Keynes

1 The following abbreviations are used in this chapter: *Indian Currency and Finance* (1913): *ICF*; *The Economic Consequences of the Peace* (1919): *ECP*; *A Revision of the Treaty* (1922): *RT*; *The Economic Consequences of Mr Churchill* (1925. Reproduced in *JMK*.9): *ECC*.
2 See Maloney (1985, chapter 3), and Groenewegen (1995a, pp. 679–687), which describe Neville's relation with Marshall as moving from a faithful to a gradually disillusioned lieutenant.
3 On Keynes's maternal ancestors, including J.L. Down, who identified the condition to be known as Down's syndrome, see Brown (1988).
4 On the Apostles, founded in 1820, see Deacon (1985, esp. chapter 8).
5 Mini (1991) emphasises anti-utilitarianism of the Apostles and the Bloomsbury Group, arguing that the 'General Theory is Keynes's Apostolic vision plus his psychological experiences' (p. 191). Hession (1984, chapter 6) emphasises the influence of the Bloomsbury Group on Keynes's creativity.
6 See, for example, Shone's paper and Williams's (both in Crabtree and Thirlwall, eds, 1980). Hession (1984) describes the Bloomsbury Group as 'a complex sociological phenomenon, tracing some of its heritage back to Coleridge's day, yet reflecting the current discontents and emerging ideas of the Edwardian years' (pp. 102–103).
7 Mini (1991, pp. 41–42) describes Keynes as having the Etonian values and the Moorean values, and Hession (1984, p. 113) describes him as employing intuition and reason in his theoretical work.
8 Note, for example, that Keynes was the president of the National Mutual Life Assurance Society (1934–1937), and founded the Arts Theatre in 1936. See Hession (1984, pp. 291–295) and Nasu (1995).
9 For the widespread rebellion of European youth against the values of the previous generation, see Wohl (1979).

Notes

10 See Skidelsky (1983, pp. 152–154). Keynes (1938, p. 445) stated that 'the large part played by considerations in his [Moore's] theory of right conduct was … an important contributory cause' to his study of probability theory.

11 Skidelsky (1983, p. 177) states that 'his attitude to British rule was conventional in every sense'.

12 The Diaries of John Neville Keynes from 30 April to 1 June 1908 are filled with his worries about Political Economy Professorship Election. See Groenewegen (1995a, pp. 622–627).

13 The thesis was published in 1921 as *A Treatise on Probability* (hereafter the *Probability*), after having undergone repeated revisions. Concerning Keynes's philosophy underlying the *General Theory*, we have a controversy between scholars who maintain the continuity between the *Probability* and the *General Theory* (Carabelli, 1988; O'Donnell, 1989) and those who maintain the discontinuity (Davis, J., 1995; Bateman, 1996).

14 See *JMK*.12, pp. 689–783.

15 The scandal related to a delivery of silver to the India Office. See Skidelsky (1983, p. 689).

16 The book resulted in Keynes being elected a member of the Royal Commission on Indian Finance and Currency. See Hession (1984, pp. 89–92).

17 See Skidelsky (1983, pp. 333–336). In spite of the entry of the United States, even in August 1918 the British War Cabinet could not predict when the war would end. See Taylor (1965, p. 108).

18 Read at the Memoir Club in the summer of 1931. See Hession (1984, p. 138).

19 See Skidelsky (1983, pp. 367–375).

20 Mantoux (1946) attacked it, attempting to demonstrate that Keynes had misconceptions about many facts. Keynes compared Versailles to the Carthaginian Peace. In Mantroux's view Versailles was reasonable to both sides.

21 This is similar in character to Keynes (1940; *JMK*.10, pp. 367–439), in which he discusses how best to reconcile the demands of war with the claims of private consumption without inflation.

22 See Kindleberger (1973, pp. 34–42) and Carr's paper (in Thirlwall, ed., 1982).

23 See Kirby (1981, pp. 39–40).

24 See Hawtrey's 'The Genoa Resolutions on Currency' (in Hawtrey, 1923). This conference is known for 'Hawtrey's proposals to stabilise the value of gold through international monetary co-operation' (Deutscher, 1990, p. 4).

25 The question of return to the Gold Standard also caused considerable controversy in Japan. Junnosuke Inoue, the Minister of Finance, was an ardent advocate of immediate return to the Gold Standard (see Inoue, 1931, chapter 4), and tight fiscal policies. Contrastingly, Tanzan Ishibashi and Kamekichi Takahashi, journalists of the Toyo Keizai Shinposha Company, advocated return at a new parity, and a public spending policy, supported by the former Ministers of Finance, Chuzo Mito and Korekiyo Takahashi.

    In 1929 the Hamaguchi Government retrenched the budget drastically and re-valued the yen upward by 10 per cent against the dollar through market intervention. In January 1930 it then put the return at pre-war parity into effect. This policy was to be abolished by the Inukai Government in November 1931. See Gotoh (1977).

26 This was an achievement of the Liberal Summer School – 'the linchpin of liberal and progressive thought during the 1920s' (Freeden, 1986, p. 78).

27 The documents concerned include The *Report* (Macmillan Committee, 1931a) and *Minutes of Evidence* (Macmillan Committee, 1931b). Clarke (1988; chapters 5–9) examines the differences in theory and economic policy between various witnesses in detail.

28 See *JMK*.20, p. 286.

29 See Howson and Winch (1977).

30 See *JMK*.20, chapter 4 and *JMK*.13, chapter 3.

31 See 'Notes on Professor A. C. Pigou's Memorandum' (*JMK*.20, pp. 409–416).

32 See the Draft Report of the Committee of Economists (*JMK*.20, pp. 437–443).

33 It contains only two statistical data.

34 See Blaug (1985, pp. 35–37).
35 See Mini (1991, chapter 6), Shionoya (1983), Skidelsky (1983, chapter 6) and Moggridge (1992, chapter 5).
36 Hession (1984, p. 110) depicts him as 'an implicit Coleridgean and an ardent anti-Benthamite'. In Cambridge communism and Marxism were becoming popular at the time, which annoyed Keynes. See Hession (1984, pp. 264–265) and Deacon (1985, chapter 10).
37 This is an application of the Lend–Lease Act to the United Kingdom. The serious issue there concerned Article 7.
38 See Iwamoto (1999, chapters 7 and 8).
39 The discussion started with the Meade plans (February and July 1941), followed by the Meade memorandum (May 1943), which drew criticism from the Treasury. The conflict continued at the Steering Committee on Post-War Employment, which produced an interim report leading to *The White Paper on Employment Policy* (Ministry of Reconstruction, 1944). *JMK*.27, chapter 5 contains the sources concerned. See Robbins (1971, chapter IX), Wilson's paper (in Thirlwall ed., 1982), Tomlinson (1985, chapters 2–4), Cairncross and Watts (1989, pp. 71–87) and Skidelsky (1998).
40 For the Treasury machinery, see Peden (1979, chapter 2). For Henderson's economics, see Komine (1999).
41 See Tomlinson (1985, chapter 3).
42 Beveridge asked Keynes and the Economic Section for advice on the financial aspect of his plan. They supported him from the outset. See Cairncross and Watts (1989, pp. 87–94). Freeden (1986, pp. 366–371) regards the *Beveridge Report* (1942) as 'a blend of left (or new)-liberalism and centrist-liberalism'.
43 The influential pamphlet in this respect was *How to Pay for the War* (1940), based on simple Keynesian economics and the national income accounting. It influenced the 1941 Budget and *The White Paper* (Treasury, 1941. Mainly by Meade and Stone). See Cairncross and Watts (1989, pp. 35–36).

4 From the *Tract* to the *Treatise*

1 Bigg (1990, pp. 96–98, 173–176), Skidelsky (1992, pp. 281–285), Moggridge (1992, pp. 434–443; chapter 19) are exceptions, albeit not sufficient. Patinkin (1976, chapter 3) explains, but does not analyse this point. It is not dealt with in Bridel (1987), Dimand (1988), Meltzer (1988), Amadeo (1989) and Laidler (1999).
2 The *Tract* equation explaining the short-term economic fluctuations follows the formulation in Pigou (1917), which allows for variability of its components. For an understanding of the two, see Bigg (1990, p. 75).
3 See *TMR*, p. 34.
4 For the theory's applicability, see *TMR*, pp. 73–80. For its rejection, see *TM*. 1, pp. 64–65.
5 Clarke (1988, p. 230) interprets the *Treatise* in 'externalist' terms and, the *General Theory*, by contrast, in 'internalist' terms. Our stance is to arrive at an understanding of the two along 'internalist' lines, for they should and could be theoretically understood. In the late 1920s there were two sides to the figure of Keynes – the advocate of Liberal Party public policy, and the theoretical–applied economist.
6 When did Wicksell's theory come to influence Keynes? It is very difficult to ascertain the period, because of lack of relevant documents from 1925 to 1930, but we have two items from the 1930s. One is Keynes's letter to Kahn (8 September 1935. Kahn Papers 13/57/137), in which Keynes says that '[Wicksell] is wonderfully on the right track'. The other is to be seen in *JMK*.14, 203n (written in 1937), where it is Fisher, rather, who is mentioned as his 'great-grandparent'.
7 This implies a dichotomy between Keynes the commentator and Keynes the theorist. See a 'publicist' and an 'economist' in Clarke (1998, p. 71). See also Bridel (1987, p. 96) and note 5 above.

8 'Currency Policy and Unemployment' (*NA*, 11 August 1923), which mentions a lack of trust in the price level as the cause of unemployment, belongs to the *Tract* theory.

9 See Skidelsky (1992, p. 164). The TOC (Tm/3/2/2) of the same period survives, arguing '[t]he control of p by control of n ... only requires that [k, k', and r] should not be linear functions of n'.

10 See Skidelsky (1992, p. 281).

11 Keynes, in fact, maintains it thereafter.

12 See his letter to Lydia (31 October): 'The conversation with Sraffa about Credit Cycle has made me very eager to begin writing my book' (Hill and Keynes, 1989, p. 245).

13 See Robertson's comment on Keynes's draft (*JMK*.13, p. 26).

14 See Moggridge (1992, chapter 17). Keynes's stance as a 'monetary reformer' is clear in 'The Problem of the Gold Standard' (*NA*, 21 March 1925). See also Eichengreen (1992), which regards the Gold Standard as 'fetters', and Barkai (1993).

15 The only surviving formula around this period is '$P = M/(C_1 + WT) \ldots C_1$ [is] the real value of the investment–deposits, T the volume of transactions, and W the inverse of the 'efficiency' of the money deposits' (Tm/2/350).

16 Possibly Keynes used Fisher's Approach in terms of the short run, for he argues 'the variability of [the equation's] elements' (Tm/3/2/23; 26). Keynes (1911) criticised the Approach.

17 Besides Fisher has a 'transitional periods' theory.

18 See Moggridge (1992, pp. 441–442).

19 Patinkin (1976, pp. 28–29) estimates that the fundamental equations appeared in the latter half of 1928.

20 Not contained in *JMK*.13.

21 Chapter 1 (Book IV) might be related to a memo (Tm/2/342–3).

22 Not contained in *JMK*.13.

23 See '(Earnings minus Savings)/(Output minus Investment) = Price Level' (undated, Tm/3/2/86), substantially similar to the first fundamental equation.

24 These are to be moved to *TM*.2, Book V, after separation from the fundamental equation. See *TM*.2, p. 4.

25 Not contained in *JMK*.13.

26 Not contained in *JMK*.13.

27 For 'Keynesian parallels' there, see Fletcher (2000, chapter 21). For Robertson's economics, see Presley's paper (in O'Brien and Presley eds, 1981). However, Presley takes things rather far in regarding the *General Theory* as 'a simplification of the earlier Robertsonian system' (1979, p. 219). For the collaboration between Robertson and Keynes, see Presley (1992).

28 See his letter to Lydia (18 May): ' ... reading the [earlier] proof sheets of Dennis's [Robertson, 1926] ... But I still don't like it ... so I ... criticised and bullied him' (Hill and Keynes, 1989, p. 325). Also see his letter to Lydia (22 May): '[Robertson] ought to tear it up'.

29 See Robertson (1928) and Bigg (1990, pp. 175–176).

30 See 'Notes on the Definition of Saving' (esp. *JMK*.13, pp. 287–288). 'I certainly date all my emancipation from the discussions between us which preceded your *Banking Policy and the Price level....* you won't slough your skins' (Keynes's letter to Robertson, 13 December 1936. *JMK*.14, p. 94). Keynes, however, never regarded Robertson as a 'classical' economist (see Keynes's letter to Robertson, 13 December 1936. *JMK*.14, p. 94). Robertson is not mentioned in *GT*, p. 3, n. 1.

31 Not contained in *JMK*.13.

32 Not contained in *JMK*.13.

33 The material which concerns the *Treatise*'s chapter 37 survives in Tm/2/246–75.

34 Not contained in *JMK*.13.

35 For this impact on Keynes, see Deutscher (1990, pp. 102–105). Keynes's rejoinder was made on 28 November 1930 (Tm/1/4/14–54). Hawtrey's criticism and his stress on

effective demand seem to contribute to leading Keynes to abandon the *Treatise* framework and move towards the *General Theory* after some hesitation.

36 'ADDENDUM' (*JMK*.13, pp. 150–164) is an excerpt, produced by the editor, from these. We shall use the original ones.

37 See Tm/1/2/102.

38 Not contained in *JMK*.13.

39 In the preface with the same date, Keynes says: 'There are many skins which I have sloughed still littering these pages' (*TM*.1, p. xvii).

5   *The Treatise*

1 Ses, for example, Kitou (1942, pp. 81–93).

2 Hicks (1967, p. 191) similarly explains the *Treatise* theory as the 'three stage theory', and Leijonhufvud (1981, pp. 173–174) refers to it as the 'two stage approach'. Hawtrey (1932, chapter 6) and Shackle (1967, chapter 13) go into detailed examination of the *Treatise* theory.

3 The 'constancy of output' should be understood in a dynamic context. Hicks (1967) understands it as 'stage one', where the price levels of investment and consumption goods change, while the output and the level of employment do not. See also Kahn (1984, Lecture 4). Contrastingly Klein (1947, p. 20) interprets the 'constancy of output' as Keynes's implicitly holding a classical theory of employment.

4 See *TM*.1, pp. 121–122.

5 See *TM*.1, p. 122. Hicks (1967, p. 196) explains this by explicitly introducing the propensity to save.

6 See *TM*.1, p. 127.

7 The *Treatise* often calls investment 'new investment' and capital stock 'old investment'. See *TM*.1, pp. 114–118.

8 See *TM*.1, pp. 127, 179, 180.

9 See *TM*.1, p. 194.

10 See *TM*.1, p. 180.

11 See *TM*.1, pp. 139, 183.

12 See *TM*.1, pp. 141, 179, 180. Myrdal (1939, pp. 65, 76–78) interprets Wicksell's investment theory similarly, referring to a formula now known as Tobin's 'q theory'.

13 In Asano (1985(6), pp. 37–40) the TM supply function is similarly stressed. In Yoshikawa (1984, p. 129), it is interpreted in relation to Tobin's 'q theory'. On the other hand, in Klein (1947, pp. 189–192) the function does not appear. This is also true of Harrod (1969, chapter 7), Hanawa-Nagasawa (1980. Translator's afterword of the *TM*.1).

14 The difference in view between Robertson-Hayek and Keynes is whether the difference between savings and investment is regarded as an increase in idle balances. See Keynes's reply to Hayek (1931. *JMK*.13, pp. 243–256) and Keynes's rejoinder to Robertson (1931. *JMK*.13, pp. 219–236), and the Preface to the Japanese edition of the *Treatise* (April 1932). The difference in view between Hawtrey and Keynes is whether dealers are sensitive to the rate of interest.

15 See *TM*.2, pp. 103–104.

16 See *TM*.2, p. 105.

17 See *TM*.1, p. 252 and *TM*.2, p. 91.

18 See *TM*.2, p. 130.

19 For a definition of money, see *TM*.1, pp. 8–9, 31–32. For the Bank Rate and the bond rate, see *TM*.1, p. 179 and *TM*.2, p. 316.

20 Indirectly it influences the volume of output in the next period through the influence upon the profit of the current period. Lindahl (1930; 1939, pp. 146–158) refers to the ratio of savings to income.

21 See *TM*.1, pp. 251–252.

22 See *TM*.2, p. 131.

23 This is a summary of *TM*.1, pp. 271–273, 258–261. The trade cycle theory in Robertson (1926, pp. 83–87) is similar to that in the *Treatise*. Hishiyama (1965, chapter 5) values the originality of Robertson's theory.

24 For the similar opinions, see Klein (1947, p. 17) and Samuelson's paper (in Lekachman ed., 1964, p. 328).

25 In this respect Hansen argues that if the rate of technical progress differs between the two sectors, the fundamental equations do not hold good. For the change in the definition of a quantity unit, see *JMK*.13, pp. 329–331.

26 They are obtained by aggregating the values of equilibrium in the micro structure, while the 'active macro variables' are those which work actively as means by which an investigator constructs a model of the real world. See Hirai (1981, chapter 6).

27 This formula is the same as the fundamental equations in Lindahl (1930. Lindahl, 1939, pp. 141–143).

28 See *TM*.1, p. 123.

29 See *TM*.1, pp. 186–187.

30 Hawtrey (1932, chapter 6) sharply points this out, emphasising, rather, the 'present demand' based on the 'consumers' income' and the 'consumers' outlay'. He also stresses the role which goods in stock and the quantity play in the trade cycle and attributes unemployment to a contraction of demand which does not accompany a fall in prices. See Chapter 4, Section V(5) and Chapter 6, Section I, of the present book.

31 The case in which profits are spent on consumption goods is argued in the logics known as the 'widow's cruse' and 'Danaides jar' (see *TM*.1, p. 125). By examining these cases, Kahn criticised Keynes's argument, claiming that the determination of the price level of consumption goods is interrelated with that of the price level of investment goods. See Kahn's note to Keynes dated 5 April 1931 (*JMK*.13, pp. 203–206), and Kahn's letter to Keynes dated 15 August 1931 (*JMK*.13, pp. 218–219). On the determination mechanism of the two price levels, there was some discussion between Keynes and Robertson. See 'A rejoinder' (*Economic Journal*, September 1931. *JMK*.13, pp. 219–236).

32 See *TM*.1, p. 128.

33 See *TM*.1, p. 194.

34 Denote the demand price as P_d, the stream of the prospective yields as $Q_1, Q_2, \ldots Q_n$ and the rate of interest as r, and we get $P_d = \Sigma_i Q_i (1 + r)^i$. Denote the price level of investment goods based on Investment Price Theory (1) as P, and the expected rate of profit as m which satisfies $P = \Sigma_i Q_i /(1 + m)^i$. If $P_d > P$, then $r < m$. So much is stated in the text.

35 One key may be found in *TM*.1, pp. 228–229, where Keynes argues that in the long run Investment Price Theory (2) holds good while in the short run Investment Price Theory (1) does (the latter is greatly influenced by opinions).

   Klein (1947, pp. 24–26) argues that the price level of investment goods is determined at the intersecting point between the demand curve for savings deposits (the bearishness function) and the supply curve of savings deposits by the banking system. This argument indicates Investment Price Theory (1) by incorporating the expected rate of return (called the 'discount rate'). However, Klein overlooks Investment Price Theory (2) and the dual determination problem of the price level of investment goods.

36 Keynes's attention to profit might have resulted from his thinking over the forced saving theory. See *JMK*.13, pp. 104–105, 277–278. On Robertson's reaction, see his letter to Keynes dated 5 December 1929 (*JMK*.13, pp. 118–119). The other possibility is an influence from the argument in Pigou (1927), where Pigou attributes the major factor in the trade cycle to the changes in expectations of profits. Besides these, Keynes's idea may also have something to do with the 'entrepreneur's profit' in Schumpeter (1911. Schumpeter, 1934, esp. chapter 4).

6 After the *Treatise*

1 The period concerned has been so far examined in a fragmentary way. To take a few examples, Patinkin (1976, p. 86) deals with the MTP manuscript very briefly. Amadeo (1989) deals with the MTP manuscript only from the development of the multiplier in one page. Dimand (1988) does not deal with it.

2 See Hawtrey (1913, pp. 42–44, 107–110 and 124–126).

3 See Hawtrey (1928, pp. 84 and 94).

4 The typescript is, however, dated 19 November 1930. See Tm/1/4/54.

5 This seems to be Keynes's response to Hawtrey's above-mentioned comment, 'The sequence here . . . prices'.

6 See Davis (1980), Cain (1982) and Deutscher (1990, p. 105).

7 See two sets of lecture notes prepared for the New School of Social Research (New York. 11 June 1931. Keynes Papers, Reel 41, AV/1/40–53 [a paging system adopted there]). He advocates raising prices by increasing investment with lowering of the long-term rate of interest. The first fundamental equation and a kind of multiplier theory underlie his argument.

8 Bridel (1987, p. 152) regards them as belonging to the *Treatise* framework. He tends to take the *Treatise* theory in terms of interest rate as equalising investment and savings, although he takes the quantity adjustments into account. Vicarelli (1984, p. 106) considers that there 'Keynes had made another fundamental break with the . . . *Treatise* [theory]'.

9 Patinkin (1976, p. 68) states that this differs from underemployment equilibrium of the *General Theory*. It is to lead to the long-period equilibrium of the MTP manuscript. Samuelson (1946) quotes it to adumbrate the *General Theory*.

10 See *JMK*.13, p. 366.

11 The quotation above shows that he does not accept marginal analysis, for it is a response to H. Schultz's argument based on the short-period marginal cost curve. See *JMK*.13, p. 372.

12 Although Patinkin (1976, p. 84) regards this letter as showing an equilibrating mechanism, it is still within the *Treatise* framework.

13 Keynes Papers, Reel 33, GTE/1/23–41. Pen-written, and not contained in *JMK*.

14 Keynes Papers, Reel 35, GTE/5/468–499. Pencil-written, and not contained in *JMK*.

15 Keynes's analysis below might be a defensive response to Hawtrey's criticism, showing insight into the TM supply function. In 'Notes on the Definition of Saving' sent to Robertson (22 March 1932), Keynes emphasises the TM supply function: 'For if Q [profit] is positive, entrepreneurs will be under a stimulus to increase output. . . . This is a good reason for wishing to split up E' [the income of the community] into its constituents E [earnings] and Q, and for "bothering" about the effect on Q of changes in F [consumption expenditure] and I' [cost of investment]' (*JMK*.13, p. 279).

16 Chapter 8 of the MTP manuscript was initially entitled 'Notes on the Effect of Changes in Output'. Crossed out there is the passage: 'if we did not distinguish between S and S', we should have no clue to the effect on output of changes in the Investment and Economy Factors. But the problem can be attacked starting from the equation $\Delta Q = \Delta I + \Delta F - \Delta E$. Let us take the case where ΔQ becomes negative as a result of I decreasing more than F is increasing'.

17 Keynes expresses this using the term 'involuntary unemployment' in a note, 'Historical Retrospect' (1932. *JMK*.13, pp. 406–408), which is still argued in terms of the *I-S* difference.

18 The term appears for the first time in the title of chapter 20 in the table of contents, 'The Monetary Theory of Production' (*JMK*.29, p. 50). Bridel (1987) argues that 'the "liquidity preference" doctrine was already part and parcel of the *Treatise*' (p. 149), expressing it as '$M^D = M_1(Y) + M(r)$' (p. 133).

19 The MTP manuscript maintains Investment Price Theory (2).

20 Patinkin (1976, pp. 71–73) finds several original ideas leading to the *General Theory*, although he regards the MTP manuscript as being within the *Treatise* framework. Amadeo (1989, pp. 74–75) sees the embryo of the multiplier mechanism in the MTP manuscript, although he points out that 'the adjustment process is based on the same causation scheme used in the *Treatise*' (p. 74).

21 There exist two sets of material related to the MTP manuscript: (i) 'Notes on the Definition of Saving', where the TM supply function (*JMK*.13, p. 279) and the possibility of a cumulative deterioration of the economy (pp. 288–289) are argued; (ii) the 1932 spring lectures (*JMK*.29, pp. 35–48). The draft for the lecture of 2 May is in line with the MTP manuscript.

22 Points (2) and (3) are not mentioned in Patinkin (1976) and Patinkin's paper (in Patinkin and Leith eds, 1977).

23 See *TM*. 1, pp. 259–261.

24 See *JMK*.13, pp. 355–358 and 364 respectively.

25 Patinkin (1976, chapter 7) identifies three stages in the supply of criticism by economists that contributed to Keynes's development: (i) criticisms of the *Treatise* by the Cambridge Circus, Hawtrey and Hayek; (ii) discussions with Kahn and J. Robinson in 1932 and 1933; (iii) Hawtrey and Robertson's criticisms of the *GT* galley proofs. Patinkin endorses (i), but not (ii) and (iii).

26 In relation to the aggregate supply function, see Marcuzzo (2002, section 3). Kahn's fellowship dissertation was submitted to King's College in 1929 (The 'short period' was evidently based on Marshall's idea). It was to influence Keynes's path to the *General Theory*. See Kahn (1989, p. xi). Kahn had delivered his first lectures on the Short Period in the Lent Term (1931): for this, see Kahn's Michaelmas lectures for 1932 (in Kahn Papers).

27 Kahn's stance had already become clear in chapter 4, 'Supply Schedule of an Industry under Perfect Competition' by Kahn (1989[1929]). He was virtual co-author of Robinson (1933c). Moreover, Keynes 'exercised a stimulating influence on [Kahn's] progress' (Kahn, 1989, p.xi).

28 There were discussions on the supply curve between J. Robinson, Kahn and Sraffa around this period. See Marcuzzo (2003, pp. 3–4). See also Robinson's remark in the summer of 1931: 'Actually the supply of goods in the short period is likely to be fairly inelastic..., but not completely so' (1933a, p. 82).

29 For a theoretical rift between Kahn-Robinson and Sraffa, see Marcuzzo (2003).

30 Sraffa (1926, p. 543) says that 'a very large number of undertakings... work under... diminishing costs'.

31 These lines were also adopted by Harrod (1936, p. 66) which criticised the *Treatise* analysis in terms of the TM supply function, arguing that it neglects a temporary equilibrium state and a marginal entrepreneur.
    For 'Keynes's *Treatise* Influence on Harrod, 1930–39', however, see Young (1989, pp. 48–50). See also Harrod (1969, chapter 7), which evaluates the *Treatise* because of: (i) the distinction between cost inflation and demand inflation; (ii) the treatment of investment and saving.

32 In contrast, Keynes did not accept Roberson's and Hayek's criticisms.

7 The turning point

1 A combination of typed and pencil-written sheets of papers. In addition to this, another manuscript (consisting of three pencil-written sheets of paper) with the same title also survives (*JMK*.13, pp. 396–397).

2 This methodology is developed in *GT*'s chapter 4.

3 For a similar line of thought, see *GT*, pp. 42 and 286.

4 See *JMK*.13, p. 403.

5 This leads to the argument in *GT*, pp. 139–140.

6 This is the first time he defined a supply schedule along these lines.

7 See Hirai (1997–1999, chapter 10, section 2).

8 This idea appeared for the first time in 'Notes on the Definition of Saving' (*JMK*.13, pp. 275–289. Esp. p. 276), enclosed in Keynes's letter to Robertson of 22 March 1932.

9 Referring to the relation between income and consumption in connection with the stability condition for P_1, Keynes does not explicitly delineate the relations between saving, consumption and income.

10 A similar description appears at *GT*, p. 250.

11 See *GT*, pp. 115–116, 122 and 286. See also Keynes (1937), *JMK*.13, pp. 457–468 (5 June 1934, and *JMK*.14, p. 58). The same idea is found in Kahn (1931) and Bryce (1935).

12 See *JMK*.29, pp. 62–66, and Hirai (1997–1999, chapter 10).

13 See Rymes (1988, pp. A1–A52, D2–D22, and I1–I28). We also have Rymes's reconstruction (Rymes, 1989, pp. 47–84).

14 This might relate to the MTP Manuscript. See *JMK*.13, pp. 382–387.

15 See the diagram in Bryce's notes (Rymes, 1988, p. A29).

16 See Rymes [Bryce], 1988, p. A29. See also *JMK*.13, pp. 422 and 424.

17 'Historical Retrospect' (*JMK*.13, pp. 406–408) precedes this. Malthus, Hobson and Douglas are yet to be mentioned.

18 Kates (1998, p. 140) regards the last lecture as decisive, stressing Keynes's reading of Malthus's letters. See Section IV below.

19 Our view of the role played by Kahn goes in the same direction as Marcuzzo (2002), although she states that, accepting Kahn's theory by the summer of 1932, Keynes developed an aggregate supply–aggregate demand analysis, and regards the lectures at the Harris Foundations and the MTP Manuscript as belonging to the *General Theory* world. Contrastingly, Patinkin (1993, p. 651) underestimates Kahn (1931).

20 The 'Manifesto' (*JMK*.29, pp. 42–45) and some related letters (*JMK*.13, pp. 376–380 and *JMK*.29, pp. 46–47) are worth noting. The connection of 'Mr Meade's relation' to Kahn's multiplier is clarified by Meade (1993). Robinson (1933b, p. 24) criticises Keynes's position in the *Treatise*. Bridel (1987, pp. 155–156) regards Robinson (1933b) as confined within the *Treatise* theory.

21 This point is stated in Kahn's letter to Patinkin dated 11 October 1978 and in the typescript by Kahn (1984, p. 11 [the fourth lecture]). See Patinkin (1993, p. 659). Keynes (1939) refers to the same thing. Kahn (1984, pp. 99–100) argues that because his 1931 article is not free from the *Treatise*, it fails to emphasise the supply–demand theory as a whole.

Bridel (1987, p. 153) does not refer to 'the standard supply–demand analysis', although he evaluates, as the crux of Kahn (1931), the disposition of the 'Treasury View', and the multiplier formulation. Bridel, however, is rather critical of Kahn (1931), stating that it belongs to the *Treatise* world.

22 See *JMK*.29, pp. 72, and 101–102. Harrod (1936, p. 71) regards the adoption of the marginal analysis in the *General Theory* as a remarkable improvement.

23 Davis (1980) states that Hawtrey formulates the multiplier theory in his working paper for the Macmillan Committee, which he omitted from his subsequent publications. Robertson (1940, pp. 117–121) opposed the multiplier theory, defending the forced saving theory. See Presley (1979, pp. 169–176). Divergent views have been expressed about Hawtrey's influence on Kahn and Keynes. See Davis (1980), Cain (1982), Deutscher (1990, pp. 102–105) and Dimand (1997).

24 See 'Does Employment Need a Drastic Remedy?' (May 1924. *JMK*.19, Part I, pp. 219–223), the Liberal Party (1928), and 'A Draft Report' (October 1930. *JMK*.20, pp. 437–443). However, Keynes did not mention the multiplier theory in his Harris Foundation lectures (June 1931).

25 Based upon Hawtrey (1925), the Treasury produced a memorandum which was a rejoinder to the Liberal Party (1928) and became the basis of *The White Paper* (May 1929). See Peden (1984) and Clarke (1988, chapter 3).

26 See *JMK*.13, p. 422.

8 Searching for a new theory of employment

1 Milgate's paper (Eatwell and Milgate eds, 1983, p. 195) judges that they 're-express the [*Treatise*'s] Fundamental Equations... in terms of different definitions'.

2 In the First Manuscript variables are for the first time expressed in terms of expectation, followed by the two manuscripts.

3 The earliest system of equations determining the level of employment. Ohlin (Patinkin and Leith eds, 1977, p. 153) stated that in the latter half of 1932 economists began to treat output as a central variable in a monetary theory. Following the Second Manuscript, we interpret '*D*' in the First Manuscript as 'disbursement'.

4 In his letter to Robertson (20 May 1933. *JMK*.13, pp. 307–308), Keynes tried to persuade Robertson that Robertson's 'hoarding' equals Keynes's 'saving – investment', which Robertson rejected (here 'saving' in the *Treatise*). Keynes also referred to '[o]ld-fashioned saving' being equal to investment. Thus it seems that the First Manuscript must have been drawn up subsequent to the letter, which referred to 'my affection for the concept $I - Q [= S]$' (p. 308).

5 The level of employment is presupposed to be uniquely related to the volume of output through a production function.

6 $C'[H']$ denote a supply function of profit, $Q_2 [Q_1]$, in the capital [consumption] goods industry.

7 Their first appearances here.

8 Keynes referred to the consumption function in the MTP manuscript, but in a different sense.

9 However, he shows some 'hesitation' and substitutes equation (4), seeing it as a definition of Q, in equation (1). See *JMK*.29, p. 64. This 'hesitation' appears in the Second Manuscript.

10 By solving the equation, $I + f_3\{f_2 (N) + f_1^{-1} (N)\} = f_2 (N) + f_1^{-1} (N)$.

11 Keynes was to tackle the problem of prices again, accepting the first postulate in the Second Manuscript.

12 The 'Economics of the Budget Constraint' follows this idea. See Christ (1968), Tobin (1980) and Turnovsky (1980).

13 See *JMK*.29, p. 76.

14 Following this, normal return is stated to be constant.

15 The argument that saving is necessarily equal to investment also appears in the Second Manuscript (see *JMK*.29, p. 69).

16 Judging from the *Treatise*, ΔN and Q should be considered to have the same sign. We advance an argument with this change below. Q is interpreted as excess profit.

17 We can consistently interpret both the equilibrium and stability of the system only by using an increment in the level of employment.

18 For the propensity to save, see *JMK*.29, p. 100.

19 In his letter to Robertson (10 September 1933. *JMK*.13, pp. 310–313), which contains criticism of Pigou (1933), Keynes called it the 'fundamental postulate of employment theory'. His approval is to be seen in the first Michaelmas lecture for 1933.

20 There exists no evidence showing the first postulate's incorporation into the system of equations (7)–(16). See also *JMK*.29, pp. 101–102 as the origin of *GT*'s chapter 2.

21 See *GT*, p. 76.

22 See *JMK*.29, p. 97.

23 For a similar argument, see *JMK*.13, p. 384.

24 For a similar argument, see *JMK*.13, pp. 369–370.
25 Amadeo (1989, p. 79) states, [in the Third Manuscript], 'we can first identify the central elements...of the principle of effective demand'. His analysis (pp. 78–85), does not seem to interpret expected 'excess profit' *Q* appropriately.
26 Keynes does not compare what adds 'some normal value' to variable costs (i.e. aggregate costs) with aggregate expenditure. Nothing like the aggregate supply function of the *General Theory* appears here.
27 This criticism might be directed against the 'transitional period' analysis in Fisher (1911, pp. 55–73) based on the rates of interest lagging behind prices.
28 There might have been Ohlin's influence at work in the 'transfer controversy' in 1929 (see Keynes's letter to Ohlin of January 1931. Patinkin and Leith eds, 1977, p. 154).
29 Patinkin (1980, p. 20) regards the Second and Third Manuscripts as revisions of the *Treatise*, basing this supposition on Keynes's assumption of the TM supply function.
30 Robertson defended Pigou (1933). See *JMK*.13, pp. 318–319. An interesting point here has to do with the effect of a money-wage cut on employment. See GTE/1/148 ('II Money wages and real wages'. Robertson), GTE/1/150 (2 Oct. 1933. Keynes), GTE/1/151–152 (19 October Keynes), GTE/1/159–160 (26 Oct. Keynes), *JMK*.13, pp. 316–317 (26 October Keynes), p. 319 (Robertson). Shove was on Keynes's side, saying that '[Pigou (1933)] struck me as the worst book on economics that I had read for a long time' (*JMK*.13, p. 321), and that 'I have spent so much time in the course of my life in abortive attempts to invent defences for him' (*JMK*.13, p. 326).

9 Establishment of the investment and consumption theories

1 There survive the following students' notes for 1933 – Bryce (pp. B1–B61), Cairncross (pp. E1–E16), Fallgatter (pp. G1–G38), Tarshis (pp. J1–J39), Salant (pp. M1–M19), and Thring (pp. N1–N18). All of them are contained in Rymes (1988).
2 In his letter to Robertson (26 October. *JMK*.13, pp. 315–317), Keynes argued that Robertson's spontaneous saving is close to his 'saving' in the *Treatise* and that he can see 'no connection whatever between...[Robertson's] revised meaning of hoarding and the Marshallian *K* and income velocity *V*'. To the second remark Robertson responded that 'I...assert that...all forces acting on *P* can be expressed in terms of *M*, *V*, or *R*' (*JMK*.13, p. 318. $M = KRP = RP/V$). In an unpublished paper, 'Saving and Hoarding' (GTE/1/164–170), Robertson argued that his revised hoarding and Keynes's revised version of it belong to the Cambridge quantity theory. Throughout their correspondence Keynes refrained from advancing his new theory examined in the present chapter.

Turning, now, to the controversy between Hawtrey (1933) and Robertson (1933b), they were indeed very critical of each other. Hawtrey criticised Robertson's economics of lacking for (i) absence of reality; (ii) neglect of the stock of commodities. Robertson (1933b) criticised Hawtrey's theory, emphasising his theory's advantage in 'setting in high relief' analytically interesting points. Hawtrey (1932, p. 279) maintained his theory of consumers' income and outlay, arguing that the quantity theory is of no use in the state of disequilibrium. His criticism of the quantity theory (see Deutscher, 1990, pp. 36–39) is similar to Keynes's in the *Treatise*.

Keynes, having undergone the influence of Robertson in the mid-1920s, was influenced by Hawtrey after the *Treatise*, and then continued to move forward.
3 Patinkin (Patinkin and Leith eds, 1977, pp. 15–16) maintains that in these lectures the effective demand theory was argued for the first time. Dimand (1988, p. 166) states that except for an investment theory all were 'in forms recognisably similar to those of the [*General Theory*]'. He notes that '[b]etween the Michaelmas 1932 lectures and the 1933 lectures, Keynes dropped profits...from its central position in his theory, although it made a fleeting reappearance as *A*, windfall appreciation' (p. 166). Dimand

overlooks Keynes's movement in this direction in the 1932 lectures. Clarke (1998, p. 95) maintains that they 'gave a more cogent account of the theory of effective demand according to the criteria of professional economists' (Clarke attributes the inception of the theory to the 1932 lectures).

4 'This is the alternative to the two classical views [the loanable fund theory and Marshall's circularity]...seen to be abortive' (Rymes [Fallgatter], 1988, p. G33).

5 See Rymes [Bryce] (1988, p. B55).

6 'The real tool is thought, and...[these equations] are not a substitute for it, but at most a guide...' (Rymes [Fallgatter], 1988, p. G35). Also see Rymes (1988, pp. B59, J37, N17).

7 We see, moreover, $f_2(\rho) = f_3(M/w)$ where w is a money wage.

8 In the second lecture Keynes alluded to Marx, Major Douglas and Hobson, making use of Marx's 'realisation problem'. He read McCracken (1933), whose possible influence on Keynes is examined in Kates (1998, pp. 153–157). Keynes did not recognise Marx (see, e.g. *JMK*.13, p. 488; *JMK*.28, p. 38; *JMK*.9, p. 285; *JMK*.10, p. 446) except for the realisation problem. For the controversy between Major Douglas, who appears in *GT*, pp. 370–371, and Hobson in the early 1920s, see Schneider (1996, pp. 113–115).

9 Milgate (1983, p. 197) doubts that 'The First Undated Manuscript' 'dates from around the same time as the two [1933 manuscripts] that precede it'.

10 See Harai (1981, chapters 1 and 5).

11 See Hirai (1981, chapter 5(4)).

12 See *JMK*.29, p. 111.

13 See *GT*, p. 137.

10 The eve of the *General Theory*

1 See *JMK*.14, pp. 464–470. The chapter concerned is referred to as 'The Pre-First Proof Index Version' (see *JMK*.14, p. 351. Hereafter the Index Version) by Moggridge. Sections III to VIII of chapter 12, 'The State of Long-Term Expectation', of the *General Theory* retain the original form of the Index Version, except for a few paragraphs, while sections I and II of the same chapter appear in the form of a summary in the Index Version.

2 Patinkin (1976) emphasises the importance of 'The General Theory', for it was here that Keynes put forward the theory of effective demand. Moreover, Patinkin (1976, pp. 3–9; 1977, p. 4) concludes, judging from the 1933 Michaelmas Lectures, that Keynes formulated the theory of effective demand in the first half of 1933. He does not notice the ambiguities in the concept of 'effective demand' and the theoretical inconsistency of Keynes's employment theory there.

3 A similar problem occurs in the Second Manuscript of 1933 in which the relation between the acceptance of the first postulate and the argument in terms of aggregate expenditure and aggregate costs is not clear. See *JMK*.29, pp. 68–69, 72 and 90–91.

4 Thereafter, however, he came to feel the difference between effective demand and income 'to be of secondary importance, emphasis on it obscuring the real argument' (*JMK*.14, p. 181). This appears in a draft for his 1937 lectures.

5 See Patinkin (1976, p. 6).

6 This also appears in the footnote in which Keynes tries to explain why the employment function might be a straight line with a slope of 45° (see *JMK*.13, p. 446). He says that there is 'a tendency for average real prime cost to increase at about the same rate as output, as supply equipment is gradually brought into use'. This indicates the first postulate ($W/P = \Delta O/\Delta N$ [where W denotes the money wage, P price, O the volume of output, N the volume of employment, ΔX an increment in X]). Patinkin (1976, p. 4, chapter 8, fn. 14, pp. 87–88) infers from this observation, Bryce's notes, and others, that the employment function passes through the origin and has a slope of 45°, and that

it is in fact the aggregate supply function and the production function of the *General Theory* (the first postulate is not used in this argumentation).

7 This shows that the three features of the *General Theory* first appeared in 'The General Theory': (i) four kinds of aggregate supply function; (ii) the aggregate supply function as a whole as an equilibrium concept; and (iii) 'Keynes's incompleteness' in the sense that because he assumes a fixed distribution of the amount of effective demand between different industries, his methodological standpoint which stresses 'the heterogeneity of goods' and expectations is not persistently maintained (see *GT*, p. 286).

8 In fact, no distinction is made there between equations (4) and (5).

9 Keynes considers that the level of employment thus determined remains 'within a modest range of fluctuation' and does not 'proceed to extreme lengths'. See *JMK*.13, p. 446. Here we see the idea of 'underemployment equilibrium' in *GT*, p. 54.

10 See *GT*, p. 280.

11 See Keynes's letter to Kahn (13 April 1934. *JMK*.13, pp. 422–423), and Keynes (1939).

12 The term 'maximise' (*JMK*.29, p. 89) means to maximise excess profit. It has no direct relation to the first postulate. This is inconsistent with the main theoretical system of the Second and Third Manuscripts of 1933, where excess profit is considered to become zero in equilibrium.

13 See *JMK*.13, pp. 427 and 436.

14 Patinkin (1976, pp. 91–92) seems to point out the same inconsistency from a different angle.

15 However, this is not unquestionable, because around this period Keynes clearly tries to separate the functions of profit. It would perhaps be more accurate to say that he shows no interest in the pseudo-TM supply function mk2, rather than that the manuscript is devoid of anything corresponding to equation (8).

16 In a letter to Harrod dated 27 August 1935, Keynes states that the discovery of the definition of marginal efficiency of capital was absolutely vital in the development of his thought. See *JMK*.13, p. 549. Historically speaking, Keynes's marginal efficiency of capital follows Fisher's 'rate of return over cost' in *The Theory of Interest* (Fisher, 1930), a key concept in Fisher's 'principle of investment opportunities'. See *GT*, pp. 140–141. Fisher said that his theory of the rate of return over cost could be traced back to John Rae (1834).

17 In Section II (2) of Chapter 5 we referred to the 'duality' problem in the theory of the determination of the price level of investment goods in the *Treatise*. The investment theory of the *General Theory* is also inconsistent. Or rather, there are two investment theories, the inconsistency between which Keynes overlooks. For more on this, see Hirai (1981, pp. 195–200).

18 Keynes's examination of some fundamental concepts can be traced back to the Second Manuscript of 1933. See *JMK*.29, pp. 68–69.

19 For comparison between the table of contents of 'The General Theory' and the tables of contents of the Third Manuscript of 1933 and Galleys 1 (I), 1 (II) and 1 (III) (see Section 1 of Chapter 11), see Hirai (1997–1999, chapter 13, section I).

20 On this occasion, Keynes read the paper entitled 'The Theory of Effective Demand' (*JMK*.13, pp. 457–468) to the American Political Economy Club. The main themes of this paper were analysis of the American economy and some suggestions on economic policy. Keynes argued that an increase in public spending through deficit financing was indispensable for the restoration of the economy, and put forward the multiplier theory in relation to the policy of public spending. Keynes wrote open letters to President Roosevelt in the New York Times of 31 December 1933 and 11 June 1934 (*JMK*.21, pp. 289–304; 322–329, respectively). Lippmann wrote a letter to Keynes to the effect that the former letter had a great effect on the U.S. Treasury's policy of lowering the long-term rate of interest. The latter, in which Keynes urged the government to effect emergency spending, was encouraged by Lippmann. See Hession

(1984, pp. 275–276). On the relation between Keynes and Lippmann, see Wright (1973, p. 78).

21 Immediately after this, the equation $C + I = E + Q = Y = C + S$ appears. In view of the argument developed up to this point, this equation should have been $C + I + U = E + Q = Y + U = C + S + U$.

22 See *GT*, p. 282.

23 As can be seen at *JMK*.13, pp. 104–108, Keynes himself, together with Robertson, developed the theory of forced saving in 1928. On this, see Presley (1978, pp. 79–80).

24 For the close relation between the galley and the lectures, see Moggridge's comment (*JMK*.13, p. 85).

25 There survive notes taken by Bryce (pp. C1–C51), Champernowne (pp. F1–F16), Hopkin (pp. H1–H43), Tarshis (pp. K1–K23), and Thring (pp. O1–O30). All of them are contained in Rymes (1988).

26 In this quotation equation (1) is dealt with, while equation (2) is overlooked.

27 In November 1934 Keynes gave a public broadcast entitled 'Poverty in Plenty: Is the Economic System Self-Adjusting?' (*JMK*.13, pp. 485–492), in which he stresses 'a fatal flaw in that part of the orthodox reasoning [economics] which deals with the theory of what determines the level of effective demand and the volume of aggregate employment; the flaw being largely due to the failure of the classical doctrine to develop a satisfactory theory of the rate of interest' (p. 489) and emphasises the importance of increasing investment through the fall in the rate of interest rather than that of increasing consumption through drastic social changes like equalisation of income.

11 The proofing process (I): from 'The Pre-First Proof Typescript' (Summer 1934) to 'Galley 1(III)' (June–July 1935)

1 See *JMK*.14, p. 351. As precursors of chapter 5, in fact, there survive three versions written a little before 'The Typescript'.

2 In Lord Keynes's Letters to Daniel Macmillan, British Library.

3 The original is $Q (O)$. See *JMK*.14, p. 387.

4 See *JMK*.13, pp. 525–526.

5 See *JMK*.13, pp. 496–506.

6 See *JMK*.13, pp. 484–485.

7 Robertson did not receive the chapter corresponding to *GT*, chapter 10, 'The Marginal Propensity to Consume and the Multiplier'. The correspondence on the galleys continued until March 1935. See *JMK*.13, pp. 493–523. Robertson (3 February 1935) remarked 'I've found it extremely hard to see the wood for the trees', and (10 February) wrote that 'a large part of your theoretical structure is...mumbo-jumbo!' The only chapters with which Robertson agreed were chapters 14 and 17, for he regarded the liquidity preference theory as an alternative version to the loanable fund theory. See Moggridge (1992, p. 567).

8 See *JMK*.14, pp. 446–447.

9 See *JMK*.14, pp. 446–447.

10 See *GT*, p. 90.

11 See *JMK*.14, pp. 448–449 and *GT*, pp. 93–94.

12 On chapter 19 we have comments by Robertson and Hawtrey (*JMK*.13, pp. 508–511, 574–576, respectively).

13 See *JMK*.13, p. 525.

14 See *JMK*.13, pp. 496–506.

15 See *JMK*.13, p. 634.

16 The discussion between Keynes and Harrod about the galley continued from July to October 1935 (*JMK*.13, pp. 527–565). The serious issue was over the classical theory

of interest. Keynes deemed the classical theory (the loanable fund theory) incoherent, taking the rate of interest to be determined by the equilibrium of investment and saving, given income. Instead he insisted upon the liquidity preference theory. Harrod recognised some value in the classical theory. He agreed completely with the constructive part of Keynes's theory, but opposed his criticism of the classical theory (Harrod held his stance thereafter, as is seen in Harrod (1969, pp. 173–174)). From Keynes's point of view, Harrod still remained partly in the world of classical economics. See especially *JMK*. 13, pp. 530–552. For the relationship between Harrod and Keynes, see also Kregel's paper (in Harcourt ed., 1985). Blaug (1985, p. 637) questions Keynes's treatment of the classical theory where he refers only to Marshall-Pigou's theory, which deals solely with the so-called 'direct mechanism'.

Milgate (Eatwell and Milgate eds, 1983, chapter 5) maintains that 'In adopting Harrod's reconciliation Keynes sacrificed his [critical] argument [developed in chapter 15 of Galley1 (I)] on the altar of the immediate success of the [constructive] theory. This has had the unfortunate consequence...' (p. 89).

17 Pigou (1941, chapter 7) criticises Keynes's critique of Marshall's theory of interest, arguing that Keynes fails to recognise that Marshall advances a long-term theory in which the level of employment is given.
18 See *JMK*.14, pp. 479–487.
19 See *JMK*.14, pp. 482–484.
20 See *GT*, pp. 189–190.
21 See *JMK*.13, p. 525.
22 This finds confirmation in the fact that the formulation of the employment function in both chapter 21 of Galley 1(II) and chapter 20 of 'The General Theory' is one and the same (in fact, D_w as deflated by the wage unit is used).
23 Here we assume that in 'The Great Revision' (see Chapter 12) Keynes came to adopt the same functions as those in the *General Theory*. This can be confirmed by the fact that Keynes used 'the aggregate supply function' and 'the aggregate demand function' in the second lecture for the 1935 Michaelmas term. Patinkin (1976, note 14 to chapter 8) erroneously states that the aggregate 'supply function' is found only in the *General Theory*.
24 See *JMK*.13, pp. 309–326.
25 See *JMK*.13, p. 525. Pigou (1933) thinks that a cut in money wages contributes to increasing the level of employment. Pigou (1941), who on the whole accepts the system of the *General Theory*, stresses two conditions for the classical view: (i) money wages must be flexible; and (ii) a cut in money wages must contribute to increasing the level of employment (see pp. 91–92). For studies which deal with Keynesian theories on the presupposition that money wages are inflexible, see Iwai (1981, pp. 128–129) and Yoshikawa (1984, pp. 87–88).
26 See *JMK*.14, p. 504.
27 In Lord Keynes's Letters to Daniel Macmillan, British Library.
28 Chapters 26, 27 and 28 will correspond respectively to chapter 25, 'Notes on Mercantilism, the Balance of Trade and Foreign Investment', chapter 27, 'Notes on the History of Similar Ideas', and chapter 26 (the same title) in the table of contents of 'The General Theory'.
29 Clarke (1998, pp. 122–124) mentions Keynes's inclusion of Hobson's theory in the *General Theory*.
30 This letter, together with some other letters by Keynes to which we refer a little later, shows that Keynes was making his last revision.
31 See *JMK*.13, p. 653.
32 See *JMK*.13, pp. 406–407.
33 See *JMK*.13, p. 407.
34 See *JMK*. 29, p. 48.
35 See *JMK*.13, p. 653.
36 See *JMK*.13, pp. 650–651.

12 The proofing process (II): 'The Great Revision' and the 1935 Michaelmas lectures

1 See *JMK*. 13, pp. 576–577.
2 See *JMK*.14, pp. 398–418.
3 See *JMK*.14, pp. 418–425.
4 See *JMK*.13, pp. 442 and 436.
5 See *JMK*.13, p. 435.
6 A possible origin is to be seen in the remarks in *JMK*.13, p. 431, (iii).
7 See *JMK*. 14, pp. 398–418.
8 Based on the remarks in *JMK*.14, p. 400 (fn.2) and 412 (fn.2).
9 See *JMK*.14, p. 400 (fn.2).
10 See *JMK*.14, p. 400 (fn.2).
11 See *GT*, p. 55.
12 Because a fully integrated firm is assumed.
13 See *JMK*.14, p. 404.
14 See *GT*, p. 53.
15 See *JMK*.14, p. 430.
16 See *JMK*.14, pp. 425–427.
17 See Tarshis (pp. L1–L45) in Rymes (1988).
18 In Lord Keynes's Letters to Daniel Macmillan, British Library.
19 Robertson's letter to Keynes (3 February 1935) and Keynes's response (*JMK*.13, pp. 496–520) are useful for an understanding of Galley 1(I), in which the principle of effective demand and the liquidity preference theory are debated. Robertson's criticism of the principle of effective demand (and the multiplier theory) can be seen in Robertson (1940, chapter IX), his criticism of the liquidity preference theory in Robertson (1940, chapter I).

See also the controversy between Harrod and Robertson. Roberston remarked in his letter to Harrod (27 September 1934) that 'if your line of reasoning is right, it makes nonsense of everything which I have been trying to say for the last eight years'. Harrod answered (3 October 1935) that 'my only ray of sunshine is Maynard's book....I agree with him (as against you) that his book...is pathbreaking'. See Young (1989, pp. 75–82).

Keynes's discussion with Hawtrey is noteworthy as well. The sources before the *General Theory* are contained in *JMK*.13, pp. 567–633 and those after the *General Theory* in *JMK*.14, pp. 2–55. The most important document is Hawtrey's comment to Keynes (*JMK*.13, pp. 567–576). In his letter to Hawtrey of 4 September (*JMK*.13, pp. 576–577), Keynes states that he is revising the galley (reference is to 'The Great Revision'), taking Hawtrey's comment into consideration. From examination of 'The Variorum' we can confirm that Keynes at this time revised as follows: (i) the quasi-rent was deleted (chapter 7 of the TOC is the main place in which Keynes makes revision); (ii) the concept of the marginal efficiency of capital was applied to working capital. However, the debate between the two remained fierce after the publication of the *General Theory*. See Keynes's letter to Hawtrey (24 March 1936. *JMK*.14, pp. 14–18).

13 The *General Theory*: the monetary economics of underemployment equilibrium

1 Ricardo, for example, is critically treated: (i) as a representative of the 'classical school'; (ii) as an advocate of Say's Law (chapter 2, section VI); (iii) as developing two theories of money – the quantity theory and the theory of interest as determined by the rate of profit (appendix to chapter 14, section II).
2 The difference between classical and neoclassical economics over the theory of value and the plutology/catallactics classification are not referred to in the *General Theory*.

3 Milgate (Eatwell and Milgate eds, 1983, chapter 5) maintains that chapter 14 became ambiguous as a result of Keynes's acceptance (*GT*, pp. 177–183) of Harrod's criticism, which caused interpreters to see the essence of the *General Theory* erroneously in expectations and uncertainty.
4 Keynes overlooks the fact that the Wicksells influences advanced monetary economics against real economics of the 'classical' economists, criticising its acceptance of the classical dichotomy, Say's Law and the quantity theory.
5 Laidler (1991a, pp. 119, 149, 152) recognises Wicksell's influence on the *General Theory*.
6 Keynes used Mandeville's *Fable of the Bees* (1714) as showing how the society which makes excessive savings should fall into the plight. Myrdal (1953, p. 45) esteemed Mandeville very highly, stating that 'he destroyed the unqualified doctrine of [the spontaneous] harmony of enlightened self-interest'. Interestingly, Hayek in his 'Dr Bernard Mandeville' (in Hayek, 1978) regards Mandeville as the first man who developed the 'spontaneous order' theory.
7 For Mummery and Hobson (1889), see Kadish and Backhouse's papers (in Pheby ed., 1994). Keynes expressed qualified approval of Hobson's under-consumption theory in the *Treatise*, pointing out its failure in linking it to the rate of interest. They agreed in recognising the main points on which they diverged, for which see Hobson's letter dated 10 February 1936 and Keynes's letter dated 14 February 1936 (*JMK*.29, pp. 209–211). Clarke (1988, pp. 226–234, 270–274) traces their correspondence. Schneider (1996, pp. 70–71) emphasises two points of difference between their theories.
8 For similar views, see Shackle on: (i) 'the formal configuration and its thermal source of power' (1967, p. 129); (ii) 'double think' [equilibrium analysis and the non-existence of knowledge regarding the future years] (1974, p. 70); (iii) 'the extra-ordinary clash of method and meaning' (1974, p. 76). Shackle regards the first aspect in (i), (ii) and (iii) as hollow, the second as deep.
   Vicarelli (1984, p. 77) regards Keynes's vision as 'the extreme instability of [the capitalist system's] capital accumulation mechanism'. Minsky (1975; 1986) sees the financial instability of the capitalist economy in the *General Theory*.
9 For his employment policy in the 1940s, see *JMK*.27, chapter 5.
10 Shackle (1974, pp. 42–43; 1967, pp. 130–132) emphasises uncertainty or un-knowledge in the *General Theory* and Keynes (1937a), while the Neo-Ricardians like Garegniani and Milgate (Eatwell and Milgate eds, 1983, p. 92) do not regard uncertainty and expectations as the essence of the *General Theory*.
11 Chapter 12 is highly rated by Shackle (1967, chapter 11), followed by chapter 17. Contrastingly, Hicks (1977, p. 126) regards chapter 12 as 'the root of the trouble'.
12 Chapter 17 is highly rated by the Post-Keynesians or the Neo-Ricardians. See, for example, Rogers (1989, p. 91), Hara (1994) and Hishiyama (1993). Hishiyama's valuation might have something to do with Keynes (1937c). See *JMK*. XIV, p. 103.
   Concerning chapter 17, moreover, we find two interesting interpretations: (i) Potestio (in Sebstiani ed., 1992) find it incompatible with chapters 1–15 in analysis and method; (ii) Tonveronachi (in Sebastiani ed., 1992) identifies two definitions of own-rates.
   Chapter 17 is traceable to chapter 18, 'Philosophical Considerations on the Essential Properties of Capital, Interest and Money' in the Table of Contents of 'The *General Theory*' in Spring 1934, which was possibly rewritten as chapter 19 drastically between December 1934 and January 1935. Keynes and Hawtrey exchanged their views on this chapter, which started with Hawtrey's comment in June 1935 (*JMK*.13, pp. 574–576). After the publication, chapter 17 was discussed between Keynes, Champernowne and Reddaway during April–August 1936. See *JMK*.14, pp. 59–70.
13 Harrod (1948, pp. 72–73) stresses this as the innovation of the *General Theory*. Harcourt and O'Shaughnessy (in Harcourt ed., 1985, pp. 16–20) sees underemployment equilibrium in terms of the short period, following J. Robinson and Kahn, while Milgate (1982) and Eatwell (in Eatwell and Milgate eds, 1983) take it in terms of the long period.

14 Shackle (1974) recognises that the *General Theory* 'resort[s], in all formal analysis, only to equilibrium, to adjusted states of affairs', although he does not forget to stress that Keynes's 'purpose is to expose that supposition as absurd and to draw the consequences of abandoning it' (p. 70). Shackle seems to grasp equilibrium in the *General Theory* as 'a haunted equilibrium' (p. 77) which is used as allowing for both an equilibrium method and uncertainty. See also Shackle (1974, pp. 42 and 76).

   Chick (Sharma ed., 1998, chapter 4) argues that the concept of equilibrium in the *General Theory*, in which time and uncertainty are fundamental, is quite different from that of the neoclassical and the classical schools, while criticising the Neo-Ricardian interpretation, represented by Garegnani (in Eatwell and Milgate eds, 1983), and Caravale (in Sebastiani ed., 1992), for taking the *General Theory* in terms of long-period equilibrium.

   Amadeo (1989) states that the *General Theory* adopts 'equilibrium static method' (pp. 17–19) although he remarks that 'in the *General Theory* as a whole one finds traces of both historical and equilibrium methods' (p. 20). Concerning long-period equilibrium, Amadeo (Davis, J. ed., 1994, chapter 2) , to a degree, recognises it, although he himself sees the *General Theory* as based on short-period equilibrium (see also Table 6–1 at Amadeo, 1989, p. 95).

15 We should also mention *GT*, pp. 84–85.

16 Milgate and Gareganani (Eatwell and Milgate eds, 1983, chapter 5 and 2 respectively) criticise Keynes's investment theory because the marginal efficiency of capital is the same as an orthodox marginalist theory of investment, and the liquidity preference theory is not effective in criticising the marginalist theory of interest. Shackle (1974, p. 76) juxtaposes Keynes's investment theory and fragility–uncertainty of investment in chapter 12, pointing out an 'extraordinary clash of method and meaning'. See also Shackle (1974, p. 47).

17 Beside this model, Keynes, in chapter 17, describes the state of equilibrium among various assets in terms of own rates of interest. This might be a mirror image of the principal model. Hara (1994) interprets the *General Theory* from this image.

18 Chick's paper (in Lawson and Pesaran, eds, 1989, p. 198) maintains that the *General Theory* adopts 'a method which captures the historical-time attributes of production in a static model. The essential trick is the use of the wage-unit'.

19 See Table 1 in chapter 6 of Hirai (1981), which shows how the heterogeneity of goods runs through the *General Theory*.

20 See the same statement at *GT*, p. 281.

21 Minsky (1975, chapter 5) argues that Keynes failed to construct an appropriate investment theory because of too much emphasis on the marginal efficiency of capital. An investment theory, says Minsky, should determine the demand price of investment goods by capitalising the prospective yields of capital. Keynes regarded the two approaches as identical, emphasising the former. Joan Robinson upholds Minsky's argument. See Eatwell and Milgate eds (1983, p. 71).

22 Harrod (1936, p. 135) seems to accept Keynes's claim that there exists no established theory of the rate of interest, but takes a rather neutral position, stating that 'the theory of liquidity preference is neither in conflict with nor necessary for what I have to argue'. Harrod (1948, pp. 63–72), however, supports the theory of liquidity preference because it is more realistic than either the loanable fund theory or the theory which attributes too much foresight to the market, and defends it against several criticisms, claiming that it should be properly regarded as an attempt to fill a void.

23 Keynes refers to a dilemma regarding the debt market: while its existence greatly decreases liquidity preference due to the precautionary motive, it also causes great fluctuations in liquidity preference due to the speculative motive. See *GT*, p. 170.

24 Keynes regards the fact that the prevailing psychology of the public is rooted in convention as causing the rate of interest to be reluctant to fall. See *GT*, p. 204.

25 Keynes refers to the following: (i) The monetary authority cannot perform ideal operations; (ii) There might occur some contingencies in which the monetary authority would fail in arriving at a certain rate of interest.

26 Skidelsky's paper (in Blaug, O'Brien, Patinkin, Skidelsky and Wood, 1995, pp. 94–95) emphasises exogenous money, arguing that 'exogenous money remained for Keynes part of the politics of the middle way'.

27 Shackle (1974) supports the latter, emphasising liquidity preference on the grounds that it is closely connected with 'our essential, incurable and merciful un-knowledge' (p. 27).

28 Although he recognises the importance and novelty of the principle of effective demand of the *General Theory*, Bridel (1987, pp. 187–189) does not deem it a success.

29 A number of different factors have been indicated as the key factor behind underemployment equilibrium: (i) the liquidity trap (Hicks, 1937; Modigliani, 1944); (ii) the negative equilibrium rate of interest at full employment (Klein, 1947); (iii) the sluggishness of adjustment speed (Patinkin, 1976).

Our view is: point (i) is emphasised neither in the *General Theory* (see p. 207), nor even after the *General Theory* (see his letter to Robertson of 5 December 1937. *JMK*.14, pp. 223–226 and Keynes (1937d)); point (ii) implicitly assumes interest-inelasticity of investment, which is not emphasised in the *General Theory*.

Point (iii) is Patinkin's attractive invention: Keynes's theory, which is constructed in terms of a single short period, is discussed as if it could be construed in terms of the long period. For example, Patinkin (1965) argues that changes in prices would make the aggregate demand function shift via the real balance effect. However, the shifts occur successively and would require some considerable time.

30 On the genealogy of macroeconomics, Hick's article in Latsis (1936, pp. 215–218) is extremely useful.

14 Interpretations of Keynes and the development of postwar macroeconomics

1 In Coddington's terminology (1983) they correspond to Hydraulicism, Reconstituted Reductionism and Fundamentalism respectively. His criterion is in reference to Reductionism (the Walrasian system).

2 Hicks (1974, p. 6) repeated the same view. See also 'Recollections and Documents' (1972) (in Hicks, 1977, pp. 134–148). For Hicks's gradual change in attitude towards the IS-LM model, see Hicks (1980).

3 See Hicks (1937, pp. 132–133 and 136; 1957).

4 Hicks (1937) compares the formal differences between the equations and variables in classical theory and those in Keynes's theory. This is remarkable, above all, in treatment of the money market.

5 See Hicks (1977, pp. xi–xiii; 1974, pp. 23–30). Hicks (1982, pp. 129–130) also describes Robertson (1926) as having 'got quite tied up with' flexprice market idea.

6 Hicks sees this transition even within the *General Theory*. See Hicks (1976, pp. 216–217).

7 Presley (in Greenaway and Presley eds, 1989, pp. 106–110) values Hicks (1935) as the real beginning of the liquidity preference theory more highly than the *General Theory*.

8 See Patinkin (1976, p. 65).

9 See Patinkin (1976, p. 80).

10 See Patinkin (1949; 1965, chapter 13), and Patinkin (Gordon ed., 1970, pp. 129–130).

11 See Patinkin (1976, p. 106).

12 See Patinkin (Gordon ed., 1970, pp. 120–129).

13 See Patinkin (1976, pp. 122–125).

14 See Patinkin (Gordon ed., 1970, p. 130).

15 See Tobin (1980, fourth lecture). This is an IS-LM analysis into which the so-called 'government budget equation' is incorporated.

16 See Tobin (Gordon ed., 1970, p. 77, fn. 1).

17 See Tobin (Gordon ed., 1970, p. 79).

236 *Notes*

18 See Tobin (Gordon ed., 1970, p. 79, fn. 5).
19 The following is based on Leijonhufvud (1968). He subsequently rejects the liquidity preference theory, defending the loanable fund theory. Moreover, in Leijonhufvud (Worswick and Trevithick eds, 1983, pp. 179–221), he argues that because the Income-Expenditure Approach Keynesians got bogged down in the Philips Curve, neglecting 'nominal shocks and real shocks', they lost ground in the debate with Monetarism and the Rational Expectations School.
20 See Leijonhufvud (1968, chapter 2). Although Leijonhufvud, *prima facie*, resembles Friedman in his understanding of prices and money-wages, what Leijonhufvud has in mind is different. See Leijonhufvud (1968, p. 67).
21 See Leijonhufvud (1968, pp. 68–75).
22 See Leijonhufvud (1968, pp. 56–57). Leijonhufvud (1981, chapter 6) also depicts Keynes's theory as a model in which the system disperses outside the 'corridor', while depicting Monetarism as a model in which the system converges within it.
23 See Leijonhufvud (1968, chapter 3).
24 Jarsulic (1988, p. 24) defines the Post-Keynesians as 'those non-neoclassicals who are not Neo-Ricardians or Neo-Marxians, and whose work centres on effective demand and non-standard theories of distribution'. He sees Davidson, Eichner, S. Weintraub as the representatives, followed by Kalecki, Kaldor and Pasinetti as well as J. Robinson and Minsky.
25 See Blaug (1974).
26 See Davidson (Gordon ed., 1970, pp. 91–92 and 100).
27 See Davidson (Gordon ed., 1970, pp. 98–99).
28 See Davidson (Gordon ed., 1970, p. 95).
29 See Davidson (Gordon ed., 1970, pp. 93–94).
30 See Davidson and Smolensky (1964), Davidson (1992; 1991).
31 The finance motive, which appeared after the *General Theory* in Keynes (1937d), is defined as arising from the need for credit in the period from the planning to the implementation of investment.
32 See Davidson (Gordon ed., 1970, p. 100, fn. 14).
33 Jarsulic (1988) defines the Neo-Ricardians as 'those whose work centres primarily around the classical theory of price and its connection to the distribution of a technically determined economic surplus, without ignoring their attempts to join those ideas to the concept of effective demand'. He mentions Sraffa, Garegnani and Eatwell. Piling (1986), a Marxist, is critical of the Neo-Ricardians who based their position on Sraffa's work on the grounds that 'Sraffa's work involves a degeneration as compared with the . . . work of David Ricardo' (p. 20).
34 This belief was not popular in the interwar Cambridge. See, for example, Pigou (1920, chapter 20) and Robertson (1926, chapter 7).
35 Pigou (1920) was, according to Hicks (1976), the founder of classical macroeconomics.
36 The main target was Pigou(1933). The debate between Pigou and Keynes centred around the theory of money. See *JMK*.14, pp. 234–268.
37 See Pigou (1950, p. 30).
38 See Pigou (1950, p. 30).
39 See Pigou (1950, pp. 17–19).
40 See Pigou (1950, p. 65).
41 The critics of Monetarism are not confined to Keynesians such as Kaldor and Davidson. Hahn (1971) is highly critical of Monetarism, advocating the development of Keynes's theory under the conditions of externalities and increasing returns. See Worswick and Trevithick (1983, pp. 72–75).
42 See Friedman (Gordon ed., 1970, p. 18).
43 See Friedman (Gordon ed., 1970, p. 25). Contrastingly, Leijonhufvud (1981, chapter 7) argues that the liquidity trap plays no role in the *General Theory*.
44 Leijonhufvud (1981, chapter 7) argues that Friedman errs in viewing Keynes's theory through the IS-LM model.

45 For my evaluation of Japanese studies in this field, see Hirai (1998).
46 See Leijonhufvud (1968, p. 322). Friedman (1970, p. 176) does not think highly of chapter 19.
47 Meltzer's *Treatise* model, as expressed in terms of the OM (output market) and AM (asset market) schedules, is formulated in Meltzer (1988, pp. 76–77). He argues that this model 'is as close…to a general equilibrium framework relating stocks and flows' (p. 77). It does not describe the transitional period which should be Keynes's focal point, but the long-period equilibrium given the level of real income.
48 Meltzer's *General Theory* model is advanced as an equations system composed of the IS, LM, and SS [aggregate supply function] curves. See Meltzer (1988, pp. 167–170).
49 Interestingly, Minsky (1975, chapter 1) also regards the two books as discontinuous. He argues that the *Treatise* accepts the quantity theory (and the classical dichotomy) and assumes full employment. The main point of the *General Theory*, he argues, lies in the determination process of the asset prices as the principal determinant of investment. Milgate (1982) also argues that 'the *Treatise* model…is just a variant of neo-'classical' theory' (p. 182) while 'the theoretical system of the *General Theory* departs from the marginalist orthodoxy (of which the *Treatise* was a part) by offering a new theory of employment which conflicts with the then prevailing theory of capital and of employment (and hence, of value) conducted in terms of demand-and-supply' (p. 187).
50 This corresponds to 'Keynes's own theory'. Amadeo's interpretation of the *Treatise* theory is in full accord with ours, although he reduces the difference between the two to the 'method of analysis' only (see Amadeo, 1994, p. 13).
51 See, for example, Klein (1947, chapter 4) and Niida's paper (in Tachi ed., 1968).
52 In this theory 'utility' of individuals plays an essential role in constructing the model. This further goes to such a degree as postulating a 'representative household' in present-day microeconomics. There utility itself has been regarded as belonging to the objective existence which escapes value judgement. It was Myrdal who continued to criticise this point.
53 The neo-classical revival in this period is succinctly described in Hines (1971, chapter 1).
54 Leijonhufvud (1999) describes this 'eclecticism' as follows: 'For most economists, this one-foot-in-each-camp stance between classical and modern ways of thinking remained perfectly comfortable up through the 1960s and into the 1970s' (p. 20). See also Hicks (1976, p. 270), who was already critical of 'equilibrium economics' and struggled to deal with the problem of 'time'.
55 The *General Theory* was propagated mainly in the form of the 'IS-LM' model, which was simultaneously worked out by Harrod, Hicks, and Meade in 1936. See Young (1987, chapter 1). This prompts the question: to what extent can the IS-LM model be said to capture sufficiently well the essence of Keynes's theory? If the answer is in the affirmative, the Keynesian Revolution is established as the IS-LM model. If the answer is in the negative, the Keynesian Revolution proves distorted.
Our view concerning the legitimacy and limitations of the 'IS-LM' formulation of the *General Theory* is as follows. The IS-LM theory has the following merits: (i) It presents a system of simultaneous equations describing the commodity and money markets, adopting an equilibrium analysis method. It correctly reflects Keynes's position in the *General Theory* in its formulations of the commodity market and the money market; (ii) It mirrors the *General Theory* in assuming the rigidity of money wages and accepting the first postulate; (iii) It preserves the *General Theory*'s method of demonstrating underemployment equilibrium.
On the other hand, as an attempt to summarise the *General Theory* the IS-LM model has the following defects: (a) It neglects the most important feature of the *General Theory* – 'the two contrasting potentialities of the market economy'; (b) It completely neglects the micro-aspect described in the *General Theory*; (c) Negligence of the *General Theory*'s micro-aspect leads to a failure to consider how the micro- and the

macro-aspects should be related to each other; (d) It oversimplifies the analysis of the commodity market developed in the *General Theory*. The volume of employment is discussed, in the *General Theory*, in terms of the aggregate supply and aggregate demand functions, while in the IS-LM theory the 45° line supersedes the aggregate supply function, without paying due consideration to the true nature of the latter; (e) These features of the IS-LM model appear to be responsible for a failure to examine critically Keynes's theory on various points – for example, the question of how far the aggregate supply and aggregate demand functions are justified if pursued consistently from the micro-aspect.

Presley (in Greenaway and Presley eds, 1989) rates the IS-LM model highly, stating that it is 'an amalgam of Keynes and the Classics combined with a strong flavour of Hicks ... which has, rightly or wrongly, dictated the thought process of the majority of post-war macroeconomics' (p. 111). A similar evaluation is made by Laidler (1999), in which he summarises that 'IS-LM was ... a highly selective synthesis of several pre-existing strands of economic thought. ... the *General Theory* was one among several sources of what came to be post-war orthodox macroeconomics' (p. 12), omitting 'many important elements of the new message which Keynes was trying to convey in 1936' (p. 4).

56 On the technical arguments of the Keynesian School in the 1960s, see Lecachman (1966, chapters 5 and 11), Stein (1969, chapter 9) and Collins (1981, chapter 1).

57 The Post-Keynesians argue against interpreting the *General Theory* as a theory of disequilibrium. See Harcourt and O'Shaughnessy (in Harcourt ed., 1985, esp. p. 13).

58 Rogers (1989) points out that Friedman pays only lip service to the general equilibrium theory.

59 See, for example, Lucas and Sargent (1979), which stands on an equilibrium business model.

60 However, the real business cycle theory, although it belongs to this school, takes a different approach. Its methodology resembles that of physics. Physics endeavours to expresses natural phenomenon in terms of mathematical equations. When coefficients are ascertained, the equation can predict a certain natural phenomenon. Here mathematical expression and natural phenomenon become unified. The only reliance placed in the precision of a mathematical equation is in its ability to forecast the natural phenomenon concerned. It is secured only by inductive precision. See Kydland and Prescott (1990).

61 This stance is explicitly criticised, for example, in Hoover (2006), a review of Woodford (2003). We agree with Hoover, for the representative household hypothesis is a belief rather than a scientific fact.

62 See Hirai (2007, chapter 17).

63 Leijonhufvud (1999, p. 28) critically discusses 'How the Moderns do away with Keynes'. Leijonhufvud's paper (in Backhouse and Bateman eds, 2006) emphasises the continuity between Marshall and Keynes, and the difference from the 'Moderns' who work on the basis of the Walrasian general equilibrium theory.

64 Liberalists are, however, not monolithic, as can readily be seen in the criticisms by Knight, Robbins and Buchanan of Hayek's theory of spontaneous order.

65 Stiglitz and Greenwald (2003), which develops this theory, is critical of theories of money which emphasise transaction demand, including, among others, the quantity theory of money. It points out the instability of the velocity of money circulation, and emphasises credit rather than money.

66 Taking up the interwar Cambridge as an example, its social philosophy is in sharp contrast with that of Monetarism and the Rational Expectations School, while it is shared by the New Keynesians, in terms of trust in the market mechanism, the role of the state, the evaluation of the situation of income distribution. For example, Stiglitz (2002) emphasises the role of the government in economic development, and is critical of the 'Washington Consensus'.

67 See Colander's paper (in DeVroey and Hoover eds, 2005). It should also be noted that the recent depression of the Japanese economy gave rise to a controversy between the Income–Expenditure Keynesians and the Structural Reformers who have no established economic theory behind them (the only exception is the Real Business Cycle theory).

68 See, for example, Blanchard, Blinder and Solow in *American Economic Review* (May 1997).

69 Leijonhufvud (1999) might be regarded as a restatement of the Disequilibrium Approach in terms of his own definitions of 'Classics' and 'Moderns'. For an evaluation of the Disequilibrium Approach in the context of the history of macroeconomics, see Backhouse and Boianovsky (2005).

70 For example, Pasinetti (1999) classifies economics into the 'Exchange Paradigm' and the 'Production Paradigm'. Considering Keynes's theory to belong to the latter, Pasinetti is critical of the Income–Expenditure Approach which tries to contain Keynes's theory within the former.

Bibliography

I Primary sources

1   Charleston Papers, King's College Archive Centre, Cambridge University.
2   The Diaries of John Neville Keynes 1864–1917, Cambridge University Library (Microfilm, 12 reels, Adam Matthew Publications, 1994) (Neville's Diaries).
3   John Maynard Keynes Papers, King's College Archive Centre, Cambridge University (Microfilm, 170 reels, Chadwyck-Healey Ltd., 1993) (Keynes Papers).
4   John Maynard Keynes's Letters to Duncan Grant, British Library.
5   Keynes's Lectures, 1932–1935, Department of Economics, transcribed by Rymes, T., Carleton University, mimeo., 1988.
6   Keynes's Will, 14 February 1941, King's College Archive Centre, Cambridge University.
7   Lord Keynes's Letters to Daniel Macmillan, British Library.
8   Richard Ferdinand Kahn Papers, King's College Archive Centre, Cambridge University (Kahn Papers).

II The Collected Writings of John Maynard Keynes (*JMK*)

The following are published by the Royal Economic Society through the Macmillan Company. Where two dates are given, the first refers to the year of publication of the original book, the second to publication in the *Collected Writings*. An expression within a parenthesis below is the one used in the text of the present book according to the situation.

Examples: *ECP*, pp. 20–25 indicates Volume 1, pp. 20–25; *JMK*. 13, pp. 20–23 indicates Volume 13, pp. 20–23.

Volume   Title

1   *Indian Currency and Finance*, 1913, 1971 (*ICF*).
2   *The Economic Consequences of the Peace*, 1919, 1971 (*ECP*).
3   *A Revision of the Treaty*, 1922, 1971 (*RT*).
4   *A Tract on Monetary Reform*, 1923, 1971 (the *Tract*, *TMR*).
5   *A Treatise on Money I: The Pure Theory of Money*, 1930, 1971 (the *Treatise*, *TM*. 1).
6   *A Treatise on Money II: The Applied Theory of Money*, 1930, 1971 (the *Treatise*, *TM*. 2).
7   *The General Theory of Employment, Interest and Money*, 1936, 1973 (the *General Theory*, *GT*).
8   *A Treatise on Probability*, 1921, 1973.
9   *Essays in Persuasion*, 1931, 1972.
10 *Essays in Biography*, 1933, 1972.
11 *Economic Articles and Correspondence: Academic*, 1983.

12 *Economic Articles and Correspondence: Investment and Editorial*, 1983.
13 *The General Theory and After: Part I, Preparation*, 1973.
14 *The General Theory and After: Part II, Defence and Development*, 1973.
15 *India and Cambridge*, 1971.
16 *The Treasury and Versailles*, 1971.
17 *Treaty Revision and Reconstruction*, 1977.
18 *The End of Reparations*, 1978.
19 *The Return to Gold and Industrial Policy, Part* 1 and *Part* 2, 1981.
20 *Rethinking Employment and Unemployment Policies*, 1981.
21 *World Crises and Policies in Britain and America*, 1982.
22 *Internal War Finance*, 1978.
23 *External War Finance*, 1979.
24 *The Transition to Peace*, 1979.
25 *The Clearing Union*, 1980.
26 *Bretton Woods and Reparations*, 1980.
27 *Employment and Commodities*, 1980.
28 *Social, Political and Literary Writings*, 1982.
29 *The General Theory and After: A Supplement* (to Vols.13 and 14), 1979.
30 *Bibliography and Indexes*, 1989.

III English bibliography

Abbreviations

Cambridge Journal of Economics ... *CJE*; *History of Political Economy* ... *HOPE*;
Journal of Monetary Economics ... *JME*
Journal of Post Keynesian Economics ... *JPKE*
Cambridge University Press ... CUP; Oxford University Press ... OUP

Ahiakpor, J., 'Wicksell on the Classical Theories, Credit, Interest and the Price Level', *American Journal of Economics and Sociology*, Vol. 53, No. 3, 1999.
Aldcroft, D., *The British Economy, Vol.1*, Wheatsheaf Books, 1986.
Aldcroft, D. and Richardson, H., *The British Economy 1870–1939*, Macmillan, 1969.
Alessandra, M. and Francesco, S., *John Maynard Keynes*, Edward Elgar, 1994.
Allan, W. ed., *A Critique of Keynesian Economics*, St. Martin's Press, 1992.
Amadeo, E., *Keynes's Principle of Effective Demand*, Edward Elgar, 1989.
Amadeo, E., 'The Wicksell-Keynes Connection', *Australian Economic Papers*, December 1994a.
Amadeo, E., 'Changes in Output in Keynes's *Treatise on Money*' (in Davis, J. ed., 1994b).
American Economic Review, 'Is there a Core of Practical Macroeconomics That We Should All Believe?', May 1997, pp. 230–246 (by Solow, R., Taylor, J., Eichenbaum, M., Blinder, A., Blanchard, O.).
Amsler, C., 'Keynes and Bank Rate Policy', *JPKE*, Spring 1993.
De Angelis, M., *Keynesianism, Social Conflict and Political Economy*, Macmillan, 2000.
Arena, R. and Quéré eds, *The Economics of Alfred Marshall*, Macmillan, 2003.
Arestis, P., *Post-Keynesian Monetary Economics*, Edward Elgar, 1988.
Arestis, P. ed., *Keynes, Money and the Open Economy*, Edward Elgar, 1996.
Arestis, P. ed., *Method, Theory and Policy in Keynes*, Edward Elgar, 1998.
Arrow, K. and Debreu, G. 'Existence of an Equilibrium for a Competitive Economy', *Econometrica*, July 1954.

Arrow, K. and Hahn, F., *General Competitive Analysis*, Holden-Day, 1971.

Aschheim, J., 'Revolutions and Counterrevolutions in Monetary Economics', *Atlantic Economic Journal*, December 1990.

Ashton, T., *The Industrial Revolution 1760–1830*, OUP, 1968.

Ashworth, W., 'Review of Wiener (1981)', *Economic History Review*, November 1981.

Asimakopoulos, A., *Keynes's General Theory and Accumulation*, Cambridge University Press, 1991.

Aslanbeigui, N., 'Pigou's Inconsistencies or Keyne's Misconceptions?', *HOPE*, Summer 1992.

Backhouse, R. and Bateman, W., *The Cambridge Companion to Keynes*, CUP, 2006.

Backhouse, R. and Boianovsky, M., 'Disequilibrium Macroeconomics: an Episode in the Transformation of Modern Macroeconomics' circulated for the Conference on the History of Macroeconomics, Louvain, January 2005.

Ballard, B., 'How Keynes Became a Post Keynesian?', *JPKE*, Spring 1995.

Baranzini, M. ed., *Advances in Economic Theory*, Blackwell, 1982.

Barkai, H., 'Productivity Patterns, Exchange Rates, and the Gold Standard Restoration Debate of the 1920s, *HOPE*, Vol. 25, No. 1, 1993.

Barnett, C., *The Collapse of British Power*, Eyre Methuen, 1972.

Barrère, A., ed., *The Foundations of Keynesian Analysis*, Macmillan, 1988.

Barrère, A. ed., *Money, Credit and Prices in Keynesian Perspective*, Macmillan, 1989.

Barrère, A. ed., *Keynesian Economic Policies*, Macmillan, 1990.

Barro, R. and Grossman, H., 'A General Disequilibrium Model of Income and Employment', *American Economic Reivew*, March 1991.

Barry, N., *Hayek's Social and Economic Philosophy*, Macmillan, 1979.

Bartlett, C., *The Global Conflict 1880–1970*, Longman, 1984.

Bateman, B., 'G.E. Moore and J.M. Keynes', *American Economic Review*, December 1988.

Bateman, B., 'Keynes, Induction, and Econometrics', *HOPE*, Summer 1990.

Bateman, B., *Keynes's Uncertain Revolution*, University of Michigan Press, 1996.

Bateman, B. and Davis, J. eds, *Keynes and Philosophy*, Edward Elgar, 1991.

Bellofiore, R., 'Monetary Macroeconomics before the *General Theory*', *Social Concept*, June 1992.

Bellofiore, R., 'Between Wicksell and Hayek', *American Journal of Economics and Sociology*, Vol. 57, No. 4, 1998.

Bernanke, B., 'Nonmonetary Effects of the Financial Crisis in the Propagation of the Great Depression', *American Economic Review*, June 1983.

Bernanke, B. and Blinder, A., 'Credit, Money, and Aggregate Demand', *American Economic Review*, May 1988.

Besomi, D., 'An Additional Note on the Harrod-Keynes Correspondence', *HOPE*, Summer 1996.

Besomi, D., *The Collected Interwar Papers and Correspondence of Roy Harrod*, Edward Elgar, 2003.

Beveridge, W., *Unemployment*, Longmans, Green and Co., 1909 and 1930.

Beveridge, W., ed., *Planning under Socialism*, Longmans, Green and Co., 1936.

Beveridge, W., *Report on Social Insurance and Allied Services*, HMSO, Macmillan, 1942 (The *Beveridge Report*).

Beveridge, W., *Full Employment in a Free Society*, Allen and Unwin, 1944.

Bigg, R., *Cambridge and the Monetary Theory of Production*, Macmillan, 1990.

Birch, T., 'Marshall and Keynes Revisited', *Journal of Economic Issues*, Vol.19, pp. 194–200, 1985.

Black, C., Coats, A. and Goodwin, C. eds, *The Marginal Revolution in Economics*, Duke University Press, 1973.

Blanchard, O., 'What Do We Know About Macroeconomics That Fisher and Wicksell Did Not?', *Quarterly Journal of Economics*, November 2000.

Blaug, M., *Ricardian Economics*, Yale University Press, 1958.

Blaug, M., *The Cambridge Revolution, Success or Failure?*, Institute of Economic Affairs, 1974.

Blaug, M., *Economic Theory in Retrospect*, CUP, 1985.

Blaug, M., *John Maynard Keynes*, Macmillan, 1990.

Blaug, M., 'Second Thought on the Keynesian Revolution', *HOPE*, Summer 1991.

Blaug, M., Eltis, W., O'Brien, D., Patinkin, D., Skidelsky, R. and Wood, G., *The Quantity Theory of Money*, Edward Elgar, 1995.

Bleaney, M., *The Rise and Fall of Keynesian Economics*, Macmillan, 1985.

Board of Trade, *Statistical Abstract for the United Kingdom*, Cmd., 1938.

Boianovsky, M., 'Wicksell on Deflation in the Early 1920s', *HOPE*, Vol. 30, No. 2, 1998.

Boianovsky, M. and Trautwein, H-M., 'An Early Manuscript by Knut Wicksell on the Bank Rate of Interest' , *HOPE*, Vol. 33, No. 3, 2001.

Booth, A., *British Economic Policy 1931–49*, Harvester Wheatsheaf, 1989.

Booth, A. and Pack, M., *Employment, Capital and Economic Policy*, Basil Blackwell, 1985.

Bortis, H., 'Notes on the Cambridge Equation', *JPKE*, Fall 1993.

Bowley, A., *Some Economic Consequences of the Great War*, Butterworth, 1930.

Boyce, R., *British Capitalism at the Crossroads 1919–1932*, CUP, 1987.

Brady, M., 'The Mathematical Development of Keynes's Aggregate Supply Function in the *General Theory*', *HOPE*, Spring 1990.

Brady, M., 'J.M. Keynes's Theoretical Approach to Decision-Making under Conditions of Risk and Uncertainty', *British Journal for the Philosophy of Science*, June 1993.

Brady, M., 'A Note on the Keynes-Pigou Controversy', *HOPE*, Winter 1994.

Brady, M., 'Keynes, Pigou and the Supply Side of the *General Theory*', *History of Economics Review*, Winter 1994.

Braithwaite, R.B., 'Editorial Foreword' (December 1972) to *JMK*.8.

Braithwaite, R.B., 'Keynes as a Philosopher' (in Keynes, M. ed, 1975).

Bridel, P., *Cambridge Monetary Thought*, Macmillan, 1987.

Brown, N., *Dissenting Forbears*, Phillimore, 1988.

Brown-Collier, E., 'What Keynes Really Said about Deficit Spending', *JPKE*, Spring 1995.

Bryce, R., 'An Introduction to a Monetary Theory of Employment' (1935. *JMK*.29, pp. 132–150).

Buchanan, J. and Wagner, R., *Democracy in Deficit*, Academic Press, 1977.

Buchanan, J., Wagner, R. and Burton, J., *The Consequences of Mr Keynes*, Institute of Economic Affairs, 1978.

Burton, J. *et al.*, *Fifty Years on Keynes's General Theory*, Institute of Economic Affairs, 1986.

Butkiewicz, J., Koford, K. and Miller, J. eds, *Keynes' Economic Legacy*, Praeger, 1986.

Cain, N., 'Cambridge and Its Revolution', *Economic Record*, pp. 108–117, 1979.

Cain, N., 'Hawtrey and the Multiplier', *Australian Economic History Review*, pp. 68–78, 1982.

Cain, P.J. and Hopkins, A.G., *British Imperialism, I–II*, Longman, 1993a and b.

Cairncross, A., *Years of Recovery*, Methuen, 1985.

Cairncross, A., *Economics & Economic Policy*, Methuen, 1985.

Cairncross, A. and Watts, N., *The Economic Section 1939–1961*, Routledge, 1989.

Caldwell, B., *Beyond Positivism*, George Allen and Unwin, 1982.

Caldwell, B. ed., *Contra Keynes and Cambridge*, Routledge, 1995.

Carabelli, A., *On Keynes's Method*, Macmillan, 1988.

Cardim de Carvalho, 'Keynes and the Long Period', *CJE*, September 1990.

Carvalho, F., 'Alternative Analyses of Short and Long Run in Post-Keynesian Economics', *JPKE*, Winter 1984–1985.

Carvalho, F., *Mr. Keynes and the Post Keynesians*, Edward Elgar, 1992.

Cassel, G., *The Theory of Social Economy*, Harcourt, Brace & Company, 1932 (translated from the German by Barron, S.).

de Cecco, M., 'Keynes Revived', *Journal of Monetary Economics*, No.1, 1990.

Cesarano, F., 'The New Monetary Economics and Keynes' Theory of Money', *Journal of Economic Studies*, No.3, 1994.

Champernowne, D., 'Unemployment, Basic and Monetary', *Review of Economic Studies*, June 1936.

Champernowne, D., 'Expectations and the Links between the Economic Future and the Present' (in Lekachman, R. ed., 1964).

Chandavarkar, A., *Keynes and India*, Macmillan, 1989.

Chandler, A. and Daems, H. eds, *Managerial Hierarchies*, Harvard University Press, 1980.

Chasse, J., 'John R. Commons and John Maynard Keynes', *Journal of Economic Issues*, June 1991.

Chick, V., 'The Nature of the Keynesian Revolution', *Australian Economic Papers*, pp. 1–20, 1978.

Chick, V., *Macroeconomics after Keynes*, Philip Allan, 1983.

Chick, V., 'Hicks and Keynes on Liquidity Preference', *Review of Political Economy*, No.3, 1991.

Chiodi, G., *Wicksell's Monetary Theory*, Macmillan, 1991.

Christ, C., 'A Simple Macroeconomic Model with a Government Budget Constraint', *Journal of Political Economy*, February 1968.

Clapham, J., Guillebaud, C., Lavington, F., and Robertson, D., *Monetary Policy*, P.S. King and Son, 1921.

Clark, C., *The National Income 1924–31*, Macmillan, 1932.

Clark, C., *National Income and Outlay*, Macmillan, 1937.

Clark, J., *Revolutions and Rebellion*, CUP, 1986.

Clarke, P., *The Keynesian Revolution in the Making 1924–1936*, Clarendon Press, 1988.

Clarke, P., 'The Treasury's Analytical Model of the British Economy between the Wars' (in Furner, M. and Supple, B. eds, 1990).

Clarke, P., 'Keynes in History', *HOPE*, Spring 1994.

Clarke, P., *Hope and Glory: Britain 1900–1990*, Penguin Books, 1996.

Clarke, P., *The Keynesian Revolution and Its Economic Consequences*, Edward Elgar, 1998.

Clarke, P., and Trebilcock, C. eds, *Understanding Decline*, CUP, 1997.

Clarke, S., *Keynesianism, Monetarism and the Crisis of the State*, Edward Elgar, 1988.

Clower, R., 'The Keynesian Counterrevolution' (in Hahn, F. and Brechling, F. eds, 1965).

Coase, R., 'The Appointment of Pigou as Marshall's Successor', *Journal of Law and Economics*, October 1972.

Coase, R., 'Alfred Marshall's Mother and Father', *HOPE*, Winter 1984.

Coase, R., *The Firm, the Market and the Law*, University of Chicago Press, 1988.

Coates, J., *The Claims of Common Sense*, CUP, 1996.

Cochran, J., 'The Keynes-Hayek Debate', *HOPE*, Spring 1994.

Coddington, A., *Keynesian Economics*, George Allen and Unwin, 1983.

Colander, D., 'The Strange Persistence of the IS-LM Model' (in De Vroey, M. and Hoovek, K. eds, 2005).

Cole, J., *The Thatcher Years*, BBC Books, 1987.

Coleman, T., *Thatcher's Britain*, Bentam Press, 1987.

Collard, D., 'Cambridge after Marshall' (in Whitaker, J. ed., 1990).

Collard, D., 'Pigou and Future Generations', *CJE*, September 1996.

Collins, B. and Robbins, K. eds, *British Culture and Economic Decline*, 1990.

Collins, R., *The Business Response to Keynes 1929–1934*, Columbia University Press, 1981.

Commons, J.R., *Institutional Economics*, Macmillan, 1934.

Commons, J.R., *The Economics of Collective Action*, Macmillan, 1950.

Coontz, S., *Productive Labour and Effective Demand*, Routledge & Kegan Paul, 1965.

Corry, B. ed., *Unemployment and the Economists*, Edward Elgar, 1996.

Cottrell, A., 'Keynes's Appendix to Chapter 19', *HOPE*, Winter 1994.

Cottrell, A. and Lawlor, M., ' "Natural Rate" Mutations', *HOPE*, Winter 1991.

Cottrell, A. and Lawlor, M. eds, *New Perspectives on Keynes*, Duke University Press, 1995.

Cottrell, P. and Moggridge, D. eds, *Money and Power*, Macmillan, 1988.

Crafts, N., 'British Economic Growth, 1700–1831', *Economic History Review*, May 1983.

Crafts, N., *British Economic Growth during the Industrial Revolution*, OUP, 1985.

Crafts, N. and Harley, C., 'Output Growth and the British Industrial Revolution', *Economic History Review*, November 1992.

Cranston, M., 'Keynes' (in Thirlwall, A. ed., 1978).

Creedy, J. and D. O'Brien, eds, *Economic Analysis in Historical Perspective*, Butterworth, 1984.

Crotty, J., 'Keynes on the States of Development of the Capitalist Economy', *Journal of Economic Issues*, September 1990.

Cutler, R., Williams, K. and Williams, J., Keynes, *Beveridge and Beyond*, Routledge & Kegan Paul, 1986.

Darity Jr., W., 'Who Owns Maynard Keynes?', *HOPE*, Spring 1994.

Darity Jr., W., 'Keynes' Political Philosophy', *Eastern Economic Journal*, Winter 1995.

Darity Jr., W. and Young, W., 'IS-LM: An Inquest', *HOPE*, Spring 1995.

Davidson, P., *Money and the Real World*, Macmillan, 1972.

Davidson, P., 'Patinkin's Interpretation of Keynes and the Keynesian Cross', *HOPE*, Fall 1989.

Davidson, P., 'Corrected Version of Patinkin's Interpretation of Keynes and the Keynesian Cross', *HOPE*, Winter 1989.

Davidson, P., *Controversies in Post Keynesian Economics*, Edward Elgar, 1991.

Davidson, P., *Post Keynesian Macroeconomic Theory*, Edward Elgar, 1994.

Davidson, P., 'What Revolution?', *JPKE*, Fall 1996.

Davis, E., 'The Role of R.G. Hawtrey in Keynesian Economics and the Economics of Keynes', *Carleton Economic Papers*, December 1977.

Davis, E., 'The Economics of R.G. Hawtrey', *Carleton Economic Papers*, January 1979.

Davis, E., 'The Correspondence between R.G. Hawtrey and J.M. Keynes on the *Treatise* ', *Canadian Journal of Economics and Political Science*, pp. 716–724, 1980.

Davis, J., *The New Economics and the Old Economists*, Iowa State University Press, 1971.

Davis, J., 'Keynes on Atomism and Organicism', *Economic Journal*, December 1990.

Davis, J., 'Keynes and Organicism', *JPKE*, No.2, 1992.

Davis, J. ed., *The State of Interpretation of Keynes*, Kluwer Academic Publishers, 1994.

Davis, J., *Keynes's Philosophical Development*, CUP, 1995.

Davis, R. and Casey, F., 'Keynes's Misquotation of Mill', *Economic Journal*, June 1977.

Deacon, R., *The Cambridge Apostles*, Robert Royce, 1985.

Deane, P. and Cole, W., *British Economic Growth 1688–1959*, 2nd Edition, CUP, 1967.

Deprez, J., 'Rediscovering the Missing Visionary of the Middle Way', *JPKE*, Spring 1995.

Desai, M., 'The Task of Monetary Theory' (in Baranzini, M. ed., 1982).

Deutscher, P., *R.G. Hawtrey and the Development of Macroeconomics*, Macmillan, 1990.

Dimand, R., *The Origins of the Keynesian Revolution*, Edward Elgar, 1988.

Dimand, R., 'Mr. Meade's Relation, Kahn's Multiplier and the Chronology of the *General Theory*', *Economic Journal*, September 1994.

Dimand, R., 'Macroeconomics with and without Keynes', *History of Economics Review*, Summer 1995.

Dimand, R., 'Hawtrey and the Multiplier', *HOPE*, Vol. 29, No. 4, 1997.

Dostaler, G., Ethier, D. and Lepage, L. eds, *Gunnar Myrdal and His Works*, Harvest House, 1992.

Dow, S. and Hillard, J. eds, *Keynes, Knowledge and Uncertainty*, Edward Elgar, 1995.

Drakopoulos, S., 'Keynes' Economic Thought and the Theory of Consumer', *Scottish Journal of Political Economy*, August 1992.

Dunlop, J., 'The Movement of Real and Money Wage Rates', *Economic Journal*, September 1938.

Dutt, A., 'Expectations and Equilibrium', *JPKE*, Winter 1991.

Dutt, A. and Amadeo, E., *Keynes's Third Alternative?*, Edward Elgar, 1990.

Dymski, G., 'Keynesian Uncertainty and Asymmetric Information', *JPKE*, No.1, 1993.

Earley, J., 'Schumpeter and Keynes', *History of Economics Review*, Winter 1994.

Eatwell, J. and Milgate, M. eds, *Keynes's Economics and the Theory of Value and Distribution*, Duckworth, 1983.

Eichengreen, B., *Golden Fetters*, OUP, 1992.

Elbaum, B. and Lazonick, W. eds, *The Decline of the British Economy*, OUP, 1986.

Eltis, W. and Sinclair, P. eds, *Keynes and Economic Policy*, Macmillan, 1988.

Eshag, E., *From Marshall to Keynes*, Basil Blackwell, 1963.

Fanning, C. and Mahony, D., *The General Theory of Profit Equilibrium*, Macmillan, 1998.

Feinstein, C., *National Income, Expenditure and Output of the United Kingdom 1888–1965*, CUP, 1972.

Felix, D., *Biography of an Idea*, Transaction Publishers, 1995.

Ferguson, N., 'Keynes and the German Inflation', *English Historical Review*, April 1995.

Fisher, I., *The Purchasing Power of Money*, Macmillan, 1911.

Fisher, I., *The Making of Index Numbers*, Houghton Mifflin Co., 1922.

Fisher, I., *The Theory of Interest*, Macmillan, 1930.

Fischer, S., 'Long-Term Contracts, Rational Expectations, and the Optimal Money Supply Rule', *Journal of Political Economy*. Vol.85, no.1, pp. 191–205, 1977.

Fitzgibbons, A., *Keynes's Vision*, Clarendon Press, 1988.

Fletcher, G., *The Keynesian Revolution and Its Critics*, Macmillan, 1987.

Fletcher, G., *Understanding Dennis Robertson*, Edward Elgar, 2000.

Frazer, W., *The Legacy of Keynes and Friedman*, Praeger, 1994.

Freeden, M., *Liberalism Divided*, Clarendon Press, 1986.

Friedman, M., *Methodology of Positive Economics*, University of Chicago, 1953.

Friedman, M. 'A Theoretical Framework for Monetary Analysis', *Journal of Political Economy*, March–April 1970 (in Gordon, J. ed., 1970).

Friedman, M., 'A Monetary Theory of National Income', *Journal of Political Economy*, March–April 1971.

Furner, M. and Supple, B. eds, *The State and Economic Knowledge*, CUP, 1990.

Gamble, A., *Britain in Decline*, Macmillan, 1981.

Garretsen, H., 'Pricing, Uncertainty and the Economics of Keynes', *Metroeconomica*, June 1990.

Garside, W., *British Unemployment, 1919–1939*, CUP, 1990.

Garside, W. ed., *Capitalism in Crisis*, St. Martin's Press, 1993.

Gayer, A. ed., *The Lessons of Monetary Experience*, George Allen and Unwin, 1937.

Gerrard, B., 'Keynes's *General Theory*', *Economic Journal*, March 1991.

Gerrard, B., 'Keynes, the Keynesians and the Classics', *Economic Journal*, March 1995.

Gerrard, B., and Hillard, J. eds, *The Philosophy and Economics of J.M. Keynes*, Edward Elgar, 1992.

Gilbert, J., *Keynes' Impact on Monetary Economics*, Butterworths Scientific, 1982.

Glahe, F., *Keynes's General Theory of Employment, Interest, and Money*, Rowman & Littlefield, 1991.

Gordon, J. ed., *Milton Friedman's Monetary Framework*, University of Chicago Press, 1970.

Graziani, A., *The Monetary Theory of Production*, CUP, 2003.

Greenaway, D. and Presley, J.R. eds, *Pioneers of Modern Economics in Britain*, Vol. 2, Macmillan, 1989.

Groenewegen, P., *A Soaring Eagle*, Edward Elgar, 1995a.

Groenewegen, P., 'Keynes and Marshall' (in Cottrell, A. and Lawor, M. eds, 1995b).

Grossman, H., 'Money, Interest, and Prices in Market Disequilibrium', *Journal of Political Economy*, September-October 1971.

Grossman, H., 'Was Keynes a Keynesian?', *Journal of Economic Literature*, March 1972.

Haberler, G., *Prosperity and Depression*, League of Nations, 1938.

Hahn, F., 'Professor Friedman's Views on Money', *Economica*, February 1971.

Hahn, F., 'Keynesian Economics and General Equilibrium Theory' (in Harcourt, G. ed., 1977).

Hahn, F. and Brechling, F. eds, *The Theory of Interest Rates*, Macmillan, 1965.

Hamouda, O. and Smithin, J. eds, *Keynes and Public Policy after Fifty Years*, Vols. 1 and 2, Edward Elgar, 1988.

Hannah, L., *The Rise of the Corporate Economy*, Johns Hopkins University Press, 1976.

Hansen, A., *A Guide to Keynes*, McGraw-Hill, 1953.

Hansen, B., 'Unemployment, Keynes, and the Stockholm School', *HOPE*, No. 2, 1981.

Harcourt, G. ed., *The Microfoundations of Macroeconomics*, Macmillan, 1977.

Harcourt, G., 'Kahn and Keynes and the Making of the *General Theory*', *CJE*, February 1994.

Harcourt, G. and O'Shaughnessy, T., 'Keynes's Unemployment Equilibrium' (in Harcourt, G. ed., 1985).

Harcourt, G. and Riach, P. eds, *Maynard Keynes' General Theory*, Routledge, 1996.

Harcourt, G. and Riach, P. eds, *A 'Second Edition' of the General Theory*, Vols. 1 and 2, Routledge, 1997.

Harley, C., 'British Industrialization before 1841', *Journal of Economic History*, June 1982.

Harris, S. ed., *The New Economics*, D. Dobson, 1947.

Harrod, R., 'The Expansion of Credit in an Advancing Community', *Economica*, August 1934.

Harrod, R., *The Trade Cycle*, Clarendon Press, 1936.

Harrod, R., *Towards a Dynamic Economics*, Macmillan, 1948.

Harrod, R., *The Life of John Maynard Keynes*, Macmillan, 1951.

Harrod, R., *Money, Macmillan*, 1969.

Harrod, R., *Economic Dynamics*, Macmillan, 1973.

Hartley, J., Hoover, K., and Salyer, K. eds, *Real Business Cycles*, Routledge, 1998.

Hawson, S., *Domestic Monetary Management in Britain*, CUP, 1975.

Hawtrey, R., *Good and Bad Trade*, Constable & Company, 1913.

Hawtrey, R., *Currency and Credit*, Longmans, Green and Co., 1919.

Hawtrey, R., *Monetary Reconstruction*, Longmans, Green and Co., 1923.

Hawtrey, R., 'Public Expenditure and the Demand for Labour', *Economica*, March 1925.

Hawtrey, R., *Trade and Credit*, Longmans, Green and Co., 1928.

Hawtrey, R., *The Art of Central Banking*, Longmans, Green and Co., 1932.

Hawtrey, R., 'Mr Robertson on "Saving and Hoarding" (II)', *Economic Journal*, December 1933.

Hawtrey, R., 'A Review of Mises (1935)', *Economic Journal*, pp. 509–518, 1935.

Hawtrey, R., *Capital and Employment*, Longmans, Green and Co., 1937.

Hawtrey, R., 'Keynes and Supply Function', *Economic Journal*, September 1956.

Hayek, F., *Prices and Production*, Routledge and Kegan Paul, 1931a.

Hayek, F., 'Reflections on the Pure Theory of Money of Mr J.M. Keynes', *Economica*, August 1931b.

Hayek, F., 'Reflections on the Pure Theory of Money of Mr J.M. Keynes', *Economica*, February 1932.

Hayek, F., *Monetary Theory and the Trade Cycle*, Jonathan Cape, 1933 (translated from the German by Kaldor, N. and Croome, H.M.).

Hayek, F., *Profits, Interest and Investment and Other Essays on the Theory of Fluctuations*, Routledge and Kegan Paul, 1939.

Hayek, F., *The Pure Theory of Capital*, Routledge and Kegan Paul, 1941.

Hayek, F., *Individualism and Economic Order*, University of Chicago Press, 1948.

Hayek, F., *New Studies in Philosophy, Politics, Economics and the History of Ideas*, Routledge and Kegan Paul, 1978.

Hazlitt, H., *The Failure of the 'New Economics'*, Van Nostrand, 1959.

Hazlitt, H. ed., *The Critics of Keynesian Economics*, Van Nostrand, 1960.

Hecksher, E., *Mercantilism* (Authorised Translation from the German by Shapiro, M.), George Allen and Unwin, 1935.

Helburn, S. and Bramhall, D. eds, *Marx, Schumpeter and Keynes*, M.E. Sharpe, 1986.

Henderson, W., *The Rise of German Industrial Power 1834–1914*, Temple Smith, 1975.

Hession, C., *John Maynard Keynes*, Macmillan, 1984.

Hicks, J., 'A Suggestion for Simplifying the Theory of Money', *Economica*, February 1935.

Hicks, J., 'Mr Keynes and the "Classics,"' *Econometrica*, April 1937.

Hicks, J., *Value and Capital*, OUP, 1939.

Hicks, J., *Critical Essays in Monetary Theory*, OUP, 1967.

Hicks, J., 'The Hayek Story' (in Hicks, J., 1967).

Hicks, J., 'A Note on the *Treatise*' (in Hicks, J., 1967).

Hicks, J., 'Automatists, Hawtreyans and Keynesians', *Journal of Money, Credit and Banking*, pp. 307–317, 1969.

Hicks, J., 'Recollections and Documents', *Economica*, February 1973.

Hicks, J., *The Crisis in Keynesian Economics*, Basil Blackwell, 1974.

Hicks, J., ' "Revolutions" in Economics' (in Latsis, S. ed., 1976).

Hicks, J., *Economic Perspectives*, OUP, 1977.

Hicks, J., *Casuality in Economics*, Basil Blackwell, 1979.

Hicks, J., 'IS-LM: an Explanation', *JPKE*, Winter 1980.

Hicks, J., *Money, Interest and Wages*, Basil Blackwell, 1982.

Hicks, J., *Classics and Moderns*, Basil Blackwell, 1983.

Hill, P. and Keynes, R. eds, *Lydia and Maynard*, Andre Deutsch, 1989.

Hillard, J. ed., *J.M. Keynes in Retrospect*, Edward Elgar, 1985.

Hines, A., *On the Reappraisal of Keynesian Economics*, Martin Robertson and Co. Ltd., 1971.

Hirai, T., *A Study of Keynes*, mimeo., 1988 (English Translation of Hirai, 1987).

Hirai, T., 'A Study of Keynes's Economics (I)–(IV)', *Sophia Economic Review*, December 1997–March 1999.

Hirai, T., 'Recent Japanese Studies in the Development of Keynes's Thought', *Annals of the Society for the History of Economic Thought*, Vol. 36, 1998.

Hirai, T., 'The Turning Point in Keynes's Theoretical Development,' *History of Economic Ideas*, Vol. 12, No. 2, pp. 29–50, 2004.

Hirai, T., 'How Did Keynes Transform His Theory from the *Tract* into the *Treatise*?', *European Journal of the History of Economic Thought*, Vol. 14, No. 2, pp. 325–348, 2007.

Hirai, T., 'How, and For How Long, Did Keynes Maintain the *Treatise* Theory?', *Journal of the History of Economic Thought*, Vol. 29, No. 3, pp. 283–307, 2007.

Hobson, J., *Confessions of an Economic Heretic*, George Allen and Unwin, 1938.

Hodgson, G., 'The Mecca of Alfred Marshall', *Economic Journal*, April 1993.

Holroyd, M., *Lytton Strachey*, Penguin, 1967.

Hoover, K., *The New Classical Macroeconomics*, Basil Blackwell, 1988.

Hoover, K., *Causality in Macroeconomics*, CUP, 2001.

Howson, S., 'A Dear Money Man?', *Economic Journal*, June 1973.

Howson, S., *Domestic Monetary Management in Britain 1919–1938*, CUP, 1975.

Howson, S. and Winch, D., *The Economic Advisory Council 1930–1939*, CUP, 1977.

Humphrey, T., 'Fisher and Wicksell on the Quantity Theory', *Economic Quarterly* (Federal Reserve Bank of Richmond), Vol. 83, No. 4, 1997.

Hutchison, T., *A Review of Economic Doctrines 1870–1929*, Clarendon Press, 1953.

Hutchison, T., *Keynes versus the 'Keynesians'?*, Institute of Economic Affairs, 1977.

Hutchison, T., *The Politics and Philosophy of Economics*, New York University Press, 1981.

Hutt, W., *A Rehabilitation of Say's Law*, Ohio University Press, 1974.

Hutton, W., *The Revolution That Never Was*, Longman, 1986.

Inoue, J., *Problems of the Japanese Exchange 1914–1926*, Robert Maclehose and Co., 1931.

Iwai, K., *Disequilibrium Dynamics*, Yale University Press, 1981.

Iwai, K., 'What is Macroeconomics?', Discussion Paper F-Series, Research Institute for the Japanese Economy, October 1987.

Jackman, R., 'Keynes and Leijonhufvud', *Oxford Economic Papers*, July 1974.

Jarsulic, M., *Effective Demand and Income Distribution*, Polity Press, 1988.

Jensen, H., 'J.M. Keynes as a Marshallian', *Journal of Economic Issues*, Vol.17, pp. 67–94, 1983.

Jensen, H., 'J.M. Keynes's Theory of the State as a Path to His Social Economics of Reform in the *General Theory*', *Review of Social Economy*, Fall 1991.

Johnson, E. and Johnson, H., *The Shadow of Keynes*, Blackwell, 1978.

Jones, S., 'The Changing Face of Nineteenth Century Britain', *History Today*, October 1991.

De Jong, 'Supply Functions in Keynesian Economics', *Economic Journal*, March 1954.

Jonsson, P., 'On the Economics of Say and Keynes' Interpretation of Say's Law', *Eastern Economic Journal*, Spring 1995.

Jonung, L, 'Knut Wicksell and Gustav Cassell on Secular Movements in Prices', *Journal of Money, Credit and Banking*, May 1979.

Jonung, L. ed., *The Stockholm School of Economics Revisited*, CUP, 1991.

Kahn, R., 'The Relation of Home Investment to Unemployment', *Economic Journal*, June 1931.

Kahn, R., *The Economics of the Short Period*, Macmillan, 1989 (his fellow dissertation, 1929).

Kahn, R., *Selected Essays on Employment and Growth*, CUP, 1972.

Kahn, R., *The Making of Keynes' General Theory*, CUP, 1984.

Kaldor, N., *The Scourge of Monetarism*, OUP, 1982.

Kalecki, M., 'The Determinants of Distribution of the National Income', *Econometrica*, April 1938.

Kates, S., 'The Malthusian Origins of the *General Theory*', *History of Economics Review*, Winter 1994.

Kates, S., *Say's Law and the Keynesian Revolution*, Edward Elgar, 1998.

Katzner, D. and Weintraub, S., 'An Approach to a Unified Micro-Macro Model', *Kyklos*, pp. 482–510, 1974.

Kavanagh, D., *Thatcherism and British Politics*, OUP, 1987.

Keynes, J.M., 'A Review of Fisher (1911)', *Economic Journal*, September 1911.

Keynes, J.M., 'A Review of Mises (1912)', *Economic Journal*, September 1914.

Keynes, J.M., 'A Review of Hawtrey (1919)', *Economic Journal*, September 1920 (in *JMK*. 11, pp. 411–414).

Keynes, J.M. ed., 'Reconstruction in Europe', *Manchester Guardian Commercial*, 1922.

Keynes, J.M., 'Alfred Marshall, 1842–1924' (in Pigou, A. ed., 1925a).

Keynes, J.M., 'Am I a Liberal?', *Nation and Athenaeum*, 8 and 15 August, 1925b.

Keynes, J.M., 'A Short View of Russia', *Nation and Athenaeum*, 10, 17, and 25 October, 1925c.

Keynes, J.M., *The End of Laissez-Faire*, Hogarth Press, 1926.

Keynes, J.M., 'Economic Possibilities for Our Grandchildren', *Nation and Athenaeum*, 11 and 18 October 1930.

Keynes, J.M., 'The Pure Theory of Money. A Reply to Dr Hayek', *Economica*, November 1931.

Keynes, J.M., 'Thomas Robert Malthus' (in *JMK*. 10, pp. 71–108).

Keynes, J. M., *The Means to Prosperity*, Macmillan, 1933.

Keynes, J.M., 'The General Theory of Employment', *Quarterly Journal of Economics*, February 1937a.

Keynes, J.M., 'Alternative Theories of the Rate of Interest', *Economic Journal*, June 1937b.

Keynes, J.M., 'The Theory of the Rate of Interest' (in Gayer, A. ed., 1937c).

Keynes, J.M., 'The "Ex Ante" Theory of the Rate of Interest', *Economic Journal*, December 1937d.

Keynes, J.M., 'Professor Pigou on Money Wages in Relation to Unemployment', *Economic Journal*, December 1937e.

Keynes, J.M., 'My Early Beliefs', 1938 (in *Two Memoirs*, Rupert Hart-Davis, 1949; *JMK*. 10, pp. 433–450).

Keynes, J.M., 'Relative Movements of Real Wages and Output', *Economic Journal*, March 1939.

Keynes, J.M., *How to Pay for the War*, Macmillan, 1940.

Keynes, J.N., *The Scope and Method of Political Economy*, Macmillan, 1890.

Keynes, M. ed., *Essays on John Maynard Keynes*, CUP, 1975.

Keynes Seminar (held at University of Kent at Canterbury), Macmillan.
   1st (1971), *Keynes*, ed. by Moggridge, D., 1974.
   2nd (1974), *Keynes and International Monetary Relations*, ed. by Thirlwall, A., 1976.
   3rd (1976), *Keynes and Laissez-Faire*, ed. by Thirlwall, A., 1978.

4th (1978), *Keynes and the Bloomsbury Group*, ed. by Crabtree, D. and Thirlwall, A., 1980.

5th (1980), *Keynes as a Policy Adviser*, ed. by Thirlwall, A., 1982.

6th (1983), *Keynes and His Contemporaries*, ed. by Harcourt, G., 1985.

7th (1985), *Keynes and Economic Development*, ed. by Thirlwall, A., 1987.

8th (1987), *Keynes, Money and Monetarism*, ed. by Hill, R., 1989.

9th (1989), *Keynes as Philosopher-Economist*, ed. by O'Donnell, R., 1991.

10th (1991), *Keynes and the Role of the State*, ed. by Crabtree, D. and Thirlwall, A., 1993.

Kindleberger, C., *The World in Depression 1929–1939*, University of California Press, 1973.

Kindleberger, C., *Keynesianism vs. Monetarism and Other Essays in Financial History*, George Allen and Unwin, 1985.

Kirby, M., *The Decline of British Economic Power since 1870*, George Allen and Unwin, 1981.

Kirman, A. P., 'The Intrinsic Limits of Modern Economic Theory', *Economic Journal.*, Vol. 99, pp. 126–139, 1989.

Kirzner, I. M., *Discovery and the Capitalist Process*, University of Chicago Press, 1985.

Kirzner, I. M., *The Driving Force of the Market*, Routlege, 2000.

Klausinger, H., 'German Anticipations of the Keynesian Revolution?', *Journal of the History of Economic Thought*, Vol. 6, No. 3, 1999.

Klein, L., *The Keynesian Revolution*, Macmillan, 1947.

Klein, L. and Goldberger, A., *Econometric Model of the United States 1929–1952*, North-Holland, 1955.

Knight, F., 'Laissez-Faire: Pros and Cons', *Journal of Political Economy*, December 1967.

Koslowski, P. and Shionoya, Y. eds, *The Good and the Economical*, Springer–Verlag, 1993.

Kuhn, T., *The Structure of Scientific Revolution*, University of Chicago Press, 1970.

Kuznets, S., *Secular Movements in Prices and Production*, National Bureau of Economic Research, 1930.

Kuznets, S., *National Income and Capital Formation 1919–1935*, National Bureau of Economic Research, 1937.

Kydland, F. and Prescott, E., 'Rules rather than Discretion: The Inconsistency of Optimal Plans,' *Journal of Political Economy*, Vol. 85, No. 3, 1977.

Kydland, F. and Prescott, E., 'Business Cycles: Real Facts and a Monetary Myth', *Federal Reserve Bank of Minneapolis Quarterly Review*, Spring 1990.

Lachman, L., 'Austrian Economics under Fire' (in Grassl, W. and Smiths, B. eds, *Austrian Economics*, New York University Press, 1986).

Laidler, D., 'On Wicksell's Theory of Price Level Dynamics', *Manchester School*, June 1972.

Laidler, D., *Monetarist Perspectives*, Philip Allan, 1982.

Laidler, D., 'Alfred Marshall and the Development of Monetary Economics' (in Whitaker, J. ed., 1990a).

Laidler, D., 'Hicks and the Classics', *Journal of Monetary Economics*, No. 3, 1990b.

Laidler, D., *The Golden Age of the Quantity Theory*, Philip Allan, 1991a.

Laidler, D., 'The Austrians and the Stockholm School' (in Jonung, L. ed., 1991b).

Laidler, D., 'Hawtrey, Harvard, and the Origins of the Chicago Tradition', *Journal of Political Economy*, Vol. 101, No. 6, pp. 1068–1103, 1993.

Laidler, D., *Fabricating the Keynesian Revolution*, CUP, 1999.

Laidler, D. and Sandilands, R., 'An Early Harvard Memorandum on Anti-Depression Policies', *HOPE*, Vol. 34, No. 3, pp. 515–552, 2002.

Lakatos, I., 'Falsification and the Methodology of Scientific Research Programmes' (in Lakatos, I. and Musgrave, A. eds, 1970).

Lakatos, I. and Musgrave, A. eds, *Criticism and the Growth of Knowledge*, CUP, 1970.

Lambert, P., 'The Evolution of Keynes's Thought from the *Treatise on Money* to the *General Theory*', *Annals of Public and Cooperative Economy*, pp. 243–263, 1969.

Lange, O., 'Say's Law' (in Lange, O., McIntyre, F., and Yntema, T. eds, *Studies in Mathematical Economics and Econometrics*, University of Chicago Press, 1942).

Latsis, S. ed., *Method and Appraisal in Economics*, CUP, 1976.

Lavington, F., *The English Capital Market*, Methuen & Co., 1921.

Lavington, F., *The Trade Cycle*, P.S. King & Son, 1922.

Lawlor, M., 'Minsky and Keynes on Speculation and Finance', *Social Science Journal*, No.4, 1990.

Lawlor, M., 'Keynes, Meltzer and Involuntary Unemployment', *Review of Social Economy*, Fall 1991.

Lawson, T., 'Keynes and Conventions', *Review of Social Economy*, Summer 1993.

Lawson, T. and Pesaran, H., *Keynes' Economics*, Croom Helm, 1989.

Leeson, R., *The Eclipse of Keynesianism*, Palgrave, 2000.

Leeson, R., Keynes, *Chicago and Friedman*, Vols. 1 and 2, Pickering & Chatto, 2003.

Leijonhufvud, A., 'Keynes and the Keynesians', *American Economic Review*, May 1967.

Leijonhufvud, A., *On Keynesian Economics and the Economics of Keynes*, OUP, 1968.

Leijonhufvud, A., *Keynes and the Classics*, Institute of Economic Affairs, 1969.

Leijonhufvud, A., 'Keynes's Employment Function', *HOPE*, Summer 1974.

Leijonhufvud, A., *Information and Coordination*, OUP, 1981.

Leijonhufvud, A., 'Mr Keynes and the Moderns' (in Pasinetti, L. and Shefold, B. eds, 1999).

Lekachman, R. ed., *Keynes' General Theory*, Macmillan, 1964.

Lekachman, R., *The Age of Keynes*, McGraw-Hill, 1966.

Lerner, A., 'Mr. Keynes's *General Theory of Employment, Interest and Money*', *International Labour Review*, October 1936.

Lerner, A., 'From the *Treatise on Money* to the *General Theory*', *Journal of Economic Literature*, March 1974.

Liberal Party, *Britain's Industrial Future*, Ernest Benn, 1928.

Liberal Party, *We Can Conquer Unemployment*, Cassel, 1929.

Lim, R., 'Keynes and the Store of Wealth Function of Money', *Indian Economic Journal*, July 1989.

Lindahl, E., 'The Rate of Interest and the Price Level', 1930 (Part 2 of Lindahl, 1939).

Lindahl, E., *Studies in the Theory of Money and Capital*, George Allen and Unwin, 1939.

Lindahl, E., 'On Keynes' Economic System: Parts I and II', *Economic Record*, May and November, 1954.

Lippmann, W., *The Method of Freedom*, Macmillan, 1934.

Lippmann, W., *The Good Society*, Little, Brown and Co., 1943.

Littleboy, B., *On Interpreting Keynes*, Routledge, 1990.

Littleboy, B. and Mehta, G., 'Patinkin on Keynes's Theory of Effective Demand', *HOPE*, Summer 1987.

Littleboy, B. and Mehta, G., 'Patinkin on Keynes's Theory of Effective Demand: A Rejoinder', *HOPE*, Winter 1989.

Loasby, B., 'Whatever Happened to Marshall's Theory of Value', *Scottish Journal of Political Economy*, Vol.25, pp. 1–12, 1978.

Loasby, B., *Knowledge, Institutions and Evolution in Economics*, Routledge, 1999.

De Long, J., 'Facets of Interwar Unemployment', *Journal of Monetary Economics*, No. 2, 1990.

Long, J. and Plosser, C., 'Real Business Cycles', *Journal of Political Economy*, Vol. 91, No. 1, pp. 39–69, 1983.

Lucas, R., 'An Equilibrium Model of the Business Cycle', *Journal of Political Economy*, Vol. 83, No. 6, pp. 1113–1143, 1975.

Lucas, R., 'Methods and Problems in Business Cycle Theory', *Journal of Money, Credit and Banking*, No. 4, 1980.

Lucas, R. and Sargent, T., 'After Keynesian Macroeconomics', *Federal Reserve Bank of Minneapolis Quarterly Review*, No. 2, 1979.

Lucas, R. and Sargent, J. eds, *Rational Expectations and Econometric Practice*, George Allen and Unwin, 1981.

Lundberg, E., *Studies in the Theory of Economic Expansion*, P.S. King and Son, 1937.

Lundberg, E., 'Gunnar Myrdal's Contribution to Economic Theory', *Swedish Journal of Economics*, pp. 472–478, 1974.

MacCallum, J., 'A Test of a Keynesian Alternative to Hercowitz's Aggregate Supply Theory', *Journal of Monetary Economics*, No.1, 1990.

Macfie, A., *Theories of the Trade Cycle*, Macmillan, 1934.

Maclachlan, F., *Keynes' General Theory of Interest*, Routledge, 1993.

Macmillan Committee, *Committee on Finance & Industry Report*, His Majesty's Stationery Office, 1931a (*Macmillan Report*).

Macmillan Committee, *Minutes of Evidence*, His Majesty's Stationery Office, 1931b.

Maloney, J., *Marshall, Orthodoxy and the Professionalisation of Economics*, CUP, 1985.

Malthus, R., *An Essay on the Principle of Population*, Macmillan, 1926 (First Edition, 1798).

Malthus, T., *An Investigation of the Cause of the Present High Price of Provisions*, J. Johnson, 1800.

Malthus, T., *Principles of Political Economy*, John Murray, 1820.

Mankiw, N.G., 'Small Menu Costs and Large Business Cycles', *Quarterly Journal of Economics*, May 1985.

Mankiw, N.G., 'Imperfect Competition and the Keynesian Cross', *Economic Letters*, pp. 7–14, 1988.

Mankiw, N.G. and Romer, D. eds, *New Keynesian Economics*, Vol.1, MIT Press, 1991.

Mantoux, É., *The Carthaginian Peace, or the Economic Consequences of Mr Keynes*, OUP, 1946.

Mantoux, P., *The Industrial Revolution in the Eighteenth Century*, University of Chicago Press, 1983 (translated from the French by Vernon, M.).

Marchal, J. and Lecaillon, J., *Théorie des flux monétaires, évolution de idées et principes généraux d'analyse*, Editions Cujas, 1967.

Marchionatti, R., 'Keynes and the Collapse of the British Cotton Industry in the 1920s', *JPKE*, Spring 1995.

Marcuzzo, M.C., 'R.F. Kahn: A Disciple of Keynes', *Cambridge Review*, March 1990.

Marcuzzo, M.C., 'The Collaboration between J.M. Keynes and R.F. Kahn from the *Treatise* to the *Geneal Theory*', *HOPE*, Vol. 34, No. 2, 2002.

Marcuzzo, M.C., 'Joan Robinson and the Two Strands of Cambridge Economists', read at Prof. Yagi's Workshop, Kyoto University, December 2003.

Marcuzzo, M.C., 'Keynes and His Favourite Pupil' (in Marcuzzo, M.C. and Rosselli, A. eds, 2005).

Marcuzzo, M.C. and Rosselli, A. eds, *Economists in Cambridge*, Routledge, 2005.

Marcuzzo, M.C. and Sanfilipo, E. with Hirai, T., Nishizawa, T. and Ogose, T., 'The Letters between John Hicks and Ursula Webb September-December 1935', Working Paper, No.207, Institute for Economic and Business Administration Research, University of Hyogo, December 2005.

Marris, R. L., 'R.F. Kahn's Fellowship Dissertation', *Economic Journal*, September 1992.

Marshall, A., 'Remedies for Fluctuations of General Prices', *Contemporary Review*, March 1887.

Marshall, A., *Principles of Economics*, Macmillan, Eighth Edition, 1920 (First Edition, 1890).

Marshall, A., *Industry and Trade*, Macmillan, 1919.

Marshall, A., *Money, Credit and Commerce*, Macmillan, 1923.

Marshall, A. and Marshall, M., *The Economics of Industry*, Macmillan, 1879.

Marty, A., 'A Geometrical Exposition of the Keynesian Supply Function', *Economic Journal*, September 1961.

Mattick, P., *Marx and Keynes*, Merlin Press, 1971.

McCallum, B., 'Price-Level Stickiness and the Feasibility of Monetary Stabilization Policy with Rational Expectations', *Journal of Political Economy*, No. 3, 1977.

McCallum, B., 'The Current State of the Policy-Ineffectiveness Debate', *American Economic Review, Papers and Proceedings*, No. 2, 1979.

McCracken, H., *Value Theory and Business Cycles*, Falcon Press, 1933.

Meade, J., 'A Simplified Model of Mr Keynes' System', *Review of Economic Studies*, February 1937.

Meade, J., *Planning and the Price Mechanism*, George Allen and Unwin, 1948.

Meade, J., 'The Keynesian Revolution' (in Keynes, M. ed., 1975).

Meade, J., 'A New Keynesian Approach to Full Employment', *Lloyds Bank Review*, No.150, 1983.

Meade, J., *The Collected Papers of James Meade*, Vols. 1–3 (1988. ed. by Howson, S.), Vol. 4 (1990. ed. by Howson, S. and Moggridge, D.), Unwin Hyman.

Meade, J., 'The Relation of Mr. Meade's Relation to Kahn's Multiplier', *Economic Journal*, May 1993.

Mehta, G., *The Structure of the Keynesian Revolution*, Allied Publishers Private Limited, 1978.

Meltzer, A., 'Interpreting Keynes', *Journal of Economic Literature*, No.1, 1983.

Meltzer, A., *Keynes's Monetary Theory*, CUP, 1988.

Meltzer, A., 'Patinkin on Keynes and Meltzer', *Journal of Monetary Economics*, No.1, 1992.

Middleton, R., 'The Treasury in the 1930s', *Oxford Economic Papers*, March 1982.

Middleton, R., *Towards the Managed Economy*, Methuen, 1985.

Middleton, R., *Charlatans or Saviours?*, Edward Elgar, 1998.

Milgate, M., 'On the Origin of the Notion of "Intertemporal Equilibrium"' *Economica*, Vol. 46, pp. 1–10, 1979.

Milgate, M., *Capital and Employment*, Academic Press, 1982.

Milgate, M., 'The "New" Keynes Papers' (in Eatwell, J. and Milgate, M. eds, 1983).

Mill, J.S., *Principles of Political Economy*, Longmans, Green and Co., 1920 (First Edition, 1848).

Millar, J., 'The Social Accounting Basis of Keynes' Aggregate Supply and Demand Functions', *Economic Journal*, June 1972.

Miller, E., 'Keynes' Monetary Theory and Bank Reserves in Britain', *Atlantic Economic Journal*, March 1989.

Miller, P. ed., *The Rational Expectations Revolution*, MIT Press, 1994.

Millmow, A., 'The Evolution of J.M. Keynes' Wage and Employment Policy 1920–1946', *History of Economics Review*, Winter 1992.

Mini, P., *Keynes, Bloomsbury and the General Theory*, Macmillan, 1991.

Mini, P., 'The Anti-Benthamism of J.M. Keynes', *American Journal of Economics*, October 1991.

Mini, P., *John Maynard Keynes*, Macmillan, 1994.

Mini, P., 'Keynes' Investments', *American Journal of Economics*, January 1995.

Mini, P., 'Keynes on Markets', *American Journal of Economics*, January 1996.

Ministry of Reconstruction, *Employment Policy*, Cmd 6527, 1944.

Minsky, H., *John Maynard Keynes*, Columbia University Press, 1975.

Minsky, H., *Inflation, Recession and Economic Policy*, Wheatsheaf Books, 1982.

Minsky, H., *Stabilizing an Unstable Economy*, Yale University Press, 1986.

Mises, L., *The Theory of Money & Credit*, Harcourt Brace & Co., 1935 (translated from the German, 1912, by Batson, H.).

Mises, L., *Human Action*, William Hodge and Company Limited, 1949.

Mises, L., *Nation, State, and the Economy*, New York University Press, 1983 (translated from the German, 1919, by Yeager, L.).

Mitchell, B. ed., *British Historical Statistics*, CUP, 1988.

Mitchell, W., King, W., Macauley, F. and Knauth, D., *Income in the United States*. Harcourt, Brace and Company, 1921.

Mizen, P. and Presley, J., 'Buffer Stock Ideas in the Monetary Economics of Keynes and Robertson', *HOPE*, Summer 1994.

Mizen, P. and Presley, J., 'Robertson and Persistent Negative Reactions to Keynes's *General Theory*', *HOPE*, Winter 1995.

Modigliani, F., 'Liquidity Preference and the Theory of Interest and Money', *Econometrica*, January 1944.

Modigliani, F., 'The Monetary Mechanism and Its Interaction with Real Phenomena', *Review of Economics and Statistics*, February 1963.

Moggridge, D., *British Monetary Policy 1924–1931*, CUP, 1972.

Moggridge, D., 'From the *Treatise* to the *General Theory*', *HOPE*, Spring 1973.

Moggridge, D., *John Maynard Keynes*, Penguin, 1976.

Moggridge, D., 'Recent Developments on the Keynes Front', *Cambridge Review*. October 1989.

Moggridge, D. ed., *Keynes, Macroeconomics and Method*, Edward Elgar, 1990.

Moggridge, D., *Maynard Keynes*, Routledge, 1992.

Moggridge, D., 'In the "Orthodox" Tradition', *JPKE*, Spring 1995.

Mokyr, J. ed., *The Economics of the Industrial Revolution*, Rowman & Littlefield Publishers, 1985.

Moore, B., *Horizontalists and Verticalists*, CUP, 1988.

Moore, G., *Principia Ethica*, CUP, 1903.

Morgan, M. and Rutherford, M., *From Interwar Pluralism to Postwar Neoclassicism*, Duke University Press, 1998.

Mummery, A. and Hobson, J., *The Physiology of Industry*, John Murray, 1889.

Muth, F., 'Rational Expectations and the Theory of Price Movements', *Econometrica*, No. 6, 1961.

Myrdal, G., *Monetary Equilibrium*, W. Hodge, 1939.

Myrdal, G., *The Political Element in the Development of Economic Theory*, Routledge and Kegan Paul, 1953 (translated from the Swedish, 1929, by Streeten, P.).

Myrdal, G., *Beyond the Welfare State*, Gerald Duckworth, 1960.

Myrdal, G., *Objectivity in Social Research*, Wesleyan University Press, 1969.

Myrdal, G., *Against the Stream*, Vintage Books, 1975.

Negishi, T., *General Equilibrium Theory and International Trade*, North-Holland, 1972.

Negishi, T., 'Involuntary Unemployment and Market Imperfection', *Economic Studies Quarterly*, April 1974.

Negishi, T., *Microeconomic Foundations of Keynesian Macroeconomics*, North-Holland, 1979.

Negishi, T., *Economic Theories in a Non-Walrasian Tradition*, CUP, 1985.

Negishi, T., *History of Economic Theory*, North-Holland, 1991.

Neisser, H., 'General Overproduction', *Journal of Political Economy*, August 1934.

Nevile, J., 'Notes on Keynes' Aggregate Supply Curve', *JPKE*, Winter 1992.

O'Brien, D., 'Monetary Economics' (in Creedy, F. and D. O'Brien eds, 1984).

O'Brien, D., 'Marshall's Work in Relation to Classical Economics' (in Whitaker, J. ed., 1990).

O'Brien, D., 'Four Detours', *Journal of Economic Methodology*, Vol. 5, No. 1, 1998.

O'Brien, D. and Presley, J. eds, *Pioneers of Modern Economics in Britain*, Macmillan, 1981.

O'Donnell, R., *Keynes*, Macmillan, 1989.

Ohlin, B., 'Transfer Difficulties, Real and Imagined', *Economic Journal*, June 1929.

Ohlin, B., 'Some Notes on the Stockholm Theory of Saving and Investment', *Economic Journal*, March and June 1937.

Ohlin, B., 'On the Slow Development of the "Total Demand" Idea in Economic Theory', *Journal of Economic Literature*, September 1974.

Ohlin, B., 'Stockholm and Cambridge', *HOPE*, No.2, 1981.

Ott, D. and Ott, A., *Federal Budget Policy*, Brookings Institution, 1965.

Panico, C., 'Sraffa on Money and Banking', *CJE*, March 1988.

Parsons, S., 'Post Keynesian Realism and Keynes' *General Theory*', *JPKE*, Summer 1996.

Parsons, W., *Keynes and the Quest for a Moral Science*, Edward Elgar, 1997.

Pasinetti, L., *Growth and Income Distribution*, CUP, 1974.

Pasinetti, L., 'J.M. Keynes's "Revolution"' (in Pasinetti, L. and Schefold, B. eds, 1999).

Pasinetti, L. and Shefold, B. eds, *The Impact of Keynes on Economics in the 20th Century*, Edward Elgar, 1999.

Patinkin, D., 'Involuntary Unemployment and the Keynesian Supply Function', *Economic Journal*, September 1949.

Patinkin, D., *Money, Interest and Prices*, Second Edition, Harcourt and Row, 1965.

Patinkin, D., 'Keynes and the Multiplier', *Manchester School of Economics and Social Studies*, September 1975.

Patinkin, D., *Keynes' Monetary Thought*, Duke University Press, 1976.

Patinkin, D., 'Keynes and the Multiplier', *Manchester School*, September 1978.

Patinkin, D., 'A Study of Keynes' Theory of Effective Demand', *Economic Inquiry*, April 1979.

Patinkin, D., 'New Materials on the Development of Keynes' Monetary Thought', *HOPE*, No.1, 1980.

Patinkin, D., *Anticipations of the General Theory? And Other Essays on Keynes*, University of Chicago Press, 1982.

Patinkin, D., 'Keynes's Theory of Effective Demand', *HOPE*, Winter 1987.

Patinkin, D., 'Keynes and the Keynesian Cross', *HOPE*, Fall 1989.

Patinkin, D., 'On Different Interpretations of the *General Theory*', *JME*, October 1990.

Patinkin, D., 'On the Chronology of the *General Theory*', *Economic Journal*, May 1993.

Patinkin, D. and Leith, J. eds, *Keynes, Cambridge and the General Theory*, Macmillan, 1977.

Peacock, A., 'Keynes and the Role of the State' (in Crabtree, D. and Thirlwall, A. eds, 1993).

Peden, G., *British Rearmament and the Treasury 1932–1939*, Scottish Academic Press, 1979.

Peden, G., 'Sir Richard Hopkins and the "Keynesian Revolution" in Employment Policy, 1929–45', *Economic History Review*, May 1983.

Peden, G., 'The "Treasury View" on Public Works and Employment in the Interwar Period', *Economic History Review*, No.2, 1984.

Peden, G., *British Economic and Social Policy*, Philip Allan, 1985.

Peden, G., *Keynes, the Treasury and British Economic Policy*, Macmillan Education, 1988.

Peden, G., 'The Road to and from Gairloch', *Twentieth Century British History*, No.3, 1993.

Peden, G., 'The Treasury View in the Interwar Period' (in Corry, B. ed., 1996).

Peden, G., *The Treasury and British Public Policy 1906–1959*, OUP, 2000.

Peden, G. ed., *Keynes and His Critics*, OUP, 2004.

Pereira, L. and Dall'Acqua, F., 'Economic Populism versus Keynes', *JPKE*, Fall 1991.

Perelman, M., *Keynes, Investment Theory & the Economic Slowdown*, Macmillan, 1989.

Pheby, J. ed., *New Directions in Post-Keynesian Economics*, Edward Elgar, 1989.

Pheby, J. ed., *J.A. Hobson after Fifty Years*, Macmillan, 1994.

Pierce, T., 'Keynes' Personal Investing', *Social Science Journal*, No.1, 1993.

Pigou, A., 'The Exchange Value of Legal-Tender Money', *Quarterly Journal of Economics*, November 1917.

Pigou, A., *The Econkmics of Welfare*, Macmillan, 1920.

Pigou, A., *Essays in Applied Economics*, P.S. King & Son, 1923

Pigou, A. ed., *Memorials of Alfred Marshall*, Macmillan, 1925.

Pigou, A., *Industrial Fluctuations*, Macmillan, 1927.

Pigou, A., *The Theory of Unemployment*, Macmillan, 1933.

Pigou, A., 'Mr J.M. Keynes' *General Theory of Employment, Interest and Money*', *Economica*, May 1936.

Pigou, A., 'Real and Money Wages in Relation to Unemployment', *Economic Journal*, September 1937.

Pigou, A., *Socialism versus Capitalism*, Macmillan, 1937.

Pigou, A., *Employment and Equilibrium*, Macmillan, 1941.

Pigou, A., *Keynes's General Theory*, Macmillan, 1950.

Pilling, G., *The Crisis of Keynesian Economics*, Croom Helm, 1986.

Presley, J., *Robertsonian Economics*, Macmillan, 1979.

Presley, J., 'J.M. Keynes and D.H. Robertson' (in Presley, J. ed., 1992).

Presley, J. ed., *Essays on Robertsonian Economics*, St. Martin Press, 1992.

Pressnell, L., '1925: The Burden of Sterling', *Economic History Review*, Vol. 31, February 1978.

Rae, J., *Statement of Some New Principles on the Subject of Political Economy*, Hillard Gray, 1834.

Ramsey, F., 'Mr Keynes on Probability', *Cambridge Magazine*, January 1922.

Ramsey, F., 'Truth and Probability', 1926 (in Ramsey, F., 1990).

Ramsey, F., *The Foundations of Mathematics*, Kegan Paul, 1931.

Ramsey, F. (ed. by Mellor, D.H.), *Philosophical Papers*, CUP, 1990.

Ratner, S., Soltow, J. and Sylla, R., *The Evolution of the American Economy*, Basic Books, 1979.

Realfonzo, R., *Money and Banking*, Edward Elgar, 1998.

Reese, D. ed., *The Legacy of Keynes*, Harper & Row, 1987.

Reisman, D., *Alfred Marshall's Mission*, Macmillan, 1990.

Ricardo, D., *The High Price of Bullion* (in Sraffa, P. ed., 1951. The First Edition, 1810).

Ricardo, D., *On the Principles of Political Economy and Taxation*, CUP, 1951 (First Edition, 1817).

Robbins, L., 'Schumpeter on the *History of Economic Analysis*', *Quarterly Journal of Economics*, February 1955.

Robbins, L., 'On the Relations between Politics and Economics', 1961 (in Robbins, L., 1963).

Robbins, L., *Politics and Economics*, Macmillan, 1963.

Robbins, L., *Autobiography of an Economist*, Macmillan, 1971.

Roberts, M., 'Keynes, the Liquidity Trap and the Gold Standard', *Manchester School of Economics and Social Studies*, March 1995.

Robertson, D., *A Study of Industrial Fluctuation*, P.S. King & Son, 1915.

Robertson, D., *Money*, Nisbet & Co., 1922.

Robertson, D., *Banking Policy and the Price Level*, Staples Press Limited, 1926.

Robertson, D., 'Theories of Banking Policy', *Economica*, June 1928.

Robertson, D., 'Mr Keynes' Theory of Money', *Economic Journal*, September 1931.

Robertson, D., 'Saving and Hoarding', *Economic Journal*, September 1933a (in Robertson, D., 1940).

Robertson, D., 'Mr Robertson on "Saving and Hoarding" (III)', *Economic Journal*, December 1933b.

Robertson, D., 'Industrial Fluctuation and the Natural Rate of Interest', *Economic Journal*, December 1934.

Robertson, D., *Essays lin Monetary Theory*, Staples Press Limited, 1940.

Robertson, D., *Lectures on Economic Principles*, Vol. 1 (1957), Vol. 2 (1958) and Vol. 3 (1959), Staples Press Limited.

Robertson, D. and Johnson, H, 'Keynes and Supply Functions', *Economic Journal*, September 1955.

Robertson, H., 'Alfred Marshall's Aims and Methods Illustrated from His Treatment of Distribution', *HOPE*, pp. 1–65, 1970.

Robinson, J., 'A Parable on Saving and Investment', *Economica*, February 1933a.

Robinson, J., 'The Theory of Money and the Analysis of Output', *Review of Economic Studies*, October 1933b.

Robinson, J., The *Economics of Imperfect Competition*, Macmillan, 1933c.

Robinson, J., *The Generalisation of the General Theory and Other Essays*, Second Edition, Macmillan, 1979.

Rochon, L-P., *Credit, Money and Production*, Edward Elgar, 1999.

Rogers, C., *Money, Interest and Capital*, CUP, 1989.

Romer, D., 'The New Keynesian Synthesis', *Journal of Economic Perspectives*, Vol. 7, No. 1, 1993.

Rostow, W., *The Stages of Economic Growth*, CUP, 1960.

Rotheim, R., 'Organicism and the Role of the Individual in Keynes' Thought', *JPKE*, Winter 1992.

Rothschild, K., 'Keynes' *General Theory*', *JPKE*, Summer 1996.

Rowse, A., *Mr. Keynes and the Labour Movement*, Macmillan, 1936.

Rubinstein, W.D., *Capitalism, Culture, and Decline in Britain 1750–1990*, Routledge, 1993.

Rymes, T., transcribed, edited and constructed, *Keynes's Lectures, 1932–35*, Macmillan, 1989.

Sampson, A., *Anatomy of Britain*, Harper & Row, 1962.

Samuelson, P., 'Lord Keynes and the *General Theory*', *Econometrica*, July 1946.

Samuelson, P., *Economics*, McGraw-Hill Book Co. (Various Editions. First Edition, 1948).

Samuelson, P., 'The *General Theory*' (in Lekachman, R. ed., 1964).

Sandelin, B. ed., *Knut Wicksell Selected Essays in Economics*, Vol. II, Routledge, 1999.

Sandilands, R., 'Perspectives on Allyn Young in Theories of Endogenous Growth', *Journal of the History of Economic Thought*, Vol. 22, No. 3, 2000.

Sardoni, C., 'Chapter 18 of the *General Theory*', *JPKE*, Winter 1992.

Sargent, T. and Wallace, N., ' "Rational" Expectations, the Optimal Monetary Instrument, and the Optimal Money Supply Rule", *Journal of Political Economy*, No. 2, 1975.

Sargent, T. and Wallace, N., 'Rational Expectations and the Theory of Economic Policy', *Journal of Monetary Economics*, No. 2, 1976.

Sayers, R., *Financial Policy 1939–45*, Longmans, Green and Co., 1956.

Sayers, R., *The Bank of England, 1891–1944*, Vols. 3, CUP, 1976.

Schneider, M., *J.A. Hobson*, St. Martin's Press, 1996.

Schumpeter, J., *The Theory of Economic Development*, OUP, 1934 (translated from the German, 1911, by Opie, R.).

Schumpeter, J., *Imperialism and Social Classes*, Meridian Books, 1955 (translated from the German by Norder, H.).

Sebastiani, M. ed., *The Notion of Equilibrium in the Keynesian Theory*, Macmillan, 1992.

Semmel, B., *Imperialism and Social Reform*, George Allen and Unwin, 1960.

Shackle, G., *The Years of High Theory*, CUP, 1967.

Shackle, G., 'Theory and Today's Establishment in Economic Theory', *Journal of Economic Literature*, pp. 516–519, 1973.

Shackle, G., *Keynesian Kaleidics*, Edinburgh University Press, 1974.

Sharma, S. ed., *John Maynard Keynes*, Edward Elgar, 1998.

Shaw, G., *Keynesian Economics*, Edward Elgar, 1988.

Shaw, G. ed., *The Keynesian Heritage*, Vols. 2, Edward Elgar, 1988.

Shionoya, Y., 'Sidgwick, Moore and Keynes' (in Bateman, B. and Davis, J. eds, 1991).

Shionoya, Y., 'A Non-Utilitarian Interpretation of Pigou's Welfare Economics' (in Koslowski, P. and Shionoya, Y. eds, 1993).

Shionoya, Y., 'Pigou's Welfare Economics and Ethical Belief', Workshop on the Cambridge School of Economics, February 2005, Hitotsubashi University.

Sidgwick, H., 'The Theory of Evolution in Its Application to Practice', *Mind*, No. 1, 1876.

Simons, H., *Economic Policy for a Free Society*, University of Chicago Press, 1973.

Singer, H., 'Austin Robinson and Keynes', *CJE*, June 1995.

Siven, C., 'Two Early Swedish Debates about Wicksell's Cumulative Process', *European Journal of the History of Economic thought*, Vol. 5, No. 1, 1998.

Skidelsky, R. ed., *The End of the Keynesian Era*, Macmillan, 1977.

Skidelsky, R., *John Maynard Keynes*. Vol. 1 (1983), Vol. 2 (1992) and Vol. 3 (2000), Macmillan.

Skidelsky, R., 'Keynes and Employment Policy in the Second World War', *JPKE*, Vol. 21, No. 1, Fall 1998.

Smithin, J., 'Hicks on Keynes and Thornton', *Canadian Journal of Economics*, April 1996.

Solow, R., 'A Contribution to the Theory of Economic Growth', *Quarterly Journal of Economics*, February 1956.

Solow, R., 'Investment and Technical Progress' (in Arrow, K., Karlin, S. and Suppes P. eds, *Mathematical Methods in Social Sciences*, Stanford University Press, 1960).

Sowell, T., *Say's Law*, Princeton University Press, 1972.

Sraffa, P., 'The Laws of Returns under Competitive Conditions', *Economic Journal*, December 1926.

Sraffa, P., 'Dr. Hayek on Money and Capital', *Economic Journal*, March 1932.

Sraffa, P., ed., *The Works and Correspondence of David Ricardo*, Vol. 3, CUP, 1951.

Stadler, G., 'Real Business Cycles', *Journal of Economic Literature*, December 1994.

Steele, G., *Monetarism and the Demise of Keynesian Economics*, Macmillan, 1989.

Steele, G., *Keynes and Hayek*, Routledge, 2001.

Steiger, O., 'Bertil Ohlin and the Origins of the Keynesian Revolution', *HOPE*, pp. 341–361, 1976.

Stein, H., *The Fiscal Revolution in America*, University of Chicago Press, 1969.

Steindl, F., 'The Monetary Economics of Lauchlin Currie', *JME*, June 1991.

Stewart, M., *Keynes and After*, Harmondsworth, 1967.

Stewart, M., *Keynes in the 1990s*, Penguin, 1993.

Stigler, G., 'The Place of Marshall's *Principles* in the Development of Economics' (in Whitaker, J. ed., 1990).

Stiglitz, J., *Whither Socialism?*, MIT Press, 1994.

Stiglitz, J., *Globalization and Its Discontents*, W.W. Norton & Company, 2002.

Stiglitz, J. and Greenwald, B., *Towards a New Paradigm in Monetary Economics*, CUP, 2003.

Stone, R., 'Keynes, Political Arithmetic and Econometrics', *Proceedings of the British Academy*, pp. 55–92, 1978.

Strachey, L., *Eminent Victorians*, Chatto & Windus, 1918.

Strøm, S. and Thalberg, B., eds, *The Theoretical Contributions of Knut Wicksell*, Macmillan, 1979.

Swan, T., 'Economic Growth and Capital Accumulation', *Economic Record*, November 1956.

Talele, C., *Keynes and Schumpeter*, Avebury, 1991.

Taussig, F., *The Tariff History of the United States*, G.P. Putnam's Sons, 1892.

Taylor, A., *English History 1914–1945*, OUP, 1965.

Taylor, J., 'Staggered Wage Setting in a Macro Model', *American Economic Review*, May 1979.

Temin, P., 'International Instability and Debt between the Wars', *JME*, No.2, 1994.

Thomas, G. and Morgan-Witts, M., *The Day the Bubble Burst*, Jonathan Clowes Limited, 1979.

Thornton, H. (ed. by Hayek, F.), *An Enquiry into the Nature and Effects of the Paper Credit of Great Britain*, George Allen and Unwin, 1939 (First Edition, 1802).

Tinbergen, J., *Business Cycles in the United States of America*, Economic Intelligence Service (League of Nations), 1939.

Tobin, J., *Asset Accumulation and Economic Activity*, Basil Blackwell, 1980.

Tomlinson, J., *British Macroeconomic Policy since 1940*, Croom Helm, 1985.

Tomlinson, J., *Employment Policy*, Clarendon Press, 1987.

Turner, C., *An Analysis of Soviet Views on John Maynard Keynes*, Duke University Press, 1969.

Turnovsky, S., *Macroeconomics and Stabilization Policy*, Macmillan, 1980.

Uhr, C., *Economic Doctrines of Knut Wicksell*, University of California Press, 1960.

Uhr, C., 'Economists and Policymaking 1930–1936', *HOPE*, pp. 89–121, 1977.

University of Cambridge (King's College), *John Maynard Keynes: 1883–1946*, 1949.

Uzawa H., 'On a Two-Sector Model of Economic Growth: I', *Review of Economic Studies*, October 1961.

Vercelli, A., *Methodological Foundations of Macroeconomics*, CUP, 1991.

Vicarelli, F. ed., *Keynes' Relevance Today*, Macmillan, 1983.

Vicarelli, F., *Keynes*, University of Pennsylvania Press, 1984.

De Vroey and Hoover, K. eds, *IS-LM Model: Its Rise, Fall, and Strange Persistence*, Duke University Press, 2005.

Waley, D., 'The Treasury during World War II', *Oxford Economic Papers*, 1953, (Supplement on Sir Hubert Henderson).

Waligorski, C., 'Keynes and Democracy', *Social Science Journal*, No.1, 1994.

Walras, L., *Elements of Pure Economics or the Theory of Social Wealth*, Allen and Unwin 1954 (translated from the French, 1874, by Jaffé, W.).

Wattel, H. ed., *The Policy Consequences of John Maynard Keynes*, Macmillan, 1986.

Weintraub, R., 'Keynes' Employment Function', *HOPE*, No. 2, 1974.

Weintraub, R., *Microfoundations*, CUP, 1979.

Weintraub, S., 'Micro-Foundations of Aggregate Demand and Supply', *Economic Journal*, September 1957.

Weintraub, S., *Classical Keynesianism*, Chilton Co., 1961.

Weintraub, S., 'The Keynesian Light that Failed', *Nebraska Journal of Economics and Business*, Autumn 1975.

Weintraub, S., 'Cost Inflation and the State of Economic Theory', *Economic Journal*, June 1976.

Weintraub, S., *Keynes, Keynesians and Monetarists*, University of Pennsylvania Press, 1978.

Wells, P., 'Keynes' Employment Function', *HOPE*, No. 2, 1974.

Whitaker, J., 'Alfred Marshall: The Years 1877 to 1885', *HOPE*, Spring 1972.

Whitaker, J., 'Some Neglected Aspects of Alfred Marshall's Economic and Social Thought', *HOPE*, Summer 1977.

Whitaker, J., 'What Happened to the Second Volume of the *Principles*?' (in Whitaker, J. ed., 1990).

Whitaker, J. ed., *Centenary Essays on Alfred Marshall*, CUP, 1990.

Wicksell, K., *Interest and Prices* (translated from the German, 1898, by Kahn, R.), Macmillan, 1936.

Wicksell, K., *Value, Capital and Rent* (translated from the German, 1893, by Frowein, S.), George Allen and Unwin, 1954.

Wicksell, K., *Lectures on Political Economy*, Vol.1 *General Theory*, G. Routledge, 1934 (translated from the Swedish, 1901, by Classen, E.).

Wicksell, K., *Lectures on Political Economy*, Vol.2 *Money*, G. Routledge, 1935 (First Edition, 1906. Translated from the second Swedish Edition, 1915, by Classen, E.).

Wicksell, K., 'The Influence of the Rate of Interest on Prices', *Economic Journal*, pp. 213–220, 1907.

Wicksell, K., 'Stabilizing the Value of Money,' *Ekonomisk Tidscrift*, 1908 (in Sandelin, B. ed., 1999).

Wicksell, K., 'The Regulation of the Value of Money' *Ekonomisk Tidscrift*, 1913 (in Sandelin, B. ed., 1999).

Wicksell, K., 'Review of Mises (1912)', *Zeitschrift für Volkswirtschaft, Sozialpolitik und Verwaltung*, Vol. 23, pp. 144–149, 1914.

Wicksell, K. (ed. by Lindahl, E.), *Selected Papers on Economic Theory*, George Allen and Unwin, 1958.

Wiener, M., *English Culture and the Decline of the Industrial Spirit, 1850–1980*, CUP, 1981.

Williams, J., 'The Monetary Doctrines of J.M. Keynes', *Quarterly Journal of Economics*, pp. 547–587, 1931.

Winch, D., 'The Keynesian Revolution in Sweden', *Journal of Political Economy*, April 1966.

Winch, D., *Economics and Policy*, Hodder & Stoughton, 1969.

Wohl, R., *The Generation of 1914*, Harvard University Press, 1979.

Wolcott, S., 'Keynes versus Churchill', *Journal of Economic History*, September 1993.

Wolfe, J., 'Marshall and the Trade Cycle', *Oxford Economic Papers*, 1956.

Wood, J. ed., *John Maynard Keynes*, Vols. I-IV, Croom Helm, 1983.

Wood, J., *British Economists and the Empire*, Croom Helm, 1983.

Wood, J. ed., *John Maynard Keynes*, Vols. V-VIII, Routledge, 1994.

Woodford, M., *Interest and Prices*, Princeton University Press, 2003 (The reviews are published by Boianovsky, M. and Trautwein, H-M., Mehrling, P., Laidler, D. and Hoover, K. together with the author's rejoinder in the *Journal of the History of Economic Thought*, No.2, 2006).

Worswick, G. and Trevithick, J. eds, *Keynes and the Modern World*, CUP, 1983.

Wright, Q. ed., *Unemployment as a World Problem*, University of Chicago Press, 1931.

Yellen, J., 'Efficiency-Wage Models of Unemployment', *American Economic Review*, May 1984.

Young, W., *Interpreting Mr. Keynes*, Polity Press, 1987.

Young, W., *Harrod and His Trade Cycle Group*, Macmillan, 1989.

IV   Japanese bibliography

(The titles below are translated by the author of the present book.)

Akashi, S., *The Genealogy of Macroeconomics*, Toyo Keizai Shinpousha, 1988.

Aoyama, H., *Theories of Industrial Fluctuations of the Cambridge School and the Stockholm School*, Soubunsha, 1953.

Asano, E., 'On the Evolution of the *General Theory*', (1)–(6), Shougaku Ronsan (Chuo University), May 1999–November 1985.

Asano, E., *The Developmental Process Leading to Keynes's General Theory*, Nihon Hyouronsha, 1987.

Choo, Y. and Sumiya, K. eds, *An History of Economic Thought in Modern Japan*, Vol.1, Yuuhikaku, 1969.

Fukuoka, M., *Keynes*, Toyo Keizai Shinpousha, 1997.

Fukuoka, M., Hayasaka, T., and Negishi, T., *Keynes and the Present Day*, Zeimu Keiri Kyoukai, 1983.

Gotoh, S., *Korekiyo Takahashi*, Nikkei Shinsho, 1977.

Hara, M., *A Reconstruction of the Economics of Keynes*, Toyo Keizai Shinpousha, 1994.

Hashimoto, S. ed., *The Economics of Marshall*, Minerva Shobou, 1990.

Hayasaka, T., 'Keynes and Nationalism' (in Tachi ed., 1968).

Hayasaka, T. ed., *Keynesianism Reexamined*, Taga Shuppan, 1986.

Hayasaka, T. ed., *Encounter with Keynes*, Nihon Keizai Hyouronsha, 1993.

Hirai, T., 'On the Disequilibrium Interpretation of the Keynesian System', *Annals of Management*, Komazawa University, No. 4, 1979.

Hirai, T., *A Reconstruction of Keynes's General Theory*, Hakutoh Shobou, 1981.

Hirai, T., 'The Developmental Process of Keynes's Theory', *Journal of Economics*, Tokyo University, Vol. 49, No. 4, 1984.

Hirai, T., *A Study of Keynes*, University of Tokyo Press, 1987 (The original version of Hirai (1988)).

Hirai, T., 'On the Relation between *A Treatise on Money* and the *General Theory*', *Journal of Economics*, Tokyo University, Vol. 55, No. 3, 1989.

Hirai, T., 'The Wicksell Connection (I)(II)', *Sophia Economic Review*, No.1 and No.2, 1990.

Hirai, T., 'Two Streams of the Cambridge School', *Annals of the Society for the History of Economic Thought*, Vol. 30, 1992.

Hirai, T., 'The Developmental Process of Keynes's Economics' (in the *Society for the History of Economic Thought* ed., 1992).

Hirai, T., *Looking at Keynes's Economics from Multiple Points of View*, University of Tokyo Press, 2003.

Hirai, T., ed., *What Is the Market Society?*, Sophia University Press, 2007.

Hirai, T., *Keynes and the Cambridge World*, Minerva Shobou, 2007.

Hishiyama, I., *A History of Modern Economics*, Yuushindo, 1965.

Hishiyama, I., *From Quesnay to Sraffa*, Nagoya University Press, 1990.

Hishiyama, I., *A Modern Evaluation of the Economics of Sraffa*, University of Kyoto Press, 1993.

Hosaka, N., *A Revaluation of the Keynesian Revolution and Monetary Theory*, Yuuhikaku, 1978.

Hosaka, N., *Modern Economic Thought and the Development of Macroeconomics*, Institute of Economics, Kobe University of Commerce, 1994.

Inoue, T. and Sakaguchi, M. eds, *Marshall and His Contemporaries*, Minerva Shobou, 1993.

Itoh, M. ed., *Keynesian Economics*, Toyo Keizai Shinpousha, 1967.

Itoh, M., *Keynes*, Koudansha, 1993.

Iwamoto, T., *Keynes and the World Economy*, Iwanami Shoten, 1999.

Kanoh, M., *Keynes's Theory of Monetary Economy*, Kourosha, 1992.

Katoh, H., *Keynesianism in Illusion*, Nihon Keizai Shinbunsha, 1986.

Kawaguchi, H., *The Foundations of Keynes's General Theory*, Yuuhikaku, 1971.

Kawano, R., *A Study of Keynes's and Keynesian Economics*, Minerva Shobou, 1994.

Kitoh, N., *A Dynamics of Money and Interest Rate*, Iwanami Shoten, 1942.

Kitoh, N., *A Study of Keynes*, Toyo Keizai Shinpousha, 1948.

Kobayashi, N., *Economic Theories of Mercantilism*, Toyo Keizai Shinpousha, 1952.

Kobayashi, N., *The Formative Years of Economics*, Miraisha, 1961.

Komine, A., 'Merchants in Hawtrey's Theory', *Hitotsubashi Ronsou*, Hitotsubashi University, No. 6, 1993.

Komine, A., 'From Hawtrey to Keynes', *Annals of the Society for the History of Economic Thought*, Vol. 32, 1994.

Komine, A., 'Henderson's Economic Thought', Discussion Paper, No. 18, Niigata Sngyo University, 1999.

Matsukawa S., *Keynes's Economics*, Chuo Keizaisha, 1991.

Mikami, R., *The Original Image of Keynes's Economics*, Nihon Hyouronsha, 1986.

Minoguchi, T., 'The Developmental Process of the *General Theory*', *Economic Review*, Hitotubashi University, No.1, 1980.

Miyazaki, Y. and Itoh, M., *A Commentary on Keynes's General Theory*, Nihon Hyouronsha, 1964.

Nakayama, Y., *An Analysis of the Monetary Economy*, Toyo Keizai Shinpousha, 1992.

Nasu, M., *Keynes as a Businessman*, Chuuko Shinsho, 1995.

Negishi, T., *A Micro Theory of Keynes's Economics*, Nihon Keizai Shinbunsha, 1980.

Negishi, T., *Classical Economics and Modern Economics*, Iwanami Shoten, 1981.

Negishi, T., *A History of Economics*, Toyo Keizai Shinpousha, 1983.

Negishi, T., *Classical and Modern Theories in Economics*, Yuuhikaku, 1985.

Nishizawa, T. and Hattori, M. eds, *Political Economy during 100 Years in Britain*, Minerva Shobou, 1999.

Ogata, T., *Undercurrents of Modern Economics*, Chuo University Cooperative Society Press, 1995.

Ohara, H., 'On the Supply Mechanism of Keynes's *Treatise*', *Meidai Shougaku Ronsan* (Meiji University), Vol. 81, No. 1–2, 1999.

Okada, M., *The Development of Macroeconomic Theory*, Nagoya University Press, 1997.

Ono, Y., *A Dynamic Theory of Monetary Economy*, University of Tokyo Press, 1992.

Sasahara, S., 'The Controversy over the Policy for Economic Recovery in Interwar Japan', *Annals of the Society for the History of Economic Thought*, Vol. 35, 1997.

Shimizu, Y., *A Prelude to a Study of J.A. Hobson*, Hakutoh Shobou, 1998.

Shionoya, Y., 'Keynes's Moral Philosophy', *Quarterly Contemporary Economy*, March 1983.

Shionoya, Y., *The Structure of the Philosophy of Value*, Toyo Keizai Shinpousha, 1984.

The Society for the History of Economic Thought ed., *A History of Economic Doctrines*, Kyushu University Press, 1992.

Sugihara, S. and Chou, Y. eds, *The History of Japanese Economic Thought*, Toyo Keizai Shinpousha, 1979.

Suzuki, R., *The Stockholm School*, Senbundou, 1976.

Tachi, R. ed., *Keynes and Modern Economics*, University of Tokyo Press, 1968.

Takahashi, M., *A Study of Keynes's Treatise on Money*, Nankousha, 1936.

Uzawa, H., 'Keynes and Neo-Classicals', *Contemporary Economy Quarterly*, No.18, 1975.

Uzawa, H., *A Theory of Economic Dynamics*, University of Tokyo Press, 1986.

Watanabe, Y., *Endogenous Money Supply Theory*, Taga Shuppan, 1998.

Yamada, N., *A Study of Keynes*, Yuurindou, 1988 (written mainly in 1948).

Yasui, T. ed., *Economics after Keynes*, Nihon Keizai Shinbunsha, 1967.

Yoshida, M., *Keynes*, Nihon Keizai Hyouronsha, 1997.

Yoshikawa, H., *A Study of Macroeconomics*, University of Tokyo Press, 1984.

Yoshioka, A., *An Economic History of Modern England*, Iwanami Shoten, 1981.

Yoshizawa, N., *A Study of the Reconstructed Gold Standard in the United Kingdom*, Shinhyouron, 1986.

Index

accounting (employment) period 106, 110, 111
aggregate: amount of employment 104, 116; costs 108, 109, 116; disbursement 96; earnings 82; effective demand 133, 134, 137; employment 134, 142, 230 (n27); expenditure 91, 108, 109, 114, 116, 121; income 91, 121, 141, 168; quasi-rent 116
aggregate demand 18, 19, 172, 192, 196, 208; function 95, 105, 119, 135, 170, 171, 180, 187, 188, 189, 231 (n23), 237 (n55); price 133, 135, 170
aggregate supply 18, 19, 115, 192, 196; function 95, 106, 117, 129, 135, 149, 155, 170, 171, 180, 186, 187, 188, 189, 223 (n26), 231 (n23), 237 (n55); price 132, 133, 134, 149, 170
Ahiakpor, J. 216 (n5)
Akashi, S. 29
Alsace-Lorraine 9
Amadeo, E. 30, 93, 202–203, 223 (n1), 224 (n20), 227 (n25), 234 (n14), 237 (n50)
American economy 12–13, 229 (n20)
American entrepreneurs 9, 10
amount of employment 105, 119, 140
Anglo-American Agreement (1923) 36
Anglo-American Financial Agreement (1942) 39
anti-profiteering policy 36
Apostles 31, 32, 217 (n5)
Arnold, T. 10
Asano, E. 94, 221 (n13)
astronomical structure model 97
Austro-Prussian War 9

Backhouse, R. 233 (n7), 239 (n70)
Baldwin government 15, 37
Bank Charter Act (1844) 8
Banking School 8

banking system 8, 18, 51, 52, 61, 62, 68, 69, 91, 179, 190, 191, 200, 222 (n35)
Bank of England (BOE) 8
bank rate 8, 21, 33, 42, 46–47, 54, 61, 67; and quantity of money 22; policy 44, 67; theories 20, 56
Bateman, B. 218 (n13)
bearishness 62, 77, 119, 145, 191
bearishness function 47, 76, 222 (n35)
Bell, V. 31
Benthamism 38
Benthamite ethic 32
Bessemer and Thomas methods 9
Beveridge Report 39, 194, 219 (n42)
Blaug, M. 231 (n16)
Bloomsbury Group 31–32, 217 (n5; n6)
Boianovsky, M. 216 (n3; n8), 239 (n70)
Bonar Law government 15
borrowing 60, 61, 152
Bretton Woods International Monetary Conference 39
Bridel, P. 223 (n8; n18), 225 (n21), 235 (n28)
Britain's Industrial Future (Yellow Book) 37, 48
British economy 7–8, 13–15, 38; dependence on foreign markets 8; domestic side 14; international side 14; relative decline 8–11
Brüning Cabinet 16
Bryce, R. 95, 98
Buchanan, J. 238 (n64)
built-in stabiliser 183
business motive 119

Cain, N. 214 (n1; n11)
Cairncross, A. 95, 98
Cambridge-Cambridge Controversy 197
Cambridge Circus 82, 83–85, 87, 98, 99, 102

capital 179, 183; asset 89, 91, 94, 95,
97, 127, 141, 182, 186; circulating capital
46; fixed capital 47, 60, 78; free capital
disposal 24, 26; equipment 106, 107,
109, 110, 111, 125, 136, 164, 165, 166,
171; goods 26, 58, 61, 68, 76, 77, 94,
119, 120, 126, 127, 163, 179; liquid
capital 60, 62, 63, 169; real capital 24,
25, 26; stock 10, 57, 58, 201; theory 17;
value of capital 25, 120; working capital
46, 47, 48, 52, 60, 62, 232 (n19)
capitalist 19
Carabelli, A. 218 (n13)
central price theory 23
Chalmers, R. 34
Chamberlain–Bradbury Committee 36
Champernowne, D. 203, 233 (n12)
Chicago lectures (1931) 73–74, 82, 87
Chick, V. 234 (n14; n18)
Chiodi, G. 29
Churchill, W. 36, 37
Clarke, P. 95, 214 (n11), 218 (n27),
219 (n5), 231 (n29), 233 (n7)
classical dichotomy 29, 30, 177, 192,
209, 233 (n4)
classical economics 88, 114, 134, 177–78,
186, 193, 230 (n16)
classical theory 170
Clower, R. 197, 205, 208
Coddington, A. 235 (n1)
collectivism 15
Committee of Economists 37
concept of 'complex' 88–89, 110
Conservative Party 15
consumption function 79, 88, 90, 114, 115,
119, 122, 123, 129, 130, 144, 188–189,
197, 206
consumption goods 56, 57, 63, 65, 79, 83;
demand 25, 83, 123; expenditure 59, 123;
price level 19, 22, 25, 60, 61, 63, 64, 69,
76, 133, 216 (n9); sector 92, 123, 186,
190; supply 83
consumption theory 61–62, 121, 131, 136,
138–139, 145, 187, 188–189; objective
factor 139, 144, 145, 146, 151, 168;
subjective factor 138, 145, 146, 152
contrasting potentialities (of the *General
Theory*) 180–181
Crafts, N. 7, 214 (n1)
credit cycle 48, 62–63, 79, 84, 87
cumulative deterioration 78–79, 87
Cunliffe Committee 36
Currency School 8

Davidson, P. 197, 236 (n24)
Davis, E. 225 (n23)
Davis, J. 218 (n13)

Dawes Plan 36
deflation 41, 42, 46
deflationary policy 14, 16, 36
'Determination' manuscript 75, 76, 87
deviation-amplifying feedback-loop 197
Dimand, R. 95, 202, 223 (n1), 227 (n3)
Disequilibrium Approach 197, 208
'Does Employment Need a Drastic
Remedy?' (1924) 45
domestic investment 45
Draft Report (1930) 100, 225 (n24)
'A Drastic Remedy for Unemployment'
(1924) 45
'Dr Melchior: A Defeated Enemy' 35
dual-decision hypothesis 197

Eatwell, J. 233 (n13)
Economic Advisory Council 37
'An Economic Analysis of Unemployment'
(1931) 73–74, 82
*The Economic Consequences of the
Peace (ECC)* 35–36
economising 107, 115, 124
economy: co-operative economy 114;
entrepreneur economy 112, 113–114;
market economy 181, 183; monetary
economy 95, 198; neutral money
economy 95; organised credit economy
18, 28
effective demand 1, 3, 4, 29, 72, 73, 101,
112–113, 131–133, 135, 137, 140,
141–142, 145, 146, 158, 162, 168, 170,
171, 187, 188, 191, 203, 227 (n3), 228(n2;
n4), 229 (n7), 230 (n27), 236 (n24; n33);
fluctuations 113
employment function 133–135, 142,
148–149, 155, 170–171, 176; and first
postulate 136–137, 145; in relation to
the determination of the level of
employment 135
employment theory 73, 96, 103–106, 129,
131, 133–135, 141, 142–143, 171, 178,
184, 186, 192
equilibrium and interrelations (of the
General Theory) 184
'Ethics in Relation to Conduct' (1904) 32
excess demand price function 109
expectation 167

Fair Trade movement 9
Federal Reserve (FRB) 16, 34, 36
finance motive 198, 236 (n31)
financial market 61, 81
financial provision 138
'The First Undated Manuscript' 118,
121–125; fundamental psychological law
121–122; investment theory 125;

multiplier theory 122; prices and volume of output for consumption goods 122–123; underemployment equilibrium 121

First World War 11, 15, 34–36

fiscalism 196

Fisher, I. 21, 49, 50, 54, 114, 210, 219 (n6), 220 (n17), 227 (n27), 229 (n16)

forced saving 27, 28, 29, 52, 143, 168, 169, 179, 222 (n36), 225 (n23), 230 (n23)

Ford, H. 12

Fordney–McCumber Act (1922) 12

free trade 15

freie Valuta 25

Friedman, M. 196, 205, 210, 236 (n44), 238 (n58)

fundamental concepts 176

fundamental equation(s) 19, 20, 42, 44, 45–46, 53, 54, 55, 56, 73, 109, 200, 220 (n19), 222 (n25); derivation 64–66; embryo 49–50; overestimation 66–67; value 63–67

fundamental psychological factors 184

Galley 1(I) 149–153; consumption 151–152; rate of interest 152–153

Galley 1(II) 149–150, 154–155

Galley 1(III) 149–150, 156–158

Galley 2 149–150, 154

Galley 3 149–150, 155–156

Garegnani 30, 198, 233 (n10), 234 (n14)

general equilibrium theory 17, 204, 207

The General Law of Employment 120

'The General Theory' 131–140, 145; arguments of chapters 6 and 9 137–138; consumption theory 138–139; effective demand 131–133; employment theory 133–135; first postulate and employment function 136–137; fundamental concepts 140; marginal efficiency of capital 139; theoretical difficulties 136–138

General Theory of Bank Rate 20

The General Theory of Employment, Interest and Money (the *General Theory; GT*) 22, 37, 38, 39, 73, 81, 88, 89, 95, 98, 116, 117, 120, 127, 129, 130, 141, 145, 177–193; earlier economists: criticism 177–179, defence 179–180; history of economics 192–193; interpretations: anti-Keynesians 198–200, Keynesians 195–198, *Treatise* and *General Theory* 191–192; monetary economics of underemployment equilibrium 180–191, contrasting potentialities 180–181, equilibrium and interrelation 184, monetary economics 181–182,

place of money 182, theoretical model 184–191, underemployment equilibrium 182–184; Wicksell's influences 178–179

Genoa International Economic Conference (1922) 36

'Gentlemanly Capitalism' historians 214 (n1), 215 (n23)

gentlemanship 10

Germany: economic performance 9; expansionism 11; industrialisation 8–9; intra-firm research and development 9

Gladstone government 8

GNP 13

gold-exchange standard 33–34

Gold Standard 14, 15, 16, 33, 36, 37, 41, 43, 48, 218 (n25)

goods and money 113

government subsidies 45

Grant, D. 34–35

Great Depression 13, 38, 74

'The Great Revision' 153, 155, 158, 159–171; chapter 2 169–170; chapter3 – employment function 170–171; chapters 6 and 7 – some fundamental concepts 160–168; chapters 8 and 9 168–169

Greenwald, B. 238 (n65)

Groenewegen, P. 217 (n2)

Hahn, F. 236 (n41)

Hansen, A. 194, 222 (n25)

Hara, M. 234 (n17)

Harley, C. 7, 214 (n1)

Harris, S. 203

Harris Foundation lectures 225 (n19; n24)

Harrod, R. 153, 155, 157, 159–160, 194, 203, 209, 224 (n31), 229 (n16), 232 (n19), 233 (n3; n13), 234 (n22), 237 (n55)

Hawtrey, R. 51, 53, 155, 159, 169, 216 (n11), 218 (n24), 221 (n14), 222 (n30), 225 (n23); controversy with Robertson 227 (n2); criticism of the *Treatise* 72–73, 87, 147, 160, 220 (n35), 223 (n15); economics 71–72; trade cycle theory 71–72

Hayek, F. 17, 26–28, 30, 111, 143, 179, 212, 217 (n33), 233 (n6), 238 (n64); state of economics 26; theory 26–28, 29

Hecksher, E. 157

Hession, C. 93, 217 (n5; n6; n7), 219 (n36)

heterogeneity–expectations approach 189

heterogeneity of goods 110

Hicks, J. 194, 195–196, 203, 206, 216 (n20), 221 (n2; n3), 233 (n11), 235 (n2; n4; n6; n7), 237 (n54; n55)

Hishiyama, I. 29, 94, 222 (n23), 233 (n12)
'Historical Retrospect' 157
Hobson, J. 158, 180, 228 (n8), 231 (n29),
    233 (n7)
Hoover, K. 238 (n61)
Hoover Moratorium (1931) 36
Hopkins, A.G. 214 (n1; n11)
House of Commons 15

Import Duties Bill (1932) 15
income 24, 96, 118, 162; aggregate income
    121, 141, 168; motive 119; and price
    level determination 118
Income–Expenditure Approach 195–197
Index Version 228 (n1)
Indian Currency and Finance (*ICF*) 33–34
industrialization: of Germany 8–9; of
    United States 8–9
Industrial Revolution 7
inflation 36, 41, 42, 46, 47, 52, 207, 210,
    218 (n21), 224 (n31)
Inoue, J. 218 (n25)
interwar years 11–16; American economy
    during 12–13; British economy during
    13–15; international monetary crisis
    15–16
investment: function 119; gross investment
    162; Investment Price Theory (1) 68, 69,
    125; Investment Price Theory (2) 68, 69,
    125; investment–saving deviation 91;
    investment–saving equilibrium 91;
    Investment Theory (1) 126, 140;
    Investment Theory (2) 126, 140;
    Revised Investment Price Theory (2)
    125; and savings 21; theory 60, 118,
    120, 126, 139–140, 145, 229 (n17),
    234 (n16; n21)
Ishibashi, T. 218 (n25)
IS-LM model 203, 206–207

Japan 218 (n25)
Jarsulic, M. 236 (n24; n33)

Kahn, R. 39, 40, 50–51, 74, 82, 87,
    151, 153, 154, 155, 158, 219 (n6),
    224 (n26; n27; n28), 225 (n19; n20;
    n21); contribution 98–100, 148,
    222 (n31)
Kaldor, N. 236 (n41)
Kates, S. 225 (n18)
Keynes, J.M.: 2 May 1932 lecture 82–83;
    atheism 31; *Beveridge Report* 39; at
    Bretton Woods International Monetary
    Conference 39; causal relations 92;
    conflict with Treasury 39; conflicting
    facets of personality 32; criticism of

Benthamism 38; criticism of Hayek 111;
    criticism of Say's Law 112; devotion
    towards friends 34–35; editor of *The
    Economic Journal* 34; in the First World
    War period 34–36; and Grant 34–35;
    job at the India Office 32; and Kitoh 85;
    Liberal Party's policy-making 37;
    and Malthus 100–102; member of
    the Chancellor of the Exchequer's
    Consultative Council 39; member
    of the Economic Advisory Council 37;
    member of the Macmillan Committee
    37; Moore's Religion 38; and postwar
    macroeconomics 203–210, representative
    macroeconomics 205–210, three periods
    203–205; at Peace Conference 35; on
    quantity theory 21–22, 42; response to
    Hawtrey's criticism of the *Treatise* 72–73;
    in the Second World War period 39–40;
    shaping of the postwar world economic
    order 39; and Strachey, L. 34 on
    underemployment equilibrium 74;
    Victorian morality 32; will 39–40
Keynesian macroeconomics 204–208;
    Disequilibrium Approach 208;
    Income–Expenditure Approach 206–208;
    Aggregate Demand-Supply Curves
    version 207; General Equilibrium
    Theory version 207; IS-LM version 206;
    Real Term version 206
Keynesian Revolution 191–193, 194
Keynes's economics: interpretation of
    development of 200–203; Amadeo, E.
    202–203; Dimand, R. 202; Leijonhufvud, A.
    200–201; Meltzer, A. 201, *General
    Theory* model 237 (n48), *Treatise*
    model 237 (n47)
Keynes's fundamental idea 181–2
'Keynes's own theory' 22, 43
Kindleberger's formulation 13
Kitoh, N. 85
Klein, L. 203, 221 (n3), 222 (n35)
Knight, F. 238 (n64)
Kojima, S. 94
Kredit Anstalt Bank 16
Kuznets' data of gross capital
    formation 169

labour/labourers 27, 28, 101, 111, 178
Laidler, D. 29, 216 (n3; n17), 233 (n5)
laissez-faire 157
Lausanne Conference (1932) 36
Lavington, F. 216 (n17)
Leijonhufvud, A. 29, 197, 205, 211,
    221 (n2), 236 (n19; n20; n22; n43; n44),
    237 (n46; n54; n63), 238 (n70)

level of employment 105, 107–109, 112, 114, 115, 117, 119, 129, 130, 135, 143, 144, 170–171, 183, 229 (n9)
level of output 79, 81, 107, 201
Liberal Party 48, 99
Lindahl, E. 28, 30, 221 (n20)
Lippmann, W. 228–229 (n20)
liquidity preference 58, 61, 76, 77, 80–81, 86, 91, 92, 96, 97, 120, 127, 129, 152, 157, 172, 182, 183, 229 (n7), 232 (n19), 234 (n16; n23), 236 (n19)
liquidity trap 97, 116, 182, 196, 225 (n16)
Lloyd George, D. 35
London World Economic Conference (1933) 12
long-period equilibrium 79–80

McCracken, H. 113, 228 (n8)
MacDonald government 15
Macmillan, D. 156, 231 (n27)
Macmillan Co. 150
Macmillan Committee 37, 48, 72
macroeconomics: situation during the last thirty years 210–213
Malthus, R. 88, 98, 158, 180; and Keynes 100–102
'Malthus's general theory' 101
Mantoux, É. 218 (n20)
Marcuzzo, M.C. 224 (n26; n28; n29), 225 (n19)
marginal efficiency of capital 117, 119, 125–127, 129, 130, 139, 142, 144, 145, 172, 183, 184, 229 (n16), 234 (n16)
Marginal Revolution 38
marginal utility theory 22
Mark Clearing Zone 11
market economy 180–181, 238 (n66)
market mechanism 59–60
Marshall, A. 20, 32, 42, 112, 121, 152, 177, 192, 217 (n2), 224 (n26), 231 (n17), 238 (n63)
Marshall–Pigou type quantity theory 42, 231 (n16)
Meade, J. 39, 82, 194, 203, 219 (n39), 225 (n20), 237 (n55)
mechanical structure model 97
Mercantilism 156
Mercantilist 157, 179
'The Method of Index Numbers' (1909) 89
method of supply and demand 84, 85, 99, 100
Michaelmas lectures 175; (1929) 50–51; (1932) 95–98; (1933) 118–120, 226 (n19), 228 (n2); (1934) 143–145; (1935) 171–172, 231 (n23)

Milgate, M. 30, 95, 198, 226 (n1), 228 (n9), 230 (n16), 233 (n3; n10), 234 (n16), 237 (n49)
Mill, J. S. 170, 177
Mini, P. 217 (n5; n7)
Minsky, H. 233 (n8), 234 (n21), 237 (n49)
Mises, L. 28, 179, 216 (n13), 217 (n33; n34)
Modigliani, F. 196, 203, 207
Moggridge, D. 93, 106, 219 (n1), 228 (n1)
Monetarism 210, 211
monetary theory: of Hayek 26–28; of Myrdal 23–6
money-value 185
Montagu, E. 34
Moore, G.E. 31, 32, 38, 218 (n10)
MTP manuscript 77–82; cumulative deterioration 78–79; evaluation 81–82; liquidity preference theory 80–81; long-period equilibrium 79–80; relation between spending and earnings 79; relation of investment to the level of output 80–81; TM supply function 77–78
Müller Cabinet 16
multiplicity of goods 186
multiplier theory 37, 84, 89, 99, 100, 103, 116, 121, 122, 123, 202, 203, 225 (n24)
Mummery, A. 158
'My Early Beliefs' (1938) 38
Myrdal, G. 2, 4, 17, 22–26, 28, 29, 233 (n6), 237 (n52); on natural and money rates of interest 25; criticism of central price theory 23; criticism of neoclassical orthodoxy 22; monetary theory 23–26; state of economies 22–23

Nation and Athenaeum 45
natural rate of interest 18, 27
Negishi, T. 208
neoclassical economics 193, 212
neoclassical macroeconomics 208–210; monetarism 210; static and dynamic models 209–210
Neoclassical Synthesis 204
Neo-Ricardians 198
Neo-Shumpeterians 213
New Classical School 211
New Deal 13, 38
New Keynesians 212
normal psychological law 118
Norman, M. 36

O'Donnell, R. 218 (n13)
Ohlin, B. 29, 204, 216 (n14), 226 (n3), 227 (n28)
Okada, M. 94

ordinary supply curve 148
'Our Monetary Policy' (1925) 45

Paish, G. 34
Pasinetti, L. 239 (n69)
Patinkin, D. 1, 29, 93, 95, 194, 196, 208,
219 (n1), 220 (n19), 223 (n1; n9; n12),
224 (n20; n25), 225 (n19; n21),
227 (n29), 227 (n3), 228 (n2; n6),
229 (n14), 231 (n23), 235 (n29)
Pax Britannica 1, 11, 13
Peacock, A. 203
Peel government 8
Philips curve 208
Pigou, A. 20, 21, 32, 33, 37, 42, 116, 153,
154, 155, 177, 199, 203, 209, 222 (n36),
226 (n19), 231 (n17; n25), 236 (n35)
place of money 182
Plutology 193
PME manuscript 88–95; concept of
'complex' 88–89; formula for a system of
commodity markets 89–92;
incompleteness 94–95; money market's
role 92; variables in a system of
simultaneous equations and their causal
relations 92–94
Policy Ineffectiveness Hypothesis 211
portfolio selection 58, 61, 68, 80, 196
post-Keynesians 197–198
post-Walrasians 197
precautionary motive 61, 119, 145, 172,
176, 190, 198, 206, 234 (n23)
price control policy 36
price level of consumption goods 64
price level of investment goods 57
prices 185–186
production cost 57
production (investment) period 110, 111
profit 66, 69–70, 107; anticipated profit 72;
excess profit 19, 69–70, 104, 109, 112,
126, 132, 133, 141, 162, 226 (n16), 227
(n25), 229 (n12); margin 24; realised
profit 70, 72, 132, 144; windfall profit
95, 96, 115, 132, 136, 137, 141, 162,
163, 202
propensity: to consume 79, 92, 118, 120,
121, 135, 139, 144, 183, 184; to hoard
75; to invest 134, 135, 142, 144; to save
77, 104, 121; to spend 121, 134, 135,
139, 142
prospective yields 58, 68, 89, 90, 127, 139,
140, 167, 181, 183, 234 (n21)
protectionism 15
Prussia 9; Austro-Prussian war 9;
Franco-Prussian war 9
pseudo-TM supply function 105, 107, 114,
117, 125, 129, 135

pseudo-TM supply function mk2 107–108,
112, 114, 115, 117, 125, 129, 137–138
purchasing power parity theory 42–43

q theory 221 (n12; n13)
quantity of employment 139, 151
quantity of money 17, 21, 22, 26, 49, 50,
91, 119, 120, 169, 184
quantity theory 42, 49, 172, 178; defects
23; integration with general price
theory 22; Keynes's criticism 21–22;
Wicksell's criticism 17
quantity unit 57, 63–64
quasi-rent 123–124, 132, 144, 167;
maximisation 136; prospective
quasi-rent 126

rate of interest 45, 47, 58, 61, 62, 68, 72,
77, 91, 92, 97, 119, 120, 126, 140,
144–145, 152–153, 157, 172, 176, 182,
183, 189–191, 206, 217 (n33), 230 (n16;
n27), 233 (n7), 234 (n25), 235 (n29);
market 18, 43, 66–67; money 17, 18,
19, 24, 27, 67, 182, 217 (n33); natural
18, 19, 25, 53, 55, 66, 67, 179;
real 114
Rational Expectations School 211
Realfonzo, R. 217 (n36)
real wage 178
reparations 12, 15, 35, 36–37, 39
representative household hypothesis 211
representative macroeconomics 205–210
'Revised IS curve' 187
A Revision of the Treaty (RT) 35, 37
Ricardo, D. 29, 101, 152, 177, 210,
216 (n3)
Robbins, L. 39, 203, 238 (n64)
Robertson, D. 21, 29, 46, 51, 55, 75, 147,
150, 151, 152, 160, 216 (n11; n15), 220
(n29; n30), 221 (n14), 222 (n23; n36),
223 (n15), 225 (n23), 226 (n4), 227 (n30),
230 (n23), 232 (n19), 235 (n5);
influences on Keynes 52–53
Robinson, J. 83–85, 155, 158, 159,
225 (n20), 234 (n21)
Rogers, C. 30, 238 (n58)
Roosevelt, F. 12
roundabout production 18, 25, 26, 27,
28, 179

Sampson, A. 215 (n23)
Samuelson, P. 206, 207, 223 (n9)
saving deposits 61
saving motives 138
Sayers, R. 215 (n39)
Say's Law 170, 192, 212
Schumpeter's theory 213

'The Second Undated Manuscript' 118, 125–127; investment theory 126; marginal efficiency of capital 126, 127; prospective quasi-rent 126; quasi-rent 127

Second World War 39

Shackle, G. 221 (n2), 233 (n10)

Skidelsky, R. 95, 218 (n11), 235 (n26)

Smithian Revolution 38

Smoot–Hawley Tariff Act (1930) 12

speculative motive 61, 81, 119, 145

Sraffa, P. 82, 84, 224 (n28; n29; n30), 236 (n33)

Stephen, T. 31

sterling 14, 15, 37

Sterling Clearing Zone 11

Stiglitz, J. 238 (n65)

Stone, R. 39, 194

Strachey, L. 31, 34

Strong, B. 36

'The Summer Manuscript' 130, 140–143; effective demand 141–142; employment theory 142–143; and 'The General Theory' 143

supply curve 74, 83, 84, 85, 148, 149

supply schedule 90–91

Table 7.1 From the *Treatise* to 'The Parameters of a Monetary Economy' manuscript 93

Table 9.1 The situation in 1933–1934 128

Table 11.1 The proofing process 150

Table 12.1 The process of development of the chapters of the *General Theory* 173–174

Table 12.2 Michaelmas lectures: 1932–1935 175

table of contents (TOCs) 45–52, 55, 85–86, 220 (n9), 223 (n18), 231 (n28); comparison 115–117; First Table 115–116; Galley Table of Contents ('TOC') 149; Second Table 116; Third Table 116–117

Takahashi, Korekiyo 218 (n25)

Tariff Reform campaign 9

Taylor, F.W. 10

TCP (theory of cumulative process) 18–19

theoretical model 184–191; assumptions 184–186; interpretation 186–191; multiplicity of goods 186; prices 185–186; theory of absolute prices 17

theory of relative prices 17

Thornton, H. 17, 216 (n3)

three manuscripts of 1933 103–115; evaluation 114–115; The First Manuscript 103–106, accounting period 106, proper criteria vs. other criteria 105, system of equations 103–106; The Second Manuscript 106–111, accounting (employment) period 110, 111, first postulate 110, fundamental equation 109, heterogeneity of goods 110, production (investment) period 110, 111, pseudo-TM supply function mk2 107–108, second postulate 111, stability of the system 108–109; The Third Manuscript 111–114, effective demand 112–113, entrepreneur economy 113, shortcomings of classical economics 114

Tinbergen, J. 204

TM supply function 2, 3, 4, 20, 22, 59–60, 70, 72–73, 75, 77–78, 80, 81, 82, 83, 84–85, 87, 88, 94, 98, 100, 102, 104, 105, 114, 144, 145, 191, 223 (n15)

Tobin, J. 196–197, 221 (n12; n13)

A Tract on Monetary Reform (the *Tract*; *TMR*) 37, 41–43, 44–45, 214 (n9), 219 (n2), 220 (n8); fundamental equation 42; purchasing power parity theory 42–43; and the *Treatise* 44

transaction motive 61, 81

Trautwein, H-M. 217 (n38)

Treasury View 14

A Treatise on Money (the *Treatise*; *TM*) 2, 4–5, 30, 37, 38, 41, 43–45, 47, 56–70, 105, 191–192, 200–203, 216 (n16–n19), 221 (n2; n7), 222 (n31), 224 (n20), 225 (n20; n21), 226 (n16), 233 (n7), 237 (n49); aftermath 22, 71; Amadeo's interpretation 202, 237 (n50); assumptions 56–58; bearishness function 47, 76; Bridel's interpretation 223 (n8); capital 60; Clarke's interpretation 219 (n5); consumption theory 61–62; Dimand's interpretation 202; duality of the determination of the price level determination of consumption goods 68; duality of the determination of the price level determination of investment goods 68–69; duality of the theoretical framework 67; equity 58; fundamental equations 49–50, 63–67; and the *General Theory* 191–192; Harrod's criticism 224 (n31); Hawtrey's criticism 53–54, 72; 'Keynes's own theory' 22, 43; Leijonhufvud's interpretation 200; market mechanism 59–60; Meltzer's interpretation 201; policy view 44; portfolio selection theory 58, 61, 68, 80, 196; profit 69–70, 107; rate of interest 58, 191; spending–earnings relation 79; state of economics 19–22; tables of contents (Table 1 and Table 2) 85–86; theoretical structure 56–63;

A Treatise on Money (the *Treatise*; *TM*)
(*Continued*)
theory of credit cycle 62–63; theory of
money 60–61; and the *Tract* 44; value of
the fundamental equations 63–67; vision
44–45; Wicksell's influences 4–5, 22,
29–30, 43, 178–179
Trebilcock, C. 214 (n11)
'The Typescript' 147–149, 159, 162,
163–168; effective demand 168; factors
of production 167; user cost 165–167

underemployment equilibrium 2, 4, 74–75,
79, 98, 121, 180, 181, 182–184, 192
unemployment 13, 44, 72, 98, 220 (n8),
222 (n30); involuntary 170, 178, 183;
natural rate of 210
'Unemployment as a World Problem' 74
United Kingdom: Bank of England
(BOE) 8; education system 10–11;
entrepreneurial spirit 10–11; foreign
investment 11; free trade policy 11;
gentlemanship 10; impact of US and
Germany's industrialisation 8–9;
industrial progress 13; Industrial
Revolution 7; a nation of rentiers 11;
reforms 8; manufactured goods share
in world trade 9; technological innovation
7, 13; traditional industries 14;
unemployment 13; war debts repayments
36; workshop of the world 7–8
United States: automobile industry 12;
chemical industry 12; creditor country
12; industrialisation 8–9; isolationist
attitude 12; manufactured goods share in
world trade 9; methods of marketing 10;
private enterprise 9; protectionism 12;
technological innovation 9–10

user cost 144, 161
Uzawa, H. 209

'The Variorum' 147, 150
Versailles Peace Conference 11, 35
Vicarelli, F. 94, 223 (n8), 233 (n8)
voluntary saving 27, 96

wage-rent fund 18
wage-unit 184, 185
Wall Street 15–16
Walrasian (general equilibrium) theory 17,
22, 185, 192, 196, 197, 204–205, 207,
212, 215 (n1), 235 (n1), 238 (n63)
Weintraub, S. 197, 236 (n24)
'Why' manuscript 75–76
Wicksell, K. 2, 17–19, 28–29, 215 (n2),
216 (n3; n4; n5; n6; n8; n9; n14);
criticism of quantity theory 17;
state of economics 17; theory of
cumulative process (TCP) 18–19
Wicksellian theory 18–19, 43, 67, 191,
219 (n6)
Wicksell's influences 17–29, 29–30,
43, 177, 178–179, 216 (n11),
217 (n36; n37), 233 (n4; n5);
negative evaluation 30; positive
evaluation 29–30
Wiener, M. 215 (n23)
Woodford, M. 30, 217 (n38)
Woolf, V. 31
would-be entrepreneurs 27

Yoshikawa, H. 221 (n13)
Young, W. 203
Young Plan 16, 36

Zollverein (Customs Union) 8